Presented to Jendra C...,
with warm thanks from
the Cornell Institute for African
Development

Thank you!

Warm wishes,
Evangeline
on behalf of IAD

The Food and Financial Crises in Sub-Saharan Africa: Origins, Impacts and Policy Implications

FSC
www.fsc.org
MIX
Paper from
responsible sources
FSC® C013604

The Food and Financial Crises in Sub-Saharan Africa: Origins, Impacts and Policy Implications

David R. Lee
Professor, Charles H. Dyson School of Applied Economics and Management
Cornell University

Muna Ndulo
Professor, Cornell Law School
Director, Institute for African Development
Cornell University

www.cabi.org

CABI is a trading name of CAB International

CABI
Nosworthy Way
Wallingford
Oxfordshire OX10 8DE
UK

Tel: +44 (0)1491 832111
Fax: +44 (0)1491 833508
E-mail: cabi@cabi.org
Website: www.cabi.org

CABI
875 Massachusetts Avenue
7th Floor
Cambridge, MA 02139
USA

Tel: +1 617 395 4056
Fax: +1 617 354 6875
E-mail: cabi-nao@cabi.org

A catalogue record for this book is available from the British Library, London, UK.

Library of Congress Cataloging-in-Publication Data

Lee, David R. (David Robinson), 1950-
The food and financial crises in sub-Saharan Africa: origins, impacts and policy implications / David R. Lee, Muna Ndulo.
p. cm.
Includes bibliographical references and index.
ISBN 978-1-84593-828-4 (alk. paper)
1. Food supply—Africa, Sub-Saharan. 2. Food prices—Africa, Sub-Saharan. 3. Financial crises—Africa, Sub-Saharan. I. Ndulo, Muna. II. Title.

HD9017.A2L44 2011
363.80967--dc23

2011027045

ISBN-13: 978 1 84593 828 4

Commissioning editor: Rachel Cutts

Printed and bound in the UK by CPI Group (UK) Ltd, Croydon, CR0 4YY, from copy supplied by the authors

Contents

Tables

Figures

Contributors

Ernest Aryeetey *is Vice-Chancellor of the University of Ghana, University of Ghana, PO Box LG25, Legon, Ghana, and Non-Resident Fellow of the Africa Growth Initiative at the Brookings Institution in Washington, DC.* aryeetey@ug.edu.gh

Julia Berazneva *is a Ph.D. Candidate and Graduate Research Assistant in the Charles H. Dyson School of Applied Economics and Management, Cornell University, 247 Warren Hall, Ithaca, NY 14853.* jb793@cornell.edu

Antony Chapoto *is Visiting Assistant Professor of International Development in the Department of Agricultural, Food & Resource Economics at Michigan State University, 207 Agriculture Hall, East Lansing, MI 48824.* chapotoa@msu.edu

David Dawe *is Senior Economist in the Agricultural Development Economics Division at the Food and Agriculture Organization of the United Nations, Viale delle Terme di Caracalla, Rome, Italy.* david.dawe@fao.org

Cynthia Donovan *is Assistant Professor of International Development in the Department of Agricultural, Food & Resource Economics at Michigan State University, 207 Agriculture Hall, East Lansing, Michigan 48824.* donovanc@msu.edu

Keith O. Fuglie *is Chief of the Resource, Environmental and Science Policy Branch of the Economic Research Service, U.S. Department of Agriculture, 1800 M Street NW, Washington, DC 20036.* kfuglie@ers.usda.gov

Nicolette Gibson *is on the Faculty of Natural and Agricultural Sciences at the University of Pretoria, Lynnwood Road, Pretoria 0002, South Africa.* nicolette.gibson@up.ac.za

Vusi Gumede *is Associate Professor of Development Studies at the University of Johannesburg, P.O. Box 1083, Halfway House 1685, South Africa.* gumede.vusi@gmail.com

Derek Headey *is a Research Fellow in the Development Strategy and Governance Division of the International Food Policy Research Institute (Addis Abbaba Office), 2033 K Street, NW Washington, DC 20006.* d.headey@cgiar.org

Robert Hockett *is Professor of Law at the Cornell Law School, Cornell University, 316 Myron Taylor Hall, Ithaca, NY 14853.* rch37@cornell.edu

T.S. Jayne *is Professor of International Development in the Department of Agricultural, Food & Resource Economics at Michigan State University, 207 Agriculture Hall, East Lansing, Michigan* 48824. jayne@msu.edu

David R. Lee *is Professor in the Charles H. Dyson School of Applied Economics and Management, Cornell University, 441 Warren Hall, Ithaca, NY 14853.* DRL5@cornell.edu

Nicole M. Mason *is a Graduate Research Assistant in the Department of Agriculture, Food and Resource Economics at Michigan State University, 200 Cook Hall, East Lansing, MI 48824.* masonn@msu.edu

William A. Masters *is Professor of Food Policy in the Friedman School of Nutrition, Tufts University, 150 Harrison Ave., Boston, MA 02111.* William.Masters@tufts.edu

Nelipher Moyo *is a Research Analyst for the Africa Growth Initiative, Brookings Institution, 1775 Massachusetts Ave NW, Washington, DC 20036.* nmoyo@brookings.edu

Siwa Msangi *is a Research Fellow in the Environment and Production Technology Division at the International Food Policy Research Institute, 2003 K Street NW, Washington, DC 20006.* S.Msangi@cgiar.org

Muna Ndulo *is a Professor in the Cornell Law School and Director of the Institute for African Development, Cornell University, 314 Myron Taylor Hall, Ithaca, NY 14850.* muna-ndulo@lawschool.cornell.edu

Mark Rosegrant *is Director of the Environment and Production Technology Division at the International Food Policy Research Institute, 2003 K Street NW, Washington, DC 20006.* m.rosegrant@cgiar.org

Hettie C. Schönfeldt *is Professor of Natural and Agricultural Sciences at the University of Pretoria, Lynnwood Road, Pretoria 0002, South Africa.* hettie.schönfeldt@up.ac.za

Kenneth R. Simler *is Senior Economist in the PREM Poverty Reduction Group at the World Bank, World Bank MSN, 1818 H Street NW, MC4-415, Washington, DC 20433.* ksimler@worldbank.org

Vera Songwe *is Lead Economist and Advisor to the Managing Director of the Africa, South Asia, Eastern and Central Europe Division of the World Bank, 1818 H Street NW, Washington, DC 20433.* Vsongwe@worldbank.org

Kostas Stamoulis *is Chief of the Agricultural Development Economics Division at the Food and Agriculture Organization of the United Nations, Viale delle Terme di Caracalla, Rome, Italy.* Kostas.stamoulis@fao.org

Hester Vermeulen *is Research Fellow in Agricultural Economics Extension and Rural Development at the University of Pretoria, Private Bag X20 Hatfield, Pretoria 0028, South Africa.* hester.vermeulen@up.ac.za

Keith Wiebe *is Deputy Director of the Agricultural Development Economics Division at the Food and Agriculture Organization of the United Nations, Viale delle Terme di Caracalla, Rome, Italy.* keith.wiebe@fao.org

Preface

Only three years after the global food crisis of 2007–2008, in early 2011, the threat of a new 'food price crisis' revisited the world. Concerns were raised anew in the media, among international development institutions, in aid agencies and among developing country governments about the magnitudes of current and predicted food price rises—their causes and likely duration, their potential impacts on poverty and nutrition—and about how the poor would cope. Debates were renewed about the efficacy of different mechanisms and policies to address both causes and outcomes. Meanwhile, poor and vulnerable populations around the developing world were left to grapple with the consequences of another round of substantial food price increases and their impacts on purchasing power, food consumption, and family nutrition.

The earlier crisis, as it turned out, was only the first in a series of calamitous events in the late 2000s that included the most severe global financial crisis since the Great Depression and a global economic recession that, though severe, appears now to have fortunately been less devastating than initially expected. Nonetheless, the appearance of another food price crisis so soon after the last one leads to the question of whether, and to what extent, such events are due principally to transitory shocks or are the outcomes of structural economic forces. The implications of this question are significant. If the events of the late 2000s were transitory, then their effects, though harsh to many of the poor in sub-Saharan Africa and other developing countries, are less likely to repeat themselves than if they were the outcome of underlying structural market forces. As is discussed at length in this volume, the earlier food price crisis was in fact due to both. The emergence of a new food price crisis represents, in part, the outcome of some fundamental changes in the world food economy, including the growing linkages between food and energy markets.

These and other issues relating to the earlier food and financial crises and their implications for the poor led to an international conference at Cornell University in May, 2009 on 'The Food and Financial Crises and their Impacts on Achieving the Millennium Development Goals in Africa.' This conference brought together most of the authors whose work is reported in this volume, as well as other scholars, representatives of international organizations and NGOs, students and other participants from the US and abroad to explore the food and financial crises and their impacts on the world's most impoverished continent. At that time, mid-2009, food prices were declining from their highs in the previous year, but the food crisis was still very much on the minds of policy makers, international institutions and food policy researchers. Moreover, the world was then still in the grips of the financial crisis and economic recession, and the means to best address them were being widely deliberated.

Since the 2009 conference, the original papers have all been updated to reflect more recent events and data. Many report extended analysis and additional results, and several other papers have been added, all of which has resulted in the present volume. It is our hope that this volume will, with the passage of time and the benefit of hindsight, be able to place in better perspective some of the key developments of the late 2000s as they played out in sub-Saharan Africa, in particular. Beyond that, our intent is that this volume highlight some of the ongoing structural changes and transformative trends in the international economy and global food system such that, if any of the events of the late 2000s recur, we will have learned enough about their causes and consequences that the world will be better able to deal with the outcomes, especially the impacts on poor and vulnerable populations. While sub-Saharan Africa has made major strides in economic growth in recent years, it is still home to many of the world's most desperately poor, and its agriculture, on which so many depend, still faces many chronic constraints.

We wish to recognize a number of individuals and institutions without whose support the conference out of which this volume grew—and the volume itself—would not have been possible. For conference sponsorship and support, we thank the following institutions, all at Cornell University: the Institute for African Development and the Charles H. Dyson School of Applied Economics and Management, principal sponsors of the 2009 conference; the Mario Einaudi Center for International Studies, administrative home of IAD; the David R. Atkinson Center for a Sustainable Future; the Institute for the Social Sciences; the Cornell Institute for Public Affairs; the Cornell Food and Nutrition Policy Program; the Vice-Provost's Office for International Relations; and the Cornell Law School.

Among the individuals we wish to thank for their efforts in producing this volume are, first and foremost, the authors whose work is represented here. We are grateful for their scholarly contributions, timely assistance and patience over many months, through various rounds and revisions. We have endeavored to produce a book that treats a time-sensitive subject in a manner that has staying power and provides broad lessons for the future, and the authors have contributed in many ways to this effort.

In addition, we wish to acknowledge a number of Cornell colleagues who contributed to the earlier conference, reviewed various versions of the conference chapters, and who otherwise assisted this effort: Shadi Atallah, Chris Barrett, Frank DiSalvo, Kifle Gebremedhin, Gil Levine, David Lewis, Alice Pell, Kenneth Roberts, David Sahn, Erik Thorbecke, and Nic van de Walle. In particular, we want to acknowledge our late colleague, Michael Latham, who brought his usual enthusiasm, intellectual passion and deep concern for the poor to discussions during the 2009 conference and afterward, as on so many other occasions. He is sorely missed.

At the Institute for African Development, we greatly appreciate the help of Program Manager Jackie Sayegh and student assistants Ishan Chellaney, Judith Osei, and Sueaee Shin, all of whom provided valuable assistance in various ways to this effort. And we especially wish to thank Evangeline Ray, Publications Manager at IAD, whose considerable talents in editing, graphic design, correspondence with authors, proofreading, and in myriad other areas over many months contributed to this volume. Without her persistence, meticulous work and attention to detail, publication of this volume would not have been possible.

Finally, we wish to thank our editors at CABI Publishing—Sarah Mellor, who worked with us in getting this project off the ground; Simon Hill, who provided valuable assistance in the editing and production of this volume; and Alexandra Lainsbury, who worked with us throughout the entire process of producing this book, answered countless questions as this project proceeded, and provided helpful guidance that led to its completion. Thanks to all.

Chapter 1

Africa's Dual Crises: The Food and Financial Crises and their Effects in Sub-Saharan Africa—Introduction and Overview

David R. Lee, Julia Berazneva and Muna Ndulo
Cornell University

Introduction

The world in 2011 is caught up in yet another era of high oil, commodity and food prices. Early in the year, the global Food Price Index published by the Food and Agricultural Organization (FAO) of the United Nations reached historic highs, both in nominal and real (inflation-adjusted) terms, surmounting levels reached even in 2008, the most recent year of high food prices. An article in *Foreign Policy* labeled the 2010–2011 run-up in food prices the 'Great Food Crisis of 2011' (Brown, 2011). The World Bank has estimated that between June 2010 and early 2011, the number of people living in extreme poverty in low- and middle-income countries increased by 44 million (World Bank, 2011b). Once again, the impacts of high food prices, especially on the poor and food insecure around the world, elicited the concern of governments, donors and international organizations.

The most recent spike in commodity and food prices follows, by only three years, the global 'food price crisis' of 2007–2008, an era that witnessed sharp increases in oil, commodity and food prices and that was immediately followed by the global financial crisis and economic recession. Beginning in mid-2007, due to a variety of factors reviewed briefly below and discussed in greater detail in several chapters of this volume, commodity prices increased to levels unprecedented since the 1970s. Between January 2004 and May 2008, for example, rice prices rose by 224 percent, wheat prices increased 108 percent, and maize prices rose by 89 percent (US Department of State, 2011, citing IFPRI). These increases in raw commodity prices were quickly translated into increases in food prices. Overall, the often-cited FAO Food Price Index increased by 57 percent in the year between March 2007 and March 2008 (FAO, 2008b).

The impacts of these price spikes were felt around the world. Civil unrest, including food riots and protests in support of lower prices and/or higher wages, occurred in at least 33 countries in late 2007 and early 2008 (Torero, 2011). Deaths occurred in Haiti, Cameroon, Egypt and other countries (Moore, 2008). Emergency appeals for food aid were generated from at least 36 countries (US Department of State, 2011). FAO's provisional estimates showed that 75 million people became undernourished in 2007 as a result of higher food and energy prices (FAO, 2008a), severely curtailing progress toward achievement of the Millennium Development Goals. International donors and development organizations around the world responded. The World Food Programme delivered about four million metric tons of food aid in 2008 to more than 102 million people in 78 countries (WFP, 2009). In the end, however, overall foreign assistance fell well short of commitments.

In no other region of the world were the impacts of the 2007–2008 global food price crisis of greater concern than in sub-Saharan Africa (SSA). This region possesses the greatest incidence of poverty in the world, the lowest regional ranking in the UNDP's Human Development Index (2011), and is characterized by various other factors often associated with high poverty outcomes—underdeveloped infrastructure and markets, low life expectancy, a high incidence of HIV/AIDS, and a large number of failed states. Yet the experience of the early 2000s had greatly increased the prospects for economic growth in sub-Saharan Africa. In the five-year period, 2004–2008, economic growth of SSA countries averaged a healthy 6.5 percent overall, with a 6.9 percent average in the low-income SSA countries (IMF, 2010a). African oil-exporting countries did even better, experiencing an average 8.5 percent growth in real GDP over the same period. These outcomes were attributable to a range of factors, not the least of which was improved macroeconomic management, as shown through relatively low inflation, sustainable fiscal balances, rising foreign exchange reserves, and declining government debt (IMF, 2010b).

Nonetheless, the impacts of the food price crisis in Africa were severe. Fourteen of 53 countries around the continent experienced food riots and mass civil disturbances, in some cases involving violence and the deaths of protesters (Berazneva and Lee, 2011). These riots proved to be a transitory phenomena—although, in Northern Africa, they presaged the massive civil unrest and democratic uprisings seen in numerous countries beginning in late 2010. Of greater concern were the more hidden yet more lethal impacts of higher food prices on the poor. More than two-thirds (22) of the 30 countries in the world estimated by the World Food Programme to be the most vulnerable to food and fuel price increases are in Africa (Sanogo, 2009). According to the FAO, food prices rose in 89 percent of sub-Saharan African countries between 2007 and 2008; all countries experienced higher rice prices, and 89 percent of countries experienced higher maize, millet and sorghum prices (NATO, 2009). In Kenya, prices rose by 43 percent. In Sudan, the price of sorghum increased by 68 percent. By 2009, FAO (2010) estimates that there were 1.023 billion undernourished people in the world (although this number is estimated to have declined to 925 million in 2010 with lower food prices and the continuing global economic recovery). Of these, in sub-Saharan Africa, an estimated 265 million people were undernourished in 2009 (FAO, 2009). The food price crisis threatened to reverse hard-fought gains in poverty alleviation and in achieving the Millennium Development Goals.

Yet, in Africa as well as the rest of the world, the global food crisis was only the beginning of the economic woes of the late 2000s. Within months after global food prices began their retreat in mid-2008, the full effects of the global financial crisis and the economic recession it precipitated began to be felt. The financial crisis actually had its roots much earlier, in the unsustainable housing bubble—created in the early to mid-2000s in the United States—which had been fueled by risky lending practices by banks and mortgage companies and reinforced in turn by the rapid and largely unregulated growth of markets for mortgage-backed securities and unregulated financial instruments such as collateralized debt obligations. The collapse of the sub-prime mortgage market began in earnest in early to mid-2007 and worsened throughout that year and in the first half of 2008, with the progressive revelations of major financial losses on the part of large international banks like

Citigroup and the Swiss bank UBS, and the collapse of the large US investment bank, Bear Stearns. Major interventions in late 2007 and the first half of 2008 by the US Federal Reserve Bank, the European Central Bank, and the central banks of the UK, Canada and Japan failed to stem the tide of increasing losses in the mortgage markets and related sectors—residential housing, commercial real estate, and consumer credit.

Continued market declines and fears of an incipient economic recession worsened in September 2008. That single month witnessed the US government's rescue of the country's two largest mortgage lenders, Freddie Mac and Fannie Mae, and its largest insurance company, AIG; the collapse of the US investment bank Lehman Brothers and the huge mortgage lender Washington Mutual; bailouts of major banks and mortgage lenders in the UK, Belgium, and Ireland; and the collapse of the giant European investment and banking firm, Fortis. In the first two weeks of October, the Dow Jones Industrial average dropped by more than 22 percent in response to the flood of negative economic news.

The meltdown in global financial markets had many dimensions—bank losses and failures, declining liquidity, financial deleveraging, and a major 'crisis of confidence' in banks and other financial institutions. Coming as it did on the heels of the inflationary price spikes for oil and food, the financial crisis precipitated a full-blown global recession in 2008–2009, particularly among industrialized countries: major declines in equity values, reflected in the stock market crash of 2008–2009, rising unemployment, and rapid declines in export prices following the earlier run-ups. After experiencing roughly 5.0 percent annual growth in 2004–2007, world output growth slowed to 2.9 percent in 2008, and actually contracted by 0.5 percent in 2009 (IMF, 2011b). Global trade, on which so many African and other developing countries depend, retreated from a strong 8.7 percent average annual growth in 2004–2007 to 2.7 percent in 2008 and then fell sharply by -10.9 percent in 2009.

Although the global economy is estimated to have rebounded in 2010 with 5.0 percent output growth and a 12.4 increase in trade volume, the global recession of 2008–2009 took a severe toll on the poor. Between 2008 and 2009, for example, the number of undernourished people in the world is estimated to have increased by 105 million (FAO, 2009). Furthermore, the World Bank and IMF have estimated that the poverty rate in sub-Saharan Africa is expected to be 38 percent by 2015, versus the 36 percent it would have been without the economic crisis; this implies that, over the long run, roughly 20 million fewer people will have escaped poverty (World Bank, 2010b).

With another food price crisis revisiting the world in 2010–2011, the story is by now a familiar one; again we hear of weather shocks and tight supplies, rising oil prices, low grain stocks, growing demands for food and oil, especially in Asia, and so forth. USDA's Chief Economist reports that it will take at least one to two years to mitigate the 'tight stocks-to-use situation' (Glauber, 2011). Are the conditions that led to the earlier crisis re-emerging? Have global food prices reached new permanently higher levels, or will sharp price declines, such as those that followed the previous food crisis in 2008–2009, recur? Were the events of 2007–2009 an aberration or are they indicative of what we should expect in the future? Have the underlying fundamentals of global food markets changed sufficiently that, as some have argued, we have entered a permanent era of high price volatility and unstable food prices? And if so, what are the underlying structural changes that are at work? Most importantly for this volume, what has been the impact of all these changes on sub-Saharan Africa, home to many of the world's most vulnerable and food insecure people? Finally, how can we improve policy responses in the event of future recurrences of food price and economic crises? These are some of the key questions that are addressed in this volume.

The Food Price Crisis

Both the food price crisis of 2007–2008 and the ensuing financial and economic crisis generated a great deal of instant analysis in the print and electronic media at the time. Much of this, however, was informed by 'issues of the moment' and not on careful analysis. With the passage of time, economists, policy analysts, financial and commodity market analysts, and other researchers have increasingly shed light on the developments of the late 2000s; this volume represents one of those efforts. This section briefly reviews some of the key developments surrounding the 2007–2008 food price crisis and its causes and consequences, both globally and in sub-Saharan Africa. The section following does the same with regard to the financial and economic crisis. This discussion sets the stage for a detailed consideration of specific developments in sub-Saharan Africa, which is the primary focus of this volume.

Causes of the Food Price Crisis

A wide range of research has attempted to identify the factors that led to the surge in food prices beginning in mid-2007 (see, for example, early studies by Abbott, Hurt, and Tyner, 2008; FAO, 2008a; Headey and Fan, 2008; Mitchell, 2008; Trostle, 2008). The extent of these price spikes is clearly evident in Figure 1.1, which shows price series for several commodities, food prices and oil. Although it was evident from the start that a complex combination of factors triggered the crisis, great debate accompanied this question at the time, due in part to the fact that some factors—notably the role of biofuels—were highly contentious given what they implied for policy. More recent retrospective analysis, including that in this volume, has provided further valuable perspectives. As suggested by several authors (Trostle, 2008; Headey and Fan, 2010; Abbott and Borot de Battisti, 2011), it is useful to distinguish two sets of contributing factors that precipitated, and exacerbated, the world food price crisis: a number of initial structural factors, with impacts playing out over the medium- and long-term, and several transitory or short-term factors that worsened the crisis. These included factors on both the supply and demand sides.

The structural factors were at least four. First, global income and population growth in the rapidly growing economies of China, India and elsewhere in the developing world underlay strong demand and slowly rising food prices earlier in the decade. For example, FAO's Food Price Index (adjusted for inflation) averaged 110.4 in 2004–2006, after having averaged only 95.9 in the preceding five years (1999–2003). With higher incomes and growing urban populations, consumer food demands continued to increase and to shift toward preferences for meat, dairy and other high-value foods. Second, low investment in agriculture and low prices (and price incentives) in the preceding decade contributed to declining growth in cereal yields (World Bank, 2009). These two factors contributed to the decrease in stockholding for all of the major food grains, leaving the international market with progressively lower stocks to buffer international demands and supply shocks over the 2000s. USDA data show that the global demand for grains and oilseeds surpassed production in seven out of eight years following 2000, and the global stocks-to-use ratio for grains and oilseeds declined steadily after 1999—from about 30 percent in 1999 to less than 15 percent in 2008 (Trostle, 2008). Third, a weak US dollar—itself the result of a rising trade deficit, budget deficit and other macro imbalances in the US economy—meant that, as most internationally traded food grains are denominated in US dollars, this fed demand growth, putting upward pressure on prices for agricultural commodities, as well as on crude oil.[1]

Figure 1.1. International commodity prices, January 2000–March 2011
(Price Index, January 2000 = 1)

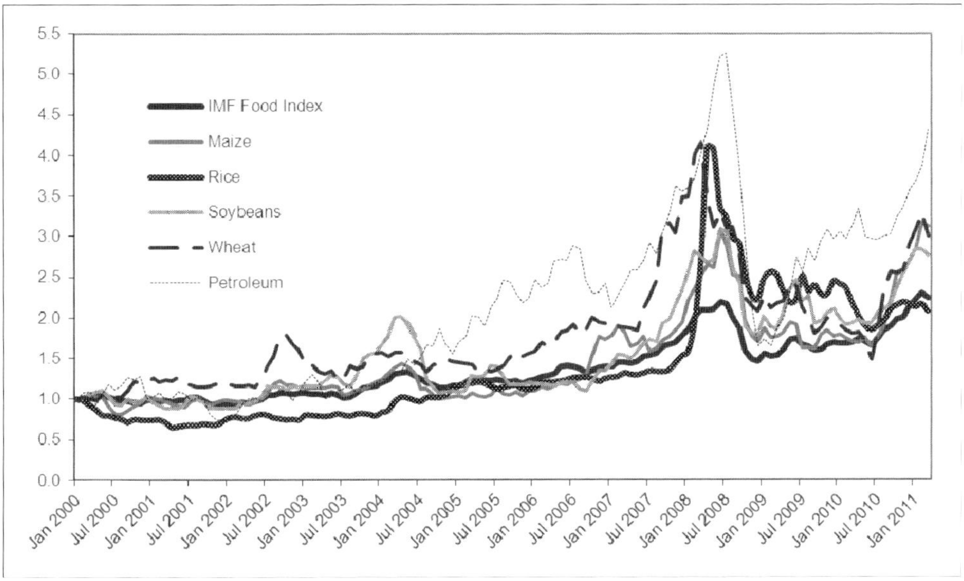

Source: Calculations by the authors using data from International Financial Statistics (IMF 2011a).
Note: Maize (US Gulf Ports), Rice (Thailand, Bangkok), Soybeans (US, Rotterdam), Wheat (US Gulf Ports), Petroleum (World Average Crude Price).

These same demand factors contributed to a fourth structural factor, rising energy prices. Oil prices increased from US$30 a barrel in early 2003 to about $140 a barrel by the end of June of 2008, which broke the earlier record, set in 1979, by some 35 percent in real terms (IMF, 2008a). Rising energy prices themselves contribute in at least three ways to increasing food prices. First, high energy prices make agricultural production and food distribution more costly, through increases in input costs for irrigation, fertilizers, and the transportation of inputs and outputs (von Braun *et al.,* 2008). Second, high crude oil prices, coupled with US and European Union policies to subsidize and encourage agriculture-based biofuels, created strong incentives to divert agricultural commodities such as maize and oilseeds from the food and feed market to biofuel feedstocks. In the US, for example, production of maize for ethanol increased from about 1 billion bushels in the 2002/2003 crop year to a projected 3.1 billion bushels in 2007/2008, rising from 10 percent to 24 percent of total US maize production[2] (Trostle, 2008). Third, high energy prices contributed to stimulating the speculative demand for commodities (more about this later). This

[1] Empirical estimates of the commodity price elasticity with respect to the real value of the US dollar are generally between 0.5 and 1.0 (Headey and Fan 2008).

[2] These numbers have since risen to much higher levels. The USDA estimates that the percentage of annual US maize production used to produce ethanol and its by-products was 40 percent in 2010–2011, and is projected at 37 percent in 2011–2012 (USDA 2011).

increasingly tight link between energy and agricultural commodity markets has been singled out as one of the major driving forces behind the food crisis—rising oil prices made biofuel production profitable, in turn increasing demands for maize in the US and oilseeds in Europe, and introducing a major stimulus into world agricultural commodity markets and prices (Headey and Fan, 2008; Mitchell, 2008; Trostle, 2008; Abbott, Hurt, and Tyner, 2009; Headey, Malaiyandi, and Fan, 2009; Lustig, 2009).

In addition to these structural factors, the crisis was exacerbated by a number of transitory factors. First, adverse weather conditions in 2007, including droughts in Australia, Russia and Ukraine, contributed to a drop in global average yields for grains and oilseeds. Second, many governments instituted *ad hoc* trade policy interventions, such as export bans, export taxes or high import subsidies (Headey and Fan, 2008; von Braun and Torero, 2009; Abbott and Borot de Battisti, 2011) in a 'beggar-thy-neighbour' attempt to protect domestic consumers from food price increases, while simultaneously exacerbating price rises in international markets. In the case of rice, for example, Vietnam banned commercial sales; India and Pakistan instituted minimum export prices; Cambodia banned exports; China instituted an export tax and eliminated a VAT export rebate; and all the while, many importers reduced tariffs and took other measures to boost imports (Childs and Kiawu, 2009). Third, non-traditional investors and speculators in commodity markets sought to diversify their holdings beyond increasingly risky financial market and mortgage-based investments, greatly increasing their investments in commodity futures markets in 2006–2008. The extent to which this factor was responsible for the run-up in food commodity markets has been widely debated (Timmer, 2008; Trostle, 2008; von Braun and Torero, 2009; Gilbert, 2010; Sanders and Irwin, 2010). Most researchers agree that, at a minimum, volatility increases at higher prices; this has suggested to some that speculation may be more of a symptom than a major source of the food crisis (Headey and Fan, 2010; Abbott and Borot de Battisti, 2011).[3]

Price Transmission and Heterogeneous Effects

Food price developments have more significant impacts on overall domestic inflation than fuel price changes in low-income countries, since households typically spend more on food than on oil-related products (IMF, 2008a). Many of the poor spend 50–60 percent or more of their incomes on food, so the specific ways in which international prices are transmitted to domestic and regional markets are important and create high stakes for consumers in developing countries, like many in SSA. Since local and regional markets are often not well integrated into world markets and are characterized by various sources of market imperfections, these heterogeneous effects and market idiosyncrasies can be key to understanding the way in which international price changes are actually translated to local producers and consumers.

The transmission mechanism of escalating international food prices into domestic markets is multifaceted. First, dollar-denominated international prices need to be converted to local currency, and then border prices need to be translated to regional market prices. Thus both real exchange rate movements, such as appreciation vis-à-vis the US dollar, and domestic policies like tariffs, subsidies, export bans, reserves, and price controls will have significant effects on the extent of price pass-through to retail markets (Dawe, 2008; Abbott, 2009; Headey and Fan, 2010). Moreover, a range of other factors such as supply

[3] Chapters 5 and 6 in this volume address this issue as well.

and demand responses to price changes, substitutability between imported and domestic foods, exogenous weather shocks, and other elements may underlie the degree of price instability in domestic markets.

The existing evidence suggests that international prices were seldom fully and immediately transmitted to consumer food costs, with great variability in the degree of transmission. However, domestic price increases did occur and were relatively large in many cases (WFP, 2008; Abbott, 2009; Blein and Longo, 2009). Both consumer price indices and commodity-specific prices can be used to examine the extent of such price transmission. One set of estimates suggests that in the first quarter of 2008 the median 12-month rate of food price inflation for a sample of 120 non-OECD countries increased from 10 to 12 percent, almost double the same rate for 2006 (IMF, 2008a). Another estimate also found rapid food inflation from February 2007 to February 2008: for example, 18.3 percent in Botswana, 6.4 percent in Peru, 14.2 percent in Bangladesh, and 24.6 percent in Kenya (OECD and FAO, 2008). Examining commodity-specific price transmission around the world with data from GIEWS (2009) and netting out regional effects as well as the effects of processed versus unprocessed and retail versus wholesale commodities, Headey and Fan (2010) find the greatest price transmission for maize, potatoes, wheat, and rice, with lower transmission for less-commonly traded commodities such as beans, millet and cassava. Their estimates suggest a great deal of heterogeneity in price transmission in 2008 globally, moderate price changes in Asia (apart from Vietnam and Thailand) and Latin America, but high price increases in some populous countries in East and West Africa.

Turning to Africa, specifically, infrastructure and communications limitations are widespread and market imperfections are ubiquitous; thus national average prices and price changes can obscure the heterogeneity of price variations across and within countries. Benson *et al.* (2008), for example, find that poor physical connectivity contributed to moderate price transmission of global price changes in Uganda, while Cudjoe *et al.* (2010) find domestic prices in Ghana to be highly correlated with global market prices—both for imported (e.g. rice) and domestically produced (e.g. maize) products. Arndt *et al.* (2008) find that the Mozambican government allowed the changes in world prices to pass through to domestic markets by supporting some economic sectors and not introducing subsidies or trade distortions. Moreover, these studies find significant price change variations within countries. For example, rural areas often experienced smaller price transmission effects because of high transportation costs (Ulimwengu, Workneh, and Paulos, 2009; Cudjoe, Breisinger, and Diao, 2010). It is clear that the transmission of international price changes across commodities, time, countries and regions is highly heterogeneous and that global average price changes may be dramatically different from price variability experienced by consumers and producers in local markets.

The Consequences of Food Price Increases for the Poor

Contributing both to rising inflation and poverty levels, high food prices posed significant challenges to developing country policy makers seeking to tackle inflation using appropriate macroeconomic measures and to support vulnerable populations by helping households maintain access to food, energy and essential services. Given limited public resources to deal with both issues simultaneously and the uncertainty regarding the causes and duration of rising food prices, governments often had to make choices (Lustig, 2009). By December 2008 most countries had implemented a series of immediate short-term measures to help isolate domestic markets from international price spikes (Demeke,

Pangrazio and Maetz, 2009). Among the most commonly used market and trade policy measures were the reduction or elimination of customs fees and tariffs, and selling grain from imports or from public stocks; these were used by 43 and 35 countries, respectively, out of 81 countries surveyed in a FAO 2009 study (Demeke, Pangrazio, and Maetz, 2009). These measures directly affected the extent of international price transmission inside national borders (Headey and Fan, 2008; Abbott, 2009; Lustig, 2009). Many countries also implemented short-term domestic measures aimed at protecting consumers—safety net programs, food subsidies, and price controls—or compensating farmers (mainly through production supports).

Well-targeted safety net programs can significantly reduce the impacts of economic shocks on households' livelihoods, as well as having longer-term positive impacts on health, education and nutrition outcomes. However, such policies were relatively less common (in the same 2009 country survey): 23 nations reported cash transfer programs, 19 countries used food assistance, and 16 countries took measures directed at increasing the disposable incomes of vulnerable populations (Demeke, Pangrazio, and Maetz, 2009). Unfortunately, many low- and middle-income countries do not have any safety net programs in place, and even where such programs exist, they are of limited coverage (FAO, 2008b). It is also not clear how many of the countries with existing safety net programs have incorporated the 'new' poor and increased the amount of cash transfers in response to the crisis (Lustig, 2009). This means that many poor people affected by the food price crisis and those who became poor as a result of it were not protected from the impact of the crisis on their living standards.

A key policy question is the effect of rising food prices on global poverty. The World Bank estimates suggest that the global headcount poverty rate increased by 1.3 percentage points as a result of the food crisis, corresponding to an additional 130 million people falling below the poverty line of US$1.25 a day (2009). Some estimates also suggest that a large share of the increase in poverty came from deepening poverty among households who were already poor (Dessus, Herrera, and de Hoyos, 2008; Wodon *et al.*, 2008). Overall, the FAO's *State of Food Insecurity Report 2009* estimates that, in 2008, the number of undernourished people in the world had reached 923 million (2009). Again, however, the impacts of rising international food prices on poverty, household food security, and nutrition differed greatly across countries, regions within countries and household types.

The extent of the country-level poverty impacts depends on several factors, such as the initial incidence and depth of poverty, the significance of food in the budgets of poor households, the share of the poor with little or no direct income from agriculture, and the ability of households to substitute between food items (World Bank, 2009). So countries with high initial poverty rates and poverty gaps are particularly vulnerable to food price increases (Dessus, Herrera, and de Hoyos, 2008). And local conditions, for example, diversified diets—such as diets with larger shares of staples derived from home produced foods and locally traded products in Uganda—can limit the impact on household welfare (Benson, Mugarura and Wanda, 2008).

Given the recent onset of the 2007–2008 food price crisis, relatively little empirical evidence exists regarding food price impacts on household welfare. The impact of rising prices on a household's net wealth is determined by the combination of decreased purchasing power (consumption effect) and potentially increased income (income effect) (World Bank, 2009). However, it is generally believed that the negative impacts on net consumers, more numerous in number, outweigh the benefits to poor producers (Ivanic and Martin, 2008; Zezza *et al.*, 2008; Wodon and Zaman, 2008; Wodon *et al.*, 2008). Some recent studies, though, point to a more nuanced picture. For example, Aksoy and Isik-Dikmelik (2008) analyze the welfare impacts of food prices on net food sellers and buyers in nine low-income countries and confirm that the largest share of poor households are net food buyers, but almost 50 percent of them are marginal net food buyers who should not be highly affected by food price rises. Rios *et al.* (2008) find that although poor farmers are net buyers of some crops, only the poorest of them are net buyers of all crops, so that food price changes should have a varied but limited effect on household welfare. When it comes to evaluating poverty impacts across socioeconomic groups and individuals, the most vulnerable households across countries are found to be urban or rural non-farm, larger in size, less well educated, and more dependent on female labor (FAO, 2008b; WFP, 2008; Zezza *et al.*, 2008; Ruel *et al.*, 2010).

Going beyond household welfare effects, it is important to recognize that rising food prices have longer-term impacts on nutritional, health and educational outcomes. Conditional on the duration and severity of food price increases, households coped with the food crisis by employing food-based strategies, non-food-based strategies, or a combination of both (FAO, 2008a). Food-based strategies involve changes in the quantity, quality and/or diversity of food items consumed, while non-food-based strategies involve a reduction in expenditures on health care and education, as well as diversification of income-generating activities. It is likely that households' responses to the food price crisis of 2007–2008 included all of these strategies, with potentially long-lasting impacts on nutrition, health and education.

Another clear impact of the rising food prices was social unrest in many countries. Peaceful protests were held, for example, in Malaysia, Indonesia, and Pakistan (Trostle, 2008). Less peaceful protests (the so-called 'food riots' of 2007 and 2008) occurred in many low-income countries, including Haiti, Bangladesh, and Uzbekistan. In sub-Saharan Africa, ten countries experienced violent mass disturbances, which differed in location, severity and organization—from trade union demonstrations in Burkina Faso to sit-ins organized by consumer associations in Senegal, to spontaneous store lootings in Guinea (Harsch, 2008; Berazneva and Lee, 2011). However, across all countries, the protesters responded to the unaffordability and lack of availability of food and other staples such as fuel and transportation, as well as to perceived government ineffectiveness and corruption. A closer look at the countries experiencing riots reveals that not only the extent of price transmission and government responses (or lack thereof) were responsible for social unrest, but also that other structural factors such as the extent of poverty and governance structures played a role.

The Financial and Economic Crisis

The financial crisis that began to become widely visible in industrialized countries in 2007 and the global recession that followed had significant impacts on financial and capital markets, international capital flows, trade patterns and economic growth around the world. One estimate suggests that the crisis and its long-term impacts on global financial markets could lead to a 3.4 to 8 percent reduction of long-run potential output in developing countries as a result of lower cumulative annual growth over a five- to seven-year period (World Bank, 2010a). Although for some developing countries the short-term impacts of the crisis were less severe since their financial sectors are not well integrated into global markets, the poor in virtually all countries experienced impacts in the form of reduced demand for exports, a drop in commodity prices, decreasing remittances and limited access to financial resources (Islam and Nallari, 2010). The World Bank estimates that the crisis added 50 million people to extreme poverty in 2009 and about 64 million by the end of 2010 as compared with a non-crisis scenario (World Bank, 2010a).

Economy-wide Effects

The impact of the global financial crisis on African economic growth became a major concern. Despite its past history of poverty and many existing development challenges, many sub-Saharan African countries had enjoyed strong growth since the mid-1990s: between 1995 and 2007, real GDP growth for the entire region averaged 5 percent and real per capita GDP growth averaged about 2 percent (IMF, 2008b). Notwithstanding the wide diversity of country experiences across the continent, the pre-conditions for sustained growth were present in many nations—an absence of political conflict, a functioning market economy and stable macroeconomic policy (IMF, 2008b). But this record of growth was severely threatened as export prices and revenues and the sources of capital available to many sub-Saharan African countries decreased dramatically in 2008 and 2009. The IMF estimates that due to the global recession, SSA's output expanded only by 2.5 percent in 2009 (IMF, 2010b); given strong population growth, this meant a decline in per capita real GDP growth of -0.1 percent. Moreover, the impacts of the financial crisis, as was the case with the food price crisis previously, manifested themselves differently across the continent.

One reason for this was the diversity of mechanisms and channels through which the global financial and economic crisis affected different countries. These can be separated into financial channels and real channels (Massa and te Velde, 2008). Financial transmission channels include stock markets, the banking sector and foreign direct investment; not surprisingly, these channels played a larger role in countries with stronger financial linkages to international capital markets. All sixteen stock markets in SSA experienced a reduction of portfolio inflows in 2007–2008, with South African, Nigerian and Kenyan stock markets particularly affected (Massa and te Velde, 2008). Limited international private banking activity shielded the banking sector in many SSA countries. However, countries with a high share of foreign owned banks, such as Ghana, Tanzania, and Zambia, faced exposure to declining lending by international banks as a result of the crisis (Brambila-Macias and Massa, 2010). Countries with pre-crisis rapid credit expansion like Cape Verde, DRC, Ethiopia and Uganda may suffer from non-performing loans in the future (World Bank, 2010a). The financial crisis also impacted the flows of foreign direct investment (FDI) to Africa as global liquidity tightened (IMF, 2008b). FDI fell in Uganda, for example, by 6.2 percent between August 2007 and September 2008 and in Ethiopia by 31 percent between the second quarter of 2008 and the first quarter of 2009 (te Velde *et al.*, 2010). For several other SSA countries, such as DRC, Liberia and Tanzania, some private planned investments were postponed or abandoned (Brambila-Macias and Massa, 2010).

In addition to the financial channels, there were several real channels through which the financial crisis and economic recession were transmitted to sub-Saharan African nations. Perhaps the most important was trade, both in terms of decreased trade volumes and declines in the terms of trade (Lin, 2008). As the global recession set in, decreasing commodity prices and falling export demand spread throughout SSA, curbing economic activity and causing a deterioration of fiscal and external balances (IMF, 2009). Export earnings peaked in July 2008, and by February of 2009 decreased more than 50 percent as both volumes and prices tumbled; imports followed the same pattern (IMF, 2010b). The collapse in trade was particularly felt in oil and commodity exporting countries; however, trade declines were visible across a wide range of sectors. For example, timber exports declined by 27 percent in Ghana (FAO, 2009); 10 percent fewer tourists arrived to visit Tanzania in the first quarter of 2009, compared with one year previously; and in the first half of 2009, the volume of Kenyan horticultural exports declined by 25 percent relative to the same period in 2008 (te Velde *et al.*, 2010).

Two other important real transmission channels are remittances and foreign aid, both serving as powerful poverty reduction mechanisms in SSA. Initially, the slow-down in global economic activity in Europe and the United States threatened to decrease remittance flows to sub-Saharan Africa, where in some countries—Ethiopia, Nigeria and Senegal, among others—remittances may account for between 5 and 10 percent of GDP (FAO, 2009). However, remittance flows overall proved to be resilient. For SSA as a whole, remittances fell only by 3.7 percent in 2009 and registered a quick recovery in 2010 (World Bank, 2011a). The flows of official development assistance (ODA) were also expected to decrease as donor countries struggled with domestic impacts of the financial crisis, prompting significant concern especially among countries that are heavily reliant on foreign assistance, such as Burundi and Liberia (FAO, 2009). However, country case studies showed heterogeneous impacts on aid, for example, declines in aid to Uganda but increases in aid to DRC (te Velde *et al.*, 2010). Moreover, ODA at the global level expanded substantially in 2008 in response to the food price crisis (FAO, 2009), and there was an increase in lending registered by the International Monetary Fund and the World Bank (te Velde *et al.*, 2010).

Sectoral and Micro-level Impacts

While the transmission channels were similar for all SSA countries, the domestic effects varied greatly, with some countries and people proving to be more vulnerable than others (Massa and te Velde, 2008; te Velde *et al.*, 2010). The variable impacts of the crisis depended in part on the importance of the different sectoral contributors to national income, dependence on trade, and on employment effects (FAO, 2009). The mining sector, for example, suffered a sharp downturn in DRC and Zambia that resulted in scaled back production and curtailed investment, the closing of companies and loss of jobs (te Velde *et al.*, 2010). At the same time, agricultural sector growth rates during the crisis tended to be greater than that of GDP (FAO, 2009). In Mozambique, for example, in the first three quarters of 2009 agricultural production actually grew by 11.7 percent, largely due to a good harvesting season (te Velde *et al.*, 2010). Experience from previous crises suggests that the demand for agricultural goods, especially food, does not decrease proportionately with drops in income, and the smallholder subsistence nature of agriculture in SSA protects the sector from credit shortages (Headey, Malaiyandi, and Fan, 2009). Moreover, the agricultural sector can potentially become a source of employment for casual labourers and returned migrants.

At a more micro level, the financial crisis affected firms and households through many avenues: employment, prices and wages, assets, public and private transfers, and access to goods and services (McCord and Vandemoortele, 2009; te Velde *et al.*, 2009). The overall poverty impact of the financial crisis did not materialize immediately (indeed, many have argued that this impact has been prolonged); in addition, it is difficult to disaggregate these impacts from the effects of the preceding food crisis. For most low-income countries, loss of employment, declining wage rates for unskilled workers, and food price changes were expected to have the largest impacts on poverty (Lin and Martin, 2010). Increased unemployment and underemployment escalated already high rates. Official unemployment rates in 2009 were 7.9 percent in SSA, with 75.8 per cent of the labor force in vulnerable employment; this is estimated to have increased by 0.5 percentage points due to the global economic crisis (International Labour Organization, 2011). Loss of formal employment was most apparent in the mining sector in SSA. In Zambia, for example, 10,000 mining workers lost their jobs in 2008, while in DRC, this figure was close to 200,000 (te Velde *et al.*, 2010).

Not only did households lose jobs, they also faced increased work hours, worsened work conditions and lowered wage rates (te Velde *et al.*, 2010). Declines in domestic and export demands for many sectors, as well as decreased product demand associated with lower remittances, were expected to put downward pressure on wage rates for unskilled labor (Lin and Martin, 2010). Households were also affected by changes in prices. Although commodity prices declined from their peaks during the food crisis, at the end of 2008 domestic prices across a range of important food staples in developing countries (not just SSA) were still 17 percent higher in real terms than two years earlier (FAO, 2009). As with the effects of the food price crisis of 2008, the impacts of commodity prices on household welfare are complex. However, the most affected groups were likely to be the rural landless, female-headed households and the urban poor—groups that, in many cases, had already reached the limit of their coping abilities during the food crisis (FAO, 2009).

The financial and economic crisis also affected the rate of poverty reduction in SSA. The World Bank, for example, estimates that the global financial crisis added 7 million people to the number of people in SSA living below US$1.25 a day in 2009 (Ravallion, 2009). There were also important impacts on the non-income dimensions of poverty, as the main coping strategies of the poor include reducing dietary diversity and household spending on education and health care (FAO, 2009). Of special concern are the long-lasting impacts on children, as highlighted in research on previous economic crises (Ravallion, 2008). Friedman and Schady (2009), for instance, estimated that as a result of the global financial crisis, SSA could expect between 30,000 and 50,000 additional infant deaths, with most of them being poorer children and female. Women and girls in poor households are, in general, more vulnerable to the effects of the global economic recession, especially in countries with pre-existing high child mortality rates and low levels of female schooling (Buvinic, Sabarwal, and Sinha, 2009).

In many ways, the financial and economic crisis beginning in 2007 and 2008 was expected to be more severe than previous economic crises. The economic crisis came at the time of deeper financial and commercial integration of developing countries into the world economy, so the impacts of shocks in the financial industry and in international markets were expected to be severe. Moreover, unlike the previous crises that had been confined to individual countries or particular regions, the global financial crisis appeared to affect large parts of the world simultaneously (FAO, 2009). However, notwithstanding the severity and scope of the financial and economic crisis, there are reasons to believe that its impacts may have been more limited in SSA than in some other regions, especially in the industrialized countries. *A priori*, we know that SSA economies remain less integrated in the international financial system and rely relatively less on international capital and bond markets to finance domestic investments and operations (Brambila-Macias and Massa, 2010). The improved macroeconomic fundamentals put in place prior to the crisis may also have mitigated the impacts of the recession on African economies compared to previous external shocks (World Bank, 2010a). The recovery in the global economy is expected to expand economic activity in SSA by 5 percent in 2010 and 5.5 percent in 2011; if these estimates bear out, they will return SSA to the high levels of growth registered in most countries of the region in the mid-2000s (IMF, 2010b). However, countries that continue to suffer from recurrent natural disasters, conflict and insufficient institutional capacity, in addition to experiencing the lingering effects of the food and financial crises, will need to be closely monitored (FAO, 2010).

Although the impacts of the food and financial crises may have been less severe than thought at the time, the policy challenge remains great: improving counter-cyclical macroeconomic policy; reorienting economic growth strategies beyond their oftentimes sole focus on natural resource extraction; improving the coverage and operations of social protection programs to better insulate the poor from the ravages of economic downturns; making needed long-term investments in infrastructure, agricultural development, education and health. The broader policy agenda facing sub-Saharan Africa is a challenging one. Ultimately, improved policies and stronger institutions will be central to the region's ability to resist and adapt to the future food and economic crises that will inevitably come.

Overview of this Volume

The chapters in this volume address several themes, all related to the food and financial crises and their impacts in sub-Saharan Africa. Broadly speaking, the principal themes discussed in this book are the causes and consequences of the dual crises, their impacts in sub-Saharan Africa at both the macro- and micro-levels, and finally, how Africa can address some of the key challenges—primarily related to improving productivity and policy—that may help the continent escape the devastation of such crises in the future. The chapters are complementary: some are wide-ranging and address continent-wide phenomena; others are empirical case studies, focusing on sub-national and local developments. Together, the chapters mix analysis of broad long-term trends with empirical analysis of short-term national and regional outcomes and authors' policy perspectives on how the region may best achieve a sustainable economic growth path in the future. The rest of this section briefly summarizes the contributions of each of the chapters.

In Chapter 2, Aryeetey and Moyo trace the origins of the food and financial crises as they affected sub-Saharan Africa. For various reasons, Africa experienced strong economic growth in the early 2000s, with associated gains in poverty reduction. Africa was nonetheless vulnerable to the global food and financial crises that arose in the late 2000s due to its high levels of poverty, heavy reliance on export earnings, and growing food imports. The financial and economic crisis had widely adverse impacts on African nations and people, both through direct channels—stock and bond markets, a decline in foreign direct investment, and depreciating exchange rates—and, in particular, indirect channels including declines in export prices and export revenues, official development assistance and remittances. The chapter traces the arc of these changes both for sub-Saharan Africa in general and three 'case study' countries, in particular—Ghana, Zambia and Nigeria. Africa's poor are argued to have experienced a 'double agony' as a result of the combined crises and their impacts on poverty, undernourishment, social unrest and other socioeconomic indicators. Although economic recovery is underway, the repercussions of past impacts are still felt and the continent remains at risk in the face of future waves of food price increases. The authors argue that although African governments have made major strides in pursuing more informed macroeconomic policies, a much better job must be done in the future to ensure that economic crises do not prevent the achievement of poverty reduction goals through better implementation of counter-cyclical social protection programs.

Chapter 3, by Wiebe, Dawe and Stamoulis, reviews the causes and effects of the food price crisis and the global financial and economic crises, particularly as they affected the food security status of the poor. The origins of the crises are shown to be numerous and complex, as were the consequences for the poor, most of whom are net food buyers and thus for whom the income to purchase food—which, in turn, is critically dependent on employment and wages—is an essential part of the food security equation. The chapter also reviews the impacts of the global economic crisis in terms of the main transmission channels that affected developing countries. The authors highlight the many different coping strategies used by the poor to deal with food price increases and economic crisis. However, they find that use of these strategies did not avert severe impacts of the crises on the poor and on rates of poverty and undernourishment, reversing at least temporarily, progress made earlier in the decade in reducing global poverty and hunger. The authors highlight a number of short- and long-term strategies for mitigating the impacts of future such crises on the poor.

In Chapter 4, Msangi and Rosegrant analyze the long-term 'drivers' of change in world food systems, specifically, selected factors influencing the food supply and demand balance, current and future, in sub-Saharan Africa. The authors argue that the exposure of the SSA region to world commodity markets that became widely apparent during the 2007–2008 food price crisis—including the growing import dependence of many SSA nations—reinforces the importance of several investment and policy factors that are key to assuring future food security. The selected drivers they identify include climate change, biofuels development, and chronically lagging expenditures in agricultural research and development. Climate change, in particular, Msangi and Rosegrant argue, is likely to present a host of new challenges to achieving future food production increases in SSA and will require public investments to offset likely future declines in crop yields and associated food price increases and adverse impacts on human nutrition. Among the investments the authors urge are those in irrigation, agricultural research and development, post-harvest processing, storage and distribution, and rural roads and infrastructure to enable markets to function more effectively. Needed policy changes include reducing trade barriers and avoiding export restraints which exacerbate food price spikes, facilitating food imports for the neediest countries, and improving the functioning of safety net programs that assist poor and vulnerable populations.

Chapters 5 and 6 address the financial market crisis specifically and its direct and indirect implications for developing economies, particularly in SSA. In Chapter 5, Hockett argues that financial asset price bubbles and busts, such as those observed in the early- to mid- and late-2000s, respectively, are in fact compatible with market efficiency and individual rationality, because they are the outcome of collective actions which aggregate individually rational behaviour. Simultaneously 'legging the spread' between cheap borrowing costs and credit-fueled capital gains on the part of many agents resulted in bubble-type asset price increases in the first half of the decade, followed by dramatic asset price drops later on once credit was exhausted. Solving this type of collective action problem requires a collective agent—in this case, a macroprudential financial regulator—who is capable of managing systemic risk through tightening credit, open market operations, capital regulation, and other measures as needed, something that some Federal Reserve Chairs have successfully done. Failing to implement successful risk management in a global credit market runs the risk of leaving the vulnerable at the mercy of financial boom-and-bust cycles they have no power to influence.

In Chapter 6, Songwe suggests that the food and financial crises were fundamentally interrelated. Innovative financial instruments, such as mortgage-backed securities, credit default swaps, and other over-the-counter (OTC) derivatives, were developed to hedge and spread financial risk. Growth in the financial and housing sectors helped buoy economic conditions in the US in the first half of the 2000s, which in turn helped support strong economic growth elsewhere, including in developing countries. The tightening of monetary and credit policies at mid-decade precipitated the exit of investors from mortgage-based instruments and into derivatives, including commodity derivatives, which coincided with government policies supporting the development of biofuels. Together these events increased the attractiveness of agricultural commodities as an asset class; the notional amount outstanding of over-the-counter derivatives on commodities grew to over US$12 trillion in 2008. The financial and economic crisis had severe consequences for many African countries, especially as it followed on the heels of the food price crisis. Finding policy solutions to avoid future financial crises will be complex and, among other things, will require the coordination of countries and international institutions in addressing financial sector reforms that include OTC derivatives and other financial instruments.

A longstanding concern in sub-Saharan Africa is its historically low rate of productivity growth in agriculture, the mainstay of the economies of many countries and by far its largest employer. Increasing agricultural productivity growth is necessary for improving food security across the continent and reducing the vulnerability of the poor, as revealed in the recent food and financial crises. In Chapter 7, Fuglie reports new production function estimates and estimates of total factor productivity growth in sub-Saharan agriculture since the 1960s. His results demonstrate an acceleration of growth in SSA agriculture since the 1980s, extending into the late 2000s. While encouraging, this improved performance is shown to be largely due to either improving terms-of-trade (e.g. higher commodity prices) or increases in agricultural land use and input intensification. Regional growth in total factor productivity—reflecting improved technology and production efficiency—remains only slightly above one percent annually, well below the global average. The chapter provides a number of recommendations regarding how to stimulate productivity growth in the future, including strengthening public policies and governance institutions and increasing public and private investments in agricultural innovation and technology transfer.

While the effects of the food and financial crises are typically reported at the aggregate national level—in large part because this is the level at which economic data are commonly reported—the studies reported in the next three chapters remind us that it is at the sub-national, regional and local levels that the impacts of crises are ultimately experienced by individual households. These impacts are shown to be highly diverse across a number of countries that are examined in depth. Mason and colleagues in Chapter 8 provide a detailed analysis of the behaviour of staple food prices, wage rates and marketing margins faced by urban consumers in selected countries in East and Southern Africa—Kenya, Malawi, Mozambique, and Zambia—between the mid-1990s and 2009. The authors find that formal sector wages in urban Kenya and Zambia and minimum wage levels in urban Mozambique rose faster than staple food prices for a decade or more prior to the food price crisis, so that while the crisis itself sharply reduced purchasing power for staple foods, overall purchasing power for staple foods for formal sector workers was still improved compared to the mid-1990s. Most employment in these (and other) countries is in the informal sector, however, so it is unclear whether the purchasing power of the poor and other vulnerable groups shared the same patterns. Marketing margins for maize and wheat generally, but not universally, trended downward between the mid-1990s and mid-2000s due to increasing local competition, efficiency gains and improved milling technology. The analysis demonstrates the importance of understanding heterogeneous local and sub-national trends in prices, wages, marketing margins and other indicators when attempting to understand the household-level impacts of events such as the food and financial crises.

In Chapter 9, Simler examines the impacts of higher food prices in 2008 on poverty in Uganda, after disaggregating households by region and their status as net food buyers or sellers. Even rural Ugandan households are shown to be overwhelmingly net food purchasers, leaving them—as well as urban households—vulnerable to food price rises. Notwithstanding the potential buffering effects played by factors such as the diversity of staple food consumption, high food self-sufficiency and weak links to global food markets, the author finds that poor Ugandan households, especially urban households, suffered significant welfare losses when food prices (along with oil prices and food imports) rose sharply in 2007–2008. The analysis demonstrates short-run impacts on the incidence, depth and geographical spread of poverty, including an additional 700,000 Ugandans living below the poverty line as a result of the food price crisis, highlighting the importance of improved social protection and safety net programs.

Gibson and colleagues in Chapter 10 examine coping strategies used by poor households in South Africa to cope with the food price spikes of 2007–2008. Poverty and undernutrition were widespread in South Africa prior to the food price crisis, making many households vulnerable to higher prices. The impacts of high food prices on portion sizes, dietary diversity and the cost of a balanced diet are analyzed. In response to price increases for staple foods, the authors document common household coping strategies, including: changing patterns of food consumption to take advantage of cheaper sources of calories, skipping meals, reducing portion sizes at mealtime, and reducing dietary diversity. Some household coping strategies are shown to have significantly negative impacts on nutritional status, exacerbating already serious nutritional deficiencies amongst the poor. The authors discuss possible policy changes and interventions to improve food security and nutritional status in the face of high food prices and examine South Africa's past experience with food fortification programs.

Turning to the future opportunities for African agriculture and economic growth, Masters, in Chapter 11, examines three key turning points in African development and argues that together they constitute significant opportunities for future growth. The first turning point is political and economic: African governments have made great progress since the 1980s in lowering trade protection and other policy-related price distortions, thereby reducing the taxation of agriculture and creating an improved policy foundation for future growth. The second is demographic: as population growth slows down from previously high levels, the 'demographic transition' will provide an increasingly fertile environment for African nations to take advantage of investment and technological change. The third turning point is technological change itself: the growth in recent years of cereal grain yields appears to reverse the historic trend of low and slowly growing agricultural productivity. This, along with the other aforementioned factors, means that the future payoffs from increased public investments—in infrastructure, research and development, and the like—may be significant and have the potential to overcome past constraints to economic development, which were exacerbated by the food and financial crises.

In Chapter 12, Gumede reviews the recent economic crisis and provides a policy perspective on how African countries can best position themselves to confront, or avoid, future crises. The chapter draws particularly from the South African experience. Four areas of policy relevance are emphasized: the pursuit of economic and sectoral strategies that prioritize the reduction of unemployment; investment in economic infrastructure and strengthening regional integration efforts; more informed fiscal and monetary policies; and developing improved social policies and programs to better protect the poor and most vulnerable populations. Other priority areas for policy reform include the financial sector, food security and the environment, and the formation of 'social compacts' to build policy consensus and help surmount some of the political obstacles to effecting meaningful policy change. Chapter 13 synthesizes this volume's main results and outlines a future policy and investment agenda to help mitigate the adverse impacts of future food and economic crises in the region.

References

Abbott, P.C. (2009) *Development dimensions of high food prices*. OECD Food, Agriculture and Fisheries Working Papers, No. 18. OECD Publishing, July.

Abbott, P. and Borot de Battisti, A. (2011) 'Recent global food price shocks: Causes, consequences and lessons for African governments and donors.' *Journal of African Economies* 20 (Supplement 1): i12-i62.

Abbott, P.C., Hurt, C. and Tyner, W.E. (2008) *What's driving food prices?* Farm Foundation, July.

Abbott, P.C., Hurt, C. and Tyner, W.E. (2009) *What's driving food prices? March 2009 update*. Farm Foundation, Oak Brook, IL, March.

Aksoy, M.A. and Isik-Dikmelik, A. (2008) *Are low food prices pro-poor? Net food buyers and sellers in low-income countries*. Policy Research Working Paper 4642. The World Bank, Washington DC, June.

Arndt, C., Benfica, R., Maximiano, N., Nucifora, A.M.D. and Thurlow, J.T. (2008) 'Higher fuel and food prices: impacts and responses for Mozambique.' *Agricultural Economics* 39: 497-511.

Benson, T., Mugarura, S. and Wanda, K. (2008) 'Impacts in Uganda of rising global food prices: the role of diversified staples and limited price transmission.' *Agricultural Economics* 39: 513-524.

Berazneva, J. and Lee, D.R. (2011) Understanding the African food riots of 2007–2008: An empirical analysis. Working Paper. Cornell University, Ithaca, NY, March.

Blein, R. and Longo, R. (2009) *Food price volatility—how to help smallholder farmers manage risk and uncertainty*. Discussion paper prepared for the Round Table organized during the Thirty-second session of IFAD's Governing Council. IFAD, Rome, Italy, February 18.

Brambila-Macias, J. and Massa, I. (2010) 'The global financial crisis and sub-Saharan Africa: The effects of slowing private capital inflows on growth.' *African Development Review* 22 (3): 366–377.

Brown, L. (2011) 'The Great Food Crisis of 2011: It's real, and it's not going away anytime soon.' *Foreign Policy*, January 10. http://www.foreignpolicy.com/articles/2011/01/10/the_great_food_crisis_of_2011.

Buvinic, M., Sagarwal, S. and Sinha, N. (2009) *The global financial crisis: Assessing vulnerability for women and children*. Prepared written statement, Division for the Advancement of Women Interactive Expert Panel on Gender Perspectives of the

Financial Crisis. Commission on the Status of Women, Fifty-third Session, New York, March 5.
Childs, N. and Kiawu, J. (2009) *Factors behind the rise in global rice prices in 2008.* Outlook Report No. (RCS-09D-01). United States Department of Agriculture (USDA) Economic Research Service, Washington DC, May.
Cudjoe, G., Breisinger, C. and Diao, X. (2010) 'Local impacts of a global crisis: Food price transmission, consumer welfare and poverty in Ghana.' *Food Policy* 35 (4): 294–302.
Dawe, D. (2008) *Have recent increases in international cereal prices been transmitted to domestic economies? The experience in seven large Asian countries*. ESA Working Paper No. 08–03. Agricultural and Development Economics Division of the Food and Agriculture Organization of the United Nations (FAO-ESA), Rome, Italy, April.
Demeke, M., Pangrazio, G. and Maetz, M. (2009) *Country responses to the food security crisis: Nature and preliminary implications of the policies pursued.* Food and Agriculture Organization of the United Nations (FAO), Rome, Italy.
Dessus, S., Herrera, S. and Hoyos, R. (2008) *The impact of food inflation on urban poverty and its monetary cost: some back-of-the-envelope calculations*. Policy Research Working Paper 4666. The World Bank, Washington, DC, July.
Food and Agricultural Organization of the United Nations. (2008a) *The state of food insecurity in the world 2008: High food prices and food security—threats and opportunities*. Rome, Italy.
Food and Agricultural Organization of the United Nations. (2008b) *Crop prospects and the food situation*. Rome, Italy, April.
Food and Agricultural Organization of the United Nations. (2009) *The state of food insecurity in the world 2009: Economic crises—impacts and lessons learned.* Rome, Italy.
Food and Agricultural Organization of the United Nations. (2010) *The state of food insecurity in the world 2010: Addressing food insecurity in protracted crises*. Rome, Italy.
Friedman, J. and Schady, N. (2009) *How many more infants are likely to die in Africa as a result of the global financial crisis?* Policy Research Working Paper 5023. The World Bank, Washington, DC, August.
Gilbert, C.L. (2010) 'How to understand high food prices.' *Journal of Agricultural Economics* 61(2): 398–425.
Glauber, J.W. (2011) *Prospects for the US farm economy in 2011*. United States Department of Agriculture (USDA), Washington, DC, February 24. http://www.usda.gov/documents/Glauber_Joe_Speech.pdf.
Global Information and Early Warning System (GIEWS). (2009) Food and Agricultural Organization of the United Nations. Rome, Italy. Available at: www.fao.org/giews/pricetool.
Harsch, E. (2008) 'Price protests expose state faults: Rioting and repression reflect problems of African governance.' *Africa Renewal,* United Nations 22(2), July. http://www.un.org/ecosocdev/geninfo/afrec/vol22no2/index.html.
Headey, D. and Fan, S. (2008) 'Anatomy of a crisis: the causes and consequences of surging food prices.' *Agricultural Economics* 39: 375–391.
Headey, D. and Fan, S. (2010) *Reflections on the global food crisis: How did it happen? How has it hurt? And how can we prevent the next one?* IFPRI Research Monograph 165. International Food Policy Research Institute, Washington, DC.

Headey, D., Malaiyandi, S. and Fan, S. (2009) *Navigating the perfect storm: Reflections on the food, energy, and financial crises*. IFPRI Discussion Paper 889. International Food Policy Research Institute, Washington, DC, August.

International Labour Organization. (2011) *Global employment trends 2011: The challenge of jobs recovery*. Geneva, Switzerland.

International Monetary Fund. (2008a) *Food and fuel prices: recent developments, macroeconomic impact, and policy responses*. Prepared by the Fiscal Affairs, Policy Development and Review, and Research Departments. Washington, DC. June 30.

International Monetary Fund. (2008b) *Regional economic outlook: Sub-Saharan Africa 2008*. World Economic and Financial Surveys, Washington, DC, October.

International Monetary Fund. (2009) *Regional economic outlook: Sub-Saharan Africa 2009: Weathering the storm*. World Economic and Financial Surveys, Washington, DC, October.

International Monetary Fund. (2010a) *Regional economic outlook: Sub-Saharan Africa 2010: Back to high growth?* World Economic and Financial Surveys, Washington, DC, April.

International Monetary Fund. (2010b) *Regional economic outlook: Sub-Saharan Africa 2010: Resilience and risks*. World Economic and Financial Surveys, Washington, DC. October.

International Monetary Fund. (2011a) *International Financial Statistics*. Washington, DC. http://www.imfstatistics.org/imf/. Accessed: May 11, 2011.

International Monetary Fund. (2011b) *World economic outlook (WEO): Tensions from the two-speed recovery: Unemployment, commodities, and capital flows*. Washington, DC, April.

Islam, R. and Nallari, R. (2010). *Of floods and droughts: The economic and financial crisis of 2008*. Policy Research Working Paper 5237. The World Bank, Washington, DC, March.

Ivanic, M. and Martin, W. (2008) 'Implications of higher global food prices for poverty in low-income countries.' *Agricultural Economics* 39: 405–416.

Lin, J.Y. (2008) *The impact of the financial crisis on developing countries*. Paper presented to Korea Development Institute. October 31. http://siteresources.worldbank.org/ROMANIAEXTN/Resources/Oct_31_JustinLin_KDI_remarks.pdf.

Lin, J.Y. and Martin, W. (2010) 'The financial crisis and its impacts on global agriculture.' *Agricultural Economics* 41: 133–144.

Lustig, N. (2009) *Coping with rising food prices: Policy dilemmas in the developing world*. The George Washington University, Washington, DC, Institute for International Economic Policy, February.

Massa, I. and te Velde, D.W. (2008) *The global financial crisis: Will successful African countries be affected?* ODI Background Note. London, UK: Overseas Development Institute (ODI), December 8.

McCord, A. and Vandermoortele, M. (2009) *The global financial crisis: Poverty and social protection*. ODI Briefing Papers 51. Overseas Development Institute (ODI), London, UK, August.

Mitchell, D. (2008) *A note on rising food prices*. Policy Research Working Paper 4682. The World Bank, Washington, DC, July.

Moore, F.C. (2008) Food price unrest around the world, September 2007 to April 2008. Earth Policy Institute, www.earthpolicy.org, April 16. http://www.earth-policy.org/data_center/C25/.

NATO. (2009) *Food price shocks and their implications for food security*. 2009 Annual Session, 176 ESCTER 09 E bis. NATO Parliamentary Assembly. http://www.nato-pa.int/default.asp?SHORTCUT=1779.

OECD and FAO. (2008) *OECD-FAO Agricultural Outlook 2008–2017*. Organization for Economic Cooperation and Development (OECD) and Food and Agriculture Organization of the United Nations (FAO), Paris, France.

Ravallion, M. (2008) *Bailing out the world's poorest*. Policy Research Working Paper 4763. The World Bank, Washington, DC, October.

Ravallion, M. (2009) 'The Crisis and the World's Poorest.' *Development Outreach*. The World Bank, Washington, DC, December.

Rios, A.R., Shively, G.E. and Masters, W.A. (2008) *Agricultural prices and income distribution among farmers: A whole-household, multi-country, multi-year analysis*. Mimeo. Purdue University, May. http://purl.umn.edu/49314.

Ruel, M., Garrett, J., Hawkes, C. and Cohen, M. (2010) 'The food, fuel, and financial crises affect the urban and rural poor disproportionately: A review of the evidence.' *The Journal of Nutrition* 140 (1): 170S.

Sanders, D.R. and Irwin, S.H. (2010) 'A speculative bubble in commodity futures prices? Cross-sectional evidence.' *Agricultural Economics* 41(1): 25–32.

Sanogo, I. (2009) 'The global food price crisis and household hunger: a review of recent food security assessments.' *Humanitarian Exchange Magazine, Overseas Development Institute (ODI)*, March. http://www.odihpn.org/report.asp?id=2988.

Timmer, C.P. (2008) *Causes of high food prices*. ADB Economics Working Paper Series No. 128. Asian Development Bank, Manila, Philippines, October.

Torero, M. (2011) Alternative mechanisms to reduce food price volatility and price spikes. The UK's Government Foresight Project on Global Food and Farming Futures, *Science Review:* SR 21. January. http://www.foodsecurityportal.org/alternative-mechanisms-reduce-food-price-volatility.

Trostle, R. (2008) *Global agricultural supply and demand: Factors contributing to the recent increase in food commodity prices*. Outlook Report No. (WRS-0801). United States Department of Agriculture (USDA) Economic Research Service, Washington, DC, July.

US Department of State. (2011) Food price crisis of 2007–2008: Lessons learned. Fact Sheet, Office of the Spokesman, Washington, DC, March 3. http://www.state.gov/r/pa/prs/ps/2011/03/157629.htm.

Ulimwengu, J.M., Wonkeh, S. and Paulos, Z. (2009) *Impact of soaring food prices in Ethiopia: Does location matter?* IFPRI Discussion Paper 846. International Food Policy Research Institute (IFPRI), Washington, DC, February.

UNDP. (2011) *The Human Development Index (HDI)*. United Nations Development Programme, New York. http://hdr.undp.org/en/statistics/hdi/. Accessed: May 11, 2011.

USDA. (2011) *World agricultural supply and demand estimates*. United States Department of Agriculture, Washington, DC, May. http://www.usda.gov/oce/commodity/wasde/.

te Velde, D.W., Ahmed, M.M., Alemu, G., Bategeka, L., Cali, M., Castel-Branco, C., Chansa, F., Dasgupta, S., Foresti, M., Hangi, M., Ingombe, L., Iqbal, A., Jalilian, H., Jemio, L.C., Kabuya Kalala, F., Keane, J., Kennan, J., Islam Khan, T., Lunogelo, H.B., Massa, I., Mbilinyi, A., Mudena, D., Mwega, F.M., Ndulo, M., Nina, O., Ossemane, R., Rahman, M., Reyes, G., Ssewanyan, S., Wild, L. and others. (2010) The global financial crisis and developing countries: Phase 2 synthesis. ODI Working Paper 316. Overseas Development Institute (ODI), London, UK, March.

te Velde, D.W., Cali, M., Keane, J., Kennan, J., Massa, I., McCord, A., Meyn, M. and Vandemoorele, M. (2009) *The global financial crisis and developing countries: Preliminary synthesis of ten draft country reports*. ODI Working Paper 306. Overseas Development Institute, London, UK.

von Braun, J., Ahmed, A., Asenso-Okyere, K., Fan, S., Gulati, A., Hoddinott, J. and Pandya-Lorch, R. (2008) *High food prices: The what, who, and how of proposed policy actions*. Policy Brief. International Food Policy Research Institute (IFPRI), Washington, DC, May.

von Braun, J. and Torero, M. (2009) 'Exploring the price spike.' *Choices* 24(1), 1st Quarter. http://www.choicesmagazine.org/magazine/article.php?article=58.

Wodon, Q., Tsimpo, C., Backiny-Yetna, P., Joseph, G., Adoho, F. and Coulombe, H. (2008) *Potential impact of higher food prices on poverty: summary estimates for a dozen West and Central African countries*. Policy Research Working Paper 4745. The World Bank, Washington, DC, October.

Wodon, Q. and Zaman, H. (2008) *Rising food prices in sub-Saharan Africa: Poverty impact and policy responses*. Policy Research Working Paper 4738. The World Bank, Washington, DC, October.

World Bank. (2009) *Global economic prospects 2009: Commodities at the crossroads*. Washington, DC, July.

World Bank. (2010a) *Global economic prospects 2010: Crisis, finance, and growth*. Washington, DC.

World Bank. (2010b) *Global monitoring report 2010: The MDGs after the crisis*. Washington, DC.

World Bank. (2011a) *Migration and Remittances Factbook 2011*. The World Bank, Washington, DC. http://data.worldbank.org/data-catalog/migration-and-remittances. Accessed: May 11, 2011.

World Bank. (2011b) *Food price watch*. The World Bank, Washington, DC, February.

World Food Programme. (2009) WFP Annual Report 2009. Summary of price impact assessment findings. Food Security Analysis Service, Rome, Italy, October 9.

Zezza, A., Davis, B., Azzarri, C., Covarrubias, K., Tasciotti, L. and Anriquez, G. (2008) *The impact of rising food prices on the poor*. Agricultural and Development Economics Division of the Food and Agriculture Organization of the United Nations, Rome, Italy.

Chapter 2

The Global Food and Financial Crises and the Poor in Africa

Ernest Aryeetey and Nelipher Moyo

University of Ghana, Ghana; Brookings Institution, Washington, DC

Abstract

Sub-Saharan Africa was significantly affected by the global food and economic crises of the late 2000s, with the continent suffering pronounced negative impacts on many of its countries and people. Given its widespread poverty, dependence on commodity exports, and status as a net food importer, the continent experienced a series of shocks as it was hit first with sharply rising food prices in 2007–2008, then by falling global prices for its exports, and finally by the depletion of foreign reserves to pay for imports and necessary goods. These impacts reversed past gains in poverty reduction and led to increased undernourishment, poor health, infant mortality and social unrest. The global financial crisis and economic recession which followed immediately thereafter further worsened the state of many African economies and people, most notably the poor. The financial and economic crises were transmitted to African economies both through direct channels—stock and bond markets, the banking sector, declines in foreign direct investment, and depreciated exchange rates—and even more strongly through indirect channels—significant declines in export prices, export revenues, official development assistance, and remittances. Economic growth in sub-Saharan Africa—in oil-producing and non-oil producing countries alike—slowed significantly in 2009 following impressive performance earlier in the decade. This chapter highlights developments in three countries—Ghana, Zambia and Nigeria—to illustrate the diverse impacts of the crises. Overall, the poor in sub-Saharan Africa experienced a 'double agony' as a result of the simultaneous crises, with negative consequences for poverty, undernourishment and infant mortality. Although the economic recovery followed more rapidly than expected and is now well underway, sub-Saharan Africa continues to be at risk once again with rising food prices in 2010–2011. While African governments made significant strides in mitigating the impact of the crises on their economies, much less progress has been made in softening the blows of the food and financial crises on the poor. Just as governments have adopted counter-cyclical macroeconomic policies, governments must, in the future, do a better job of implementing counter-cyclical social protection programs to assist poor and vulnerable populations and help ensure that external economic shocks do not derail long-term poverty reduction goals.

Introduction

From 2007 through mid-2008 world food prices, especially for cereal grains, increased significantly. The nominal prices of staples such as maize, wheat and rice doubled between 2007 and 2008. In the wake of such increases, the poor are particularly vulnerable because they spend upwards of 50 to 80 percent of their incomes on food and have little capacity to adapt to price increases. To cope with the crisis, poor households had to reduce the quality and quantity of the food they consumed, increasing their risk of undernutrition and malnutrition. As a result of the global food crisis, the Food and Agriculture Organization of the United Nations estimated that the number of undernourished people in the world increased from 915 million in 2008 to 1.02 billion in 2009 (FAO, 2009). With the global economic recovery in 2010, the number of undernourished is estimated to have decreased to 925 million, though it remains much higher than before the crisis.

As a net-food importing region, sub-Saharan Africa was the hardest hit by the global food crisis. Low agricultural productivity has also made sub-Saharan Africa the most food-insecure region. Half of the region's 819 million inhabitants live on less than $1.25 a day (World Bank, 2010b). The global food crisis not only increased the number of people living below the poverty line in Africa, it also made the lives of those already living in poverty much worse.

The global financial crisis, which intensified in the last quarter of 2008, helped to bring down world food prices but also introduced a series of new challenges for the poor in sub-Saharan Africa. The combination of low global demand, falling commodity prices, declining remittances, slowing aid flows, net capital outflows and rising unemployment presented new challenges for the region. Until both crises hit, African economies were performing well, with unprecedented growth driven by commodity booms and improved economic management. The continent experienced its highest growth since independence as GDP grew at an average of 4.9 percent between 2000 and 2007. Some governments in the region were beginning to implement or expand social protection programs. The dual crises threatened to reverse the progress made by African governments to reduce poverty and maintain macroeconomic stability.

Even as economic growth in Africa has returned to pre-crisis levels (GDP growth is expected to be 5.3 percent in 2011), it is becoming increasingly clear that the food and financial crisis is having a lagged impact on the poor in the region. Furthermore, rising food prices in late 2010 and early 2011 once again threaten the well-being of poor and vulnerable households.

This chapter will examine the impact of the crisis on African countries. It will examine how the poor in sub-Saharan Africa have been affected by the double agony of simultaneous crises in both the food and financial sectors. The chapter will argue that while African governments have made significant strides in mitigating the impact of the crises on their economies, much less progress has been made toward softening the blows from such crises on the poor.

Subsequent sections of this chapter will discuss the scope of the food and financial crises and some of their causes, followed by an examination of the transmission mechanisms of the crises on African economies, with illustrations from Ghana, Zambia and Nigeria. These illustrations provide useful information about the crises' impacts on mineral-dependent, non-oil producing African countries (Zambia), on mixed agriculture/mining-based African countries (Ghana), and on oil-producing African countries (Nigeria). Since the majority of African countries fall into at least one of these categories, the impacts of the crises on these three countries is likely to be a good representation of impacts elsewhere in sub-Saharan Africa. Following these discussions we will assess the impacts of the dual crises on the poor in the region and then analyze government responses to the crisis with a discussion of social protection programs in sub-Saharan Africa. Finally, the last section will summarize key findings and conclusions.

The Scope of the Crises

Most discussions of the effects of the crises on African countries have tended to look at them as separate events, not necessarily linked. The need to look at them together arises from the fact that they occurred quite close to one another and so had a more pronounced combined immediate impact on people and economies than would otherwise have been the case.

The Global Food Crisis

Sharp increases in the prices of grains and other food staples from 2007 through mid–2008 had serious implications for food and nutrition security, macroeconomic stability, and political security worldwide. Between March 2007 and March 2008, the global price of wheat increased by 130 percent, the price of rice by 74 percent and that of maize by 87 percent (Islam and Buckley, 2009). This was a major shock as world food prices had declined 75 percent from 1974 to 2005. Despite the global economic recovery that followed the financial and economic crises of 2007-2009, by late 2010 and early 2011 world food prices as measured by the FAO had risen again, to levels higher than peak 2008 prices. While the 2007–2008 global food crisis is now a thing of the past, the risk of another food crisis remains high.

It is estimated that the average household in sub-Saharan Africa spends 60 to 80 percent of its income on food. Consequently, the impact of the food crisis on households in the region was especially devastating. As a net food-importing region, sub-Saharan Africa is more vulnerable to food price shocks than any other region in the world. The region imports 25 percent of the food it consumes and receives about one-third of the world's food aid (UNCTAD, 2009a).

There are numerous factors that contributed to the sharp increases in global food prices. The most commonly cited include:

- *Increasing demand from emerging market economies*: As China and India continue to develop, their demands for grains and other foods have increased, putting upward pressure on global food prices.
- *Biofuels*: The rising use of food crops, especially maize, for biofuels contributed to higher prices of grains. According to the US Department of Agriculture (2009), about 23 percent of all maize produced in the US was used to produce ethanol in 2007–2008; that proportion rose to 31 percent in 2008–2009 and has since risen still further.
- *Increasing fuel prices*: The price of oil went from approximately $92 per barrel in January, 2008 to $147 per barrel in July of 2008. The spike in oil prices led to an increase in the price of agricultural inputs such as fertilizer and pesticides, which in turn led to higher costs of production for farmers. Pressure from fuel prices has subsequently eased as the price of oil averaged $79 in 2010 and was projected to average $86 in 2011,

though this projection is subject to shocks that could push prices up once again (Energy Information Administration [EIA], 2010).

- *Agricultural productivity:* Production has grown much more slowly than demand for grains. Furthermore, floods, droughts and other natural disasters in 2008 contributed to slower productivity growth.
- *Low stocks of grain:* Although demand continued to increase, stocks of all major cereals fell in the years prior to the price surge. The Food and Agriculture Organization of the United Nations (FAO) indicated that cereal stocks in 2007 were 13 percent less than in 2003 (FAO, 2008). Cereal stocks increased from 501 million tons in 2008–2009 to 525 million tons in 2009–2010, helping to relieve the pressure on food prices. However, as of March 2011, the FAO projects a 'tightening of the global cereal supply-and-demand balance in 2010–2011,' which is contributing to renewed increases in food prices (2011).
- *Investor behavior*: Speculative capital also played a role in driving up food prices. The volume of globally traded grain futures and options rose significantly in the second half of 2008. Supply and demand fundamentals do not fully explain the drastic increase in trading in grain futures and options. One explanation is that investors fleeing the housing bubble fueled an asset bubble in world commodity markets.
- *Climate change*: Water shortages, land scarcity and climate change all contribute to higher prices of food. Climate change is likely to exacerbate land and water shortages and will have a huge effect on agriculture in the future.

Headey and Fan (2008) examine the relative strength of each of these factors in explaining the global food crisis. Some factors are found to have more explanatory power than others. Ultimately they conclude that 'a conflagration of factors caused food prices to rise much more quickly than is desirable, and whatever the precise impacts so far, it is clear that many of the world's poor have already experienced the harsh reality of more costly sustenance.'

Even though the news about the food crisis was later eclipsed by the global financial and economic crisis, it is important to note that food prices continue to be elevated above pre-crisis levels and it is the poor who continue to bear the brunt of this crisis.

The Global Financial Crisis

The global financial crisis began in the summer of 2007 with the collapse of the US subprime mortgage market and intensified in the fall of 2008 following the failure of Wall Street giant Lehman Brothers. The financial problems of investment banks and insurance companies like Bear Stearns, Merrill Lynch, and AIG further intensified the crisis, which quickly spread from the US to other advanced economies, especially in Europe. Global bank losses from the financial crisis were initially estimated to be over $2.2 trillion dollars as the crisis moved to other sectors of the global economy (IMF, 2010). The world economy contracted in 2009 by 1.1 percent from growth of 3.0 percent in 2008. World trade volumes decreased by 12 percent (IMF, 2009), and Foreign Direct Investment (FDI) inflows to developing countries declined by 29 percent in 2009 (UNCTAD, 2010). The world economy has since rebounded and is now expected to grow by 4.8 percent in 2010 and by 4.2 percent in 2011 (IMF, 2010c). World trade volumes began to recover in the second half of 2009 and increased noticeably in 2010. Experts, however, project that imports will remain depressed in the short to medium term.

The causes of the financial crisis are still widely debated. Some argue that low interest rates encouraged the search for higher yields and consequently created large global imbalances; others blame lax regulation of the financial sector, excessive leverage and risk taking among investors, and poor disclosure about complex financial assets (Mohan, 2009).

Whatever the cause(s), the financial crisis spread to developing countries through trade linkages, a reduction of foreign direct investment and remittances, and a collapse in commodity prices. As the financial crisis turned into an economic crisis, the growth outlook for sub-Saharan Africa took a turn for the worse. Despite being the region the least integrated into global financial markets, sub-Saharan Africa was hard hit by the financial crisis. Real GDP growth in sub-Saharan Africa decreased as a result of the crisis, from 7.0 percent in 2007 to 5.6 percent in 2008, dropping further downward to 2.5 percent in 2009 (IMF, 2010b). Before the crisis the majority of African economies had enjoyed robust economic growth for close to a decade. The continent grew at an average annual rate of 4.8 percent between 2000 and 2007. The global financial crisis, by all accounts, significantly worsened economic performance and the living conditions of the poor in sub-Saharan Africa. While they were hit hard by the financial crisis, African economies have recovered much faster than they did during previous crises. Prudent economic management before and during the crisis, rising commodity prices and the implementation of counter-cyclical fiscal policies helped to bring about the quick recovery. In fact, sub-Saharan Africa is estimated to have grown about 4.7 percent in 2010 and is expected to grow by 5.3 percent in 2011 (World Bank, 2011a).

The Crises and Broad Economic Performance

The experiences of individual African countries in response to the financial and economic crises varied. As one of the more globally integrated countries in the region, Ghana was hit quite hard by the global financial crisis. Before the crisis Ghana boasted significant GDP growth, averaging 5 percent between 1984 and 2007. The country experienced a marked decrease in GDP growth, from 8.4 percent in 2008 down to 4.7 percent in 2009 (World Bank, 2011). Ghana's new status as an oil-producing country bodes well for economic growth in 2011; it is now expected to grow 13.4 percent in 2011 (World Bank, 2011a).

The region's oil producers did not fare much better. Nigeria, one of the region's largest oil producers, saw a decrease in its GDP growth outlook, from 7.0 percent in 2007 to 6.0 percent in 2008 (IMF, 2010b). The country is now projected to grow 7.1 percent in 2011 (World Bank, 2011a) as the economic recovery in Africa strengthens and oil prices continue to increase.

The economic outlook for the Zambian economy decreased as global demand for commodities weakened. Due to falling copper prices, the Zambian economy grew at a slower rate in 2008 than in 2007, declining from 6.2 percent growth in 2007 to 5.7 percent in 2008 (IMF, 2010b). In line with the rest of the region, the Zambian economy experienced a resurgence in 2009 and 2010; GDP grew at 6.3 percent in 2009 and 6.4 percent in 2010 (World Bank, 2011a). The Zambian economy is now forecast to grow by 6.5 percent in 2011, in line with pre-crisis levels.

Figure 2.1. Recent Real GDP growth performance

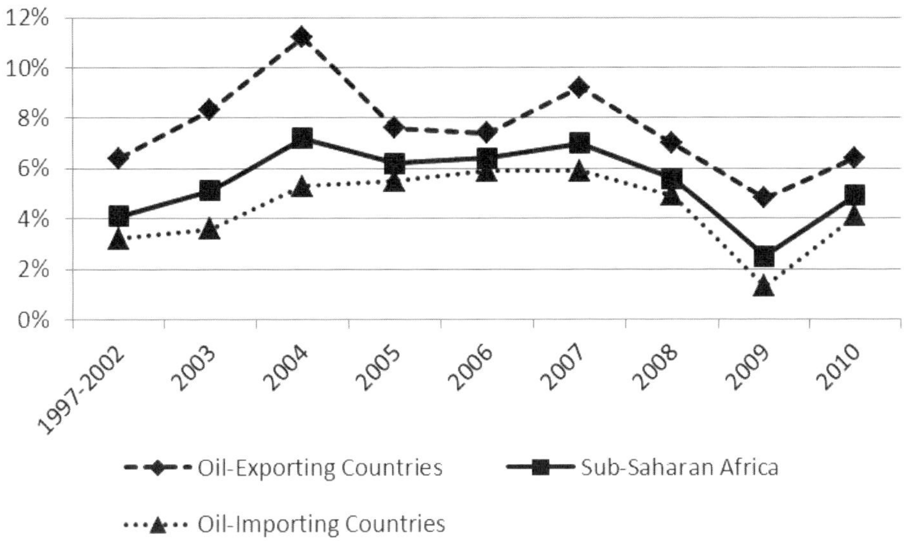

Source: IMF, Regional Economic Outlook, October 2010.

Unemployment

The recent global financial crisis exacerbated the unemployment problem in sub-Saharan Africa. But unemployment was a primary issue in sub-Saharan Africa even before the crisis. While the official estimate of unemployment in the region was 7.6 percent in 2008, this does not adequately reflect the fact that over 75 percent of the labor force was employed in low-productivity informal sector activities. Those in vulnerable employment sectors are also likely to fall into the category of the working poor. Reducing poverty in Africa will therefore require African countries to increase efforts to create jobs for those in vulnerable employment situations (UNECA, 2010). According to the International Labour Organization (ILO), four-fifths of the employed in sub-Saharan Africa are classified as working poor. Despite the impressive growth rates between 2000 and 2007, unemployment in sub-Saharan Africa decreased by only 0.3 percent.

Zambia was one of the countries hardest hit, in terms of unemployment, by the financial crisis. With the sharp decrease in the price of copper, mines in the Copperbelt were forced to drastically reduce their operations and maintain skeleton crews. Consequently, about 8,500 workers in the mining sector were laid off (ODI, 2009). The true impact of these layoffs is much greater than this number suggests. By some estimates, each formal sector mining job in Zambia supports an additional 20 jobs in services, suppliers and the informal sector (Green, 2009).

Both Nigeria and Ghana have experienced modest increases in unemployment as a result of the global financial crisis. The Overseas Development Institute (ODI) reports that FDI-generated employment in Ghana dropped from 15,526 in the fourth quarter of 2007 to 10,022 in the fourth quarter of 2008 (2009). Similarly, the ODI estimates that unemployment in Nigeria will increase as a result of decreasing remittances and FDI.

Overall, unemployment in sub-Saharan Africa is estimated to have risen to 8.2 percent in 2009 (ILO, 2010).

Rising unemployment has devastating effects on the poor who do not have adequate savings to cushion the blow. In the Copperbelt province of Zambia, the retrenchment of 25 percent of mining sector workers resulted in an increase in commercial sex workers as households struggled to survive (Oxfam, 2008). As copper prices began to rebound in 2009, the unemployment situation in Zambia also improved. By the end of 2010, many of the retrenched mine workers had been rehired. However, the country remains extremely vulnerable to volatility in the copper market.

Unemployment has once again emerged as a key concern in Africa as of early 2011. What began as riots over unemployment and poor economic conditions in Tunisia resulted in the overthrow of that government in early 2011. This spread to Egypt, with the end of the longstanding Mubarak government weeks later. Similar riots have erupted across North Africa and are an important reminder that Africa must achieve job-creating growth in the years to come.

Transmission Channels of the Food Crisis in African Economies

The two major things that influenced the transmission of rising global prices in 2007–2008 to African households were the growing immersion of African economies into global food trade and domestic policy responses that often compounded the problems facing households.

Net Food Importers

Due to increasing demand for food and low agricultural productivity, the majority of African countries are net food importers. Of the 47 countries in sub-Saharan Africa, only 12 are net exporters of raw food. In addition, almost all of the countries in the region are net importers of cereals (Wodon and Zaman, 2008).

The agricultural sector employs 65 percent of the labor force in Africa and accounts for 32 percent of GDP (World Bank, 2008). Despite the importance of the agricultural sector for the livelihood of Africans, the majority of African households are net consumers instead of net producers of foods. It is their status as net consumers (especially of cereals) that makes African households particularly vulnerable to global food price shocks. Due to various structural constraints, African farmers have not been able to take broad advantage of rising food prices. The increasing prices of fertilizer and other imported inputs, limited access to credit, and poor market access are some of the most commonly cited reasons for farmers in the region not capitalizing on higher prices by increasing the volume of their output.

In Nigeria, for example, the agricultural sector is still an important part of the economy despite the significance of oil. Agriculture accounts for one-third of Nigeria's GDP and employs 40 to 60 percent of the labor force. Although the agricultural sector contributes significantly to the Nigerian economy, agricultural production in the country is low and has not been able to match increasing demand. Consequently, Nigeria is a net food importer.

Rice is the fastest growing food source in sub-Saharan Africa. This is especially true in Nigeria, where about 40 percent of the rice consumed is imported (Ogundele and Okoruwa, 2006), making it one of the largest importers of rice in the world. Consequently, the spike in the price of rice and other cereals was quickly transmitted domestically. For example, the price of a 50 kg bag of premium imported rice increased exponentially, from ₦7,500 in December, 2007 to ₦14,000 by March, 2008. A similar trend was seen in low quality brands of rice. Over the same period, the prices of palm oil, maize, guinea maize and beans rose by 36, 28, 16 and 12 percent, respectively (Central Bank of Nigeria [CBN], 2008).

In spite of significant efforts by the Nigerian government to boost local rice production, including a 100 percent tax on rice imports, the production increase was not sufficient to match the consumption increase. With the rising price of rice, the Nigerian government removed the tax on rice imports for six months in 2008 to help ease the hardships on consuming households. The country's food import bill increased 33 percent, from US$3 billion in 2007 to $3.99 billion in 2008 (CBN, 2008). This has significant implications for undernourishment in a country where 65 percent of the population lives on less than a dollar a day.

Despite having a slightly more diversified agricultural export base, Ghana is also a net food importing country. The country is highly dependent on wheat and rice imports. About two-thirds of all the rice consumed in Ghana is imported, and similarly 100 percent of all the wheat consumed is imported (Cudjoe *et al.*, 2008). A shortage of public and private physical storage facilities has limited Ghana's ability to hedge against price fluctuations, leaving the country vulnerable to global food price shocks. Ghana produces a significant amount of other staples such as maize, cassava, and yams in different regions, and for this reason the impact of the global food price hikes varied across those different regions. The regional variations offered little relief as the prices of local staples also increased during the crisis period. For example, the real price of maize in December, 2008 was 72 percent higher than in December, 2006. Likewise, the real price of cassava in December, 2008 was about 33 percent higher than in December, 2006. To cope with these price increases, 38 percent of Ghanaian households reported that they were reducing both the quantity and quality of food they consumed, and this was expected to have significant implications for undernourishment and malnutrition (Brinkman *et al.*, 2009).

Maize continues to be the primary staple food in Zambia; it provides 60 percent of the dietary energy supply. The price of maize in Zambia is very volatile, even when compared with other countries in the region (Jayne and Chapoto, 2009), as the majority of farmers in the country are subsistence farmers and are heavily dependent on rainfall and other seasonal effects. In dollar terms, the price of maize in Zambia was 40 percent higher in June, 2008 than in June, 2007. The appreciation of the *kwacha* against the dollar in the first half of 2008 helped to shield the country from food price increases; in fact, in *kwacha* terms, maize prices only increased 9 percent between June, 2007 and June, 2008. However, as the *kwacha* began to depreciate against the dollar in the second half of 2008 and early 2009, the impact of elevated food prices in Zambia was significant. According to the Zambia Vulnerability Assessment Committee, because of elevated food prices coupled with flooding in certain parts of the country, approximately 445,000 people in the country needed additional food assistance—totalling about 33,333 tons of maize—from July, 2008 to March, 2009 (ZVAC, 2008). Improved rains in 2009 resulted in a significant increase in the output of staple grains in 2010. Maize production grew at a record 48 percent, to 2.7 million tonnes between 2009 and 2010. Cassava and wheat followed a similar trend. This helped to provide a cushion against rising food prices.

The outlook for net-food importing countries improved moderately in the second half of 2009 and the first half of 2010; however, by the summer of 2010 food prices began to increase once again. The Food and Agriculture Organization projected that the food import bills for food-deficit countries increased by 11 percent in 2010, and unless production of major food crops increases significantly in 2011, the outlook is expected to worsen.

In Ghana, increased output of cocoa, poultry, maize and sorghum in 2010 helped to relieve pressure on consumers. However, as world food prices increase back to 2008 crisis levels, consumers will feel the pinch on their household food budgets.

Figure 2.2. World food price index, 2007–2010

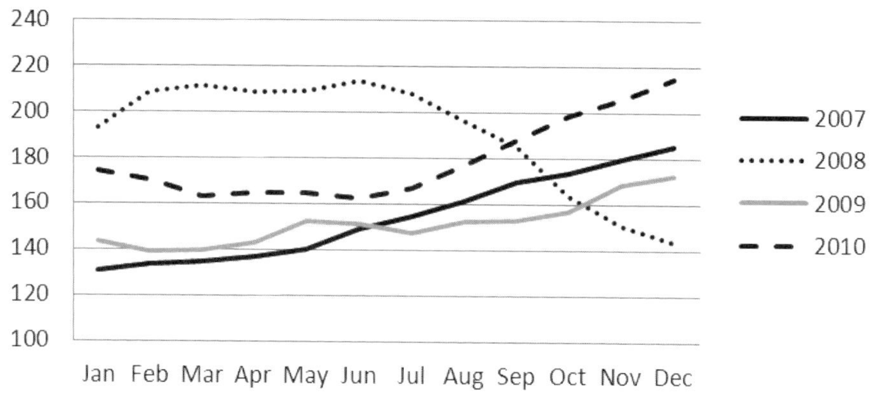

Source: FAO Food Price Indices, January 2011

Inflation

In sharp contrast with previous decades, African countries have made significant progress in tackling inflation; the continent achieved single-digit inflation rates averaging 7 percent between 2000 and 2007. This is a significant improvement compared with the 10 percent average inflation rates between 1990 and 1999. Increasing population growth coupled with the region's status as a net-food importing region has left sub-Saharan Africa highly vulnerable to food price inflation. In the wake of the recent food and fuel price shocks, inflation increased markedly in sub-Saharan Africa, to 11.7 percent in 2008 from 6.8 percent in 2007 (IMF, 2010b). The IMF estimates that food price increases accounted for almost 70 percent of 'headline' inflation (nominal inflation unadjusted for seasonality and including volatile food and energy prices) in the region in 2008 (IMF, 2009). Prudent economic management during the crisis has helped to moderate inflation back down to 7.5 percent in 2010 (IMF, 2010b).

In Nigeria, the increasing appetite for imported food items among urban households facilitated a quick transmission of global price increases into the domestic economy (CBN, 2008). Increases in the prices of cereal imports were quickly transmitted to local markets. As a result, year-on-year headline inflation more than doubled, from 5.4 percent in 2007 to 11.6 percent in 2008 (IMF, 2010b). The Central Bank of Nigeria reports that much of this increase was driven by the increase in food and fuel prices (CBN, 2008). Although the economic recovery was well underway in Nigeria in 2010, inflation continued to be elevated due primarily to rising oil prices. The IMF projected inflation of 11.9 percent in 2010; a combination of rising food and fuel prices in the first half of 2011 could push inflation higher (2010b).

In Ghana, inflationary pressures from high food and fuel prices in the first half of 2009 led to a sharp increase in inflation. Despite the country's adoption of an inflation-targeting framework in 2007, the annual inflation rate in Ghana increased markedly, from 12.7 percent at year's end, in December, 2007, to 18.1 percent by December, 2008. This was due to both food and non-food (mostly fuel) price inflation. Annual food price inflation rose from a 10.5 percent rate at the end of 2007 (December) to 17.7 percent in December, 2008. Similarly, annual non-food price inflation rose from a 14.4 percent rate in December, 2007 to 18.9 percent by December, 2008. Inflation continued to increase in 2009 to 19.3 percent but decreased to 10.6 percent in 2010. With Ghana's new oil-producing status, inflation remains a major concern for the government.

Similar trends were observed in Zambia, where inflation increased significantly, from single-digit inflation in 2006 (9.0 percent) to double-digit inflation by 2009 (13.4 percent) (IMF, 2010b). The spike in food prices quickly translated into high inflation in Zambia; annual food price inflation increased considerably, from 5.9 percent measured at year's end in December, 2007, to 20.5 percent in December, 2008, while non-food price inflation increased modestly, from 11.9 percent in December, 2007 to 12.9 percent in December, 2008 (BOZ, 2008). Zambia has been able to contain inflation in the post-crisis period at an annual average of 8.2 percent in 2010. The IMF (2010b) projects that inflation will decrease even further in 2011, down to 7.5 percent; however, there is a risk of upward pressure on inflation as a result of rising food prices.

The sharp rise in inflation across sub-Saharan Africa has broader implications for wages, poverty, and even social unrest on the continent. In their study, Ravallion and Datt (2002) found that a marked increase in the rate of inflation also led to an increase in headcount poverty. The impact of the food crisis on the poor in Africa will be examined in more detail further below.

Transmission Channels of the Financial Crisis on African Economies

Despite being the least integrated into global financial markets, sub-Saharan Africa was not insulated from the direct and indirect effects of the financial crisis. The direct effects included stock market volatility, exchange rate volatility, capital flow reversals and capital scarcity in the banking sector. As the financial crisis turned into a global economic crisis, the indirect effects of the crisis in Africa included decreasing demand for commodities, a slowdown in official development assistance, a decrease in remittances, increasing unemployment, and ultimately slower GDP growth.

Direct Channels

Stock Markets

Before the global financial crisis, investors poured billions of dollars into the so-called 'frontier' markets in Africa. The number of stock markets in sub-Saharan Africa increased from only five in 1989 to about 16 in 2008. Furthermore, the capitalization of African stock markets increased from $113 billion in 1992 to $245 billion in 2002 (IMF, 2009).

Sub-Saharan Africa's emerging (South Africa) and frontier (Ghana, Kenya, Nigeria, Uganda, and Zambia) economies were hit the hardest by the direct effects of the global financial crisis. Since the onset of the global financial crisis, stock market volatility in sub-

Saharan Africa has increased significantly and wealth losses have been observed in the majority of stock exchanges.

Stock market indices for Kenya, Nigeria, Uganda and Zambia dropped significantly in 2008, and only three markets in sub-Saharan Africa (Ghana, Malawi, and Tanzania) registered positive returns that year (IMF, 2009). The Nigerian Stock Exchange was severely impacted by the financial crisis; between March, 2008 and March, 2009 the all-share index went down by 67 percent, while market capitalization was reduced significantly (ODI, 2009). The Nigerian Stock Exchange (NSE) has had the strongest resurgence in the wake of the financial crisis. Securities listed on the NSE increased from 7.03 trillion *naira* in December 2009 to 9.92 trillion *naira* by the end of 2010 (Agabi, 2011).

In Zambia, the all-share index deteriorated from the peak of 4,440.46 points in March, 2008 to 2,143.4 points in December, 2009. The Lusaka Stock Exchange has also begun to rebound; the all-share index was reported at 3,642.35 points in February, 2011, not as high as the pre-crisis levels but a marked improvement from 2009.

Despite experiencing significant volatility in the third quarter of 2008, the Ghana Stock Exchange (GSE) is one of the few stock exchanges in Africa that recorded a net gain at the time. The GSE all-share index increased from 6,599.8 points in December, 2007 to 10,431.6 points in December, 2008 (GSE, 2011). After reporting record gains in 2008, the GSE experienced a 46 percent decline in 2009, closing the year at just 5,423.98 points. Like other stock markets in the region, the GSE has experienced a resurgence and was reported at about 7,369 points by the end of 2010 (GSE, 2011).

Bond Markets

As global liquidity dried up, bond markets in some African countries came under pressure. Several countries in the region registered net outflows in their local debt markets. In Zambia, foreign holdings of government securities decreased from a peak of $296 million in June 2008 to $166 million in December 2008.

In addition, the cost of raising funds in international capital markets increased significantly. The African Development Bank reported that sovereign debt spreads rose by an average of 250 basis points in 2008 for developing countries (AfDB, 2009). Due to the increased cost of borrowing in 2008, Kenya, Nigeria, Tanzania and Uganda postponed their plans to raise funds in international capital markets. In fact, South Africa was the only country to issue new foreign denominated bonds in international capital markets in 2010. As the economic outlook continues to strengthen, numerous countries in sub-Saharan Africa, including Nigeria, Zambia, and Ghana, have planned to issue international bonds in 2011 (Nigeria and Zambia, $500 million each; Ghana, $500–700 million).

Foreign Direct Investment

In the past decade, FDI inflows to sub-Saharan Africa increased significantly, from about $9.2 billion in 2000 to $63 billion in 2007 (UNCTAD, 2009b). Inflows continued to increase in the first half of 2008, to $72 billion. However, the global financial crisis had a significant negative impact on these FDIs, which decreased to $59 billion for Africa in 2009.

Prudent macroeconomic and fiscal policies, rising oil and other commodity prices, and increased global liquidity facilitated much of the increase in FDI to Africa over the past decade. However, private capital flows to sub-Saharan Africa have been largely concentrated among oil producers and other mineral-rich countries. It is estimated that two-thirds of total inflows went to South Africa and Nigeria (IMF, 2010a).

The global financial crisis led to a contraction of private capital flows to Africa. Total inflows to sub-Saharan Africa fell from $53.0 billion in 2007 to $22.8 billion in 2009, a decline of 57 percent (IMF, 2010a). In Ghana, FDI inflows doubled, from about US$2.3 billion to US$5.3 billion in the period 2006–2007. However, by the end of December, 2008, FDI had declined by about 16 percent to US$4.4 billion (ODI, 2009a).

Nigeria was the largest FDI recipient in Africa in both 2007 and 2008. The country is the nineteenth largest recipient of FDI in the world. However, FDI inflows to Nigeria decreased moderately as a result of the financial crisis, from $6.8 billion in 2008 to $5.8 billion in 2009 (UNCTAD, 2010).

Zambia experienced a significant increase in FDI inflows between 2000 and 2007, from about $121 million in 2000 to $1.3 billion in 2007. The financial crisis has had a marked impact on this flow (the majority of which was concentrated in the beleaguered mining sector). FDI inflows to the country fell from $1.3 billion in 2007 to $939 million in 2008 and then began to increase in 2009 as the price of copper also increased. The country received an estimated $959 billion in FDI in 2009, though this remains below pre-crisis levels (UNCTAD, 2010).

Overall, FDI inflows to Africa increased in 2010 due in part to a more robust recovery in emerging markets and rising commodity prices. However, with the recovery in advanced economies projected to be gradual, FDI inflows to Africa are also expected to increase at a slower rate in 2010–2011 than in the previous decade.

Banking Sector

The banking sector in sub-Saharan Africa has had very limited exposure to sub-prime mortgages and other asset-backed securities. Despite this, countries with a high number of foreign-owned banks were more exposed to the sudden slowdown in cross-border bank lending caused by the global financial crisis than those with fewer such banks. Credit to local banks from foreign-owned banks came under significant pressure as global credit markets dried up. Some foreign-owned banks reduced the limit on credit lines to local banks. There were reports of bank spreads increasing as the cost of borrowing rose. Countries that have significant foreign ownership of banks (more than half) include Botswana, Cape Verde, Central African Republic, Chad, Côte d'Ivoire, Equatorial Guinea, Lesotho and Zambia (IMF, 2010).

While there have been no major bank failures reported in the region, the majority of domestic banks have had to rely heavily on the small base of domestic deposits. As a result, the lending conditions in some countries have become more stringent as banks shift towards more high-quality clients.

The increased cost of funds and increased risk perception has led to a decrease in the liquidity available for trade transactions worldwide. The global shortage in trade finance liquidity was estimated to be about $100–300 billion in 2009, while in sub-Saharan Africa it was estimated to be approximately $30–40 billion (Subramanian, 2009). In particular, short-term import finance has become increasingly scarce in the region. The International Finance Corporation (IFC) reports that short-term (less than 360 days) import finance support represented 90 percent of its African trade business by volume of transactions (AfDB, 2009).

The IFC responded to the global trade finance shortage by creating the Global Trade Liquidity Program (GTLP). This program allocated $4 billion to address the shortage of trade finance resulting from the global financial crisis. In addition, the African Development Bank created its own $1 billion Trade Finance Initiative to provide liquidity for trade in Africa. As of March 2011, global trade finance had returned to adequate levels. World trade is projected to grow 7 percent in 2011, up from a decrease of 10.7 percent in 2009 (IMF, 2010c).

Foreign Exchange Markets

The fall in commodity prices and subsequent decrease in foreign exchange reserves, portfolio outflows, and steep increases in import bills have led to a significant depreciation of the majority of African currencies. In Zambia, a 66 percent decrease in the price of copper, the country's primary export commodity, led to a 50 percent depreciation of the *kwacha* against the US dollar between July and December of 2008. Conversely, an increase in copper prices beginning in 2009 led to an improvement in the country's foreign exchange reserves. In 2010, the *kwacha* appreciated 2.1 percent against the US dollar to an average of about K4,731/US$ (Fundanga, 2011).

With a drop in Nigeria's foreign reserves from $67 billion in June, 2008 to $53 billion in December, 2008, the *naira* also depreciated against the US dollar, from N117 to N135 per US dollar over the same period (ODI, 2009). The *naira* has continued to depreciate against the US dollar, reaching N151 by the end of January, 2011.

In the first quarter of 2009, Ghana's *cedi* depreciated against the US dollar by 14 percent, which reduced the country's potential benefits from lower fuel and food prices. Overall, the *cedi* depreciated by about 20 percent against the US dollar in 2009. The Bank of Ghana embarked on an aggressive stabilization program to steady the *cedi's* volatility with some positive results; while the *cedi* continued to depreciate in the first quarter of 2010, it began to appreciate against the US dollar in the second half of 2010. Year on year, the *cedi* depreciated by only 0.3 percent against the US dollar in 2010, which was a significant improvement from 2009 (BOG, 2011).

The depreciation of African currencies has had broader implications for the region. Since the majority of African countries have high foreign debt, the cost of servicing the debt increased with the depreciation of currencies. In addition, the cost of imports, including food imports, increased even further, placing an additional burden on poor households in the region.

Indirect Channels

The effects of the global financial crisis transmitted to sub-Saharan Africa through indirect channels were much more severe than those transmitted through direct channels because they affected the real economy. The decrease in global trade coupled with slower remittances, shortfalls in official development assistance (ODA), and rising unemployment led to a marked slowdown in GDP growth in sub-Saharan Africa in 2009. Economic growth in the region was only 1.9 percent that year. The region has since begun to recover, growing at a rate of 4.7 percent in 2010, and is expected to return to trend levels of growth (about 5 percent) in 2011 (World Bank, 2011a).

External Sector

Africa's growth spurt in the past decade was driven primarily by increasing commodity trade flows. Lower global demand and the subsequent fall in global commodity trade was one of the primary transmission mechanisms of the global financial crisis to sub-Saharan Africa.

In the second half of 2008, global demand for commodities began to fall and with it the prices of major commodities began to plummet. Commodity-exporting countries, both oil and non-oil producers, were severely impacted by the decrease in global commodity trade. Sharp decreases in global commodity markets led to major swings in their terms of trade. In 2009, terms of trade losses for oil producers in sub-Saharan Africa averaged 26.8 percent of GDP (IMF, 2010).

After reaching record highs in 2008, the price of oil dropped from US$147 per barrel in July, 2008 to $47 per barrel in January, 2009. Oil is the lifeblood of the Nigerian economy, as oil-related products amount to 97 percent of all exports from the country and accounted for 81 percent of the government's revenue in 2008 (World Bank Country Statistics, 2008). The decrease in oil prices in 2009 led to a large contraction in the value of Nigeria's exports, from US$83.6 billion in 2008 to US$59.3 billion in 2009. The country's current-account surplus fell from 20 percent of GDP in 2008 to 6 percent of GDP in 2009.

The price of oil began to increase from the 2009 low to an average annual price of about $79 in 2010. The Nigerian government has cautiously benchmarked oil at $62 per barrel for its 2011 budget. Rising oil prices led to a rebound in Nigerian exports, which increased to approximately $78 billion in 2010. The current-account surplus also increased to 13.5 percent of GDP in 2010 (EIU, 2011).

With rising copper prices, Zambia's external sector performed extremely well between 2000 and 2007. Merchandise exports, 80 percent of which are copper, increased from $746 million in 2000 to $5,089 million in mid-2008 (Central Statistical Office). Weak demand for copper was the main transmission mechanism of the global financial and economic crisis to Zambia. The price of copper fell 67 percent in six months, from a peak of US$8,985 per metric tonne in July, 2008 to US$2,902 in December, 2008. Consequently, Zambia's export earnings decreased from US$4,957 million in 2008 to US$4,375 million in 2009. Coupled with the high price of oil in the first half of 2008, the current-account deficit widened to 4.2 percent of GDP by the end of 2008, from 2.6 percent in 2007 (EIU, 2009).

The price of copper began to rebound in 2009, driven primarily by sustained demand in emerging markets, from $6,981 in December, 2009 and even further to an average of $9,147 in December, 2010. With rising copper prices, Zambia's export earnings increased to about $6,850 million in 2010. Similarly, the country's current-account deficit narrowed from 1.2 percent of GDP in 2009 to a surplus of about one percent of GDP in 2010 (EIU, 2011).

Having a more diverse external sector, Ghana was not subject to the same volatile swings seen in several other parts of sub-Saharan Africa. High gold and cocoa prices helped to maintain export levels. However, this was offset by high oil and food prices, and the current-account deficit for 2008 widened to about 21.3 percent of GDP (BOG, 2008); it has since narrowed, to about 7.3 percent of GDP in 2010. Ghana became an oil producing country in December, 2010; this is expected to help the country maintain a lower current-account deficit in 2011 (EIU, 2011).

Official Development Assistance

Sub-Saharan Africa is the world's largest recipient of official development assistance (ODA). The majority of African countries rely on ODA to balance their national budgets, to improve infrastructure, and to fund other poverty reduction and development initiatives. Between 2000 and 2008, ODA to Africa tripled, from $8 billion to about $27 billion (OECD, 2010).

At the G-8 summit in 2005, heads of state from the G-8 countries agreed to double aid to Africa and other regions by 2015. The global financial crisis has restricted their ability to meet the so-called Gleneagles targets. Hallet (2009) found that aid flows respond negatively and with a lag to severe downturns in donor countries. While net bilateral aid flows to sub-Saharan Africa rose by 3 percent in 2009, the OECD reports that ODA in 2010 will be below target by $18 billion. In particular the OECD reports that, due in large part to pronounced economic hardships among European donors, Africa will only receive $11 billion of the $25 billion aid increase promised at Gleneagles. There is no doubt that the shortfall in aid commitments will have negative implications for poverty reduction and development in sub-Saharan Africa.

Since 2001, aid has accounted for over 50 percent of Ghana's development budget and 12 percent of its gross national income. In Zambia, ODA accounts for 14 percent of gross national income and supports about 27 percent of the budget. In contrast, ODA accounts for a very small amount of Nigeria's gross national income; in 2008, ODA to Nigeria accounted for less than one percent of gross national income, and it contributed one percent of the national budget. Accordingly, the shortfall in aid disbursements is likely to have a more significant negative impact on Ghana and Zambia than on Nigeria.

Remittances

Remittances have become an important source of additional income in sub-Saharan Africa. The flow of remittances increased sharply in the past decade, from $4.6 billion in 2000 to $21.4 billion in 2008 (World Bank Fact Sheet, 2010). This number reflects only a fraction of the true volume of remittances to the region; by some estimates 45–65 percent of all remittances to sub-Saharan Africa are informal (Freund and Spatafora, 2005).

The financial crisis also led to a decrease in the flow of remittances to Africa; remittances fell from $21.4 billion in 2008 to $20.6 billion in 2009. Low-remittance countries such as Ghana and Zambia suffered much less from this trend than high-remittance countries like Nigeria, which is the largest recipient of remittances in sub-Saharan Africa. In 2008, Nigeria received $9.9 billion in remittances; this fell to $9.5 billion in 2009 as a result of the financial crisis.

Prior to the crisis, migrant remittances to Ghana increased noticeably, from about $449 million in 1999 to $1.9 billion in 2008 (BOG, 2008). Remittances to Zambia are much smaller by comparison. In 2007, Zambia received $59 million in remittances, which translates into $5 per person, much lower than the sub-Saharan African average of $26 per person.

This decrease in remittances has undoubtedly had a negative impact on poor households in the region. Using a large nationally-representative household survey, Adams (2006) found that international remittances reduced the depth and severity of poverty in Ghana. In addition, using a panel dataset of 33 countries over the period 1990–2005, Anyanwu and Erhijakpor found that international remittances have a strong, statistically significant impact on reducing poverty in Africa. They found that a one percent increase in official international remittances as a percentage of GDP will lead, on average, to a 0.29 percent decline in the share of people living in poverty (2010). The decrease in remittances in 2009 threatened to delay and possibly reverse poverty reduction efforts in the region.

Remittances are crucial for households in Ghana, constituting about 5 percent of household income on average. Adams *et al.* (2008) show that for observed expenditures, households receiving international remittances have the highest mean per capita expenditure and the lowest observed poverty on average of all the household groups. The economic status of this group of households improves even further with the receipt of remittances. Comparing their predicted poverty values with counter-factual poverty values, Adams *et al.* (2008) suggest that, for households with international remittances, the poverty headcount of households is reduced by 88.1 percent and the poverty gap by 90 percent.

The World Bank reports that remittance inflows to sub-Saharan Africa have rebounded from $20.6 billion in 2009 to an estimated $21.5 billion in 2010 (2011b). The sluggish economic recovery and high unemployment in advanced economies raises concerns that remittances to developing countries will grow at a much slower rate than that existing before the global financial and economic crisis.

Impact of the Double Agony on the Poor

In most areas of the region where poverty has decreased significantly in the past decade, the decrease has been the consequence of significant improvements in agricultural earnings and increases in public spending on services for the poor. Both of these have been severely compromised by the double crisis, hence the worsening of the situation for the poor.

Poverty

The proportion of the population living on less than $1.25 a day in sub-Saharan Africa decreased from 55.7 percent in 1990 to 51 percent in 2005. While this decrease was not enough to meet the Millennium Development Goal of halving poverty by 2015, it represents significant progress in the region. The double agony of the food crisis and the financial crisis threatens to eliminate the poverty reduction gains that sub-Saharan Africa has made.

The poor are disproportionately hurt by increases in food prices because many are net consumers of food and already spend 60 to 80 percent of their incomes on food. Even though the majority (about 80 percent) of the rural poor in Africa are engaged in agricultural activities, they too are frequently net consumers of food items (Wodon and Zaman, 2008). Chen and Ravallion (2009) estimated that the dual crisis coupled with the fuel price shocks in 2008 would see the number of the poor in the world rise from 53 million to 64 million in 2009. UNECA (2010) estimated that 27 million more people were plunged into poverty as a result of the global financial and economic crisis. In addition, reduced economic growth in sub-Saharan Africa will cost the continent's 390 million people living in extreme poverty about 20 percent of their per capita incomes, or about US$46 per person (UNECA, 2010).

Dessus *et al.* found that 88 percent of the increase in urban poverty resulting from the global increase in food prices was from poor households becoming poorer, while only 12 percent could be attributed to non-poor households falling into poverty (2008). It is difficult to quantify the reduced well-being of poor households as a result of the crisis. However, all evidence points to the fact that poor households will continue to struggle with the effects of the financial crisis well after the global economy has recovered.

Ndikumana and Shimeles show that during previous crises, African countries have experienced sharp decreases in per capita consumption and subsequent increases in headcount poverty (2009). They find that in addition to these trends, poverty has been slow to decrease in the wake of previous crises. The majority of African governments reacted strongly to the global financial and economic crisis and put forward additional monetary and fiscal measures to help their economies recover. As a result, African economies have recovered much more quickly than expected. However, without similar additional measures, poverty will remain elevated in line with previous crises.

Figure 2.3. Africa: poverty and income trends

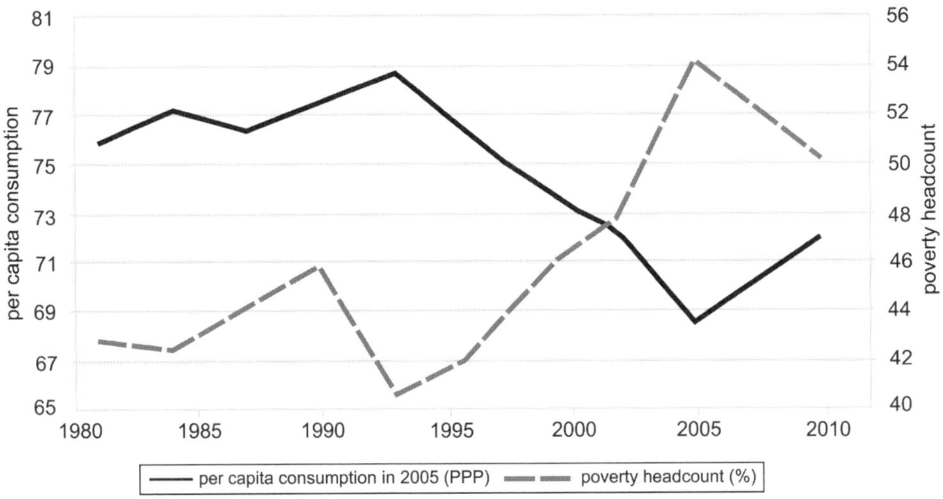

Source: Ndikumana and Shimeles (2009)

About 28.5 percent of the population of Ghana lives below the national poverty line (Government of Ghana, 2007). Cudjoe *et al.* examined the impact of the food crisis on the poor in Ghana and found that the welfare effect for households was relatively modest at the aggregate national level due to relatively diverse consumption patterns (2008). However, the national average hides important regional differences, both between regions and within different income groups. The urban poor in Ghana were the hardest hit by high food prices. The negative effect of the food crisis was particularly strong in the north of Ghana; this can be attributed to higher grain consumption and much lower initial per capita income levels.

According to the World Development Indicators, 64.3 percent of Nigerians and 64.4 percent of Zambians live on less than $1.25 a day. The Oversees Development Institute estimated that the number of poor people in both countries would increase as a result of the global financial and economic crisis (2009a).

World food prices are once again on the rise. The World Bank estimates that an additional 44 million people were pushed into poverty in developing countries between

June, 2010 and February, 2011 as a result of rising food prices (World Bank, 2011c). Many African countries boasted good harvests in 2010, and this has prevented even more people from falling into poverty. However, since the majority of countries in the region are net food importers, rising food prices are likely to exacerbate poverty again in 2011.

Undernourishment

One of the most tragic outcomes of the combined food and financial crises is that the number of undernourished people in the world is estimated to have increased significantly, from about 850 million in 2007 to 915 million in 2008. The double impact of the crises led to a further increase in the number of undernourished people, to 1.02 billion in 2009 (FAO, 2009).

The stronger than expected economic recovery in emerging markets helped to ease this trend, with the number of undernourished people estimated to have declined to 925 million in 2010 (FAO, 2010). However, global undernourishment remains well above pre-crisis levels. Furthermore, as food prices continue to rise in the first quarter of 2011, many are concerned that this welcome decline will not continue.

About one in three people in sub-Saharan Africa is chronically hungry, the largest proportion of undernourished people in the world. Prior to the crisis, sub-Saharan Africa had made significant progress in reducing the proportion of undernourished people, from 34 percent (1995–1997) to 30 percent in 2003–2005. It is estimated that following the food and financial crises, the number of undernourished people in sub-Saharan Africa increased from 236 million in 2007 to 265 million in 2009 (FAO, 2009). The recent economic recovery in Africa has helped to ease undernourishment in the region; the number of undernourished in the region is estimated to have fallen to 239 million in 2010. Unfortunately, this remains well above the pre-crisis levels.

Ghana is the only country in sub-Saharan Africa that has successfully met the Millennium Development Goal to reduce hunger by half. The number of undernourished people in Ghana was reduced from 16 percent of the total population in 1995–1997 to 8 percent in 2004–2006 (FAO Statistics, 2009). Nigeria has historically boasted some of the lowest rates of undernourishment in sub-Saharan Africa. However, it has yet to cut the number of undernourished people in the country by half. The undernourishment rate has been somewhat stagnant, moving from 10 percent in 1995–1997 to 8 percent in 2004–2006. Zambia is one of the low performers when it comes to undernourishment. The number of undernourished people as a proportion of the total population increased from 41 percent in 1995–1997 to 45 percent in 2004–2006. Regardless of their past successes or failures, however, all three countries have projected undernourishment to increase as a result of the global crises. This will have long-term consequences for Africa. Studies show that in the long run, undernourishment is associated with diminished learning ability, reduced work productivity, impaired mental development and nutrition-related diseases (WHO, 2008).

Infant Mortality

Economic shocks, regardless of the source, have had very negative implications for child health and education outcomes in Africa and other poor countries (Ferreira and Schady, 2009). Alarmingly, the World Bank estimates that, as a result of the food and financial crises, there will be between 200,000 and 400,000 additional infant deaths per year from 2009 to 2014 (2009).

It is estimated that approximately 30 million children are born in Africa each year, and more than 3 million of them die before they turn one year old (Friedman and Schady, 2009). Using National Demographic and Health Surveys, Friedman and Schady estimated that the recent crises would result in an additional 30,000 to 50,000 infant deaths in sub-Saharan Africa in 2009. The majority of these deaths was expected to be in poor households in rural areas.

Friedman and Schady (2009) also found that negative shocks to GDP had particularly dire consequences for the infant mortality of girls. They reported that, while the boy/girl ratio at birth does not change during crises, given limited resources, households invest more in the health and well-being of boys than of girls, leading to a greater increase in the infant mortality of girls than that of boys. Rising inflation, the high cost of food, falling remittances, and falling real wages significantly constrain household resources available for health spending. With limited and constantly diminishing resources, households are forced to make difficult choices that ultimately disproportionately hurt girls more than boys.

Food Riots

The global food crisis placed a heavy burden on net-food importing countries. Many countries were not able to meet the demand for food with the rapidly increasing prices of 2007 and 2008. Consequently, food riots erupted in many countries around the world. In Africa, food riots ensued in numerous countries, including Burkina Faso, Cameroon, Côte d'Ivoire, Egypt, and Senegal (Ngongi, 2008). As food prices continue to be elevated above pre-crisis levels and food production in sub-Saharan Africa remains well below demand, there is a persistent risk that the challenges could lead to a security crisis in the region.

By the first quarter of 2011, the FAO's Food Price Index was once again on par with the 2008 peak level. There is increasing concern that rising food prices could again lead to civil unrest in 2011. Indeed, some scholars have argued that high food prices were a contributor to the civil and political unrest in North Africa that occurred early in 2011.

African Responses to the Global Food and Financial Crises: Prospects

Due to improved macroeconomic and fiscal positions achieved in the first half of the decade, many African governments were able to implement counter-cyclical measures to mitigate the effects of the financial crisis. These measures included fiscal stimulus packages, banking sector reform, targeted sector stimulus actions, and increased monitoring of the financial sector.

The Zambian government, for example, implemented various fiscal programs to stimulate the beleaguered mining sector. These included removing the windfall tax, increasing the capital allowance to 100 percent, reducing the excise duty on heavy fuel oil, and removing customs duties on certain copper products. In addition, the Bank of Zambia pursued extensive expansionary monetary policy. It increased the supply of foreign exchange in the market in an effort to reduce volatility in the exchange rate. It sold over $360 million worth of assets between September, 2008 and November, 2009, contributing to a more stable *kwacha*. Coupled with a rebound in commodity prices in 2009, these policies helped to reduce the severity of the economic slowdown in Zambia. The country is expected to grow at a respectable rate of 6.4 and 6.5 percent in 2010 and 2011, respectively. As of 2010, Zambia had returned to a single-digit inflation level of 8.2 percent, a significant improvement from 13.4 percent in 2009.

Having built up reserves due to the elevated price of oil before the crisis, the Nigerian government had the space within which to implement monetary and fiscal policies to ease the effects of the crisis on the Nigerian economy. With rapidly declining oil prices, the Nigerian government reduced the oil price benchmark used for the 2009 budget from $59 per barrel to $45 per barrel and re-prioritized projects to reflect lower expected revenues. The government also reduced the allocation of funds to state governments and placed restrictions on overseas trips of government officials to save money. In line with this, the Central Bank of Nigeria (CBN) also implemented a series of monetary policies to mitigate the negative effects of the crisis on liquidity in the country. The CBN reduced the monetary policy rate (MPR) from 10 percent to 8 percent. It also reduced the cash reserve requirement (CRR) from 4 percent to one percent, and the liquidity ratio was gradually reduced from 40 percent to 25 percent. As a result of these policies and rising oil prices, the Nigerian economy is expected to grow by 7.1 percent in 2011. Inflation fell moderately, from 12.3 percent in 2009 to 11.9 percent in 2010, and is projected to fall even further, to 9.8 percent in 2011 (IMF, 2010c).

Some countries in the region lacked the space to implement expansionary policies when the financial crisis hit. High debt levels significantly constrained the ability of some countries in sub-Saharan Africa to implement fiscal stimulus measures. In Ghana, for example, the fiscal deficit widened from 9 percent of GDP in 2007 to 14.5 percent of GDP in 2008. During the same period, the current-account deficit rose to 20 percent of GDP as a result of rising food and fuel prices. Given the twin deficits, the government of Ghana did not have the fiscal space needed to implement counter-cyclical measures. Instead the government was forced to implement an austerity budget for the 2009 fiscal year to reduce the fiscal deficit to about 9.5 percent of GDP within a year.

Social Protection Programs

Social protection programs are not a new phenomenon in sub-Saharan Africa. In the years following independence many African countries implemented a variety of social protection schemes, but these were abandoned during the crises of the 1980s. In the past decade, social protection programs have been revived in the region within the context of the Poverty Reduction Strategy Papers (PRSPs) and Millennium Development Goals (MDGs). However, only a few countries in the region—namely, South Africa, Namibia, Ethiopia and now Ghana—have significant social protection programs.

In many countries, the social protection budget is dominated by pension spending for government workers. This is especially true in Zambia, where 75 percent of the social protection budget is devoted to pensions for public workers, thus leaving civil society organizations to play a key role in social protection.

In Ghana, as part of a greater strategy to eliminate poverty, the government has implemented a number of programs to improve living conditions for the poor. Since 2000 the government has created the following programs: the Livelihoods Empowerment Against Poverty (LEAP) program, which provides conditional cash transfers to selected extremely poor households; the School Feeding Program, which provides meals to children to increase enrollment and retention in schools; the Education Capitation Grant Program, which pays poor households to cover tuition and other school fees; and a National Health Insurance Scheme to provide health insurance for all Ghanaians (ODI, 2009b).

Even though Ghana has made some progress in implementing social protection programs, the programs cover only a fraction of the country's poor. Even after being expanded in 2009, the programs cover only about 3 percent of the population in a country where a quarter of the population lives below the poverty line and 18 percent are considered to be in extreme poverty (UN Data, 2010).

Both Zambia and Nigeria have implemented some social protection programs. However, these programs lack adequate funding and are poorly coordinated at the national level, a problem that plagues social protection programs across the continent.

In Nigeria, the establishment of the National Poverty Alleviation Programme (NAPEP) in January, 2001 was the first attempt to coordinate the country's social protection schemes. The primary objective of Nigeria's social protection policy is to reduce poverty and protect vulnerable groups. To this end the Nigerian government has established a series of programs since 2001 to protect the poor in the country, including the Child Protection Program, designed to provide allowances and nutrition supplements for poor households with children. In addition, the Social Assistance Program provides conditional cash and non-cash assistance to poor households, free primary education, school feeding allowances, medical allowances and protection of elderly persons. The Social Insurance Program is another which provides health and unemployment insurance, agriculture insurance and old-age pension insurance schemes. Lastly, the Nigerian government has implemented a Labor Market Program to provide job training, microfinance, and other initiatives to increase employment in the country. While Nigeria has made significant progress in implementing these social protection programs, the programs only cover a small fraction of the estimated 75 million Nigerians living in poverty.

The Zambian government created the Public Welfare Assistance Scheme (PWAS) to help poor households cope and to build capacity to help poor and vulnerable households overcome poverty. The program provides food, clothing, and education and health services to beneficiaries. Due to erratic and insufficient funding (only $5 million a year) the PWAS program covers only half of the intended recipients. PWAS is funded by the Zambian government and bilateral and multilateral donors; as a result, it is highly vulnerable to disruptions in donor funding. The Zambian government is in the process of piloting an unconditional social cash transfer scheme in five of the country's 72 districts. The program gives $8 per month to households headed by older people caring for orphans and vulnerable children; however, this cash transfer program is also donor-funded, making it similarly vulnerable to volatility in funding.

What little revenue governments have had to implement social protection programs in sub-Saharan Africa has been further constrained by the recent food, financial, and economic crises. Falling commodity prices have broadly resulted in a reduction of government revenues. In Zambia, copper accounts for 70 percent of government revenue, and so the 67 percent decrease in the price of copper between July and December, 2008 led to a significant reduction in revenue from the mining sector. Similarly, oil accounts for about 80 percent of government revenue in Nigeria, so the decrease in the price of oil from $147 per barrel in July, 2008 to under $40 per barrel by the end of December, 2008 placed a significant strain on government resources (oil prices have since rebounded significantly). Coupled with the shortfall in ODA, these drops in revenue mean that African governments will have a more difficult time implementing, let alone expanding, their social protection programs. However, this does not mean they should not try to do so.

A Call to Expand Social Protection Programs in Africa

The recent food and financial crises are an important reminder of why Africa cannot wait to implement national social protection programs. Nationally implemented social protection programs are needed to reduce the impact of external shocks on poor and vulnerable households. By most estimates, it is much cheaper to offer small protections to vulnerable households to prevent them from falling into poverty than to lift them out of it.

The success of programs like the Productive Safety Nets Program (PSNP) in Ethiopia, which was created to 'provide transfers to the food-insecure population in chronically food-insecure districts,' is evidence that low-income counties can implement social protection programs effectively. The PSNP is now the largest social protection program in sub-Saharan Africa (excluding South Africa). It covers about 7 million people at a cost of about $500 million annually (Gilligan *et al.*, 2009). In addition, advancements in mobile phone technology, for example, mobile phone money transfer services, present a new method for providing social protection services to poor households in a cost-effective manner.

Even with these social protection programs, it is difficult to quantify the impact of the food and financial crises on Africa's progress towards the Millennium Development Goals. Given the increase in undernourishment, infant mortality and poverty as a result of the crises, it is safe to say that the dual crises set the region back in meeting the MDGs.

With about 70 percent of Africa's workforce engaged in the informal sector, providing social protection through formal social insurance schemes is inadequate. It is therefore important that governments expand their social protection programs to include social assistance (e.g. cash transfers, food transfers, vouchers) as well as social services (e.g. maternal and child health and nutrition programs).

African governments should spearhead the coordination and implementation of *national* social protection programs. *Ad hoc* or trial-based programs that are implemented by external partners are a start, but governments must be at the forefront of these programs to ensure that they are sustainable and long-term. More importantly, these programs should be counter-cyclical, offering the highest benefits during times of crisis.

Conclusion

As a net-food importing region, Africa has been significantly impacted by the global food crisis. Rising food import bills, depletion of foreign reserves to pay for imports and a spike in food prices have had pronounced negative impacts on African economies and the African people. This has resulted in a reversal in poverty reduction gains and associated increases in undernourishment, poor health, infant mortality and social unrest. Even as the economic recovery is well underway in sub-Saharan Africa, the long-term consequences of increasing poverty are sure to linger. Furthermore, the continent continues to be at risk as world food prices are once again on the rise in early 2011, placing an ongoing strain on poor households.

The global financial crisis was transmitted to African economies through both direct and indirect channels. It is the indirect channels that have been most detrimental to the real sectors of African economies. Economic growth in sub-Saharan Africa slowed significantly in 2009 after impressive performance in the first half of the decade. Both oil-producing and non-oil producing countries in the region experienced slower growth. This has long-term lagged consequences for poverty reduction on the world's poorest continent.

From a macroeconomic perspective, the economic recovery in sub-Saharan Africa is now in full swing. The majority of countries in the region are expected to grow at pre-crisis levels in 2011. However, it is evident that the lagged consequences of the crises—poverty, infant mortality and undernourishment—remain above pre-crisis levels.

A shortfall in aid targets, net capital outflows, and a contraction of the external sector limited the ability of African governments to implement or expand social protection programs during the crises. As a result, in many places the poor have been left to fend for themselves in the wake of the recent crises. The increase in poverty rates across the continent as a result of the food and financial crises could take years to reverse. Going forward, just as African governments have adopted counter-cyclical macroeconomic policy, so too must governments adopt counter-cyclical social protection programs. This is vital to ensure that external shocks do not derail poverty reduction goals.

References

Adams, R., Alfredo, C. and Page, J. (2008) Remittances, Consumption and Investment in Ghana. *Working Paper Series* 4515. World Bank, Washington, DC.

Adams, R. (2006) Remittances and Poverty in Ghana. Policy Research Working Paper No. 3838. World Bank, Washington, DC.

African Development Bank Group. (2009) The African Development Bank Group Response to the Economic Impact of the Financial Crisis. Tunis-Belvedère, Tunisia.

Agabi, C. (2011) Market Capitalization Stood at N9.92 Trillion in 2010. *Daily Trust Newspaper*, 11 January, 2011.

Anyanwu, J. and Erhijakpor, A. (2010) Do International Remittances Affect Poverty in Africa? *African Development Review*, Vol. 22(1): 51–91.

Bank of Ghana. (2008) *Annual Report and Accounts 2008*. Accra, Ghana.

Bank of Ghana. (2011) Monetary Policy Committee Press Release. Accra, Ghana.

Bank of Zambia. (2008) *Annual Report 2008*. Lusaka, Zambia.

Brinkman, H., Bauer, J.M. and Mahama, A. (2009) Assessing the Impacts of the Global Economic and Financial Crisis on Vulnerable Households in Ghana. VAM Food Security Analysis. World Food Programme, New York.

Central Bank of Nigeria. (2008) *Annual Report: 2008*. Abuja, Nigeria.

Chen, S. and Ravallion, M. (2009) The Impact of the Global Financial Crisis on the World's Poorest. Available at: http://tinyurl.com/ccagl8.

Cudjoe, G., Breisinger, C. and Diao, X. (2008) Local impacts of a global crisis: Food price transmission and poverty impacts in Ghana. IFPRI Discussion Paper No. 842. IFPRI, Washington, DC.

Dessus, S., Herrera, S. and de Hoyos, R. (2008) The Impact of Food Inflation in Urban Poverty and its Monetary Cost. Policy Research Working Paper 4666. World Bank, Washington, DC.

Economist Intelligence Unit. (2009) *Country Report: Zambia* December 2009. EIU, London.

Economist Intelligence Unit. (2011) *Country Reports for Ghana, Nigeria and Zambia*. Published February 2011. EIU, London.

Ferreira, F. and Schady, N. (2009) Aggregate Economic Shocks, Child Schooling and Child Health. *World Bank Research Observer* 24(2): 147–181.

Food and Agriculture Organization (FAO) of the United Nations. (2008) *The State of Food Insecurity in the World 2008*. Economic and Social Development Department, FAO, Rome.

FAO. (2009) *The State of Food Insecurity in the World 2009*. Economic and Social Development Department, FAO, Rome.

FAO. (2010) *Food Outlook: Global Market Analysis*. November, 2010 Ed. Economic and Social Development Department, FAO, Rome.

FAO. (2011). FAO Cereal Supply and Demand Brief. Economic and Social Development Department, FAO, Rome. Available at: http://www.fao.org/worldfoodsituation/wfs-home/csdb/en/

Freund, C.L. and Spatafora, N. (2005) Remittances: Transaction Costs, Determinants, and Informal Flows. World Bank Policy Research Working Paper No. 3704. Development Research Group, World Bank, Washington, DC, August.

Friedman, J. and Schady, N. (2009) How Many More Infants are Likely to Die in Africa as a Result of the Global Financial Crisis? Policy Research Working Paper. Washington, DC: World Bank.

Fundanga, C. (2011) Fourth Quarter 2010 Media Briefing. Bank of Zambia Briefing February 2011, Lusaka, Zambia.

Ghana Stock Exchange. (2011) Market Capitalization. Available at: http://www.gse.com.gh/

Gilligan, D.O. Hoddinott, J. and Taffesse, A.S. (2009) The impact of Ethiopia's Productive Safety Net Programme and its Linkages. IFPRI Discussion Paper 00839. IFPRI, Washington, DC.

Government of Ghana. (2007) A Brighter Future: 2008 Budget Highlights. 2008 Budget Statement and Economic Policies. Accra, Ghana, November. Available at: http://www.mofep.gov.gh/documents/2008_budget_highlight.pdf

Green, D. (2009) A Copper-Bottomed Crisis? The Impact of the Global Economic Meltdown on Zambia. Oxfam International Discussion Document. Oxfam International, December.

Hallet, M. (2009) Economic Cycles and Development Aid: What is the Evidence from the Past. *ECFIN Economic Brief Issue* 5. November 2009.

Headey, D. and Fan, S. (2008) Anatomy of a Crisis: the Causes and Consequences of Surging Food Prices. *Agricultural Economics* 39 (Supplement): 375–391.

International Labor Organization (ILO). (2010) *Global Employment Trends*. Geneva, Switzerland, January.

International Monetary Fund (IMF). (2009) *Regional Economic Outlook: sub-Saharan Africa*. October 2009. IMF, Washington, DC.

IMF. (2010a) *Regional Economic Outlook: sub-Saharan Africa*. April 2010. IMF, Washington, DC.

IMF. (2010b) *Regional Economic Outlook: sub-Saharan Africa: Resilience and Risks*. October 2010. IMF, Washington, DC.

IMF. (2010c) *World Economic Outlook (WEO) Recovery, Risk, and Rebalancing*. October 2010. IMF, Washington, DC.

Islam, R. and Buckley, G. (2009) Rising Food Prices and their Implications for Employment, Decent Work and Poverty Reduction. International Labour Organization, Geneva.

Jayne, T.S. and Chapoto, A. (2009) The Impacts of Trade Barriers and Market Interventions on Maize Price Predictability: Evidence from Eastern and Southern

Africa. *Working* Paper No. 102. MSU International Development, East Lansing, Michigan.
Mohan, R. (2009) Global Financial Crisis: Causes, Impact, Policy Responses and Lessons. Working Paper No. 407. Stanford Center for International Development, Stanford, CA.
Ndikumana, L. and Shimeles, A. (2009) *Global Economic Crisis, Long Term Growth and Policy Implications for Africa.* Africa Development Bank, Development Research Brief No. 5.
Ngongi, N. (2008) Policy implications of high food prices for Africa. In *Responding to the Global Food Crisis: Three Perspectives*. IFPRI, Washington, DC.
ODI. (2009a) *The Global Financial Crisis and Developing Countries, Synthesis of Findings of 10 Country Case studies*. Overseas Development Institute, London.
ODI. (2009b) Social protection to tackle child poverty in Ghana. *Briefing Paper,* February 2009. Overseas Development Institute, London.
OECD. (2010) Development Aid Rose in 2009 and Most Donors Will Meet 2010 Aid Targets. Development Assistance Committee. OECD Newsroom, 14 April, 2010.
Ogundele, O. and Okoruwa, V. (2006) Technical efficiency differentials in rice production technologies in Nigeria. *Research Paper* 154. AERC, Nairobi.
Ravallion, M. and Datt, G. (2002) Why Has Economic Growth Been More Pro-Poor in Some States of India than Others? *Journal of Development Economics*, 68(2): 381–400.
Subramanian, V. (2009) Promoting Trade Finance in Africa: A Strategic Perspective. Exim Bank of India. 6 July, 2009. Africa Business Forum, London.
UNECA. (2010) *Economic Report on Africa 2010*. UNECA and AU Publication, Addis Ababa, Ethiopia.
United Nations Conference on Trade and Development (UNCTD). (2009a) *Food Security in Africa: Learning Lessons from the Food Crisis.* Geneva: Trade and Development Board, Forty-Seventh Executive Session.
UNCTD. (2009b) *World Investment Report 2009: Transnational Corporations, Agricultural Production and Development.* New York and Geneva.
UNCTD. (2010) *World Investment Report 2010: Investing in a Low Carbon Economy*. New York and Geneva.
UN Data. (2010) National Poverty Statistics. Available at: http://data.un.org/
US Department of Agriculture. (2006) USDA Agricultural Baseline Projections to 2015. *Baseline Report* OCE–2006-1. Interagency Agricultural Projections Committees, Washington, DC.
US Department of Agriculture. (2009) *World Agricultural Supply and Demand Estimates*, 9 October, 2009.
US Energy Information Administration (EIA). (2010) *Short Term Energy Outlook: December 2010*. Department of Energy, Washington, DC.
WHO. (2008) *The Global Food Crisis: Implications for the Health of People in the African Region*. Information Note, Regional Office for Africa.
Wodon, Q. and Zaman, H. (2008) Rising food prices in sub-Saharan Africa: poverty impact and policy responses. *Policy Research Working Paper Series* 4738. World Bank, Washington, DC.
World Bank. (2008) *World Development Report: Agriculture for Development*. World Bank, Washington, DC.
World Bank. (2009) The Impact of the Financial Crisis on Progress towards the Millennium Development Goals in Human Development. Internal Policy Note. World Bank, Washington, DC.

World Bank. (2010a) Global Economic Prospects 2010: Crisis, Finance, and Growth. World Bank, Washington, DC.
World Bank. (2010b) World Development Indicators Update 2010. World Bank, Washington, DC.
World Bank. (2011a). Global Economic Prospects January 2011: Regional Annex. World Bank, Washington, DC.
World Bank. (2011b) Migration and Remittances Factbook 2011. World Bank, Washington, DC.
World Bank. (2011c) Food Price Hike Drives 44 Million People into Poverty. Press Release No:2011/333/PREM. World Bank, Washington, DC.
Zambia Vulnerability Assessment Committee. (2008) Multi-Sectoral In-Depth Vulnerability and Needs Assessment. Lusaka, Zambia.

Chapter 3

Food Prices and Economic Crises: Causes and Consequences for Food Security in Developing Countries

Keith Wiebe, David Dawe and Kostas Stamoulis
Food and Agriculture Organization of the United Nations, Rome

Abstract

High food prices in 2007 and 2008 had significant impacts on food security, particularly among poor consumers in developing countries. After mid-2008, commodity prices fell as a result of the global financial and economic crisis, but in many poor countries prices remain higher than they were before the crisis, and the benefits of lower food prices have been offset by declines in income, employment, export earnings, remittances, foreign direct investment and official development assistance. The recent food price and economic crises reversed earlier progress in reducing hunger, and the Food and Agriculture Organization (FAO) estimates that more than one billion people, representing around one-sixth of the world's population, were chronically undernourished in 2009, even while global cereal production remained near record levels. The number of undernourished people is estimated to have declined to 925 million in 2010, but commodity prices rose again in mid-2010 amidst concerns about production and export restrictions in some regions. Demands on agriculture will increase in the coming decades, and supply will face new challenges, but most experts agree that the world has the resources and technological potential to produce enough food if appropriate investments are made and policies put in place. The biggest challenge to reducing hunger will be to improve access to food by the poorest.

Introduction

The FAO estimates that more than one billion people, representing around one-sixth of the world's population, were chronically undernourished in 2009. That number represents an increase of an estimated 150 million over levels existing in the mid-2000's—the result of two crises that were quite different in their natures and origins but have had similar impacts on food security. The first was the 'food price crisis' that peaked in mid-2008, and the second was the global financial and economic crisis that began immediately thereafter. Both sharply reduced access to food, particularly for the poorest. As a result, earlier progress in reducing hunger—towards both the 1996 World Food Summit goal (reducing the number of hungry people in the world) and Millennium Development Goal 1 (reducing the proportion of hungry people in the world)—was reversed. The number of undernourished people was estimated to have declined to 925 million in 2010 due to improved economic conditions, particularly in developing countries, and to prices remaining below their peak levels (FAO, 2010a). But the number of undernourished people remains higher than it was before the crises of 2008–2009, and concerns about food price levels and volatility emerged again in mid-2010.

While the recent crises and their impacts have focused public and private attention on food and agriculture after decades of neglect, that attention must look beyond these crises if hunger is to be reduced and eventually eliminated.

Looking to the future, a variety of factors affecting both demand and supply of food and other agricultural commodities will increase the challenge of feeding the world. Growth in population, income and urbanization will increase the total demand for food and change the composition of diets. Agriculture will be linked ever more closely with the energy sector, both as a consumer and—increasingly—as a producer of fuel. Most experts agree that the world has sufficient potential to meet these demands if appropriate investments are made and policies introduced, but climate change will complicate the task of increasing agricultural production—improving growing conditions in some areas, making them worse in many others, but changing them virtually everywhere in ways that are still uncertain.

The biggest challenge to reducing hunger is not meeting the demands of those with sufficient incomes to buy food, whether today or in 2050, but in meeting the needs of those who have neither the income to buy enough food nor the resources to produce it. This challenge is illustrated by two key facts. First, the recent increase in the number of hungry people occurred even as farmers responded to higher food prices with record global cereal production in 2008. And second, even before the recent food price and economic crises, over 800 million people were undernourished—a number that has remained stubbornly and unacceptably high for the past half century and will remain unacceptably high over the next half century unless the poor are enabled to participate in broad-based economic growth.

This chapter explores these challenges in turn and will conclude with four key messages:

- The recent food price and economic crises reversed earlier progress in reducing hunger, and concerns remain despite improvements in 2010.
- Demands on agriculture will increase in the coming decades, and supply will face new challenges.
- The world has the resources and technological potential to produce enough food, if appropriate investments are made and policies put in place.
- The biggest challenge to reducing hunger will be to improve access to food by the poorest.

The 'Food Price Crisis'

Food prices rose rapidly from 2005 to 2008 after several decades of relative stability (in nominal terms) and decline (in real terms). The FAO food price index rose by 7 percent in 2006 and by 27 percent in 2007, and that increase persisted and accelerated in the first half of 2008 (FAO, 2009d). In June 2008, the prices of basic foods on international markets reached their highest levels in 30 years, raising widespread concerns about hunger and political instability at local, national and global scales. Cereal prices subsequently declined in 2009 but rose again sharply in mid-2010 in response to drought and a ban on exports by the Russian Federation (FAO, 2010b).

There has been considerable debate about the causes of the recent rise in food prices. Growth in population and income and the changes in diet associated with urbanization, particularly in large developing countries like China and India, have certainly contributed to increased demand for food over the past several decades, but these long-term trends did not change significantly in the past few years so were not a key factor in the recent price spike. Declining investment in agriculture is also a longer-term phenomenon, and in fact is not surprising given the long-term decline in real prices of food and other agricultural commodities. But like growth in food demand, this did not change significantly in recent years. Likewise global cereal stocks have been declining over the past decade—but not in themselves changing sufficiently in the past several years to cause the spike in prices. Nevertheless these factors helped to set the stage for greater volatility in food prices when harvests were reduced in several key countries in 2005 and 2006. The impact of these supply shortfalls was compounded by rising energy prices, which had the dual effect of increasing the cost of producing agricultural commodities and simultaneously making the production of biofuels more attractive—and thus increasing the demand for feedstocks from agricultural commodities.

The role of biofuels in the rise in food prices has been the subject of considerable discussion and debate, but its effect is difficult to disentangle from that of the various other factors that contributed. It is not surprising that estimates vary, given differences in methods, commodities, and time periods covered. At one extreme, a World Bank working paper (Mitchell, 2008) suggested that 70–75 percent of the price increase was attributable to the increase in biofuel production and 'related consequences,' while at the other extreme, the White House Council of Economic Advisors (Lazear, 2008) estimated that biofuels were responsible for just 3 percent of the increase in global food prices. Most studies (e.g. Rosegrant, 2008; Collins, 2008; Glauber, 2008) found that biofuels accounted for about a third of the increase in the prices of maize and other staple commodities. For poor consumers in developing countries for whom basic staple foods represent a large share of their consumption and even total expenditures, the rapid expansion in the production of biofuels seems to have had significant effect.

This conclusion is further supported by the movement of crude oil and maize prices during 2006–2008, when oil prices exceeded the $60 threshold estimated to represent the 'break-even price' in terms of profitability of ethanol production from maize in the United States (FAO, 2008a). (Note that this threshold assumed maize prices in the range of $80 per ton, but in fact the threshold would increase as maize prices rose, since feedstock costs represent the largest share of the total cost of producing biofuels.)

Finally, exchange rate movements and policy responses to high prices in some countries—particularly restrictions on exports as an attempt to keep domestic prices low—helped trigger a contagion effect and exacerbated the increase in prices of food and other agricultural commodities. A survey of policy responses to high food prices by governments in around 100 developing and transition economies indicates a mix of measures to support consumers, producers, and trade-related measures (FAO, 2008c). The most common measures were the reduction or suspension of import tariffs and taxes and short-term support of domestic production by means of agricultural inputs and credit; many countries also introduced or reinforced food assistance and other kinds of social safety nets as well as price controls or price subsidies. Importantly, a number of large exporter countries such as India, Vietnam, China, Pakistan, Egypt, Argentina, Kazakhstan, Russia and Ukraine selectively banned cereal exports or imposed quotas and increased export taxes as well as minimum export prices. These measures prompted further price increases and volatility in international markets. In sum, multiple factors interacted to contribute to the rapid increase in prices, and it is difficult to isolate the impact of any one factor.

What Did High Food Prices Mean for Food Security?

Most of the world's poor live in rural areas, and most of them depend at least in part on agriculture for their livelihoods, so it is not unreasonable to expect that they might be insulated from the effects of rising prices because they produce their own food, or perhaps that they might even benefit from higher prices if they produce a surplus of food for sale.

In fact, however, most of the world's poor, like most of the world's population in general, are net buyers of staple foods. This is not surprising in the case of the urban poor, but even in rural areas, the majority of poor households are net buyers of staple foods in most developing countries—whether because they lack sufficient land to produce enough food for their own consumption, or because they produce other crops for sale and purchase food.

This is a critical distinction, because it means that while attention is often focused on increasing food production, most of the world's poor rely on other sources of access to food, including income (which depends on the levels of both employment and wages) and remittances. This also means that rising food prices reduce the purchasing power of such households and thus affect them adversely.

Reliance on income from on-farm agricultural production is highest among rural households in sub-Saharan Africa, but even there agricultural wages, off-farm employment and other sources of income account for a quarter to a third of rural household income on average (Davis *et al*., 2010). The share of rural household income from sources other than agricultural production is typically higher (by one-half to two-thirds) in other regions of the world. This diversification helps sustain real incomes when agricultural prices are low but may increase vulnerability when food prices are high (or when those alternative sources of income are adversely affected by economic conditions, as we will see below).

When food prices rise, poor households, who may spend as much as 70–80 percent of their total expenditures on food, are forced to adjust in various ways (FAO, 2008b). They may reduce consumption of preferred staples and higher-value foods such as fruits, vegetables, meat and dairy products (and may even eat greater quantities of cheaper staples), and they may also increase time spent working (or seeking work) and reduce expenditures on health care and other non-food items. Even if these responses succeed in maintaining caloric intake, they may still result in reduced nutritional status, due to reduced consumption of protein and micronutrients, as well as diminished health status. As labor is often the most important asset held by the poor, this has implications for incomes and access to food in the future as well as for the current period.

Households also have access to food through other means, for example, drawing down savings, borrowing, or depleting or (in extreme cases) even selling assets such as land. These options may come at the high price of compromising future ability to generate income and obtain access to food, but for the poorest households these may be the only options that remain.

Reduced access to food as a result of high food prices, among other factors, is estimated by the FAO to have increased the number of undernourished people in the world to 915 million in 2008, up from 848 million in 2005–2007 (FAO, 2009a, 2010a). (As we will see in the next section, in 2009 the number rose even higher as a result of the global economic crisis before declining again in 2010.)

While the number of undernourished people in the world is estimated to have increased during the years leading up to 2009, high food prices during the same period also gave farmers incentives to increase production. In fact, global cereal harvests in 2008 reached record levels, up 7 percent over 2007 (FAO, 2009b). But the supply response was uneven; cereal production rose 13 percent in developed countries but only 3 percent in developing countries (FAO, 2009c). Part of the difference may be explained by shifts among crops in 2008, but the difference also reflects weaker incentives for farmers in developing countries—due both to policy measures taken by governments in some developing countries to limit domestic price increases and to poor infrastructure, which hinders farmers' access to markets for agricultural inputs as well as outputs.

Food prices fell sharply in the second half of 2008, in part due to farmer responses and a strong global harvest in 2008. Given that most of the world's poor are net buyers of staple food commodities, this suggests that their access to food should have improved. However, while world food prices have retreated from their mid-2008 peak levels, they are still high by historical standards. Furthermore, although domestic food prices for most countries also declined somewhat during the second half of 2008, in the vast majority of cases, and in all regions, their decline did not keep pace with that of international food commodity prices. At the end of 2008, domestic staple food prices were still 17 percent higher in real terms than they had been two years earlier, and this was true across a range of important foodstuffs (FAO, 2009a). Prices are projected to remain higher over the next decade than they were in the past decade (OECD-FAO, 2010).

The Global Financial and Economic Crisis

Importantly, prices fell not only as a result of increased supply but also as a result of the declining demand precipitated by the financial crisis that began in developed countries and the sharp global economic downturn that followed. Falling wages, rising unemployment and declining remittances reduced incomes and offset the effects of lower food prices, causing a sharp deterioration in access to food for many. Foreign investment in developing countries (including in the agricultural sector) fell sharply after having increased rapidly in the preceding years, and official development assistance remained (and still remains) uncertain, while public budgets in developed countries face unprecedented demands for stimulus funds in those economies.

The recent crisis was historically unprecedented in several ways. First, because it followed so closely on the heels of the sharp increases in staple food prices during 2006–2008, the mechanisms that are normally used by poor countries and households to cope with economic shocks were already stretched thin. Second, the crisis affected large parts of the world simultaneously. When economic crises are confined to individual countries, or to several countries in a particular region, governments can make recourse to instruments such as currency devaluation, borrowing or increased use of official assistance to counter the effects of the crisis. The scope of such instruments is more limited in the case of a global crisis. And third, with developing countries more financially and commercially integrated into the world economy than in the past, they are far more exposed to changes in international markets. A drop in global demand or supply or restrictions in credit availability have immediate repercussions on developing countries.

The global economic slowdown hit developing countries through both financial and commercial channels, with important implications for their food security and overall economic growth. The main transmission channels are as follows.

Foreign Direct Investment (FDI). Foreign investments going to developing countries are estimated to have declined by about 40 percent in 2009 (World Bank, 2010). Although most investment is for mining, industry and services, the agricultural sector is also affected. Reduced employment has economy-wide ripple effects and forces unsuccessful urban job-seekers to return to rural areas.

Remittances. Migrants' transfers to developing countries declined by 5 percent in 2009 (World Bank, 2010). Remittances had previously grown by as much as 20 percent per year, becoming an important source of capital for developing countries. In low-income countries, for example, they represent 6 percent of total economic output. What is more, remittances have usually been resistant to shocks and have often even increased during economic crises in recipient countries. It is likely due to the global dimensions of the recent crisis that the counter-cyclical effect of these transfers was less strong this time.

Official Development Assistance (ODA). Foreign aid is the principal source of capital inflows for many of the poorest countries, but the global economic slowdown affected the budgets of donor countries along with the needs of recipients. After a substantial increase in 2008, ODA to developing countries dropped by 6 percent in 2009 (World Bank, 2010).

Financial Markets. As the crisis evolved, developing countries faced higher costs for external credit from both private and public sources. The risk premium for loaning money to developing countries increased, and in many cases, credit may not have been available at all as banks rationed their financial reserves and lent only to those perceived to be the most reliable borrowers.

International Trade. Trade volume for emerging and developing economies declined by 8 percent in 2009 as compared to 2008, and in sub-Saharan Africa declining commodity prices in 2009 reduced the terms of trade by about 15 percent (IMF, 2010).

The combined effect of the tightening in these transmission channels is that reduced international capital flows, tighter credit conditions, lower remittance transfers and shrinking export opportunities cut into investment and lead to reduced growth prospects in developing countries. Unless concrete steps are taken to increase investment, these factors can have long-term adverse effects on poor countries, even after the global crisis has passed.

What Has the Global Financial/Economic Crisis Meant for Food Security?

Following on the heels of the food price crisis, these threats to food security come at a time when the traditional response strategies of poor households have already been strained, meaning that few options to protect current consumption levels remain and longer-term prospects have already been compromised.

Faced with increased unemployment, declining wages and reduced demand for their work, households try to maintain income by migrating, selling assets such as livestock, borrowing money, or participating in new types of economic activity. International evidence indicates that women and even children may enter the labor force in greater numbers as a response to economic downturns.

Furthermore, households alter spending patterns and reduce expenditures on durable goods relative to food and other essential items. Food expenditure also tends to shift towards cheaper, calorie-rich, energy-dense foods such as grains, and away from more expensive protein- and nutrient-rich foods such as meat, dairy products, or fruits and vegetables.

Coping mechanisms thus involve undesirable but often unavoidable compromises: poor working mothers, for example, are less likely to seek health care for themselves or their children; migration might weaken community cohesion; withdrawing children from schools destroys long-term human capital; the sale of assets reduces the stock of physical or financial resources and is not easily reversible; and shifting from more nutritious foods towards less nutritious items or simply eating less causes malnutrition, affects labor productivity and reduces children's cognitive potential.

Poorer households are naturally hit harder by rising prices and falling incomes. The rural landless and urban poor are the most affected by the crisis because they typically spend the greatest share of their incomes on food (and the greatest share of their food expenditures on basic staples), and because they lack the resources to produce food themselves. Other vulnerable groups include female-headed households where some members' family responsibilities (e.g. caring for children and the elderly, collecting water and fuel, and cooking) limit their ability to devote a greater share of their time to paid employment.

Table 1.1. Examples of Main Effects of the Economic Crisis and Household Responses

	Armenia	Bangladesh	Ghana	Nicaragua	Zambia
Effect of the crisis	Drop in: Remittances	Drop in: Remittances, FDI, ODA	Drop in: Remittances, FDI, Trade, ODA	Drop in: Remittances, FDI, ODA	Drop in: Remittances, FDI, Trade, ODA
Household responses	Diet changes, reduced health expenditures, borrowing, livestock sales	Fewer meals, cheaper foods, reduced health expenditures, borrowing	Diet changes, reduced health and education expenditures, livestock sales	Diet changes, borrowing, livestock sales	Fewer meals, cheaper foods, reduced health and education expenditures, transfers

Source: FAO (2009a).

Country case studies from a recent FAO report on global food insecurity illustrate the manifold ways in which households respond to the fall in remittances, exports, foreign direct investments and other impacts of the economic crisis (see Table 1.1). In Armenia, the households most adversely affected by the shock are those relying on remittances from seasonal and long-term migrants or wage labor in the construction and production sectors (particularly the mining and chemical industries). Remittances also represent an important source of income for many households in Bangladesh and Nicaragua, while Ghana and Zambia have been affected proportionately more by reduction in demand for their agricultural and mineral exports. Various coping mechanisms have been used by the poor to adapt to the crisis, depending on their specific situations, but a common theme across countries has been a deterioration in consumption patterns and a reduction in human capital and other productive assets.

As a result of these factors, the FAO estimates that 1.02 billion people were undernourished in 2009—the highest figure in recent decades and nearly one sixth of the world's total population (FAO, 2009a). It is important to note that the increase in undernourishment was *not* a result of limited international food supplies. As noted previously, 2008 saw record global cereal production, partly in response to high food prices, and the latest estimates indicate that global cereal production declined only modestly in 2009, down 1.1 percent from the record high in 2008 but still the second largest crop ever gathered (FAO, 2010b). The number of undernourished people in the world is estimated to have declined from its peak in 2009 to 925 million in 2010 (see Figure 3.1). This is attributable primarily to improvements in access to food due to improved economic conditions, particularly in developing countries, and the fact that food prices have remained below their peak levels of 2008.

Projections for 2010 indicated that the number of undernourished people would decline in all developing regions, although at different paces. Two-thirds of the world's undernourished live in just seven countries (Bangladesh, China, the Democratic Republic of Congo, Ethiopia, India, Indonesia and Pakistan), and over 40 percent live in China and India alone. The region with the highest number of undernourished people continues to be Asia and the Pacific (see Figure 3.2), but with a 12 percent decline from 658 million in 2009 to 578 million, this region also accounts for most of the global improvement expected in 2010.

It is also critical to remember that more than 800 million people were already undernourished before the recent food price and economic crises began, and they will remain undernourished even after those crises have passed. Indeed, the number of undernourished people in 2010 was higher than the number in 1990–1992, the base period against which the hunger-reduction targets of the 1996 World Food Summit and the Millennium Development Goals are measured. While some regions (e.g. East and Southeast Asia) have made notable progress, in many other regions and at the global scale relatively little progress has been made towards achieving the World Food Summit goal of reducing the number of hungry people in the world by half by 2015. In fact, developing countries as a group have seen an overall setback in terms of the World Food Summit goal (from 827 million undernourished in 1990–1992 to 906 million in 2010) (FAO, 2010a).

Somewhat better progress has been made towards achieving Millennium Development Goal 1(c) of reducing the proportion of hungry people by half by 2015, but here too, earlier progress at the global scale has slowed in recent years, and many regions are lagging. The proportion of undernourished people remains highest in sub-Saharan Africa, at 30 percent in 2010, but progress varies widely at the country level. As of 2005–2007 (the most recent period for which complete data are available), the Congo, Ghana, Mali and Nigeria had already achieved MDG 1(c) and Ethiopia and others were close to achieving it, but in the Democratic Republic of Congo, the proportion of undernourishment had risen to 69 percent, up from 26 percent in 1990–1992. In Asia, Armenia and Viet Nam had achieved MDG 1(c), and China and others were close to doing so, while in Latin America and the Caribbean, Guyana, Jamaica and Nicaragua had achieved MDG 1(c) and Brazil and others were approaching the target (FAO, 2010a).

Figure 3.1. Trends in undernourishment, 1969 to 2010

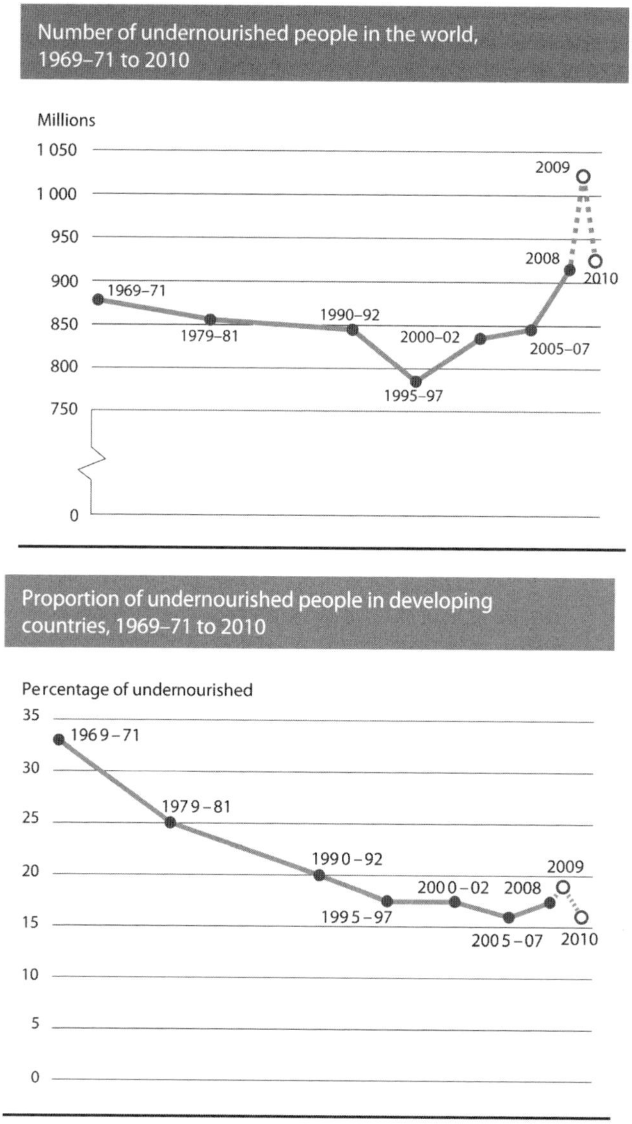

Source: FAO.

Note: Figures for 2009 and 2010 are estimated by FAO with input from the United States Department of Agriculture, Economic Research Service. Full details of the methodology are provided in the technical background notes (available at www.fao.org/publication/sofi/en/). Source: FAO.

Figure 3.2. Undernourishment by region, 2010

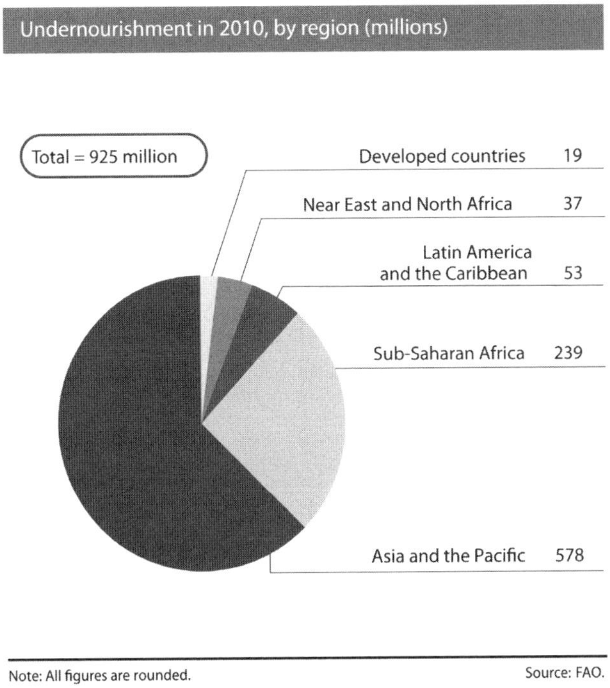

Source: FAO (2010a).

Longer-term Challenges

Looking beyond the recent crises, a variety of factors affecting both demand and supply of food and other agricultural commodities will increase the challenge of feeding the world in the future. Growth in population is slowing but will still add nearly 3 billion people to the world's total by mid-century. Virtually all of this growth will occur in the developing countries, and most of it will be in urban areas. Combined with increased income, which will also grow most rapidly in the developing countries, this is expected to increase global food demand by about 70 percent by 2050.

At the same time, agriculture will become linked ever more closely with the energy sector, both as a consumer and—increasingly—as a producer of fuel. Use of cereals as a feedstock in the production of biofuels (primarily maize for ethanol in the United States) was expected to slow somewhat in 2009 as a result of the economic crisis, but was still projected to reach 125 million tonnes, representing 6 percent of total cereal utilization (FAO, 2009b). Future trends in the use of cereals, sugar, vegetable oils or other agricultural commodities or by-products in the production of biofuels will depend partly on markets, but even more critically on policies, particularly in the United States and the European Union.

These trends remain uncertain, of course, but will play a critical role in the evolution of demand for agricultural products and thus will have an impact on food security via their effects on the levels and volatility of agricultural producers' incomes—and on food prices faced by consumers.

Most experts agree that the world has sufficient potential to meet these demands if appropriate investments are made and policies introduced, but climate change will complicate the task of increasing agricultural production—improving growing conditions in some areas, making them worse in many others, but changing them virtually everywhere in ways that are still uncertain. Autonomous adaptation by farmers, for example by shifting planting dates, switching crops and varieties, and adopting or expanding the use of technologies like conservation tillage or irrigation where economical, will offset some of the effects of gradual warming, at least initially, but studies suggest that impacts on agriculture due to changes in temperature and precipitation as well as the frequency and intensity of extreme events such as droughts, heat waves or severe storms are likely to become more severe after mid-century. Given these expected impacts as well as closer links with energy and financial markets, policies and investments to support agricultural adaptation, mitigation and risk management more generally will become increasingly important.

What Can Be Done?

The food price and economic crises have had a severe impact on millions of people. Those suffering from undernourishment need immediate assistance to prevent a worsening of their situation, and the recent crises have rightly focused attention on meeting their needs. The unfortunate reality, however, is that the number of undernourished people was already high and rising even before these crises began, revealing the inadequacies of the present food system and the urgent need for structural changes.

In the short term, safety nets and social protection programmes must be created or improved to reach those most in need. Simultaneously, small-scale farmers need improved access to indispensable means of production and technologies—such as high-quality seeds, fertilizers, feed and farming tools and equipment—that will allow them to boost production. This should also lower food prices for poor consumers, both rural and urban.

In the medium and longer terms, solving the problem of hunger requires investing in agriculture, particularly in low-income food deficit countries. This is important both as a means of increasing food production and, equally, as an engine of economic growth, since most of the world's poor depend at least in part on agriculture for their livelihoods. These countries must be assisted with the necessary technical and financial solutions and policy tools to enhance their agricultural sectors in terms of productivity and resilience in the face of crises. Stable and effective policies, regulatory and institutional mechanisms, and functional market infrastructures that promote investment in the agricultural sector are paramount. Investments in food and agricultural science and technology need to be stepped up. Improved institutions and governance at local, national and international levels are also essential.

While investment and policy improvements in agriculture are necessary to eliminate hunger, they will not be sufficient. Even though most of the world's poor live in rural areas and depend in part on agriculture for their livelihoods, many already earn significant shares of their incomes from non-agricultural sectors, and that process of transition will continue in the future. For the world's poor, access to food will increasingly depend—as it already does for the vast majority of the world's rich—on incomes earned outside agriculture.

In sum, the recent food price and economic crises reversed earlier progress in reducing hunger, raising the number of undernourished from 848 million before the crises began to 1.02 billion in 2009. While economic recovery helped bring the number down to 925 million in 2010, concerns remain about continuing volatility in commodity markets. Demands on agriculture will only increase in the coming decades, and supply will face new challenges. But the world has the resources and technological potential to produce enough food, if appropriate investments are made and policies put in place. The biggest challenge to reducing hunger will be to improve access to food by the poorest. Now, while public and private attention on agriculture and food security are high, it is essential to maintain and focus that attention on increased investment in agriculture, protection of vulnerable groups, and improved governance of food security at national and global scales. Only a healthy agricultural sector, combined with a growing non-farm economy and effective safety nets and social-protection programmes, will sustainably eradicate poverty and food insecurity in line with the Millennium Development Goals and those of the 1996 World Food Summit.

References

Collins, K. (2008) The Role of Biofuels and Other Factors in Increasing Farm and Food Prices. A Review of Recent Developments with a Focus on Feed Grain Markets and Market Prospects. Prepared by Keith J. Collins LLC as supporting material for a review conducted by Kraft Foods.

Davis, B., Winters, P., Carletto, G., Covarrubias, K., Quiñones, E.J., Zezza, A., Stamoulis, K., Azzarri, C. and DiGiuseppe, S. (2010) A Cross-country Comparison of Rural Income-generating Activities. *World Development* 38(1), 48-63.

FAO (2010a) *The State of Food Insecurity in the World 2010*. FAO, Rome.

FAO (2010b) *Crop Prospects and Food Situation*, No. 3, September. FAO, Rome.

FAO (2009a) *The State of Food Insecurity in the World 2009*. FAO, Rome.

FAO (2009b) *Food Outlook*, June. FAO, Rome.

FAO (2009c) *Crop Prospects and Food Situation*, No. 3, July. FAO, Rome.

FAO (2009d) *The State of Agricultural Commodity Markets 2009*. FAO, Rome.

FAO (2008a) *The State of Food and Agriculture 2008, Biofuels: prospects, risks and opportunities*. FAO, Rome.

FAO (2008b) *The State of Food Insecurity in the World 2008*. FAO, Rome.

FAO (2008c) *Crop Prospects and Food Situation*, No. 5, December. FAO, Rome.

Glauber, J. (2008) Statement of Joseph Glauber, Chief Economist before the Committee on Energy and Natural Resources, United States Senate, 12 June, 2008.

IMF (2010) *World Economic Outlook April 2010*. IMF, Washington, DC.

Lazear, E. (2008) Testimony of Edward P. Lazear, Chairman, Council of Economic Advisers, before the Senate Foreign Relations Committee Hearing on 'Responding to the Global Food Crisis,' Wednesday, May 14, 2008.

Mitchell, D. (2008) A Note on Rising Food Prices, Policy Research Working Paper 4682. World Bank, Washington, DC.

OECD-FAO (2010) *OECD-FAO Agricultural Outlook 2010-2019*. OECD, Paris, and FAO, Rome.

Rosegrant, M. (2008) Biofuels and Grain Prices: Impacts and Policy Responses. Testimony of Mark W. Rosegrant, Director, Environment and Production Technology Division,

International Food Policy Research Institute, for the US Senate Committee on Homeland Security and Governmental Affairs, 7 May, 2008.

World Bank (2010) *Remittances and Migration Factbook 2011*. Available at: http://econ.worldbank.org/WBSITE/EXTERNAL/EXTDEC/EXTDECPROSPECTS/0,,contentMDK:21352016~pagePK:64165401~piPK:64165026~theSitePK:476883,00.html (accessed 10 November 2010).

Chapter 4

Future Challenges for the World Food Economy and Sub-Saharan Africa: Major Environmental and Socioeconomic Drivers of Change

Siwa Msangi and Mark Rosegrant
International Food Policy Research Institute, Washington, DC

Abstract

In this chapter, we explore the nature of several key drivers of change in global food systems and describe the food security situation in sub-Saharan Africa within that context. One of the challenges facing the continent and the sub-Saharan region in particular is that of continuing exposure to market-driven price shocks that expose import-dependent countries to the increasing volatility of world commodity markets. Given their differing levels of price transmission, not all countries in sub-Saharan Africa face the same level of exposure to global price movements, but the overall trend of increasing import dependency will leave more of the region in a vulnerable position with respect to global market trends if improvements are not made in the internal infrastructure that supports the agricultural and non-agricultural sectors. Among the improvements needed are investments in irrigation and on-farm production technologies, post-harvest processing, and storage and distribution infrastructure, as well as increased agricultural R&D focused on improving yields of key staple crops under the increasing levels of abiotic and biotic stresses that will inevitably come with global environmental change. Aside from long-term climate change, the increased variability in climate that is already being experienced in many parts of the sub-continent will also require additional attention, investment and policy action. Within the context of sub-Saharan Africa, the gendered dimensions of poverty and malnutrition must also be closely examined in order to design effective and long-lasting policy interventions—either in terms of direct agricultural policy or social protection mechanisms.

Introduction

The state of food insecurity in the world continues to be a subject of intense interest for policy analysts who are concerned about the vulnerability of households in the poorer regions of the world. The sharp changes in food prices that have occurred in global and national markets over the past several years have brought heightened awareness to policy makers and agricultural economic analysts of the stresses facing global food systems and the ecosystems that support them. During the period 2006–2008, the prices of oil increased by four-fold and led to second-round price effects on many other goods and services that depend significantly on fossil fuels as inputs to production, including agriculture. In the six years leading up to 2008, the international market prices of basic grain commodities more than doubled, while the world prices of wheat and rice tripled their levels. While this might represent a relatively small impact on the consumer price indices in more developed countries where food typically represents a small share of the household's budget, these shocks constituted a significant and sharp change in household welfare in poorer countries, where the share of these commodities in total consumption is much higher (von Braun, 2007).

The underlying factors contributing to the rapid changes in food prices in the late 2000s were seen to be widely varied in terms of their relevance to different national circumstances—ranging from policy interventions by national governments that had spillovers into regional markets to linkages with regional environmental outcomes and even broader macroeconomic effects. There was a good deal of discussion over the causality of price increases for different commodities in the empirical literature, and several comprehensive analyses appeared. Prior to the widespread availability of reliable secondary data that could allow analysts to examine actual production and consumption behaviour over the 2006–2008 period, a number of authors tried to assess the relative merit of several alternative factors that could have led to the sharp price increases—drawing from their intuitive knowledge of the commodity markets in question and using whatever secondary data were available on key macroeconomic indicators of relevance. The paper by Abbott *et al.* (2008), for example, took account of the global macroeconomic picture and the relative decline of the dollar in relation to other currencies in order to draw out arguments for how these factors could affect the fundamentals of demand and supply in key commodity markets. Other authors (Trostle, 2008; OECD, 2008) painted a picture of the complex interactions among several determinants of rapidly changing food market dynamics, and of how the confluence of these factors with the more recent turmoil in financial markets compounded the constraints faced by producers and consumers in poorer countries trying to adapt to a rapidly changing economic environment (von Braun, 2008).

More recent papers, making use of a wider range of secondary data from the mid- to late-2000s, have countered some of the assertions that were made earlier in the debate over the causes of the food price spikes. Headey and Fan (2010), for example, have taken issue with earlier statements about the contributions of India and China's rising food demands to market price increases, suggesting that this is not supported by a careful analysis of the underlying data on market fundamentals over the 2006–2008 period. They argue that country-level policy decisions on grain storage and trade policy had greater impacts on food price outcomes, and they echo the views of others who disparage the 'beggar-thy-neighbour' effect of export bans and taxes, which seem to be attractive policy instruments at the national level but cause inefficiencies and asymmetric externalities at the level of regional trade (Bouet and Laborde-Debucquet, 2010). Other authors such as Gilbert (2010) argue against the premise that biofuels played a major part in the price increases, and like Songwe in this volume, argue that investments in agricultural futures had a much stronger role in the price movements over the 2007–2008 period. Baffes and Haniotis (2010), however, strike a balance among the various points of view, arguing that while the impact of biofuels may not have been as strong as previously supposed, there is a relevant link between energy and non-energy commodity prices. They also emphasize the role of agricultural commodities in the portfolios of financial investors as a contributing factor and point to the strong evidence for variability dominating the historic trends in commodity prices.

Compared to previous decades, the current trends in world food prices seem remarkably different in character and appear to break the trend of secular declines in real price levels that had previously been the norm. Looking into the future, a number of global models project the continued elevation of world prices for agricultural goods above historical trend levels, despite the price increases and declines in recent years. For instance, the medium-term projections generated by the joint modeling effort of the Organization for Economic Cooperation and Development (OECD) and the Food and Agricultural Organization of the United Nations (FAO) show that, even with price declines following 2008, a prevailing tightness remains in most major agricultural markets, keeping price levels significantly above historical trends—with some grain commodities reaching levels 15 to 40 percent higher than the average levels seen over the 1997–2006 period (OECD-FAO, 2010). World market price projections from a recent study of the International Food Policy Research Institute (IFPRI) show that world grain prices may undergo increases ranging from 20 to 30 percent over the period 2010 to 2050 if future climate effects on crop yields could be offset—otherwise, increases ranging from 50 to 100 percent could be seen if those longer-term climate impacts are factored in (Nelson *et al.*, 2010). Some see the reversal of historically declining real prices of agricultural commodities as an opportunity for the agricultural producers in both developed and developing countries. But others remain concerned about the implications of high food prices and increased volatility in food markets for the welfare and well-being of vulnerable populations that are mostly net consumers of these products and largely reside in the poorest regions of the developing world (Evans, 2008; FAO, 2008).

The challenges and increased stresses that face global food production and distribution systems in the present economic climate are particularly acute and pressing for sub-Saharan Africa, where high levels of food insecurity persist. Roughly 33 percent of the population lives with insufficient food supplies (FAO, 2005), and an even greater proportion, 43 percent, has been estimated to live below the international poverty line (Dixon *et al.*, 2001). The constraints that prevent Africa from benefiting from higher producer prices for agricultural commodities are myriad and include the fact that most of sub-Saharan Africa's agricultural production relies on rainfed cultivation and uses lower levels of inputs like fertilizers and improved seeds compared to other regions. Additionally, the area affected by land degradation within the region is expanding and thereby causing a decline in soil fertility, which in turn reduces yields and domestic production levels, effects that are compounded by a lack of technological innovation and fertilizer use (FAO, 2005).

In this chapter, we explore the longer-term dynamics of global agricultural markets within the context of a rapidly changing global environment, where various key environmental, technological and socioeconomic drivers are at play. We do not attempt to explain the shorter-term price spikes and periods of market volatility which have been caused by factors such as market speculation, trade restrictions, grain storage behaviour and other local policies. Instead, we take a longer-term view and examine the drivers of the world food economy with a particular focus on the implications for the developing world, especially sub-Saharan Africa. It is in this region that many of the greatest risks lie but where, nonetheless, tremendous potential still remains to boost and reinvigorate the health of the agricultural sector and make significant strides toward improving human well-being. The period of analysis that we address spans from 2010 to 2050, well beyond the 2007–2008 period of high price volatility, but falling within the period when many of the challenges in meeting future food needs are expected to be encountered. We examine these challenges and opportunities for Africa within the wider context of the global world food situation and evaluate the potential role of alternative policy interventions, including investments in agriculture and other key sectors such as education, public health and sanitation. Based on analysis of the investment implications, we conclude with some final recommendations for both policy interventions and further research.

Drivers of Change in Food Systems

The upward pressures on agricultural commodity prices mentioned in the previous section are the result of several underlying factors or 'drivers of change' that are diverse in nature. These range from environmental to socioeconomic 'drivers' and from slow- to fast-moving factors, affecting price and market outcomes differently in the short- versus the long-term. Policy factors are also diverse, ranging from agricultural to energy policies, including those policies that encourage biofuel production from agricultural feedstocks. Figure 4.1 illustrates the interactions among the various key 'drivers' of change in global food systems and their linkages to other components of the food economy and to important outcomes of human well-being such as nutrition.

The figure also illustrates the forces that come from both the demand and supply sides of the market (on the left side of the diagram), resulting in higher prices for food, and the implications for net consumers of food (on the right). On the supply side, the drivers that restrict expansion of production over time are those negative effects on yield coming from environmental stresses and the lack of growth in R&D-driven productivity, as well as limits to area expansion due to pressures from other land uses such as human settlement. On the demand side, the increased demands for animal products arising from economic growth and dietary changes, the associated increases in demand for feed grains, and other non-food uses for grains such as conversion to first-generation biofuels—all act together to increase market demands and pressure on prices. While this schematic is not exhaustive in its identification of all the major factors, it incorporates the main elements of global environmental and economic changes in food production and consumption systems that we address in this chapter.

Characterizing the Drivers of Change

It is useful to consider the various drivers of change identified above—and in the broader literature—in further detail to better understand their importance in explaining the recent tightening in global food markets. In particular, it is useful to distinguish between short-term versus long-term phenomena. This distinction is helpful not only from the point of view of policy-making, but also in identifying which factors are more transitory in importance versus those which may persist into the future and cause prices to rise even further later on. In this chapter, we particularly focus on selected longer-term drivers of change and their effects on food supply and demand outcomes to 2050, rather than on the factors underlying shorter-term market price spikes.

Figure 4.1. The interrelationships among key drivers of change in food systems and their connection to human well-being

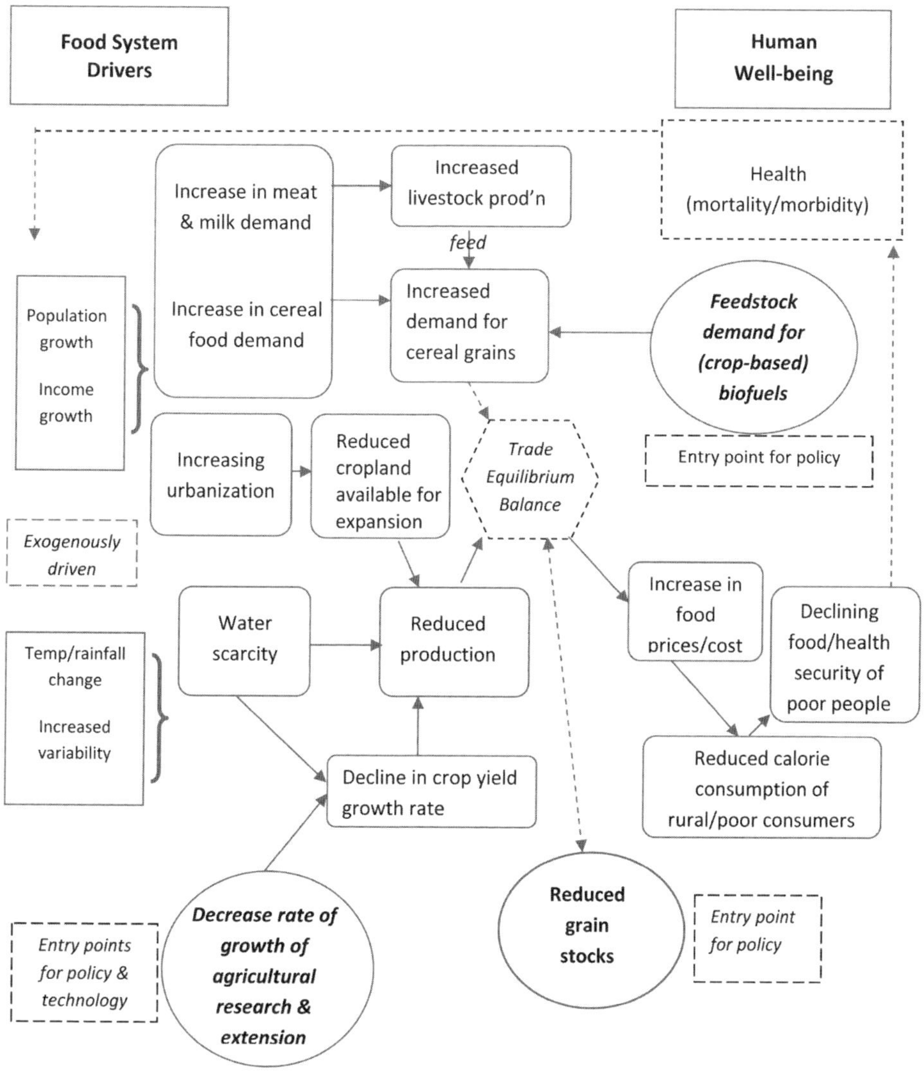

While Figure 4.1 illustrates the interconnections among the various drivers of change and identifies where some of the critical feedback loops might be, it does not indicate what characteristics distinguish the short- versus the longer-term effects on food systems. Figure 4.2 addresses this distinction and shows where some key drivers of change lie in relationship to each other and with respect to their intertemporal or dynamic characteristics—the speed with which they act, as well as the degree to which they explain short-term versus long-term phenomena.

Figure 4.2. Characteristics of various drivers of change in food systems

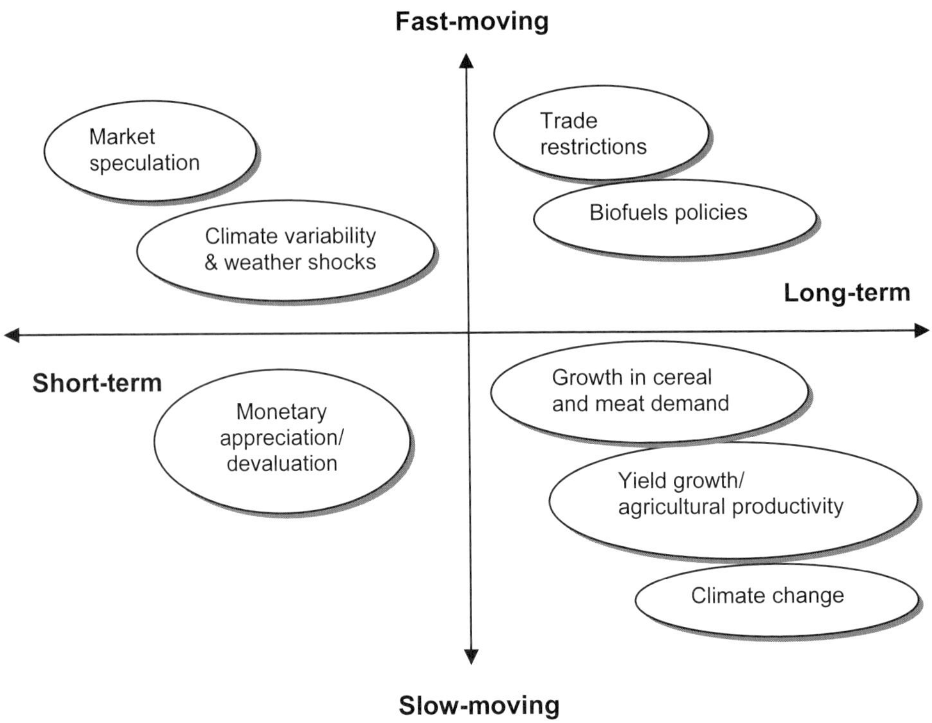

One end of the spectrum (the upper-left quadrant) contains the fast-acting drivers that help to explain short-term market effects. Here we see that market speculation stands out as a factor that helps explain the 'bubbles' that form in markets and prices due to expectations about short- to medium-term market trends, but which may reverse themselves rapidly on the basis of economic conditions and fast-changing market information. This type of activity has been cited by some authors as a factor that explains the spikes that developed in markets in the late 2000s, as opposed to other indicators stemming from supply and demand fundamentals that usually determine price formation (von Braun *et al.*, 2008). Other observers, however, remain more skeptical of the role of market speculation relative to the direct policy actions by governments, such as changes in trade policies (Headey and Fan, 2010).

At the other end of the spectrum, in the lower-right quadrant, we find relatively slow-moving phenomena that play a part in determining the long-term evolution of food systems and the performance of the underlying ecosystems that support them. Here, for example, climate change is a key factor, incorporating the long-term changes in temperature, precipitation, atmospheric chemistry and other elements that impact crop growth potential and the characteristics of agroecological systems. Climate change as a phenomenon should be distinguished from effects of climatic *variability* and extreme weather incidents that are manifest in many regions and which are short-term phenomena.[4] These types of weather shocks drive the supply-side of the food equation and can lead to sudden drops in output that can push up market prices, whereas sudden surges from the demand side of the equation (such as those due to the growth in crop-based biofuel production) may also tighten market conditions and contribute towards similar price increases.

Drivers of supply-and-demand change that operate on a slower-moving trajectory are those associated with growth in demand for key consumer food products, such as cereals and meats (which also have implications for feed demand), as well as trends in crop yield growth, which determine how well the supply side can adjust to increases in demand. Changes in the demand for food and fibre products tend not to 'surge' as rapidly as those for energy-intensive products, such as petroleum used in transport. However, these products represent a component of food system changes that can be expected to contribute to keeping prices at elevated levels well into the future, as cited by the OECD in their projections of agricultural production and prices to 2019 (OECD-FAO, 2010), as well as in longer-term projections (von Braun *et al.*, 2008; de Hoyos and Medvedev, 2009).

In this chapter, we focus on two particular drivers of change that are best suited to treatment within the quantitative framework that we will introduce in later sections, namely investments in agricultural R&D and climate change. These two long-term, supply-side drivers represent different types of factors: one is mostly policy-driven in nature, given that R&D investments (either public or private) respond to incentives or direct funding provided by governments; the other is fundamentally an environmental phenomenon, though its effects can be influenced by national (or international) economic and environmental policy actions. In the following sections, we discuss the nature of these drivers in more detail.

Investments in Agricultural Research and Development

In addition to the basic drivers of socioeconomic change such as increasing human population numbers and household incomes, which govern the changes in food and energy demands over time, there are several key supply-side drivers that must be taken into account. A number of key environmental factors including resource scarcity or degraded land and water quality can constrain the supply side of food systems from responding readily and consistently to changes in demand. Reduced research investments in crop and energy technology development can lead to a long-term slow-down in the expansion of supply, which eventually leads to higher prices as demand continues to grow. This is one of the key aspects of the global food problem identified in this chapter: how declining trends in agricultural research investment can result in a less resilient agricultural system and a more food-insecure future, especially given the challenges that climate change and bio-energy development present to the global food economy.

A number of future assessments of global food production and consumption show projections of future agricultural land requirements that assume 70 percent of food needs will be met through yield enhancements (FAO, 2006). Yet agricultural research has stagnated or declined over the years in many countries, particularly since the early 1990s (Table 4.1). For developing countries, public agricultural research investments increased by 37.4 percent between 1981 and 1991, but then declined to 21.8 percent between 1991 and 2000. For developed countries, this decline is even sharper; growth in public agricultural research declined from 28.7 percent between 1981–1991 to 5.9 percent between 1991–

[4] The two phenomena are related in that the increased incidence of extreme weather events is one of the outcomes of long-term climate change.

2000. For sub-Saharan Africa, which is particularly vulnerable to food security problems, public research investments actually declined in real terms. Given the vast number of studies that show the existence of significant R&D spillovers, a decline or stagnation of research in any of these regions may have adverse impacts on agricultural productivity in other regions as well. Table 4.1 also presents agricultural research expenditures as a percentage of agricultural GDP. It can be seen that this share has declined substantially for sub-Saharan Africa over the years, while declining slightly for low and middle income countries in general, and increasing for other country groups.

Table 4.1. Public Expenditures in Agriculture-related Research, 1981–2000

Region/Country	Expenditures as a % of Agricultural GDP			Public agricultural R&D spending (2005 PPP dollars, millions)		
	1981	**1991**	**2000**	**1981**	**1991**	**2000**
Low and Middle Income Countries	0.56	0.56	0.55	6,049	8,310	10,119
Sub-Saharan Africa	0.86	0.76	0.65	1,084	1,253	1,239
Asia and Pacific	0.33	0.37	0.39	1,971	3,287	4,758
Latin America and Caribbean	0.91	1.08	1.19	2,274	2,697	2,710
Middle East and North Africa	0.60	0.60	0.74	720	1,074	1,412
High Income Countries	1.51	2.08	2.35	9,774	12,577	13,313
Total	0.91	1.00	0.98	15,823	20,887	23,432

Source: ASTI (2009).

As the United States and other developed regions have shifted their research focus to reflect consumer preferences for processed, organic and other high-value products, the diffusion of more relevant yield-enhancing technology in developing countries has slowed (Alston and Pardey, 2006). Only one-third of global public agricultural research in the 1990s was in developing countries, with over 50 percent of that being concentrated in Brazil, China, India, and South Africa (Alston and Pardey, 2006). Therefore, better technology diffusion and more public funds dedicated to agricultural research programs are critical to meet growing food needs, especially in low-income countries where food needs are most acute.

The Challenge of Climate Change

Climate change and increasing demands for water resources will impact agricultural growing conditions, significantly impacting food production in the future. Integrated assessment models have shown that climate change effects on temperature and rainfall are expected to have positive yield effects in cooler climates, while likely decreasing cereal yields in low latitude regions—the geographical location of most developing countries (Easterling *et al.*, 2007).

One set of estimates shows that developing countries are expected to experience a 9 to 21 percent decline in overall agricultural productivity due to global warming, while industrialized countries will face a 6 percent decline to an 8 percent increase, depending on the offsetting effects that additional atmospheric carbon could have on rates of photosynthesis (Cline, 2007). As a result of these differences in predicted production capabilities, some regions will benefit from increases in yields while others will be left to import an increasing amount of food to meet future demands. Fischer *et al.* (2005) estimate that cereal imports will increase in developing countries by 10 to 40 percent by 2080. While there is a large variation in these predictions, the combined effects of rapid population growth, lower yields, and increasing reliance on trade policy for food imports could leave an additional 5 to 170 million people malnourished in 2080—up to 75 percent of the total in Africa—depending on the projection scenario (Schmidhuber and Tubiello, 2007). Parry *et al.* (2005) have shown that regional variations in the number of food insecure is better explained by population changes than by climate impacts on food availability. As a result, economic and other development policies—especially policies pertaining to agricultural research and technology—will be critical in influencing future human well-being.

Food and Agricultural Outlook to 2050

In this section we present some projections for food production and consumption based on the IMPACT (International Model for Policy Analysis of Agricultural Commodities and Trade) model of the International Food Policy Research Institute (IFPRI) (Rosegrant *et al.*, 2001, 2002, 2005; Msangi and Rosegrant, 2009). We also outline the implications that we see for long-term food security. These simulations will help show the impact of policy-based and socioeconomic drivers on the evolution of agricultural prices, as well as the role that technological interventions and investments can play. These results will also help illustrate the types of entry points for policy and investment that are possible to help stabilize food prices and improve human well-being in the face of the various drivers of change that we have discussed.

Model Description

To examine the potential impact of biofuel production growth on country-level and domestic agricultural markets, a partial-equilibrium modeling framework is adopted to capture the interactions between agricultural commodity supply and demand, as well as trade, at the global level. The model used is IFPRI's IMPACT model, which was developed for projecting global food supply, food demand and food security to the year 2020 and beyond (Rosegrant *et al.*, 2008). The IMPACT model is a partial equilibrium agricultural model for crop and livestock commodities, including cereals, soybeans, roots and tubers, meats, milk, eggs, oil-seeds, oil-cakes/meals, sugar/sweeteners, and fruits and vegetables. It is specified as a set of 115 country and regional sub-models, within each of which supply, demand, and prices for agricultural commodities are determined. The model links the various countries and regions through international trade using a series of linear and non-linear equations to approximate the underlying production and demand functions. World agricultural commodity prices are determined annually at levels that clear international markets. Growth in crop production in each country is determined by crop and input prices, the rate of productivity growth, investment in irrigation, and water availability. Demand is a function of prices, income, and population growth. The IMPACT model incorporates four categories of commodity demands—for food, feed, biofuel feedstocks, and other uses.

Baseline Model Projections

Production Growth

The profile of projected global cereal production over time is shown in Figure 4.3, where we see steady trends of expected output growth to 2050. Cereal production is projected to grow steadily across all seven regions, with North America and Europe leading the regions in cereal production volume.

Figure 4.3. Total cereal production to 2050 (millions of metric tons)

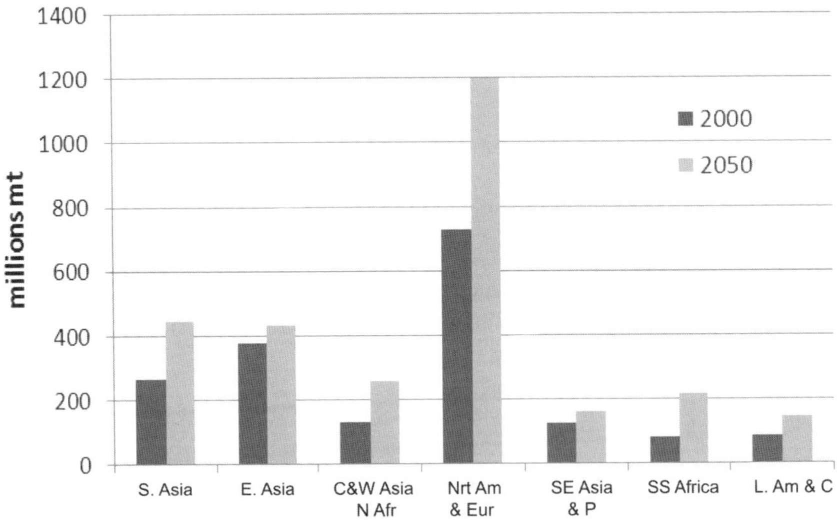

Source: IFPRI IMPACT projections.
Note: E. Asia = East Asia, S. Asia = South Asia, SE Asia & P = Southeast Asia & Pacific, SS Africa = sub-Saharan Africa, L.Am & C = Latin America & Caribbean, C&W Asia N Af = Central & West Asia and North Africa, Nrt Am. & Eur. = North America and Europe.

If we look at these trends on a per-capita basis, however, we see a somewhat more static picture in terms of how the various regions are projected to maintain production levels relative to their populations (Figure 4.4). In this case, we see that North American, European and Central Asian regions experience significant increases in production relative to their own population growth and are able to provide the surpluses that supply the food and feed needs of the rest of the world. The Middle East/North Africa region is able to increase its per capita production levels over the projection period, as is the Latin American/Caribbean region. By contrast, the South and East Asian regions decrease their per capita production over time, as does sub-Saharan Africa.

Figure 4.4. Per capita cereal production to 2050 (kg per capita per year)

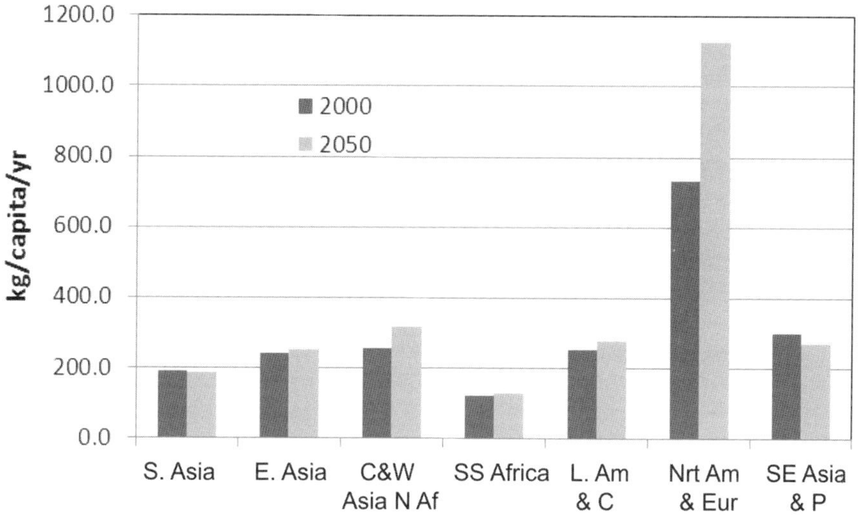

Source: IFPRI IMPACT projections.
Note: E. Asia = East Asia, S. Asia = South Asia, SS Africa = sub-Saharan Africa, L.Am & C = Latin America & Caribbean, C & W Asia N Af = Central & West Asia and North Africa, Nrt Am & Eur. = North America and Europe, SE Asia & P = Southeast Asia & Pacific

Demand Growth

In terms of demand growth over the fifty-year period, total food demand for cereals is projected to increase in all regions, with North America, Europe and East Asia leading all other regions in total volume. Table 4.2 shows how the total demand for cereals is divided into its largest two components (food and feed uses). In terms of food use, the region that shows the strongest growth in demand for cereals is sub-Saharan Africa, even though other regions like South Asia, East Asia, and the Pacific and Latin America exceed it in terms of food consumption volume. The Middle East/North Africa region has food demand growth for cereals similar to that of South Asia, while those regions with the lowest levels of growth are Eastern Europe and Central Asia, as well as the East Asia and Pacific regions. In terms of feed uses of cereals, the North American and European regions lead the world in total volume of projected feed consumption, followed by East Asia, Latin America and the Caribbean as well as the Middle East and North Africa regions.

If we look at the patterns of food demand in per capita terms, we get a more comparable basis on which to examine the changes in consumption patterns across regions (Figure 4.5). Looking at the demand for cereals, we see that East and South Asia are projected to fall in per capita cereal consumption compared to the rest of the world. In terms of the increasing demand for meat, which is the main driver of feed demand for cereals, the IMPACT model projects that East Asia will far outstrip other regions in per capita consumption levels, which is in keeping with its rapid growth in per capita income compared to other developing and developed regions. Other regions that show large increases in per capita consumption of meat are North America and Europe, which have far higher levels of consumption than South Asia and sub-Saharan Africa. In these latter regions, per capita consumption of meat is projected to grow steadily from relatively low levels due to steady income growth over this period.

Table 4.2. Total, Feed and Food Demand for Cereals (Millions of Metric Tons)

Region	Total			Food			Feed		
	2000	2050	% chg	2000	2050	% chg	2000	2050	% chg
South Asia	250	427	71%	218	360	66%	3	12	266%
East Asia and Pacific	524	688	31%	347	376	8%	102	205	100%
Europe and Central Asia	235	267	13%	79	80	1%	108	124	14%
Latin America and Caribbean	180	287	60%	63	88	40%	50	112	122%
Middle East and North Africa	90	182	103%	56	102	83%	23	58	147%
Sub-Saharan Africa	84	243	190%	65	187	189%	7	18	155%
North America and Europe	619	853	38%	114	148	30%	324	401	24%

Source: IFPRI IMPACT projections.

Long-term Trends in Malnutrition

Given the patterns of supply and demand that have been highlighted above, the IMPACT model infers a trend in the levels of malnourished people among the most vulnerable demographic of the population—those aged zero to five. The determinants of malnutrition are derived primarily from four key indicators—per capita calorie availability, access to clean drinking water, rates of secondary schooling among females, and the ratio of female-to-male life expectancy. The links between malnutrition and these determinants were established in the work of Smith and Haddad (2000), who used them as explanatory variables to account for changes in levels of child malnutrition across the developing world between 1975 and 1995. According to their work, a greater share of the reduction in child malnutrition levels over this period could be accounted for by improvements in female schooling and access to clean water than by simple calorie availability. This finding is in keeping with the four-pillared concept of food security that underlies FAO's conceptual framework—where food availability is only one of the factors that accounts for food security status among vulnerable populations and must be evaluated along with access, utilization and stability. The methodology used for tracking child malnutrition in IMPACT, therefore, covers aspects of availability, access and utilization. The concept of access is grounded in the price response of consumption to market conditions, and the utilization aspect is related to access to clean water, which is a major determinant of human health and the ability of the body to absorb and utilize available and accessible nutrients.

Figure 4.5. Per capita cereal demand to 2050 (kg per capita per year)

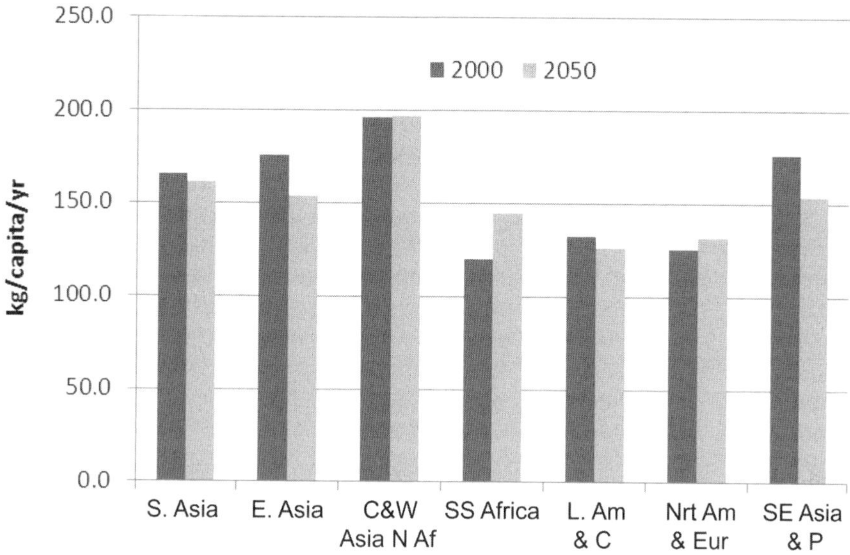

Source: IFPRI IMPACT projections.
Note: E. Asia = East Asia, S. Asia = South Asia, SS Africa = sub-Saharan Africa, L.Am & C = Latin America & Caribbean, C & W Asia N Af = Central & West Asia and North Africa, Nrt Am & Eur. = North America and Europe, SE Asia & P = Southeast Asia & Pacific

The baseline trends for child malnutrition are shown in Figure 4.6, where we see variation in the projected rates of change in malnutrition. The declines in the prevalence of malnutrition across the various sub-regions of Africa and Asia show a steeper decline for the Asian region than for sub-Saharan Africa in the period up to 2025, after which a number of the African sub-regions also show steady declines.

The South Asia region has the highest overall levels of prevalence of malnutrition but is able to achieve significant reductions by 2050 compared to Southeast Asia and Western sub-Saharan Africa, where the overall levels of malnutrition prevalence decrease only slightly. East Asia, which begins with the lowest levels of malnutrition, is able to draw these levels down even further in the longer-term, achieving single-digit levels that no other region can match. The overall picture of child malnutrition, however, is completed only when one looks at the total *numbers* of malnourished children, for which the IMPACT model projections show the Asian region to have the highest levels, even in 2050, although the rate of decrease is among the fastest. This contrasts with sub-Saharan Africa, where there is an overall increase in the numbers of malnourished to 2025, before the acceleration of production and per capita income levels allow this region to reduce its numbers over the remaining period to 2050. In total numbers, however, the count of malnourished children in sub-Saharan Africa remains nearly the same in 2050 as it was in 2000, even though that number represents a smaller share of the overall population. This picture helps to illustrate the challenge that remains in combating hunger and improving human well-being outcomes in the developing world in the long term, given the impending pressures that environmental and policy-driven shocks can be expected to have on the global food system.

Figure 4.6. Prevalence of preschool child malnutrition in Asia and Africa (percent of population aged 0 to 5)

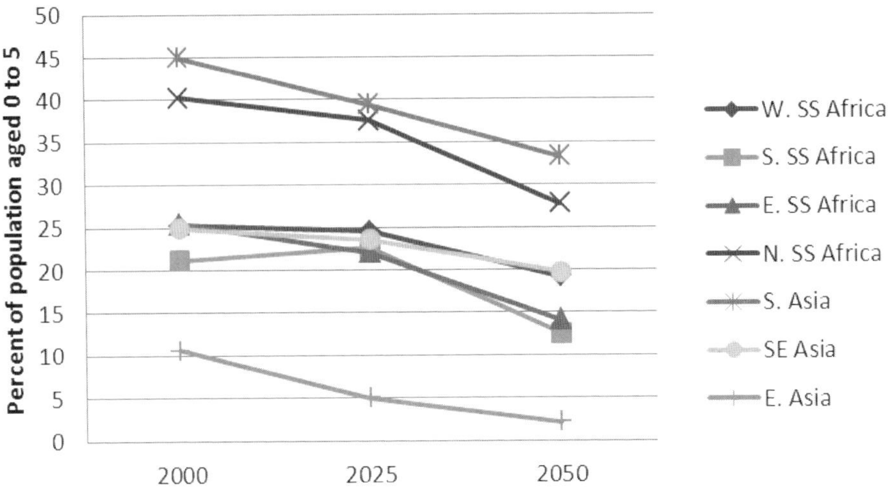

Source: IFPRI IMPACT projections.
Note: N/S/E/W. SS Africa =Northern/Southern/Eastern/Western sub-Saharan Africa, S. Asia = South Asia, E. Asia = East Asia, SE Asia = Southeast Asia.

Baseline Projections of Spending Needed for Agriculture

In this section, we present some projections for spending on agriculture that are anticipated under a baseline set of assumptions regarding the future growth of crop yields and productivity in agriculture. We will contrast the baseline case with one in which there is an effort to offset the effects of climate change—as envisioned under one of the more severe climate scenarios—in order to illustrate the levels of spending and improvement needed to address the challenges that global environmental change will pose to the global food system.

By looking at the baseline case to 2050 projected with IFPRI's IMPACT model, we see that the implied spending across both the agricultural and non-agricultural sectors implies sizable outlays of resources in order to meet future needs for food, feed and fuel (Table 4.3). From this table, we see that a sizable outlay of expenditures is still needed in South Asia to maintain its irrigation system in order to continue the successes and the momentum of the Green Revolution. This is reflected in the strong increases in irrigated area that are projected to continue in South Asia (Figure 4.7) compared to what is seen in other regions.

Table 4.3. Baseline Results for Agricultural and Non-agricultural Sector Investments for the Years 2000–2050 (Billions of 2000 US dollars)

Region	Agric. Research	Clean Water	Female Educ.	Irrig. Expansion	Irrig. Efficiency	Rural Roads
South Asia	25	63	24	36	30	10
East Asia and Pacific	35	45	20	6	19	43
Europe and Central Asia	30	5	1	1	4	2
Latin America & Caribbean	58	27	6	8	11	65
Middle East & North Africa	21	13	4	5	1	2
Sub-Saharan Africa	21	66	16	44	5	112
All Developing	190	219	72	99	70	235

Source: IMPACT model projections.

Figure 4.7. Simulated increases in net irrigated area over time

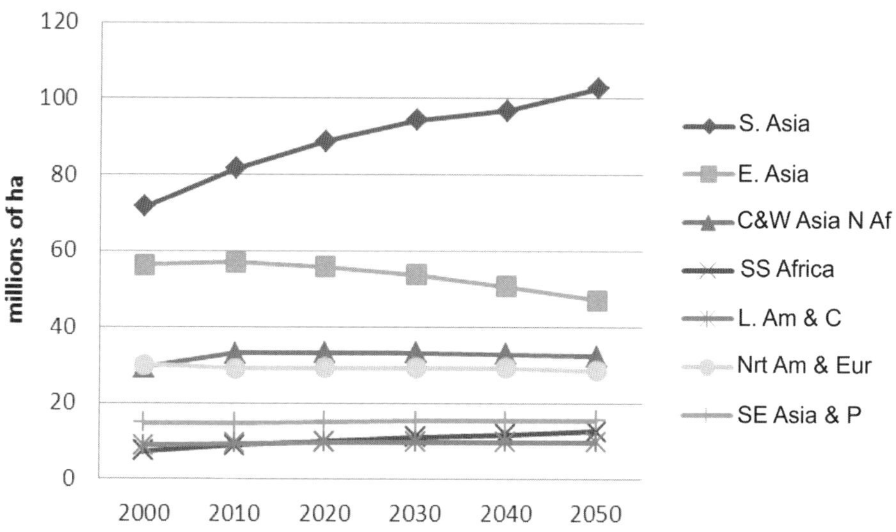

Source: IFPRI IMPACT projections.
Note: E. Asia = East Asia, S. Asia = South Asia, SS Africa = sub-Saharan Africa, L.Am & C = Latin America & Caribbean, C & W Asia N Af = Central & West Asia and North Africa, Nrt Am & Eur. = North America and Europe, SE Asia & P = Southeast Asia & Pacific

Even though there are increases in irrigated area in sub-Saharan Africa, they are modest in size compared to other regions, which reflects the historical difficulty in realizing successful irrigation investments in this region and the notoriously high investment costs of those which are implemented (Inocencio *et al.*, 2007). For the rest of Asia and the Pacific, clean water investments remain the largest category in which projected future spending needs lie. There is also a higher share of regional spending that is allocated to rural road access compared to South Asia.

Table 4.4. Breakdown of Agricultural Sector Investment Needs under Baseline Case for the Years 2000–2050 (Billions of 2000 US dollars)

Region	Total Agricultural Spending	Share of Total Agricultural Spending			
		Agricultural Research	Irrigation Expansion	Irrigation Efficiency	Rural Roads
South Asia	101	24%	36%	30%	10%
East Asia and Pacific	102	34%	6%	19%	42%
Europe and Central Asia	38	80%	3%	11%	5%
Latin America and Caribbean	142	41%	6%	8%	46%
Middle East and North Africa	29	74%	16%	2%	9%
Sub-Saharan Africa	182	12%	24%	2%	62%
Developing	593	32%	17%	12%	40%

Source: IMPACT model projections

Turning to the project shares in agricultural investment, the region that has the highest proportion of its baseline expenditures allocated to rural road access is sub-Saharan Africa, followed closely by Latin America and the Caribbean (Table 4.4). The largest amount of spending that is envisioned for agricultural research is in Latin America and the Caribbean, as seen in Table 4.3. This will be necessary to change the pattern of historical production growth, which has mostly come from agricultural land expansion, into a future pattern of growth that relies more on technology-dependent yield increases.

For the sub-Saharan Africa region, a more even spread of the investment outlays is envisioned across all components of the agricultural sector. The high spending on rural roads in sub-Saharan Africa is due to the continent's vast scale and the underdeveloped state of rural roads compared to most other regions. Improving access to clean drinking water is also a 'big ticket' component of Africa's projected spending bill given its important role in household health and welfare and the fact that this has been slow to spread to those parts of rural sub-Saharan Africa that need it most. Irrigation investment to counteract the historically low rate of irrigation expansion and adoption across the continent constitutes the third largest component. South Asia will also need a large outlay of expenditures for improving access to clean water given the large numbers of poor and malnourished in that region. Figure 4.8 shows the changes in levels of access to clean water—used as exogenous assumptions in the IMPACT simulations—across various regions.

Figure 4.8. Share of population with access to clean water over time

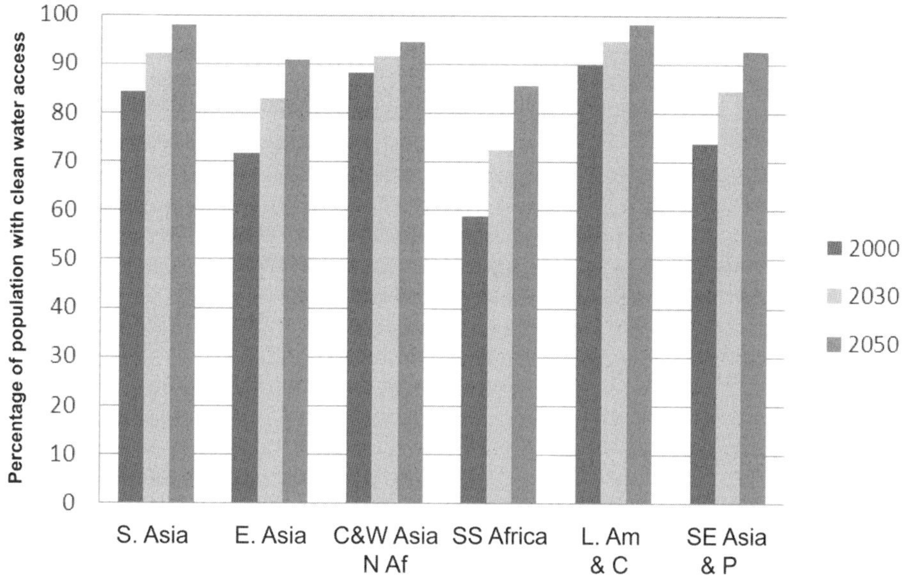

Source: IFPRI IMPACT projections.
Note: E. Asia = East Asia, S. Asia = South Asia, SS Africa = sub-Saharan Africa, L.Am & C = Latin America & Caribbean, C & W Asia N Af = Central & West Asia and North Africa, Nrt Am & Eur. = North America and Europe, SE Asia & P = Southeast Asia & Pacific.

Spending on female secondary education, and education in general, also comprises a large portion of the projected non-agricultural spending portfolio for both Asia and sub-Saharan Africa (Table 4.3), as this type of spending is responsible for a large share of the reduction in child malnutrition seen in recent years. With their rapidly growing populations, these regions are projected to have sizable increases in the population of school-aged children who will require educational services in the coming years. Figure 4.9 shows, for example, the rates of female secondary school enrollment embedded in our baseline simulations, and these imply increasing numbers of girls to be educated over time. Therefore, in order to maintain and continue to improve the secondary school enrollment rates, the pace of future expenditures has to increase in order to accommodate these new pupils.

The Added Challenge of Climate Change

In addition to the scenarios that we have presented, we must also begin to reconcile our accounting of future food balances with the added challenges that climate change will represent to the global food system. It must be said that the ultimate impacts of climate change—both in terms of magnitude and regional specificity—remain somewhat uncertain, as there is a wide spectrum of modeling results that show various degrees of impact for the same regions of the world. Much of this uncertainty is due to the fact that the different Global Circulation Models (GCMs) depict the interactions between the atmosphere, the ocean and terrestrial systems differently, leading to greater divergences in model results as one moves forward in time. For this reason, the Intergovernmental Panel on Climate Change (IPCC) tried to portray the wide variation in model results in both its Third and Fourth Assessment Reports; some authors have chosen to take the more extreme of those outcomes to illustrate the possible range of impacts on agriculture.

Figure 4.9. Female secondary schooling rates over time

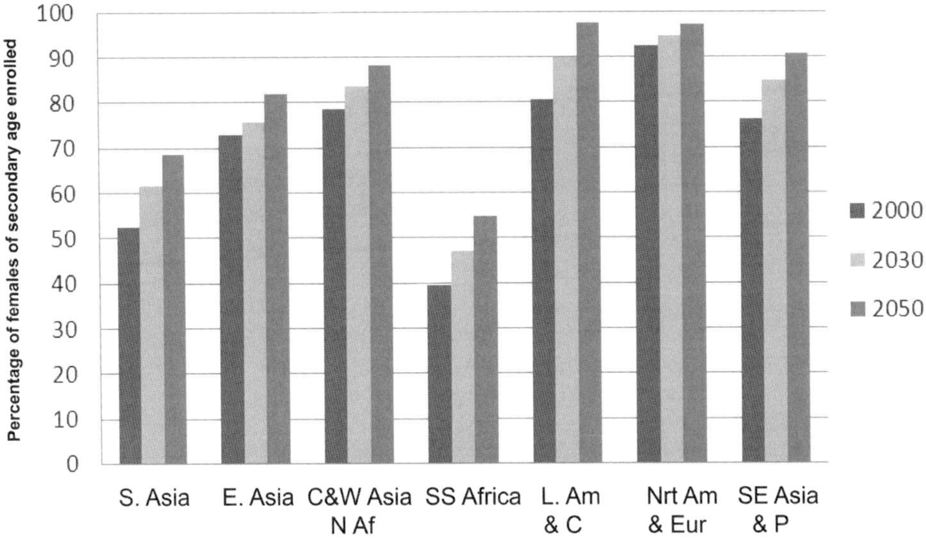

Source: IFPRI IMPACT projections.
Note: SS Africa = sub-Saharan Africa, S. Asia = South Asia, L. Am & C = Latin America & the Caribbean, E. Asia = East Asia, SE Asia & P = Southeast Asia and the Pacific, C&W Asia N AF= Central & Western Asia and North Africa.

In the example that we will show, we draw from the results of alternative climate models—one from the Australian modeling group within the Commonwealth Science and Industrial Organization (CSIRO), which tends to give 'drier' climate outcomes—and the US model based at the National Center for Atmospheric Research (NCAR). The outputs generated by these models are based on a common underlying socioeconomic set of driving assumptions, which come from the 'A2' scenario, in which there is assumed to be a higher reliance on fossil-based fuels and lower rates of dissemination of 'clean' technologies across the globe. This kind of socioeconomic 'storyline' is similar to the less-favourable scenarios of both the Millennium Ecosystem Assessment (MA, 2005) and the United Nations Environment Programme's GEO-4 assessment[5] (UNEP, 2007), in which the geopolitical environment is portrayed as being less harmonious and more centered upon economic growth, even if at the expense of environmental quality. Some results based on

[5] The Fourth Global Environmental Outlook (GEO-4) of UNEP is an environmentally-focused global assessment with a scenario structure similar to that of the Millennium Ecosystem Assessment, with a linked multi-model quantitative framework to assess future outcomes to 2050 (UNEP, 2007).

the outputs of the French Model for Interdisciplinary Research on Climate (MIROC) are also shown for contrast.

The methodology that we have used to account for climate change 'shocks' within our modeling framework is still under revision and is subject to change in the future. The main challenge lies in the reconciliation of biophysical modeling results—which are run at a relatively micro-level scale of resolution—with the workings of an aggregate-level, market equilibrium-driven policy model such as IMPACT, which has to take the average of crop level effects across space. The biophysical impacts of temperature and precipitation changes on agricultural crop yields are best represented by agronomic models, which account for local soil characteristics and other environmental influences (e.g., solar radiation) that affect crop growth; these can be simulated at a very disaggregated level of spatial resolution. In order to simulate the effect of these field-level crop yield effects on the aggregate supply of a particular commodity within a country or region, these disaggregated effects have to be aggregated up to the spatial units of the market equilibrium model in order to portray the impacts they will have on supply, trade and market prices within the economic model. The marriage of these two elements—the biophysical process-driven elements and the economic equilibrium-driven mechanisms—is complex, and is a subject of continuing research and refinement at IFPRI; this is described in better detail in the technical appendix of Nelson *et al.* (2009). We have also not fully attributed the possible effects that carbon fertilization could have on future crop yields due to the uncertainty that still exists in trying to quantify this result for various agronomic zones, where the on-the-ground reality could differ significantly from carbon fertilization experiments in the laboratory.

Notwithstanding these difficulties, we present some results that show the overall magnitude of climate change impacts on global agricultural markets so that we can begin to discuss the implications of these in terms of both national and household-level economic effects. Table 4.5 shows the projected impacts of climate change on the yields of three major cereal commodities—maize, rice and wheat—that are of key importance to both food and feed uses.

Table 4.5. Simulated Impacts on Yields in 2050 from Various Climate Change Simulations

Crop	Percent change from yields under year 2000 climate					
	CSIRO		NCAR		MIROC	
	irrigated	rainfed	irrigated	rainfed	irrigated	rainfed
Maize						
developing regions	-2.0	+0.2	-2.8	-2.9	-5.3	-3.5
developed regions	-1.2	+0.6	-8.7	-5.7	-12.3	-29.9
Rice						
developing regions	-14.4	-1.3	-18.5	-1.4	-11.9	+0.1
developed regions	-3.5	+17.3	-5.5	+10.3	-13.3	-12.8
Wheat						
developing regions	-28.3	-1.4	-34.3	-1.1	-13.4	-10.4
developed regions	-5.7	+3.1	-4.9	+2.4	-11.6	-9.0

Source: Nelson *et al.* (2009, 2010).

Note: The CSIRO and NCAR results are from Nelson *et al.* (2009) and are based on A2 SRES (Special Report on Emissions Scenarios). The MIROC-based results are from Nelson *et al.* (2010) and are based on A1b SRES scenario-based climate outputs.

In 2050, the range of impacts due to climate change on important grains such as maize implies non-trivial effects for the livestock industry in developed regions, which rely on maize for feed, as well as for food consumers of maize in sub-Saharan Africa. One cannot really assign probabilities or weights to the scenario results shown since they represent different underlying assumptions of the way in which the changes in atmospheric carbon from the simulated socioeconomic scenario lead to different temperature and moisture interactions between the atmosphere, ocean and land surfaces within a particular physical modeling system. While there are some positive effects on yield, there remains significant potential for downside risk to the more vulnerable developing regions—either from effects that are realized directly in those regions, or through market-mediated ripple effects that could be propagated widely throughout the world food system.

The world price impacts associated with these yield effects are shown in Table 4.6 for the three major grain crops. These show significant increases in price beyond the 2050 levels already projected even without climate change. It should be kept in mind that these market effects do not represent sudden price spikes that occur in 2050, but rather a gradual build-up of market pressures that accumulate over the projection period to 2050 as supplies tighten due to the shifts in the biophysical suitability of growing these major cereal grains. Even though wheat is not as important a staple crop as maize for sub-Saharan Africa, the simulated doubling of prices in 2050 compared to the no-climate change case is striking nonetheless and represents a significant shift in global market conditions.

Table 4.6. Simulated Impacts on Price in 2050 from Various Climate Change Simulations (US$/mt)

Crop	Baseline		NCAR-based scenario		CSIRO-based scenario	
	2000	2050 no CC	2050 with CC	% chg	2050 with CC	% chg
Maize	95	155	235	51.9	240	55.1
Rice	190	307	421	36.8	406	32.0
Wheat	113	158	334	111.3	307	94.2

Source: Nelson *et al.* (2009). Note: The CSIRO and NCAR results are from Nelson *et al.* (2009) and are based on A2 SRES scenario.

We show the implications of these climate-driven changes for child malnutrition outcomes based on the impacts that simulated climate outcomes have on yields, country-level supplies and market-level prices. Looking at the impacts in 2050 for various regions (Table 4.7), we see that there are appreciable differences between the 2050 outcomes with and without climate change. For both climate model outcomes, climate changes result in additional levels of malnutrition in South Asia and sub-Saharan Africa, with a projected 10 million additional malnourished children in SSA in 2050 given projected climate changes. This would mean a further worsening of malnutrition that is already foreseen over the entire projection period. The impacts in South Asia suggest that climate change may moderate the significant declining trend in child malnutrition that occurs over the period to 2050. The effects that are simulated here represent just the impacts that climate has on crop production and prices, with the resulting decreases in food consumption and average calorie availability from all foods. Given that calorie availability is only one component of the food security measure that we use, it is important that other socioeconomic components of household food security be kept on track to avoid food security being seriously derailed by future additional stresses created by global climate changes. For the moment, we focus on the kinds of adaptation that might be possible through direct interventions in agriculture.

Table 4.7. Total Number of Malnourished Children in 2000 and 2050 (Millions of Children Aged 0 to 5).

Region	Baseline		NCAR-based scenario		CSIRO-based scenario	
	2000	2050 no CC	2050 with CC	total chg	2050 with CC	total chg
South Asia	76	52	59	7	59	7
East Asia & Pacific	24	10	15	5	14	4
E Europe & Central Asia	4	3	4	1	4	1
Latin America & Caribbean	8	5	6	1	6	1
Middle East & North Africa	3	1	2	1	2	1
Sub-Saharan Africa	33	42	52	10	52	10
All developing countries	148	113	139	26	137	24

Source: Nelson *et al.* (2009).

Implied Investments for Adaptation

The effects on grain yields, prices and levels of child malnutrition in the developing world shown above suggest that threats to global food supplies would be significantly increased if the effects on crop yields in the climate change scenarios were to be actually realized. In order to offset these effects, responsive policy actions and adaptation measures would have to occur. These adaptive actions are not actually embedded in our results, as agent-based endogenous technology choice is not fully represented in our model. These types of adaptations and technology choices would have to be introduced through new scenarios in order to account for the possibilities of improved seed varieties and other adaptive on-farm improvements which are not endogenous within our framework. We plan to do these types of adaptation-focused scenarios in further work.

We nonetheless try to illustrate the magnitudes of investment efforts that would be needed if adaptations to climate change were carried out by boosting productivity within the agricultural sector through direct investments in agricultural R&D or through investments in complementary and supporting agricultural sectors. We do this by conducting a policy experiment in which we introduce yield improvements to the affected crops and regions, and determine the *additional* levels of agricultural sector spending above the baseline case that are necessary to offset the shocks introduced by climate change. The results provide us with insights as to where the additional spending on agriculture is needed most and which regions stand in greatest need of these investments. The results of this scenario analysis will provide policy makers and agricultural researchers and scientists with a sense of prioritization of their efforts in coming years.

For this experiment, we consider (for the sake of simpler exposition) the results of one model, the Hadley Center's climate change model, which provides the basis for the IPCC's 'A2a' scenario and simulates rather sharp decreases in precipitation for South Asia as well as key parts of sub-Saharan Africa and Latin America. The top half of Table 4.8 shows the breakdown of cumulative investment expenditures to 2050 across various categories that underlie the baseline trajectory of the model (where climate change effects are not included). The lower half of the table shows the additional expenditures within the agricultural sector—in terms of percentage increases over baseline expenditure levels—that we see as necessary to offset the effects of climate change on the world food system based on the above climate change assumptions.

From this table, we see that sub-Saharan Africa requires the largest level of spending on agriculture in order to offset the impacts of climate change as measured within the above modeling framework. Within that total spending level for Africa, the amounts for irrigation and agricultural R&D are close in magnitude. The level of investment needed for rural roads is more than quadruple the amount of investment needed in all the other sectors combined. Given the poor state of road networks in Africa and the large share of the population that is projected to remain rural in the future (implying higher road-building costs necessary to reach them), the levels of spending in this category are relatively large compared to other regions and constitute a significant increase over the baseline spending needs for roads. The next largest level of outlays on roads is for Latin America; its relatively low population density (compared, say, to Asia) also raises the cost of reaching people by road.

The additional spending on agricultural research needed to offset climate change impacts is highest in sub-Saharan Africa among all regions, followed by the Latin American and Caribbean region and the Middle East and North African region. These additional spending requirements demonstrate the need to maintain the increases in yield growth (over area expansion) that are required in order to produce the high volumes of cereals needed to meet food and feed needs as environmental and socioeconomic changes occur to 2050.

Implications for Food Security and Policy

We now turn to the implications suggested by the scenario results discussed in the previous section in light of the current global food situation. In particular we address the implications of the scenario results for household-level welfare.

Micro-level Impacts and Household Welfare

Price changes in food and energy markets influence households directly through market prices and indirectly through the costs of production and transportation for marketed goods. Net sellers and net buyers are affected differently; even though net sellers gain from price increases, their gains may not be enough to offset the negative impacts that net buyers undergo. From FAO data, we see that in some of the poorest countries, a relatively small share of households are net sellers of the staple foods that have recently experienced the strongest price effects. In a country like Bangladesh, for example, only slightly under 16 percent of all households are net sellers of staples (according to year 2000 data), while in Vietnam the proportion was over 40 percent in 1998 (FAO, 2008). Developing countries like Madagascar, where over half (51 percent) of households in 1993 were net sellers, are unusual, compared to countries like Guatemala and Malawi, where net sellers accounted for slightly over 10 percent and nearly 12 percent of all households in 2000 and 2004, respectively.

Table 4.8. Spending Needs for Agricultural Sector to Offset Climate Change Impacts, 2000-2050.

Cumulative Baseline Expenditures to 2050: Total Spending in Agriculture (billions US $)

Region	Agricultural Total	Agricultural Research	Irrigation Expansion	Irrigation Efficiency	Rural Roads
South Asia	78	10	14	35	19
East Asia and Pacific	52	10	2	29	11
Europe and Central Asia	13	6	-	7	0
Latin America and Caribbean	62	12	3	13	35
Middle East and North Africa	16	12	-	3	4
Sub-Saharan Africa	171	15	12	7	138
Developing	392	65	30	93	208

Required Increases in Spending over Baseline Levels (percent)

Region	Agricultural Total	Agricultural Research	Irrigation Expansion	Irrigation Efficiency	Rural Roads
South Asia	78%	43%	38%	115%	190%
East Asia and Pacific	50%	29%	30%	151%	26%
Europe and Central Asia	33%	21%	0%	157%	19%
Latin America and Caribbean	44%	21%	35%	116%	53%
Middle East and North Africa	56%	55%	0%	638%	178%
Sub-Saharan Africa	94%	69%	27%	146%	123%
Developing	66%	34%	30%	133%	89%

Source: IMPACT model projections.

Ivanic and Martin (2008) show that the impacts of high food prices also had differential effects on poverty rates and incidence, depending upon this same question of net selling and buying position of households. In their analysis, a country like Vietnam could (and probably did) experience a net reduction in poverty rates due to the fact that increased rice prices put those rural households who were net sellers in a much better position than before. Likewise, Peru might also achieve poverty reductions due to increased maize prices favouring those rural households who were net sellers, while increased wheat prices are shown to increase the incidence of poverty. The benefits in Madagascar arise from maize and dairy, while in Pakistan the market benefits arise from rice, dairy and wheat. So the impacts vary according to region, commodity, the particular structure of individual national economies, and the agricultural sector, in particular. Most of the positive benefits that Ivanic and Martin document are in rural areas, while urban households tend to bear the negative impacts of higher prices across the board. In their study, they account for wage effects, which will be more pronounced (and positive) for the rural households who sell their labor to the agricultural sector.

De Hoyos and Medvedev (2009) expand on the approach of Ivanic and Martin by making a clearer distinction between the movements of food and non-food consumer price indices when simulating the micro-level effects of rising food prices. They expand their analysis to the global level through the use of the World Bank's global computable general-equilibrium model (ENVISAGE), which is able to examine the effects of increases in biofuel production in more detail. They also find that the impacts of price increases depend on the relative net buyer/seller position of the household, concluding that the overall food price movements of 2006–2008 had more of an impact on poor households in East Asia and the Middle East/North Africa region, while the impacts of biofuels tend to affect households, especially urban households, in sub-Saharan Africa and South Asia more heavily. The difference between these effects comes from the fact that in a case where price increases are mostly biofuel-driven, the relatively small part that South Asia and sub-Saharan Africa play in the production of biofuel feedstocks (as opposed to Latin America, Southeast Asia and the OECD countries) means that households are mostly experiencing price shocks coming from international grain markets, where they are largely net consumers. None of the wage effects stemming from the domestic production of biofuel feedstock crops would accrue to households in South Asia and sub-Saharan Africa—making both rural and urban households there lose under such a scenario. The structural CGE model approach allows the authors to simulate the various degrees of 'adjustment' (illustrated conceptually below) that households are able to take advantage of when encountering price shocks.

The means by which households adjust their production and consumption in response to economic shocks is shown in Figure 4.10, which illustrates the various dimensions of response that can be undertaken to make these adjustments. Given that a number of expenses such as rent (especially for urban dwellers) might be quasi-fixed, a good deal of household adjustment must come from the food consumption side, often leading to poorer diets and lower levels of essential nutrient intakes. Households with other assets can disinvest to the extent possible in order to smooth consumption in the short-term. Often, however, these disinvestments are not reversed in future periods when economic conditions ease, resulting in reduced endowments and enhanced vulnerability to future shocks. The tendency to pull children, especially girls (Schultz, 2002) from school in times of hardship leads to longer-term effects that arise from decreased investments in human capital and reduced earning capacity and productivity in the future.

Some might argue that biofuels, despite causing increases in food prices, could lower the costs of energy to households and thus generate some benefits that might not otherwise be accounted for. The specific outcome depends on the shares of household income that go towards food and energy purchases, and these shares vary by income level. From the data that we can observe on household-level expenditure patterns, we see that those households which lie at the poverty line tend to spend upwards of 50 percent of their household income on food, while that spent on energy is much smaller (Ahmed *et al.*, 2007).

Figure 4.10. Schematic of household income and expenditure adjustments

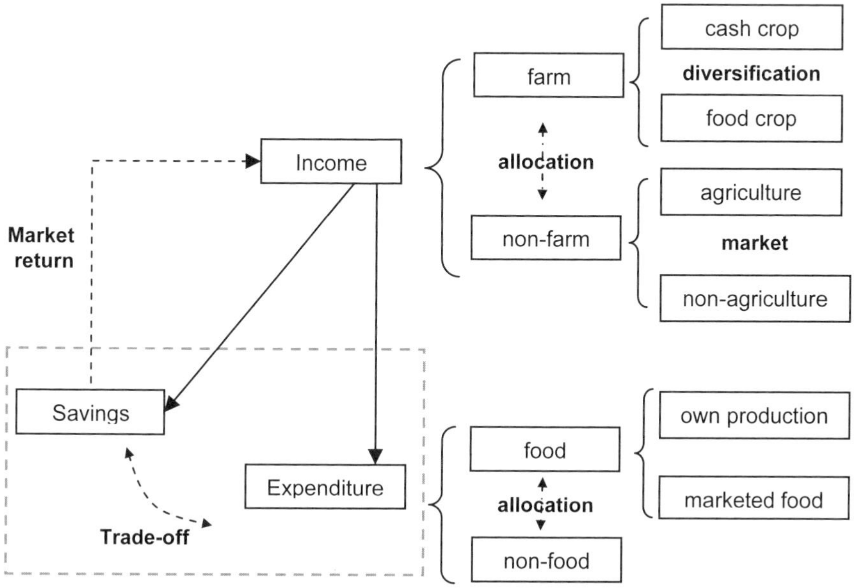

Policy Implications

In light of the evidence and experimental results that we have presented, a number of policy recommendations are pertinent to addressing the world food situation, food prices and the implications for current and future human welfare. *We consider several possible entry points for policy interventions, each of which is relevant to the global food situation and the challenges that will be faced prior to 2050.* Some of these interventions are more of a technological nature, while others pertain to policy-focused interventions at both national and global levels. We divide our discussion of these factors between those interventions which are focused on the supply side versus the demand side of the world food equation.

Supply-side Interventions

As shown in Figure 4.1, there are a number of possible interventions that will impact the supply-side response to continuing demand growth. The first is to boost the output of cereals by raising yield levels over time through policies that accelerate the improvement of crop technologies. This can be done directly through mechanisms such as improved seed technologies, which enhance the productivity and hardiness of plant varieties, or through the expansion of land areas under irrigated production, which typically have higher yields than rainfed alternatives. Improved seeds can even reduce the loss in productivity that occurs when irrigated cropland becomes water-logged or subject to increased salinity, thus allowing the expansion of irrigated areas to be even more effective in raising overall production levels.

In terms of specific technological interventions that can address the observed declines in productivity of key staple crops, there is a wide range of improved crop varieties that can be adopted in regions that have relied mostly on traditional but lower-yielding varieties. Some of this varietal improvement will be necessary just to maintain yields at current levels in the face of increasingly adverse environmental conditions such as climate changes, including elevated temperature levels, decreased rainfall and the associated increased incidence of crop pests and diseases. A key agricultural technology that was instrumental in allowing the Green Revolution in South Asia to take off was irrigation, which is drastically underinvested in in many regions of the world, including sub-Saharan Africa. These increases in irrigation, however, would have to be accompanied by corresponding investments in installing adequate drainage facilities so that problems of salinity are avoided in those regions with existing and/or increasing soil salinity. Improvements in drainage may also have to be accompanied by adoption of more salt-tolerant crop varieties.

In the case of climate change, a country experiencing decreases in crop productivity due to more variable or adverse climatic conditions can decide to decrease the area under cultivation of that crop and to meet its domestic demands through imports. Alternatively, producers might decide to switch towards a more resilient crop variety that is more tolerant of extremes in either temperature or rainfall conditions. However, this requires mechanisms that go beyond trading patterns and requires a robust and productive system of agricultural research to make these improved varieties available. The improved varieties—and the many other improved technologies that are developed through the system of international agricultural research—are frequently provided as global public goods, supplementing the efforts of those countries that still lack the capacity to produce them domestically. Other needed interventions focus on the management side—improved practices in crop and grazing management, innovations in water harvesting and water management, and improved crop and soil nutrient management, among others.

Due to the existence of significant R&D spillovers between countries and regions, investments in agricultural research in one country will also benefit other countries and regions. This further illustrates the importance of continuing R&D activities and generating knowledge that will help farmers increase production and help meet growing domestic and international demand. This suggests a vital role for climate-focused agricultural research for future decades.

Demand-side Considerations

The growth of biofuel production has created a major competing source of demand for maize and other agricultural feedstocks and has contributed significantly to commodity price pressures. Policy interventions that might mitigate these upward pressures on food prices include limiting or perhaps even avoiding the use of food crops as feedstocks in the production of 'first-generation' conventional biofuels like ethanol and biodiesel. There are various policy instruments that support biofuel production, such as direct supports to biofuel producers and blenders, as well as national blending targets and mandates and trade policy instruments that raise the barriers to imported biofuels from other regions (or encourage their export from others). Technology adoption will largely remain driven by private sector developments, but can be helped by policies such as increased spending on research and development that is aimed at pushing forward the next generation of conversion technologies and feedstocks. While there are a number of trade-related policy instruments that need to be addressed at the country-level, there is also a need for policy (and political) coordination at the global level in order to effect multilateral agreements that can lead toward the liberalization of international trade. As far as biofuels are concerned, trade policy has a large influence on trade and prices through biofuel feedstocks and, more importantly, trade in biofuels themselves. In practice, allowing for freer trade in ethanol means that gasoline can more easily be replaced by renewable fuels whenever energy prices rise. In addition, if designed poorly, tariffs, tax credits, subsidies and mandates can lead to perverse effects—such as the possibility of actually increasing fossil-fuel consumption, as noted by de Gorter and Just (2007).

In terms of social protection of the most vulnerable sections of the population, there is a lot that can be accomplished through policy-driven strengthening of national social 'safety net' programs that allow for relief for those who are the most threatened by escalating food prices, while avoiding 'blanket' policies like price controls that are easier (and cheaper) for governments to enact, but which have the perverse effect of reducing the producer response that could otherwise soften future price rises through increased output. The main challenge of policy in this case is to find a balance between maintaining producer incentives and avoiding distortions that might counteractively dampen the self-correcting responses that are needed, while still supporting human welfare through protecting the most vulnerable. The careful targeting of interventions to those most in need requires deliberate and careful policy design, which is often lacking in indiscriminate food subsidy-type schemes, which may benefit many of the poor (especially if they're the majority consumers of the targeted staples), but may also benefit better-off households who have greater adjustment capacity and assets to exploit.

Enabling Institutions and the Policy Environment

The sum total of needed supply and demand interventions that we have presented here suggests that a combination of policy interventions is necessary when dealing with the world food situation—in the same way that a complex combination of factors was responsible for the recent food price crisis. The maintenance or acceleration of yield growth over time is part of the policy combination that should also be pursued, as it will have a profound effect upon the trajectory that future food system dynamics will follow. There is also a long lag period between the time that such investments are made and the time their impacts are realized. Some of these needs have been taken up by the global development donor community and by country commitments to increase R&D spending and other interventions from both public and private sources. Concurrent improvements in the delivery of extension services and in the marketing and distribution infrastructure must also be made, and these can only come from national governments and from concrete allocations of public spending. Regional development agendas, such as the Comprehensive African Agricultural Development Program (CAADP), are trying to lead regional policy bodies and national governments towards agriculture-focused public spending increases; this requires the analytical support of researchers and policy analysts to better refine policy targets and define the appropriate domains for intervention. Among the organizations that are contributing towards the implementation of the CAADP agenda within sub-Saharan Africa are various research centers within the Consultative Group for International Agricultural Research (CGIAR), grant-making organizations such as the Alliance for a

Green Revolution in Africa (AGRA), and a number of other multilaterally-funded policy organizations.

There are also policy and research spillovers that occur between countries which can benefit from the interventions of a wide-reaching set of institutions. Due to the existence of significant R&D spillovers between regions, investments in agricultural research in one country will also benefit other countries, whether they are made by a CGIAR center or by other research institutions. For every dollar spent on R&D activities in one country, then, the resulting gains will be shared by multiple countries and regions. This further illustrates the importance of continuing R&D activities and generating knowledge that will help farmers increase their production and meet growing domestic and international demands. As was seen in the recent food price crisis, the spillovers that are created by unilateral trade policy actions such as country-level export bans can have a profound effect on commodity markets such as that for rice, which is a relatively thin market and highly concentrated among a small group of big exporting nations. The willingness of country-level policy makers to impose trade restrictions is driven by their desire to respond quickly (and visibly) to the concerns of their constituents and is usually done in the absence of alternative mechanisms for providing social protection and relief to those who are most vulnerable.

In light of the policy failures of the recent past, in terms of how countries responded (or did not respond) to food price spikes, a number of observers have suggested alternative institutional arrangements that can better serve to ensure relative stability and calm within key commodity markets for critical staples. The proposal that has been put forth by a number of IFPRI-based authors (von Braun and Torero, 2009; von Braun *et al.*, 2009) calls for a system of physical and virtual grain reserves to be put in place, such that specific targeted interventions could be made either through the release of grain into the market or through taking on contracts and positions in futures markets when key market-level indicators are triggered; the entire process would need to be monitored by a well-informed and strategically-placed intelligence unit. While the authors have been careful to distinguish the proposed mechanisms from those used in the past by country- and regional-level commodity stabilization schemes, there has been continued debate over the ability of centralized international or regional institutions to correctly influence market fundamentals in an efficient and effective manner without repeating the shortcomings and mistakes of past institutions. Others associated with FAO (Sarris *et al.*, 2009) have proposed an alternative approach, which relies on providing financing, guarantees and brokerage services to countries seeking to procure needed food supplies on the world market in order to maintain confidence in the trading system and prevent panic buying. While the precise institutional details have yet to be elaborated, this proposal has generated interest among those who prefer that the roles of international institutions remain those of providing guarantees and reassurance, rather than making direct interventions in the market.

Both the IFPRI and FAO proposals suggest a radical change in the roles of public and international institutions and in how they engage with agricultural markets. Nonetheless, the proposals provide a useful contrast to each other and illustrate the differences of opinion that exist within the research and policy community regarding how international institutions might best serve to reduce the volatility of world food prices and protect vulnerable populations. Neither of these proposals has been acted upon, and both are still subject to debate. At present, key institutions—FAO, the World Bank, the World Food Program (WFP), the World Trade Organization (WTO), IFPRI and others—continue to closely monitor key indicators within the food system and consult on concerns emerging from market trends (Fan, 2010). This may allow for a more coherent and coordinated response from the international community in the future, so that helpful and timely advice can be given to national governments, with bodies like WTO being able to provide a forum for negotiations and dispute resolution, while an institution like WFP would have a clear operational role in crisis intervention.

In the opinion of these authors, there is a strong argument to be made for good monitoring and data analysis mechanisms so that knowledge and decision-support systems can be more effective and useful to policy analysts and national policy makers. There is a need to re-think global food governance and to consider how better coordination might discourage arbitrary and harmful unilateral actions that negatively impact a globalized food system. Rather than investing in new and more cumbersome institutions that, though well-intentioned, may introduce further volatility if interventions are undertaken with asymmetric and (far) less-than-perfect information, we see value in encouraging cooperation and coordination among the institutions that do exist so that greater investments in short-term safety nets and longer-term resilience and productivity measures can be brought to bear. Much of the analysis reported in this chapter points to the benefits of doing so.

Conclusions

This chapter has explored several key drivers of long-term changes in global food systems and has examined a number of possible entry points for policy intervention in order to determine their long-term effects on food prices and other market-driven outcomes. Due to the nature of our analytical framework and the difficulty of fully describing the agent-level dynamics inherent in factors such as storage decisions and the behaviour of financial speculators, we have not addressed several shorter-term factors. Among the drivers of change that we discuss are those which are policy-driven—the growth in biofuel production and the impact of increasing investment in key agricultural and non-agricultural sectors—as well as those which are environmentally focused, such as global climatic change. We have demonstrated the impact that these drivers might have on future market outcomes as well as other important implications for consumption and nutrition status, which are of key interest to policy makers. The drivers of change that we have reviewed are seen to affect both the demand and the supply side of the world food balance and to have implications for the kinds of policy interventions and institutions that are needed to address global food security. We have tried to remain cognizant of the multiple components of food security so as not to focus solely on food production and output but to maintain progress towards the ultimate goals of reducing levels of malnutrition and improving human well-being.

While it is important to understand the causes and underlying factors influencing the rapid rise and fall of food and energy prices in recent years, it is equally important to understand the policies that can mitigate the impacts of price increases on human welfare in the future as well as the types of institutions that are best suited for mediating these policies. While most researchers and analysts would argue that certain policy responses should be avoided in dealing with high prices—such as export bans, which tend to exacerbate regional and global-level price extremes—not all of these analysts are in agreement as to the kind of institutional arrangements that can prevent or discourage counter-productive measures of this kind. Countries now face a variety of policy choices that can help to calm nervous constituents, including import subsidies, the restoration of production subsidies and grain reserves, subsidies for the vocal middle class, policing and threatening traders, and attempting to curb food price inflation with macroeconomic policies. While many of these policies are sub-optimal and inefficient, they are within easy reach of policy makers and can be implemented in a visible and face-saving manner to assuage the anxieties of the voting public. On the other hand, three broad policy areas represent desirable and effective tools for fighting the challenges and negative side-effects posed by high food prices: increasing international trade, improving agricultural growth, and enhancing the protection of vulnerable populations. But these require policy coordination and cooperation at a global level, which is not easy to achieve, especially in the case of trade policy. There are a number of countries that are well-placed to institute their own social protection programs, but others will require the help of multilateral donors such as the World Bank to maintain these programs in their national budgets in the face of other fiscal pressures.

The pressures created by high food prices that threaten the food security and well-being of millions in vulnerable regions, such as South Asia and sub-Saharan Africa, can be partly alleviated by eliminating trade barriers and export bans and by better enabling international institutions to raise the financing and mobilize the resources needed to effect emergency food imports for the neediest countries. Agricultural growth can be revitalized by expanding aid for rural infrastructure, services, agricultural research and technology. Finally, the vulnerable can be shielded from the worst effects of high food prices by expanding food and nutrition-related aid, including safety nets, child nutrition and employment programs.

In summary, a two-track approach is needed to address the ongoing food and financial crises experienced by particularly vulnerable countries in the developing world. This should include a global and national food, health, and nutrition security initiative focused on the vulnerable as well as an agricultural productivity initiative focused on small farmers. Combining our quantitative results with evidence cited from other studies suggests a range of policy interventions that could be instrumental in offsetting the negative impacts of high food prices and in helping to promote their associated benefits. These include increasing investments in the agricultural sector and reversing the steadily declining trend of research and development spending and decades of counter-productive agricultural trade and national-level sector policy.

Acknowledgements

The authors gratefully acknowledge the invaluable assistance of Miroslav Batka in the preparation and revisions of this paper.

References

Abbot, P.C., Hurt, C. and Tyner, W.E. (2008) What's Driving Food Prices? Issue Report, Farm Foundation.

Agricultural Science and Technology Indicators. (2009) ASTI Survey. Unpublished surveys. Facilitated by the International Food Policy Research Institute, Washington, DC.

Ahmed, A.U., Hill, R.V., Smith, L.C., Wiesmann, D.M., Frankenberger, T., Gulati, K., Quabili, W. and Yohannes, Y. (2007) The world's most deprived: characteristics and causes of extreme poverty and hunger. 2020 Discussion Paper 43, International Food Policy Research Institute, Washington, DC.

Alston, J. and Pardey, P.G. (2006) Developing-country perspectives on agricultural R&D: New pressures for self-reliance? In: Pardey, P.G., Alston, J.M., and Piggott, R.R. (eds.) Agricultural R&D in the developing world: Too little, too late? International Food Policy Research Institute, Washington, DC.

Baffes, J. and Haniotis, T. (2010) Placing the 2006/08 commodity price boom into perspective. World Bank Policy Research Working Paper 5371. July 2010.

Bouet, A. and Laborde-Debucquet, D. (2010) Economics of Export Taxation in a Context of Food Crisis: A Theoretical and CGE Approach Contribution. IFPRI discussion paper 994. IFPRI, Washington, DC.

Cline, W. (2007) Global Warming and Agriculture: Impact Estimates by Country. Center for Global Development. Washington, DC.

de Gorter, H. and Just, D.R. (2007) The economics of US ethanol import tariffs with a consumption mandate and tax credit. Department of Applied Economics and Management Working Paper # 2007–21, Cornell University, 23 October.

de Hoyos, R.E. and Medvedev, D. (2009) Poverty Effects of Higher Food Prices: A Global Perspective. World Bank Policy Research Working Paper 4887, March 2009.

Dixon, J., Gulliver, A. and Gibbon, D. (2001) Farming Systems and Poverty: Improving Farmers' Livelihoods in a Changing World. Food and Agriculture Organization and World Bank, Washington, DC and Rome, Italy.

Easterling, W.E., Aggarwal, P.K., Batima, P., Brander, K.M., Erda, L., Howden, S.M., Kirilenko, A., Morton, J., Soussana, J.-F., Schmidhuber, J. and Tubiello, F.N. (2007) Food, fibre and forest products. In: Parry, M.L., Canziani, O.F., Palutikof, J.P., van der Linden, P.J. and Hanson, C.E. (eds.) Climate Change 2007: Impacts, Adaptation and Vulnerability. Contribution of Working Group II to the Fourth Assessment Report of the Intergovernmental Panel on Climate Change. Cambridge University Press, Cambridge, UK, 273–313.

Evans, A. (2008) Rising Food Prices: Drivers and Implications for Development. Briefing Paper 08/02, Chatham House, United Kingdom.

Fan, S. (2010) Five Steps to Prevent a Repeat of the 2007–08 Food Crisis. Policy Statement, International Food Policy Research Institute, Washington, D.C.

FAO (Food and Agricultural Organization of the United Nations). (2008) Soaring Food Prices: Facts, Perspectives, Impacts and Actions Required. Paper prepared for the High-level Conference on World Food Security. The Challenges of Climate Change and Bio-energy. HLC/08/INF/1. FAO, Rome.

FAO (2005) Background Paper for 31st Session of the Committee on World Food Security. Impact of Climate Change, Pest and Disease on Food Security and Poverty Reduction, May 23–26.

FAO (2006) World agriculture: towards 2015/30. Food and Agricultural Organization of the United Nations, Rome.

Fischer, G., Shah, M., Tubiello, F.N. and van Velhuizen, H. (2005) Socioeconomic and climate change impacts on agriculture: an integrated assessment, 1990–2080. Phil. Trans. R. Soc. B 360: 2067–2083.

Gilbert, C.L. (2010) How to Understand High Food Prices. *Journal of Agricultural Economics,* 61(2): 398-425.

Headey, D.C. and Fan, S. (2010) Reflections on the Global Food Crisis: How did it happen? How did it hurt? And how can we prevent the next one? IFPRI Research Monograph 165. IFPRI, Washington, DC.

http://papers.ssrn.com/sol3/papers.cfm?abstract_id=1024532
Inocencio, A., Kikuchi, M., Tonosaki, M., Maruyama, A., Merrey, D., Sally, H. and De Jong, I. (2007) Costs and performance of irrigation projects: A comparison of sub-Saharan Africa and other developing regions. IWMI Research Report no. 109. International Water Management Institute (IWMI), Colombo, Sri Lanka.
Ivanic, M. and Martin, W. (2008) Implications of higher global food prices for poverty in low-income countries. *Agricultural Economics* 39 (Suppl.): 405–416.
Millennium Ecosystem Assessment. (2005) Ecosystems and human well-being: Scenarios. Findings of the scenarios working group. Island Press, Washington, DC.
Msangi, S. and Rosegrant, M.W. (2009) World Agriculture in a Dynamically-Changing Environment: IFPRI's Long-Term Outlook for Food and Agriculture under Additional Demands and Constraints. Paper written for the Expert Meeting on How to Feed the World in 2050. Food and Agricultural Organization of the United Nations (FAO), Rome.
Nelson, G.C., Rosegrant, M.W., Koo, J., Robertson, R., Sulser, T.B., Zhu, T., Ringler, C., Msangi, S., Palazzo, A., Batka, M., Magalhaes, M., Valmonte-Santos, R., Ewing, M. and Lee, D. (2009) Climate change: Impact on agriculture and costs of adaptation. IFPRI Food Policy Report. IFPRI, Washington, DC.
Nelson, G.C., Rosegrant, M.W., Palazzo, A., Gray, I., Ingersoll, C., Robertson, R., Tokgoz, S., Zhu, T., Sulser, T.B., Ringler, C., Msangi, S. and You, L. (2010) Food Security, Farming and Climate Change to 2050: Scenarios, Results, Policy Options. IFPRI Research Monograph. IFPRI, Washington, D.C.
OECD (Organization for Economic Cooperation and Development). (2008) Rising Food Prices: Causes and Consequences. OECD, Paris.
OECD-FAO. (2010) Agricultural Outlook 2010–2019. OECD, Paris.
Parry, M., Rosenzweig, C. and Livermore, M. (2005) Climate change, global food supply and risk of hunger. *Philosophical Transactions of the Royal Society* 360: 2125–2138.
Rosegrant, M.W., Paisner, M.S., Meijer, S. and Witcover, J. (2001) Global food projections to 2020: Emerging trends and alternative futures. IFPRI, Washington, DC.
Rosegrant, M.W., Cai, X. and Cline, S. (2002) World water and food to 2025: Dealing with Scarcity. IFPRI, Washington, DC.
Rosegrant, M.W., Cline, S.A., Li, W., Sulser, T.B. and Valmonte-Santos, R. (2005) Looking Ahead: Long-Term Prospects for Africa's Agricultural Development and Food Security. 2020 Discussion Paper No. 41. IFPRI, Washington, DC.
Rosegrant, M.W., Ringler, C., Msangi, S., Sulser, T.B., Zhu, T. and Cline, S.A. (2008) International Model for Policy Analysis of Agricultural Commodities and Trade (IMPACT): Model Description. IFPRI, Washington, DC. Accessible at: http://www.ifpri.org/sites/default/files/IMPACTwater.pdf
Sarris, A. (2009) Evolving Structure of World Agricultural Trade and Requirements for New World Trade Rules. Discussion Paper. FAO, Rome.
Schmidhuber, J. and Tubiello, F. (2007) Global food security under climate change. *Proceedings of the National Academy of Sciences* 104 (5):19703-19708.
Schultz, T.P. (2002) Why governments should invest more to educate girls. *World Development* 30(2):207–225.
Smith, L. and Haddad, L. (2000) Explaining Child Malnutrition in Developing Countries: A Cross-Country Analysis. IFPRI Research Report. IFPRI, Washington, DC.
Trostle, R. (2008) Global Agricultural Supply and Demand; Factors Contributing to the Recent Increase in Food Commodity Prices. WRS-0801. Economic Research Service, US Department of Agriculture.

UNEP (United Nations Environment Programme). (2007) Global Environmental Outlook (GEO4): Environment for Development. Progress Press.
von Braun, J. (2007) The World Food Situation: New Driving Forces and Required Actions. Food Policy Report, IFPRI, Washington, DC.
von Braun, J. (2008) Food and Financial Crises: Implications for Agriculture and the Poor. Food Policy Report. IFPRI, Washington, DC.
von Braun, J., Ahmed, A., Asenso-Okyere, K., Fan, S., Gulati, A., Hoddinott, J., Pandya-Lorch, R., Rosegrant, M.W., Ruel, M., Torero, M., van Rheenen, T. and von Grebmer, K. (2008) High Food Prices: The What, Who and How of Proposed Policy Actions. Policy Brief, IFPRI, Washington, DC.
von Braun, J., Lin, J.Y.F. and Torero, M. (2009) Eliminating Drastic Food Price Spikes: three-pronged approach for reserves. Discussion Note. IFPRI, Washington, DC.
von Braun, J. and Torero, M. (2009) Implementing Virtual and Physical Food Reserves to Protect the Poor and Prevent Market Failure. IFPRI Policy Brief, IFPRI, Washington, DC.

Chapter 5

Here We Go Again: The Abiding Structure of Financial Crisis—and What To Do about It

Robert Hockett
Cornell Law School, Cornell University, Ithaca, New York

Abstract

This chapter argues that financial asset price bubbles and busts, such as those we have recently experienced in the mortgage and securities markets, are compatible with market efficiency, individual rationality, and even ethically unobjectionable behaviour. The reason is that they constitute classic recursively self-amplifying collective action problems, the hallmark of which is the efficient aggregation of individually rational behaviours into collectively calamitous outcomes. In the present case, individuals rationally 'legged the spread' between cheap borrowing costs and credit-fueled capital gains rates, neither of which market actors could affect in their individual capacities, even when knowing that credit would eventually have to run out at some indefinite point in future. The upshot was a continuous series of self-reinforcing, credit-fueled asset price increases, followed by a symmetrical series of hoarding-induced asset price drops once credit was exhausted. It is important to emphasize the rationality- and efficiency-compatible side of this story because prescribing a proper cure to our ills presupposes a proper diagnosis. The solution to a collective action problem, of course, is a collective agent. In the present context, that is a macroprudential financial regulator cognizant of her requisite role in tightening credit-money supplies when positive feedback loops emerge in asset markets.

Introduction

Asset price bubbles and bursts, along with the credit and monetary contractions that generally follow them, have recurred with depressing regularity throughout the course of financial history. The same regularity, understandably if also humblingly, characterizes the soul-searching and lesson-seeking that seem typically to follow these cataclysms. I say 'humblingly' because, given the regularity both of these occurrences and of our subsequent efforts to diagnose them so as to prevent their recurrence, one might have hoped we'd have reached 'the end of [this] history' by now.[6] But it seems we have not. Why? I aim in this brief chapter both 1) to suggest why it is we have failed thus far, and 2) to preempt further

[6] I am of course alluding here to a well-known 1989 essay, and subsequent 1992 monograph of the same title, by Francis Fukuyama (1992).

failure. I would like, that is to say, both to counteract two recurring confusions that so far have stood in the way of our understanding and preventing financial crises, and then to suggest how best to understand and prevent them.

First, then, on the reasons we have thus far failed to prevent the recurrence of crises: One reason, some might suppose, is that each asset price bubble bears its own characteristic features—in particular, its own underlying asset or set of such assets, and its own peculiar species of financial chicanery that seem always to come to light just as each bubble's outer limits are neared.[7] Hence it is never easy to predict the precise form that the next bubble might take. There is surely some truth in this suggestion, just as there is in the oft-encountered truism that financial regulators are doomed always to remain a step or two behind the most clever of rule-arbitraging financial 'wizards.' Yet I doubt this is the relevant truth that we're after, for reasons I'll presently explain.

Another, more apposite reason for asset price bubbles' regular recurrence, I think, might be our tendency—precisely by dint of our understandable proclivities to notice and then further probe the unique characteristics of each new bubble-and-burst that occurs—to overlook the more or less invariant foundational structure that all asset price bubbles seem to share. We might, moreover, expect this latter tendency to be especially pronounced when influential expert opinion—including, sometimes, regulatory opinion—rests upon views of financial markets pursuant to which asset price bubbles are erroneously thought to be either impossible or undetectable.[8]

My own view is that asset price bubbles are *both* possible *and* detectable while they are inflating, and that we can see how only by attending to the basic asset price bubble structure to which I alluded a moment ago. Belief to the contrary, I think, is the result of one or both of two misapprehensions. These are to the effect that asset price bubbles or their detection prior to bursts are incompatible with 1) efficiency on the part of financial markets, 2) rationality on the part of market actors, or 3) both. Because efficiency in turn is so well theoretically warranted and empirically corroborated, and systematic irrationality for its part so wildly implausible (not to say oxymoronic in the very naming), the line of thought that I have in mind here goes on to conclude that it is the suggestion that bubbles are possible or detectable that must then be rejected. Call these the 'efficiency-incompatible' and 'rationality-incompatible' theses, respectively.

So why do I say 'misapprehension' in connection with these two incompatibility theses? I do so, first, because the kind of efficiency that is in play when we speak of efficient capital markets is primarily, at least in the short run, *informational* efficiency, while only derivatively—and in the longer run with plenty of pitfalls along the way—allocative efficiency. What the markets do efficiently in the short run is to impound price-relevant *information*. And the 'information' in question here notoriously excludes potential value-relevant data that simply remain, for some not-pre-determinable period of time, unavailable.

The information that capital markets efficiently aggregate excludes, in other words, the stuff of radical 'uncertainty' as distinguished from actuarial 'risk'—that is, data in respect of which market participants must in effect take positions, but which positions in turn have to be decided upon on the basis of generally serviceable conventions and heuristics, 'best

---

[7] The mentioned chicanery, as it happens, seems seldom if ever to constitute a significant cause of asset price bubbles and bursts, only a symptom that manifests itself late in the game. See R. Hockett (2010).

[8] Call the first view the 'ontic' view, and the second view the 'epistemic' fallback. Former Federal Reserve Chairman Greenspan, for one, appears to have held each of these views at various points of his tenure. For reasons I'll presently provide, I think the epistemic view less implausible than the ontic, but I think both views are nevertheless unsustainable.

guesses,' 'gut feelings,' or 'animal spirits' rather than on plausible probability distributions of the sort associated with 'risk.'

Think of risk as that which is associated with a bet on ordinary rolled dice. There is a one in six chance that any particular number will come up on a roll of one die, and so the monetary risk of losing your bet is the amount of your bet multiplied by five-sixths. Uncertainty, by contrast, would be better exemplified by a game of dice in which players do not even know what numbers are represented on the faces of the cube. Even admittedly *efficient* markets cannot aggregate *that* sort of 'information.' And as we shall see, that sort of information lies at the core of asset price bubbles and bursts.

It is important to understand informational efficiency not only with respect to what it excludes, but also with respect to what it includes: the 'information' that capital markets efficiently impound also notoriously *in*cludes, again at least in the short run, both 1) advertently and inadvertently propagated 'misinformation' nicely suited to filling the gap that is radical uncertainty, and relatedly 2) 'beautiful baby' and cognate forms of 'noise' information. It includes, that is to say, information about how others are presently valuing the asset in question via their trading behaviour, which itself can in turn be the product of how yet others appear to be presently valuing the asset in question via their trading behaviour, and so on.[9] Prices can become self-amplifying in such cases—the very antithesis of self-equilibrating. Thus people can begin buying simply because they anticipate that others will buy, driving the market prices of that which they buy upward.

Where efficient informational inclusion is concerned, in other words, positive feedback loops can amplify and distort, at least for several-year intervals, the more accurate 'fundamental value' signals that prices tend in the longer run to convey. Think of them as the positive flipside of those self-fulfillingly prophetic 'runs' on assets that always follow on bubbles, the stuff of 'crashes.' For that is just what they are—they are 'bank runs in reverse,' so to speak.[10] All that is needed for the whole sorry 'bipolar' process to get underway is for a critical mass of bets to be placed, such that they attract further such bets made in anticipation of yet more such bets. A spontaneously emergent 'pyramid' scheme or Ponzi process, which requires no 'scheme' and no Ponzi, will then do the rest.[11] The usual quips of wags, pundits, and depressingly many scholars notwithstanding, little-to-none of this is in tension with informational efficiency as understood by the usual renditions of the Efficient Capital Markets Hypothesis.

So much for the efficiency-incompatibility thesis. How about the putative rationality-incompatibility of asset price bubbles? Well, just as asset price bubbles are not incompatible with the relevant forms of efficiency characteristic of asset markets, neither are they incompatible with the relevant form of 'rationality.' Once again, much current popular parlance to the contrary, there is little-to-no tension between rationality on the part of individual financial market actors, on the one hand, and suboptimality on the part of the

---

[9] 'Beautiful baby' and 'noise' information originate, respectively, with Chapter 12 of J.M. Keynes (1936) and Fischer Black (1986). For more on all of this, see again Hockett, *supra* note 2. Keynes was referring to contests run by the British press of his day, pursuant to which contestants cast votes for the most beautiful of a slate of baby photographs, with those voting on the highest vote-getters winning prizes. It did not take long for voters to cease voting on photos that they themselves found beautiful, and commence voting on those they predicted that others would find beautiful. In speaking of 'noise' traders, Black, for his part, referred to those who traded on rumours and what they thought other traders were doing.

[10] See again Hockett (2010) for much more on this.

[11] A fair bit has been written of late on positive feedback loops in asset pricing and their roles in bubble-inflation. See, for example, F. Allen *et al.* (2006). A superb synthesis of his many insightful articles on the subject is H.S. Shin (2010). See also Hockett, *supra* note 2, for much more on the matter, as well as Hockett (2011). The idea of a 'naturally occurring Ponzi process' figures prominently in R.J. Shiller (2000).

outcomes of *interactions among multiple such actors* on the other hand. To suppose that there is, is to commit a fallacy of composition, and in so doing to overlook the commonplace outcome, long familiar to game theory and folk wisdom alike, that multiple acts of individual rationality can under some circumstances aggregate into forms of collective irrationality or the functional equivalent thereof.

Indeed, our recent bubble-and-burst in mortgage-backed securities and associated financial instruments, just like previous asset price bubbles, can readily be modeled as a variant of the familiar 'prisoners' dilemma' and 'chicken' games regularly encountered in microeconomic and game theory texts.[12] In particular, it can be viewed as the upshot of a stylized game of James Dean-style drag race 'chicken.'[13]

In my version of the game, justifiably self-confident, forward-wise blindfolded contestants drive speedily toward a cliff's edge known to be far distant but not *how* far distant. They are paid by the foot to proceed for as long as—but only for as long as—they outpace others whom they can see to their sides and behind. Finally, they know there are multiple safety nets over the cliff's edge in any case for at least some who don't manage to 'bail' in time to avoid going over. It is far from clear that there's any irrationality on the part of any participant in this game. Each stands a good chance of bailing before going over, and of falling into a net if she does. And each stands to grow rich on the way.

The blindfolds in my stylized game of course correspond to the radical uncertainty that attaches to any bubble's limit point; even those who know we're in bubble territory know that there's generally no way to know when the party will end. Payment by the foot corresponds to the fact that all players grow richer the closer they draw to the endpoint, legging the spread between low borrowing costs and high capital gains rates. Finally, the nets of course correspond to the bailouts that many know they are apt to receive. No asset price bubble or bust over the past millennium fails to feature these characteristics.

It is precisely here, I suggest, that we find the 'basic structure' to which I have referred—the structure that is common to all asset price bubbles and bursts. When bubbles develop and inflate per this structure, all manner of behaviour that ordinarily looks profligate or cavalier comes to look rather more prudent and prosaic. Purchasing a home or related asset with a low-front-end, 'balloon'-rate mortgage, for example, looks sensible; for throughout the bubble's duration you can always cheaply refinance your loan on the strength of the rapidly appreciating collateral—the house or other asset—before the balloon rate kicks in. Lending to borrowers with less stellar credit histories looks safer for the same reason—the collateral's continually rising price offsets the added default risk—so credit continues to flow, and debt rates continue to grow. Like remarks hold with respect to the good ratings that mortgage-backed instruments received for a while, and of the relaxed attitudes shown by some of our piecemeal—non-'systemic'—regulators like the Securities and Exchange Commission. For again, the hallmark of the collective action problem known as an asset price bubble is that *each* actor's actions are indeed *rational*, so long as all *other* actors remain able to keep acting as they have been acting. And it is only when indefinitely extensible credit's never-precisely-foreseeable limit-point is reached that the latter proviso can no longer be counted on.

---

[12] See again Hockett, 'Fixer-Upper,' *supra* note 3. See also my posting on the subject on the Dorf on Law weblog, available at www.dorfonlaw.org/2009/09/what-maynard-keynes-james-dean-and-now.html.

[13] The typical game of 'chicken' differs from the generic 'prisoners' dilemma' game in one important respect: retaliation constitutes the best non-cooperative strategy in the latter case but not in the former, since retaliation in the former results in the death of both players. The variant of 'chicken' that I model here, possessed as it is of 'safety nets,' accordingly lies somewhere between garden variety 'chicken' and 'prisoner's dilemma.'

Once the limit point is reached, however, all turn abruptly and retrace their steps in reverse. The bubble deflates down the same path along which it inflated. The race back to the starting line artificially deflates asset values just as the race to the cliff's edge artificially inflated them—even good assets are viewed as lemons. Previously boom-sustained debt now becomes 'overhang,' no longer supported by highly market-valued collateral. Defaults ensue, first among borrowers, then among their lenders, then among lenders to lenders, and so on. Credit contracts system-wide, just as mercurially as it formerly expanded. Business investment soon follows suit. Firms tighten belts, employees are laid off, consumer expenditures thus drop, firms accordingly contract further, and so on—as the boom's feedback process morphs into the bust's feedback process. It is the same collective action problem, now tacking south rather than north.

So there we have bubbles, busts, and their structure, as well as why they're compatible both with informational efficiency and with individual market actor rationality. How, then, to end this sorry history once and for all? The key, I believe, is found in the collective action structure I've been at pains here to emphasize.

Solutions to collective action problems, unsurprisingly, require collective agents—agents who act in the name of all to render it no longer rational for individual actors to make decisions that aggregate into collectively irrational outcomes. In effect, that is how the Fed and Treasury behaved in the autumn of 2008 during the downside—the bust side—of our most recent bubble and bust. The Troubled Asset Relief Program (TARP) recouped most of its bailout monies precisely because it brought into one portfolio securities that were undervalued by holders of multiple portfolios during the 'downside' collective action problem that is a bust. But what about the 'upside'—who serves as collective agent during a 'boom' or a bubble?

That, I maintain, would be a macroprudential, or 'systemic risk,' regulator—an authority charged with overseeing and modulating price behaviour in the credit-monetary-financial system as a whole rather than simply one sector of it. In particular, this regulator would monitor both 1) the growth of leverage rates across the economy as a whole, and 2) the growth of spreads between market prices on the one hand and proxies for 'fundamental' value on the other. As those rates and spreads move into self-amplifying territory, she would steadily tighten credit, increasingly tax short-term capital gains, or both. There are multiple levers by which this can be done—including Federal Funds rate management, open market operations, reserve requirements, capital regulation, deposit insurance charges, 'Tobin' taxation, and others.[14] But in order for this to be done, the regulator must of course understand her role as a collective agent—a desideratum that sits in some tension with devotion to, say, the ideology of Ayn Rand.[15]

The US had something much like the required collective agent overseeing the credit-monetary-financial system for a surprisingly lengthy, more or less bubble-free, period: the Fed in the course of the 1950s, early- to mid-1960s, and early- to mid-1980s, when the likes of Chairmen William McChesney Martin and, later, Paul Volcker took seriously the Fed's role as counter-cyclical macroeconomic stabilizer.[16] Both of those well regarded custodians of our credit-money system seem to have understood the systemic prisoners' dilemma-like structure of asset price bubbles and consumer price inflations alike.[17] And so

---

[14] See again Hockett, 'Fixer-Upper,' *supra* note 2 for detail.

[15] The allusion is to former Fed Chairman Alan Greenspan's devotion to Ms. Rand.

[16] See again Hockett, 'Fixer-Upper,' *supra* note 2 for more on this history.

[17] Consumer price inflation is characterized by the same prisoners' dilemma structure that characterizes asset price bubbles, which indeed can be viewed simply as cases of asset price hyperinflation. Again see Hockett, *supra* note 2.

both employed the Fed's principal systemic levers to 'lean against the wind' and 'take away the punch bowl just as the party was getting good' in order to stabilize asset and consumer price inflations.[18] Volcker's immediate successor, Chairman Greenspan, alas, saw things differently, succumbing by turns to the efficiency- and rationality-incompatibility theses that I have just sought to dispel. Unless and until we fully reinstate the role of the Fed—or of some counterpart systemic regulator such as the new Dodd-Frank-instituted Systemic Risk Council—as envisaged by such former chairs as Martin and Volcker, I fear we are probably destined to continue our cycle of repeated asset price bubbles and bursts, with all the lost wealth and lost health and 'lost decades' that this always seems to entail.[19]

The US could succeed in this partly by choosing its Fed chairs more wisely than it has from the late 1980s until recently. More securely, the US would clarify the Fed's mandate to make clear that overheated asset price inflation, as measured against suitable proxies for 'fundamental value' (such as home building costs and rental rates in frothy housing market areas), is as inimical as is consumer price inflation to those 'stable prices' that the Fed already is charged with 'promoting.'[20] Ultimately, however, regulators worldwide will also have to bring more institutions and markets—notably hedge funds, money funds, repo and currency markets—under the credit-supervisory umbrella. For, unlike in Martin's and even in Volcker's day, in our day it is no longer commercial banks that are the principal sources of bubble-fueling credit. It is the 'shadow banks'—the institutions and markets that I have just mentioned—that primarily play this role. The stakes, we all know, could scarcely be higher; asset price bubbles and bursts of the magnitude just experienced in the US are seldom if ever contained within national boundaries. Credit markets are now thoroughly 'global' in character. Finance knows no boundaries. Hence credit contractions, and with them contractions in the 'real' economy, are themselves global in character. Fewer funds are available to be lent in the interest of development and project finance. The same goes for sovereign lending and other forms of aid, as domestic governments urgently turn to domestic expenditures—and indeed more public borrowing—to pull their own economies out of slump. What is more, such investable capital as remains tends to fly to safe havens like US Treasury securities, rather than to developing countries' sovereign debt instruments or firms. Global consumers and producers, for their parts, 'tighten their belts' during bust-following recessionary slumps, shrinking demand for the exports of developing countries. The worst off find it harder even to *earn* their way out of trouble, let alone borrow their way out.

As ever, it seems, it is not only 'big finance' that suffers the horrors attendant on depressed 'animal spirits' and credit-money contraction. It is also—indeed it is primarily—those who were already most vulnerable. It is those who are still working to climb into a self-sustainable 'takeoff' position. Hence the timeless irony is present again: the most innocent are the hardest hit, while the least innocent are bailed out. I wish I could recommend some means of insulating the most vulnerable especially from the ravages of financial boom-and-bust cycles. I fear, however, that the only workable solution will be to

---

[18] The quoted nostrums were popularized by Martin.

[19] With 'lost decade,' I am alluding to the protracted slump, now rather more than a decade in duration, that Japan has suffered since the collapse of its stock and commercial real estate price bubbles of the late 1980s. With 'lost health,' I am alluding to a recent report in the *New York Times* on the health consequences of long-term unemployment. Finally, with 'lost wealth,' I am alluding to all of the production that is foregone during periods of capacity-underutilization, as during recessions.

[20] See Federal Reserve Act, Section 2A, codified at 12 U.S.C. § 225(a) (1977), as subsequently amended.

end these cycles themselves. I hope I've at least managed to convince you that this can be done. Will we learn this time?

References

Allen, F., Morris, S. and Shin, H.S. (2006) Beauty contests and iterated expectations in financial markets. *Review of Financial Studies* 19, 719–752.

Black, F. (1986) Noise. *Journal of Finance* 41, 529–543.

Fukuyama, F. (1992) *The End of History and the Last Man.* Free Press, New York.

Hockett, R. (2010) A fixer-upper for finance. *Washington University Law Review* 87(6), 1213–1291.

Hockett, R. (2011) Bretton Woods 1.0: An essay in constructive retrieval. Working Paper, Cornell Law School, Ithaca, New York.

Keynes, J.M. (1936) *The General Theory of Employment, Interest, and Money.* Macmillan Cambridge University Press, London.

Shiller, R.J. (2000) *Irrational Exuberance.* Princeton University Press, Princeton, New Jersey.

Shin, H.S. (2010) *Risk and Liquidity.* Oxford University Press, Oxford.

Chapter 6

The Food and Financial Crises and Complex Derivatives: A Tale of High Stakes Innovation and Diversification

Vera Songwe
The World Bank, Washington, DC

Abstract

This chapter argues that the 2007–2008 food price crisis and the financial crisis that followed were integrally related. Throughout the early 2000s, low interest rates fueled rapid growth in the US housing market, increased liquidity and led to greater risk-taking through the development of innovative financial instruments. In order to hedge and spread financial risk, instruments such as the mortgage-backed security (MBS), the credit default swap (CDS), and other over-the-counter (OTC) derivatives were developed faster than the regulatory framework required for their oversight. Growth in the financial sector helped support increased demand for housing, which in turn helped buoy the US economy. Developing countries also grew rapidly, in part as a result of the favourable economic conditions in the US. However, a tightening of monetary policy and other economic developments in the mid-2000s eventually triggered a crisis in the market for mortgage backed securities, precipitating the exit of investors and institutions from this market into other markets such as the commodity derivatives market. Meanwhile, policies to diversify US fuel sources also increased the attractiveness of agricultural commodities as an asset class, putting further pressure on prices. By June 2008, the notional amount outstanding of over-the-counter derivatives on commodities had grown to more than US$12 trillion. As incomes in African countries increased earlier in the decade, many countries increased their dependence on food imports, while commodity output growth slowed and global grain stocks dwindled. Consequently, the financial crisis that began in 2007 and the subsequent economic crisis had damaging consequences for many African countries, reinforcing the impacts of the food price crisis. Just as events leading up to the food and financial crises were global and complex, similarly, solutions to avoid such crises in the future will be complex, requiring coordination amongst all countries and international institutions. G-20 countries and institutions such as the IMF and the World Bank must work on solutions with the Financial Stability Board (FSB) as part of a broad and comprehensive reform agenda. The implications of reforms such as the Dodd-Frank legislation proposed by the FSB will have significant implications for developing countries. It is important that these reforms do not undermine growth or hinder the development of innovative financial instruments needed to help finance investments—including agricultural investments—and promote the long-term deepening of the financial sector.

Introduction

In the summer of 2008 food prices reached historic highs, following steep increases in staple food crop prices between 2007 and 2008. The prices of wheat and rice doubled, and maize prices more than tripled, from $2.50 per bushel to nearly $8.00 per bushel between 2006 and 2008. The rapid rise in food prices in 2007–2008 led to social unrest and/or civil conflict in more than 30 countries. Meanwhile, in 2008, the number of hungry people globally increased from about 896 million to over 1.023 billion in 2009; it later dropped to 925 million in 2010 (FAO, 2010).[21] With these developments the attainment of the Millennium Development Goals (MDG), especially MDG 1 of halving poverty by 2015, which in early 2007 was in sight for a number of low income African countries (LICs), has been severely compromised (World Bank, 2010b).

A large body of literature exists on the causes and impacts of the food crisis (von Braun, 2007; World Bank, 2008a; Timmer, 2009; FAO, 2009b; Prakash, 2011); this topic is reviewed in Chapter 1 of this volume and is addressed in other chapters. However, what is little acknowledged is that in 2007, 'No Street'[22]—even before Main Street—was already feeling the pain of the impending financial crisis; the food crisis was foreshadowing the financial crisis. Between 2001 and 2007, investment banks expanded their reach and became increasingly more global in nature. By 2007, poor farmers in low income countries had become part of a large and sophisticated financial infrastructure as commodities—and food commodities in particular—increasingly became an asset class. Commodities, including staple food products consumed by many of the world's poor, became a central part in a cycle of rapid financial innovation and diversification. The developing countries had benefited for close to a decade from favourable monetary and regulatory policies in the West. In 2008 they shared the downside risk of these policies.

The objective of this paper is to demonstrate that there is a strong link between the financial crisis and the food price crisis of 2007–2008, and furthermore, that the financial crisis began in earnest with the housing market and moved to commodity markets as financial agents began in 2005–2007 to increasingly diversify away from complex credit default swaps (CDSs) and collaterized debt obligations (CDOs) into commodities, then believed to be more secure and more liquid.

Developing countries are still recovering from the impacts of the food and financial crises. In managing the risk associated with recurring price crises, financial development and regulation—especially of agricultural commodity markets—must be part of the solution. A lack of understanding of the intimate link between events precipitating the financial crisis and events precipitating the food crisis will undermine policy proposals to help low-income countries address this new reality of interconnected markets. Many of the world's poor farmers cannot cope with persistent volatility and its impact on their livelihoods—and worse still, cannot cope with the devastating consequences of volatile markets. In addition, for many developing countries, these persistent crises are crippling their prospects for growth. Many solutions have been proposed. These solutions generally focus on the need to increase production and productivity of farmers in developing countries and to improve trade regulations to allow free flow of goods. However, no solution to the food price crisis will be complete if it does not address issues of comprehensive financial market regulation and, in particular, regulation of commodity

---

[21] Between 2008 and 2009, prices remained high. For example, the average price of rice in 2009 was 90 percent higher than the average level in 2006 (FAO, 2009).

[22] 'No Street'—a term used to refer to poor and largely rural areas in low income countries.

markets and the type of financial products and institutions linked to commodity trade. Regulation of financial markets is especially important for developing countries that do not have adequate institutional frameworks to deal with complex financial trade, but whose financial and trading sectors could be easily crippled in the event of a downturn.

This chapter is organized as follows: we first describe the financial market sentiment and activity in the run-up to the crisis, which together formed the 'perfect storm' that precipitated the food crisis and impending financial crisis. These include rapid financial innovation, high risk tolerance by the financial sector demonstrated primarily through mortgage financing activity, a weak dollar, and domestic US policies on ethanol subsidies. The next section reviews the events leading up to the food and financial crisis to establish the links between the two. Following this, we examine the markets for agricultural commodities in Africa to see how these have evolved over the past decade and to observe Africa's growing links to financial markets. Finally, we discuss regulatory progress made since the crisis and suggest ways to ensure that the emerging post-crisis financial regulatory framework and architecture are comprehensive, that they support the development of innovative financial products and are consistent with financial market development in Africa and other developing countries.

Rapid Globalization, Deepening Market Linkages and Unprecedented Growth: 2000–2007

Interest Rates, the Housing Market and Growth

The sequence of events leading up to the food price crisis of 2007–2008 began with rapid financial innovation and a favourable regulatory environment in the United States in the mid-1990s (that extended through 2008), and with monetary policy easing by the Federal Reserve Bank in 2001. After the recession of 2001, the Federal Reserve Bank began to expand money supply in a bid to stimulate demand and restore growth. As a result, the Federal Funds rate—the interest rate at which depository institutions lend balances to each other overnight—was lowered from 6.25 percent in January 2001 to 1.75 percent by the end of 2001, one of the most aggressive interest rate reductions ever taken by the Fed. By mid-2003, this rate had dropped to one percent, at which point the real Federal Funds Rate was negative—that is, nominal rates were lower than the rate of inflation. As a strategy for reviving growth in the United States, this monetary policy stance was highly successful. By the end of 2004, the growth rate of the US economy had more than tripled, peaking at 3.6 percent from 1.1 percent in 2001 (see Figure 6.1). Growth slowed in 2005 but remained high at 3.1 percent (World Bank, 2010a). This growth was largely fueled by growth in the housing sector.

The second related event was the change in mortgage policies in the housing industry. The lowering of short-term interest rates not only fueled growth in the dollar volume of mortgage lending but also changed buyers' preferences for the types of mortgages they demanded. With short-term rates lower than the traditional thirty-year rates, buyers opted increasingly for adjustable rate mortgages[23] (ARMs), with an assumption that rates would

---

[23] A home loan in which the interest rate and the resulting monthly payment are tied to a short-term interest rate like the one-year Treasury bill rate. Typically, the mortgage interest rate will be two or three percentage points above the related short-term rate. In addition, the interest rate can be adjusted annually or based on payment history.

stay low for a long time. This increase in risk-taking by consumers was matched by an increase in the complexity of the innovative financial sector products offered and purchased by investment firms among themselves and to other institutions. With the increase in the volume of ARMs, banks needed to spread and diversify risks. So a new instrument—mortgage backed securities (MBSs)—became very popular. After a mortgage is sold, it can be bundled with other subprime mortgages and immediately resold as part of a complex portfolio of MBSs, often involving over-the-counter (OTC)[24] financial derivative contracts (as opposed to exchange-traded derivatives[25]), which combine aspects of insurance, options, and futures. Growing quantities of mortgage-backed securities were sold in the early- to mid-2000s to financial institutions all around the world. These institutions considered MBSs another way of diversifying their portfolios with what they believed to be highly-rated debt instruments insured by other derivative instruments known as credit default swaps (CDS). MBSs and CDSs were again bundled into another asset class called collaterized debt obligations, or CDOs, and sold to other financial investment firms the world over, essentially globalizing the risks initially borne by US homeowners.

Figure 6.1. Growth in the US, sub-Saharan Africa, Euro area and BRIC countries 2001–2010

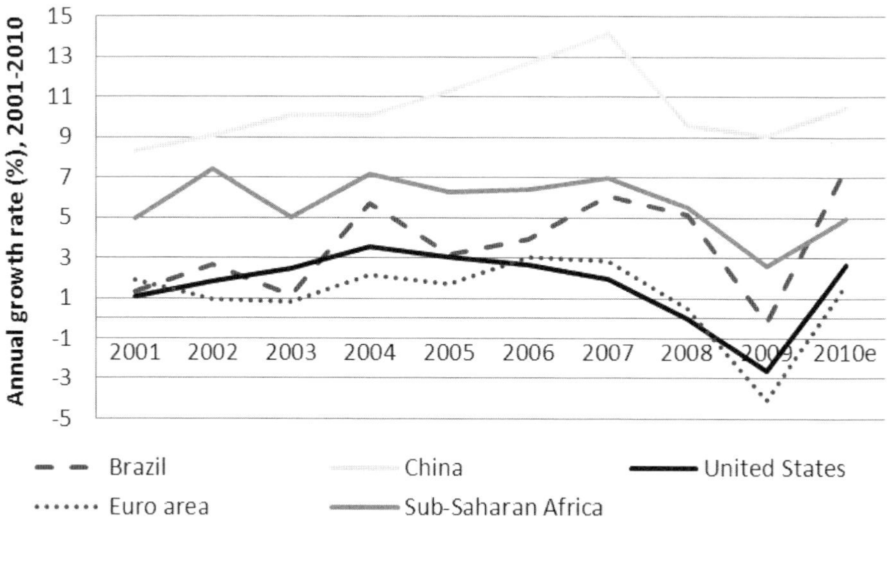

Source: World Economic Outlook, 2010, IMF data, Authors calculations.

On the assumption that interest rates would stay low, the number of subprime mortgages grew threefold between 2000 and 2006 (Shiller, 2008). A subprime loan is a

[24] OTC derivatives are privately negotiated financial contracts whose market value is determined by the value of an underlying asset, reference rate, or index.

[25] For exchange-traded derivatives, credit risk is borne by clearinghouses that serve as intermediaries between the parties to all transactions by becoming the buyer to every seller and the seller to every buyer. Clearinghouses guarantee the performance of exchange-traded contracts so that parties to these transactions do not have to evaluate one another's creditworthiness.

loan made to a borrower with blemished credit or one who provides only limited documentation of income, employment history, and other indicators of creditworthiness. By late 2006, subprime or near-prime mortgages had grown from 12 percent of all mortgages in 2000 to 34 percent (worth an estimated $1 trillion), at which point almost one-quarter of all mortgages were conventional nonprime loans (GAO, 2009; Dell'Ariccia *et al.*, 2008) with an associated increase in risk. About 45 percent of subprime borrowers in 2001 had less than 20 percent equity in their homes at the time of purchase; by 2006, this proportion had increased to an unprecedented 60 percent (Wallison, 2008). As the demand for houses grew so did the price of homes. Between January 2002 and June 2006 housing prices increased by 87 percent.[26] These increases raised the purchasing power of US households, and rising housing demand helped push domestic consumption in the US and in turn ignited a period of strong export-led growth in China. By 2006, global GDP had expanded by 4 percent as Europe, Asia and Africa all grew along with the US and China.

Unprecedented Growth in Africa

Participating in the broader global economic expansion, Africa experienced unprecedented economic growth between 2001 and 2007 (World Bank, 2009). Africa's GDP increased from US$307 billion to $817 billion in current dollar terms. More than half of sub-Saharan African (SSA) countries grew by 4 percent or more on average between 2000 and 2005, compared with fewer than a quarter of SSA countries during the period 1980 to 1995. The year 2005 was the fifth consecutive year for which regional growth was at least 3.5 percent, and it ushered in the first five-year period since 1960 in which per capita growth for Africa remained positive in every year. Africa's poverty rate went from 59 percent in 1995 to 50 percent in 2005 (Sala-i-Martin and Pinkovskiy, 2010).

What accounted for this era of unusually strong growth? In the early 2000s many African countries focused on getting the fundamentals of economic management right—they worked to reduce their debt, to control inflation and to put in place sustainable fiscal policies. Foreign exchange reserves including gold increased more than 300 percent, from $37 billion in 2001 to $154 billion in 2008. In addition to this, African countries also began to address some of the fundamental structural rigidities in their economies, such as the divestiture of governments from private sector activity, the opening up of hitherto publicly dominated sectors such as telecommunications, and the reduction of public sector borrowing from the banking sector, which was crowding out private investments. These reforms coupled with an overall favourable external economic environment produced strong results. Net FDI inflows more than doubled, from $14 billion in 2001 to $34 billion in 2008. For the first time, FDI flows into Africa exceeded overseas development assistance (Global Development Finance, 2008).

Much of this growth was driven by increased commodity exports to developed countries and to newly emerging economies such as Brazil, India, Russia and China. Nigeria, for example, bolstered by robust oil revenues, nearly doubled its export share of world markets, from 0.27 percent to 0.50 percent.[27] Even its non-oil exports showed an increase in market share, from 0.02 percent to 0.08 percent. Another high performer was South Africa, which markedly improved its export share from 0.46 percent to 0.63 percent, owing to strong performance in food and feed products, crude raw materials, and

[26] See Mbaa.org

[27] This and the rest of the data cited in this paragraph are drawn from UN COMTRADE Statistics and the World Development Indicators database of the World Bank.

manufactures. Botswana, which historically is one of the region's fastest growing economies, steadily increased its market share between 2000 and 2005. In addition to commodity exports in the big and small resource-rich countries, better subsistence and cash crops bolstered agriculture incomes and industrial production in some West African countries. In 2001, food exports as a share of GDP for Africa averaged 0.9 percent of GDP, with Cote D'Ivoire and Cameroon exporting over 2 percent of GDP in raw food exports. African countries also exported processed foods; in 2001 exports of raw and processed agricultural goods accounted for 4.3 percent of total GDP. Stability in many countries such as Liberia and Sierra Leone also helped support growth on the continent.

This growth was also spurred by a weak dollar, which led to unprecedented increases in demand for cheaper Chinese products, especially in the US; this in turn fueled economic growth in China and India. Asia in this decade became a growing manufacturing center for the world, and the demand for commodities to support this growth—metal, minerals, oil and food products—increased at a rapid pace. This in turn contributed to the growth of Africa's exports, creating a 'virtuous circle' of global economic growth. Between 2001 and 2006, demand pressures in particular drove non-oil commodity prices up by about 30 percent, while oil prices shot up over 40 percent.[28] By 2006, the US economy had begun to overheat.

The Crisis: Interest Rates, Biofuels, and Commodities

By early 2006, a slow 'tsunami' was beginning to build in the US, and economists began to actively talk about global trade and monetary imbalances. In the US, core inflation (inflation excluding volatile food and energy components) had been rising for much of 2006; average inflation in 2006 was 3.2 percent—twice the 2002 level of 1.5 percent. The US responded to the threat of high oil prices and high inflation by raising interest rates and passing a biofuels law to encourage increased diversification in energy sources. The federal funds and one-year Treasury bill interest rates rose from less than 2 percent between 2002 and 2004 to peak at 5.3 percent in June 2006.[29] However, a number of studies show that even as interest rates edged up beginning in 2005, the subprime mortgage lending market continued to grow through 2007, in sharp contrast to the prime mortgage market where denial rates began increasing sharply in 2005. As a result, the stock of subprime mortgage loans continued to increase through 2007. This led to higher interest payments and mortgage payments on ARM loans.[30] With the rise in interest rates, the housing market witnessed a sharp contraction, demand for ARMs dried up, and the rate of increase in housing prices leveled off (FHFA, 2011). By the third quarter of 2006, the growth of US residential investment swung from 0.5 percent in 2005 to an alarmingly negative -1.1 percent. This decline, plus the end of the additional consumption generated by withdrawals of home equity value from home equity loans, ushered in a slowdown in US growth as GDP in the third quarter of 2006 began to contract (see Figure 6.1) for the first time in five years (Bureau of Economic Analysis, 2007).

[28] Commodity Price Index, IMF Data and Statisics (2010) and author's calculations.

[29] See US Department of Treasury, www.treasury.gov/resource-center/data-chart-center/interest-rates.

[30] See US Federal Reserve Bank (www.federalreserve.gov) for rate interest data. Interest rates began falling in the second quarter of 2007 and have continued to decline since; the average for March 2011 was 0.23 percent.

By early 2007, Wall Street began to feel the first tremors from the CDO markets. Defaults were rising in the mortgage market and financial institutions were feeling the pressure since many CDOs included derivatives that were built upon mortgages—including risky, subprime mortgages. The asset values at the core of CDOs were shrinking and the market for MBSs was disappearing. Investors had bought CDOs on the assumption that these were much more liquid and could easily be sold or cashed in. However, as panic spread, the market for CDOs' underlying assets also began to disappear, and investors tried to divest and diversify into other asset classes. One asset class—commodities—was performing well.

Figure 6.2. Evolution of credit default swap indices with subprime mortgage components, 2006–2009

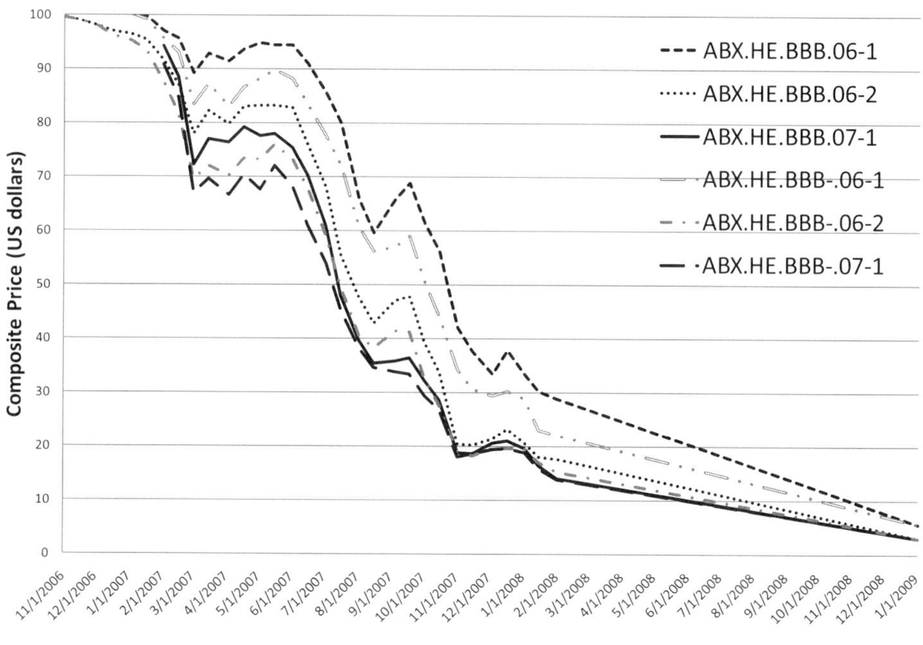

Source: Market Financial Information Service and author's calculations.

The spike in the second quarter of June 2007, as shown in Figure 6.2, was the turning point of the financial crisis. The mortgage crisis was now in full bloom and the CDOs and MBSs were proving to be illiquid assets. As the value of residential mortgage-backed securities (RMBSs) dropped, index traders diversified into commodities. The impacts on the market for RMBSs are shown in Figure 6.2. The ABX.HE indices are equally weighted indices of the 20 largest volume subprime residential mortgage-backed securities. The ABX indices are based on credit derivatives written on MBSs backed by subprime mortgage loans; they help investors track the price of credit default insurance on a basket of subprime mortgage deals. The ABX index family served as a barometer of the stability of the subprime mortgage market when it was launched in 2005, and later, in 2007, helped track the collapsing valuations of the US subprime mortgage market, which have been at the core of observed credit market developments.

The six ABX.HE indices depicted in the graph represent 20 subprime RMBSs issued from 2006 to 2010.[31] The indices all have high risk levels measured by the ratings BBB and BBB-. The figure shows that the stress on markets began in late 2006 and early 2007; in the second quarter of 2007 the markets were in free-fall, with a slight rebound at mid-year for the less risky of the two indices.[32] However, by 2008 these securities had lost over 70 percent of their value, and by early 2009 over 90 percent of their value had been lost. Early in 2008, America's leading banks had all absorbed substantial losses from the mortgage market; by year's end, Citigroup reported a devastating net loss of $18.7 billion for 2008 while Merrill Lynch, acquired by Bank of America, incurred a net loss of $15.3 billion in the fourth quarter alone (*New York Times*, January 8, 2009). The Bank for International Settlements (BIS) estimates that in 2008 the value of MBSs in the system was over 2 trillion dollars (Fender and Scheicher, 2008).

Diversification into Commodity Markets

Relative to consumer prices in developing countries, internationally traded agricultural commodity prices were broadly stable until 2007, when the prices of food commodities such as maize, wheat and soybeans rose very rapidly (World Bank, 2009a) (Figure 6.3). While commercial prices for agricultural commodities increased gradually through 2007, commodity prices in the derivatives market began increasing in late 2005. Global agricultural futures markets experienced rapid growth starting in late 2004. The open interest for many agricultural futures markets doubled or even tripled from late 2004 through 2006. For example, the CBOT wheat futures market saw open interest increase 275 percent from June 2004 to June 2006 (CFTC, 2010). Other markets, such as soybeans, continued to see rapid growth in open interest into 2008. There were many reasons for the growth in trading commodity futures markets. Some have attributed the increased interest to improved trading infrastructure on futures markets—electronic trading made it easier for non-commercial and index funds to interact in these markets, and information about the prospects for grain availability became more readily accessible with improved technology. The inflationary environment for many commodity markets also made it an attractive market for traders. Together these factors increased the demand for commodities.

Another reason for the increase in commodity prices in 2007 is directly related to the crisis in the housing market. As the credit crisis hit, more institutional investors further diversified into the commodity futures market; the trade in agricultural commodities and futures increased by 32 percent in the first two quarters of 2007 (BIS) and the value of OTC commodity derivatives in that period increased by over 150 percent.[33] Index funds and other non-commercial financial institutions were diversifying out of derivatives with US mortgage instruments, but they continued to bet on commodity derivatives including those in the OTC derivative markets.

Commodity index funds trade on a basket of up to 20 or more commodities, primarily oil and metals (ores), but also on agricultural commodities. Agricultural commodities usually account for 10 to 20 percent of the index according to CFTC market studies.

[31] Source: Market Financial Information service and author's calculations.

[32] As Fender and Scheicher (2008) observe, "According to *The Wall Street Journal* (2007), when Swiss bank UBS wrote down its subprime mortgage investments by $10 billion in December 2007, it looked to the ABX as a guidepost in determining values for its holdings. Likewise, Morgan Stanley and Citigroup reportedly cited the ABX as a factor in the sizeable write downs announced in late 2007."

[33] Bank for International Settlements, March 2011, and author's calculations.

However, between 2003 and 2008 the volume of index fund trades increased by 1900 percent, from US$13 billion to $260 billion (CFTC, 2008). It was possible to trade these amounts by index funds because index fund trades are not linked to real promissory notes for actual purchase of a commodity. They are not providing, for example, any insurance to a farmer for delivery of a fixed amount of a commodity on a given date. These funds basically function based on complex formulas that provide notional returns to investors. Therefore, despite the fact that the total stocks of commodities such as grains was very low and demand by commercial buyers was high, index traders such as hedge funds could continue to invest in this market via the derivatives market, pushing prices even higher.

Figure 6.3: Commodity prices, 2002–2009

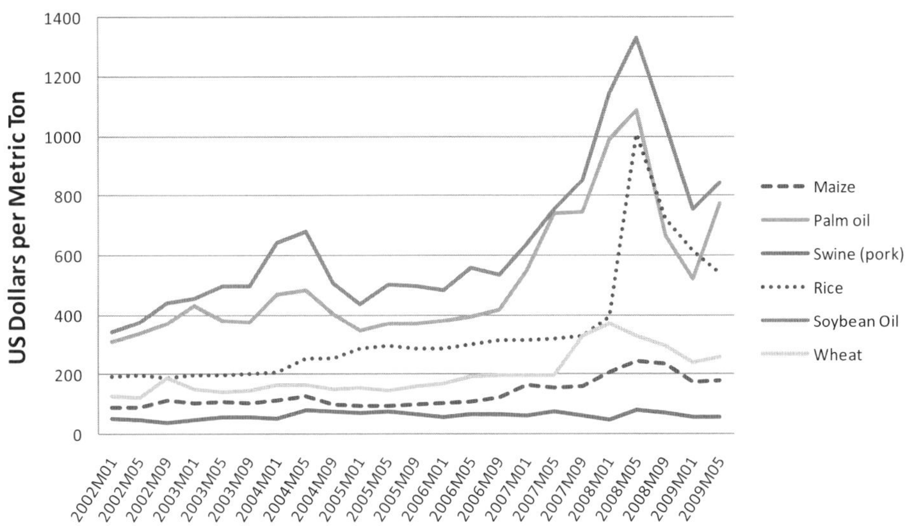

[1]Maize (corn), U.S. No.2 Yellow, FOB Gulf of Mexico, U.S. price, US$ per metric tonne
[2]Palm oil, Malaysia Palm Oil Futures (first contract forward) 4-5 percent FFA, US$ per metric tonne
[3]Swine (pork), 51-52% lean Hogs, U.S. price, US cents per pound.
[4]Rice, Five percent broken milled white rice, Thailand nominal price quote, US$ per metric tonne
[5]Soybean Oil, Chicago Soybean Oil Futures (first contract forward) exchange approved grades, US$ per metric tonne
[6]Wheat, No.1 Hard Red Winter, ordinary protein, FOB Gulf of Mexico, US$ per metric tonne

In the soybean market, for example, on June 30, 2008, at the height of the food crisis, three non-commercial principals each held aggregate futures and OTC positions exceeding a position limit—a European hedge fund held a long equivalent position above the all-months-combined limit (of 10,000 contracts) by 200 contracts. The other two non-commercial traders held equivalent long futures positions that were above the single-month limit (of 6,500 contracts): a US investment advisor with institutional clients was over, on the long side, by 3,100 contracts, and an Asian hedge fund was over on the long side by 1,300 contracts. Seven intermediaries in soybeans were reported as clients above the limits, but all were subject to the Commission's special call. Counting only OTC positions, none of the above exceeded limits.[34] Index traders by mid-2008 were increasingly diversifying into the commodity markets. Overall, as the quantity of OTC derivatives in the markets increased, the share of commodities included in the OTCs increased.

More Diversification from Oil to Commodities

In response to continued increases in oil prices and a faltering US economy, the US Congress passed two pieces of legislation—the Energy Policy Act of 2005 and the Energy Independence and Security Act (EISA) of 2007. Initially the EPA required that 5.4 billion gallons of biofuels be blended with gasoline by 2008, increasing to 7.5 billion gallons in 2012. In addition, the EISA mandated 36 billion gallons of biofuel to be blended by 2022. These two bills created incentives for US producers to sharply increase ethanol production over the next two decades. The purpose of the two acts was to reduce the demand for oil in the US and, in turn, reduce prices. As a result, ethanol production increased by an average of almost 22 percent per year through 2007. Over this period, the number of ethanol plants more than doubled, resulting in a production capacity of 7.9 billion gallons by January, 2008. The immediate consequence of the Energy Policy Act was that once oil prices rose above about $75 per barrel, it became profitable with subsidies to switch to corn-based ethanol (Mitchell, 2008).

This diversification away from oil and into corn-based ethanol was one of the causes of the food price crisis. Although estimates varied widely, increased demand for biofuels has been estimated to account for as much as 70 percent of the increase in corn prices and 40 percent of the increase in soybean prices in 2007–2008 (IMF, 2009). These policies also helped turn corn and other grains into an asset class. Corn trading by index traders increased as production of ethanol and demand for corn increased. The net notional values associated with corn commodity index trading increased significantly from December 31, 2007 to March 31, 2008 (by about 36 percent) and increased again from March 3, 2008 to June 30, 2008 (by about 27 percent). Overall, the CBOT corn trading index notional value increased from $7.6 billion in March 2007 to $13.1 billion in June 2008, while the CBOT corn price increased from $4.56/bu to $7.26/bu over the same period (CFTC, 2008).

The trend in ethanol plant expansion leveled off in early 2009 because of declining ethanol profitability and the expansion of US ethanol production to levels approaching the US government's renewable fuels standard mandate of 15 billion gallons for the year 2015. In addition, in some cases the mismatch between the high cost of corn inputs for ethanol production and the drop in anticipated prices as production increased led to severe losses by many firms (Wisner, 2009).[35] Ethanol production, however, picked up again in mid-2009 after market adjustments and a renewed increase in oil prices. According to data from the Renewable Fuels Association (2011), in 2009 ethanol production was 10.75 billion gallons, and 2010 was another record year for US ethanol production, with 13.23 billion gallons produced. Going forward, ethanol production may slow as domestic production rates approach the legal mandates for conventional biofuels in 2011 and 2012. Ethanol production is also approaching 10 percent of the US gasoline market.[36] Federal regulations have until recently limited the percentage of ethanol that could be blended for use in all

---

[34] The details in this paragraph come from CFTC, 2008.

[35] Between June 2008 and early 2009, over 17 ethanol plants shut down or filed for bankruptcy, including the second largest ethanol producer in the US.

[36] http://www.eia.doe.gov/neic/speeches/newell_03302011.pdf.

gasoline-powered vehicles to a maximum of 10 percent (E10); as production increases and oil prices continue to climb, this limit could be increased.

The combination of diversification away from the ARMs and MBSs and the increased activity of hedge and index funds in OTC commodities derivatives trade transformed the mortgage crisis into a food crisis. In this regard the food crisis delayed the financial crisis by a few quarters.

In 2008, when derivative trading was at its highest levels, the notional amounts outstanding of over-the-counter derivatives amounted to US$675 trillion,[37] of which two percent were on commodities as quoted by the Bank for International Settlements (BIS, 2010). This number subsequently dropped to US$604 trillion in 2009 and $582 trillion in June of 2010;[38] the accompanying drop in commodity-based OTC derivatives is illustrated in Figure 6.4. In 2008, about US$12 trillion worth of this amount was non-gold and non-precious metal trade. By comparison, worldwide annual GDP in 2008 was $68.6 trillion (IMF, 2010)[39] and the total GDP of Africa in 2008 was less than one trillion dollars.[40] On the other hand, in the regulated exchange derivatives market, the gross notional amounts of on-exchange derivatives amounted to nearly $80 trillion.[41] The BIS also provides an indicator which is the total value of all derivative contracts globally if they had to be closed out and settled at market value on a specific date; in June of 2009, this amount was US$22.5 trillion.

Figure 6.4. Notional amounts of total commodity-based OTC derivatives traded 2002–2010: commodity trading spike in 2007–2008

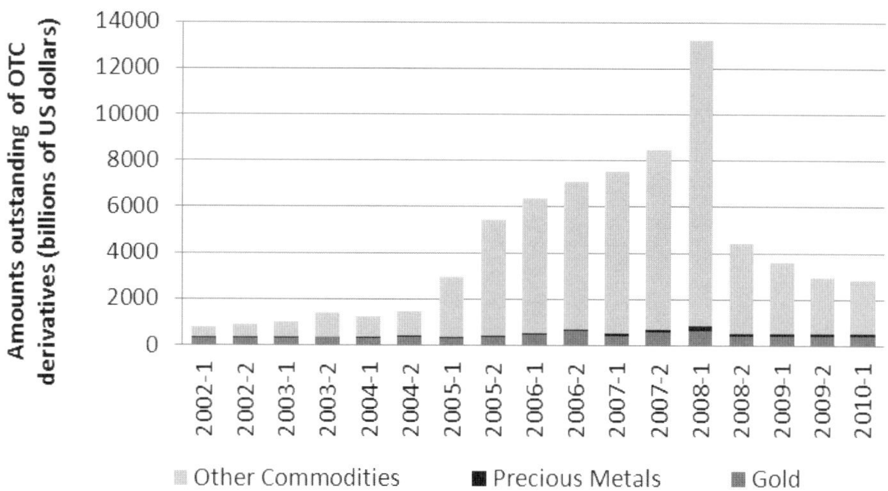

Source: Bank of International Settlement Statistics, 2011. Author's calculations.

---

[37] See *BIS Quarterly Review*, March 2010, Table 19: 'Amounts outstanding of over-the-counter (OTC) derivatives, by risk category and instrument,' and author's calculations.

[38] Ibid.

[39] IMF, 2010, IMF statistics and author's calculations.

[40] World Bank Economic Indicators and author's calculations (for sub-Saharan Africa).

[41] *BIS Quarterly Review*, March 2011, Table 23A: Derivative financial instruments traded on organized exchanges.

By the end of 2008, investors had increasingly moved from holding MBSs into investing in commodities. As companies watched the collapse of the housing market, they sought to diversify into commodities but also turned to the OTC market as a means of buying insurance against defaults on corporate bonds. Since the credit default swaps are privately executed bilaterally between two mutually consenting institutions off the exchange, there was no way to tell who was trading in the OTC derivatives or how much and when the trades were taking place. Investors in the OTC derivatives market followed an upward trend through 2006. In 2007, as the housing crisis set in, there was a massive shift into other derivative instruments. Some of the errors from the mortgage market were carried over into the derivatives market. First, some investors in the OTC markets tended to use sophisticated and innovative algorithms to determine market movements and investment size. Second, even though the rationale behind the purchase of derivatives was for insurance purposes, there were no real assets set aside to honour claims should they come due. As a result, when the market turned in 2008 and hedge funds and other investors tried to liquidate their paper and found they could not, a panic was created in the market and huge deleveraging began. Pressure from the OTC market spilled over into the food market. Food prices followed these movements, witnessing a large jump from 2007 to 2008 and then subsequently dropping in 2009.

Africa's Food Market and the Crisis

Trends in Exports and Imports, 2000–2008

For close to a decade, Africa—'No Street' and its farmers—had benefited from the low interest rates and a favourable exchange rate with the US, in particular, and a favourable financial regulatory policy environment, to increase exports and grow their incomes. 'No Street' had not heard of CDOs, RMBSs and subprime mortgages; neither did they realize that the rapid growth on the continent was underpinned by this wave of financial innovation taking place in advanced financial centres. In 2006, even though food prices had begun to inch up, there was no immediate link made between this rise and food prices; however, a crisis was in the making.

In 2001, agriculture represented over 22 percent of total GDP in SSA; this dropped to an average of 16 percent by 2008 as other sectors, especially mining and the service sectors but also finance, grew during the boom years. Another reason for the drop in agriculture as a share of GDP was a drop in the agricultural productivity that had begun in the early 1980s and continued through the 2000s in many African countries (World Bank, 2008b). Despite this drop in contribution to GDP, a significant proportion of sub-Saharan Africa's rural population—over 70 percent—depends on agriculture for its livelihood. This figure masks the wide heterogeneity of the region. In 2001, agriculture's share of GDP was over 50 percent in five African countries—Liberia (72.7 percent), Nigeria (59.2 percent), the Democratic Republic of Congo (54.3 percent), Guinea-Bissau (51.1 percent) and the Central African Republic (50.7)—and it accounted for over 25 percent of GDP in another 25 countries on the continent.[42] On the other hand, in some countries such as Mauritius, Congo, South Africa, the Seychelles and Botswana, the share of agriculture in GDP has been less than five percent since the early 2000s. Over this period, agriculture as a share of GDP increased in only four countries: Mozambique, Guinea, Angola and Eritrea.

---

[42] UN Comtrade Statistics; trade database, World Integrated Trade Solution, World Bank; and author's calculations.

Table 6.1. Exports and Imports of Food and Agriculture Products by SSA Countries

	Food Imports as % GDP			Agric Imports as % GDP			Curr Acct Bal as % GDP		
SSA Country	2000–2001	2006–2007	2007–2008	2000–2001	2006–2007	2007–2008	2000–2001	2006–2007	2007–2008
Angola	1.5	0.9	1.0	2.1	1.0	1.1	-3.7	20.8	13.2
Benin	4.4	6.8	9.2	5.6	8.3	10.8	-3.4	-7.1	-8.8
Botswana	0.1	0.0	0.0	0.1	0.1	0.2	9.8	15.9	9.0
Burkina Faso	0.3	0.4	0.4	0.7	0.9	0.9	-11.3	-12.7	-18.5
Burundi	0.6	1.6	1.4	1.2	2.3	2.4	-6.4	-12.8	-16.6
Cameroon	0.6	0.8	1.0	1.0	1.2	1.4	-3.2	1.3	-0.3
Cape Verde	2.1	2.6	3.4	3.0	3.3	4.1	-10.5	-11.2	-14.2
Ctr. Afr. Rep.	0.0	0.1	0.1	0.3	0.3	0.3	..	..	..
Chad	0.0	0.1	0.1	0.2	0.2	0.3	..	..	..
Comoros	3.9	6.2	6.3	4.6	6.8	6.8	..	..	..
DR Congo	1.2	1.8	1.8	2.0	2.7	2.7	..	..	..
Congo, Rep.	1.6	1.6	1.9	2.5	2.3	2.6	9.6	-12.3	-26.1
Cote d'Ivoire	2.6	3.1	3.2	3.6	3.6	3.7	-1.5	1.1	0.6
Eq. Guinea	0.5	0.3	0.3	0.7	0.5	0.4	..	..	..
Eritrea	3.7	1.7	1.6	4.6	2.5	2.2	-16.5	..	..
Ethiopia	1.1	0.4	0.9	1.2	0.6	1.1	-2.2	-8.1	-5.7
Gabon	1.0	1.0	1.1	1.1	1.3	1.3	15.4	22.9	..
Gambia, The	2.4	5.9	7.4	4.7	8.8	10.0	..	-9.0	-5.1
Ghana	2.0	2.1	2.7	2.9	3.1	3.9	-7.0	-6.9	-10.6
Guinea	0.7	2.5	3.1	1.0	3.1	3.9	-3.3	-9.1	-20.5
Guinea-Bissau	1.3	3.5	4.7	1.8	3.9	5.0	-5.6	-5.6	-3.9
Kenya	0.9	1.0	1.2	2.4	2.2	2.7	-2.1	-3.1	-5.2
Lesotho	0.1	0.2	0.1	0.2	0.7	0.5	-17.1	9.3	13.3
Liberia	4.1	9.6	9.8	6.0	11.1	13.1	..	-29.3	-36.3
Madagascar	0.5	1.1	1.2	0.9	1.5	1.5	-4.9	..	..
Malawi	0.8	0.9	0.8	2.3	2.3	2.4	-3.9	..	..
Mali	0.4	0.7	0.6	1.2	1.1	1.0	-11.2	-5.9	-10.2
Mauritania	2.6	4.5	6.0	3.9	5.8	7.4	..	..	..
Mauritius	1.6	2.1	2.0	2.3	3.0	3.0	2.7	-7.6	-8.2
Mozambique	1.5	3.4	3.1	3.1	4.9	4.4	-17.1	-10.4	-10.9
Namibia	0.2	0.3	0.3	0.4	0.3	0.3	2.6	11.1	5.5
Niger	0.4	0.3	0.3	1.2	1.2	1.1	-5.3	-8.5	-10.3
Nigeria	1.2	0.6	0.7	1.4	0.8	1.0	10.7	20.9	15.3
Rwanda	0.3	0.2	0.3	0.9	0.9	1.0	-5.8	-5.4	-5.0
Sao Tome & Principe	2.0	1.5	1.7	2.7	2.6	2.5	-35.3	-45.4	-49.2
Senegal	4.0	4.3	5.3	6.4	5.4	6.6	-6.1	-10.4	-13.0
Seychelles	1.6	2.2	2.7	2.7	4.1	4.1	-15.8	-19.8	-34.9
Sierra Leone	2.5	2.5	3.5	3.5	3.3	4.3	-14.9	-8.2	-10.6
South Africa	0.4	0.6	0.6	0.9	1.0	1.0	0.1	-6.3	-7.3
Sudan	0.6	0.7	0.8	1.0	1.1	1.2	-4.1	-10.1	-4.7
Swaziland	0.2	0.1	0.1	6.9	3.2	1.0	-1.2	-4.8	-5.2
Tanzania	0.4	1.1	0.9	1.0	1.5	1.4	-4.5	-9.3	-11.9
Togo	2.5	4.5	5.1	6.2	6.7	8.2	-11.6	-8.3	-8.2
Uganda	0.1	0.6	0.5	0.4	0.9	0.8	-5.9	-4.0	-4.8
Zambia	0.6	0.3	0.6	1.1	0.5	0.8	-18.3	-2.4	-6.6
Zimbabwe	0.1	4.2	7.9	0.6	6.1	9.3	..	..	..
All SSA Countries	0.8	0.9	1.1	1.4	1.4	1.5	-5.6	-5.3	-9.0

Source: UN COMTRADE data, World Bank World Economic Indicators, and author's calculations.

With growing demands and slowly expanding domestic production, many countries in SSA increased their food imports (Table 6.1). Between 2001 and 2008, raw food imports (defined as imports of meat and dairy products, grains and cereals—i.e., wheat, rice barley, maize/corn and other cereals, vegetables, fruits and dried fruits) in SSA grew from about US$3 billion to over US$10 billion, or from about 0.8 percent of GDP in 2001 to 1.1 percent of GDP in 2008. South Africa and Nigeria, the two most populated countries, accounted for over 30 percent of the region's raw food imports. Many countries in Africa therefore were vulnerable to food price increases due to this import dependence. In 2007, when food prices began to climb and global stocks were low, SSA countries were less well-placed than they had been at the beginning of the decade to take advantage of the rapid rise in prices. In addition, the demand for and imports of all agricultural commodities (raw and processed) had tripled, from US$4.8 billion in 2001 to $14 billion in 2008.[43]

While in 2001 raw food imports represented three percent or more of GDP in only five countries, by 2008 the imports of raw foods as a share of GDP was over 3 percent in 12 countries, and in 15 countries raw food imports as a share of GDP increased by over 100 percent as prices increased rapidly in 2008.[44]

In 2007, food import values in Liberia, Benin, Togo, the Gambia and Mauritania increased from 2001 levels by over 30 percent of GDP. The food price increases impacted different countries differently and the impacts varied by country and by commodity. The price increases in African markets between 2006 and 2008 were highest for maize (87 percent), followed by wheat (65 percent), and rice (62 percent), while commodities that are less widely traded in international markets saw smaller price increases in African markets (Minot, 2010).

As a consequence of increasing prices and reliance on imports, the food price crisis had an immediate impact on the balance of payments for many African countries. In Tanzania, Benin, Guinea, Burundi, and Liberia, for example, where agricultural imports doubled between 2001 and 2008, the current account balance as a share of GDP doubled or tripled. In Tanzania the current account deficit increased from 4.5 percent of GDP in 2001 to 11.9 percent in 2008; in Benin it increased from 3.8 percent of GDP deficit in 2001 to an 8.8 percent deficit in 2008.[45]

Many SSA countries have also historically provided food subsidies to large parts of their populations. In particular the prices of rice, wheat, corn and oil are often subsidized. Social safety net programs are frequently prescribed as better able to target the needs of the poor compared to generalized food subsidies. However, since the institutional framework to implement more targeted policies was frequently lacking and a significant share of the population was affected by the crisis, governments often found it more expedient to employ food subsidies and/or tax cuts. Data from a 2008 IMF survey covering 161 countries show that between 2006 and 2008 nearly 57 percent of countries reduced taxes on food, while 27 percent reduced taxes on fuels. On the expenditure side, 18 percent of countries increased food subsidies while 22 percent increased fuel subsidies (IMF, 2008b). When food prices began to rise above historic rates in 2006, many countries were able to tap into built-up reserves to address the initial price increase. However, by the end of 2008, many of these countries could no longer subsidize staple food consumption without external balance-of-payments support. The food price increases in SSA were further compounded by poor

---

[43] UN Comtrade Data, 2009; World Bank World Economic Indicators 2009, and authors calculations.

[44] World Development Indicators, 2009, and UN Comtrade data, 2009.

[45] Author's calculation with data from UN COMTRADE Statistics (trade data) and World Bank World Development Indicators database (GDP data).

infrastructure network, which in places resulted in even higher average price increases than were observed in international markets. One reason for this was that fuel and fertilizer price increases in some cases were twice the rate of food price increases. Farmers therefore found it difficult to grow food to support their livelihoods (Benson, 2008; World Bank, 2008c). In addition, a large percentage of rural households are net buyers of staple food crops, so they are hurt by higher food prices. By early 2008, many SSA countries were struggling to cope with a spiraling food price crisis.

The pressure on governments to act was high and mounting as civil unrest broke out in many countries and cities in May 2008. Seychelles, Burundi, Sierra Leone, and the DRC introduced restrictive trade measures and tax reductions on food commodities. As shown in Table 6.1, these countries were amongst the raw food importers in 2008, and three of them are also fragile or conflict states. In Liberia, Senegal, Benin and Gabon, governments reduced taxes on fuel products while Senegal, Mauritius, Swaziland and Ethiopia increased food subsidies. An IMF study (2008a) suggests that the median fiscal impact of policy responses to rising food prices was around 0.9 percent of country GDP in 2008. Some countries imposed export bans and traders hoarded what grain was left while elevator providers struggled to find corn, rice and wheat to deliver to markets. The food price crisis had become a global problem. With the housing crisis in the US underway, the food crisis in developing countries and rising fuel prices straining world economies, the three basic elements needed for a crisis—vulnerability, globalization and illiquidity—were fully aligned.

In the summer of 2008, 'No Street' was struggling to manage the food crisis and the ensuing macroeconomic instability, while policy debates in the west focused on the causes of the mortgage crisis and their resolution. However, in September 2008, Wall Street met 'No Street.' With the collapse of Lehman Brothers, the food crisis transformed into a financial crisis once again and the cycle from finance to food and back was complete.

Dealing with Financial Crisis in a Globalized Age: Regulation, Innovation and Markets

As the magnitude of the crisis became evident, it was common to talk about the impact of the crisis in waves. The first wave was the meltdown of Wall Street, the second was the meltdown of the banking and financial sectors, and the third was the meltdown of the real sector—the collapse of trade and developing country exports, and a slowdown in infrastructure projects. Academics and policy makers alike generally felt it was principally this third wave that would impact low income countries and SSA in particular. As a result, much of the debate about the solutions needed to tackle the food price crisis remained divorced from the debate around regulatory reform of the financial markets, the commodity markets and as a result the financial sector. A lack of understanding of the intimate link between the two events will undermine future policy proposals for low income countries as they emerge from these crises.

The past decade has demonstrated the benefits of innovation and risk taking, in that trillions of dollars of wealth were created, which permitted economies the world over to take advantage and compete, grow and reduce poverty. However, the 'creative destruction' that comes with growth and competition has been chilling and reminds us that wealth creation must certainly be accompanied by tangible, measurable asset creation and regulation to ease and manage the destructive components of innovation. Such asset creation and regulation were lacking in the past decade in the financial markets.

The depth and breadth of the financial crisis were unprecedented. The challenge now is for world leaders to decide how to implement reforms that will improve the resilience, stability and transparency of the financial system. The head of the Commodity Futures Trading Commission, in his testimony to Congress in 2010, best summarized the situation as follows (Gensler, 2010):

> *Nearly thirty years after they were developed, OTC derivatives remain unregulated, which is in stark contrast with the other major parts of our financial markets—the securities and futures markets. OTC derivatives were at the centre of the 2008 financial crisis. They added leverage to the financial system with more risk being backed up by less capital. Taxpayers bailed out AIG with $180 billion when that company's ineffectively regulated $2 trillion derivatives portfolio nearly brought down the financial system—that means that every person in this room has $600 in AIG. Over-the-counter derivatives—initially developed to help manage and lower risk—actually concentrated and heightened risk in the economy and to the public.*
>
> *After the 2008 financial crisis, there is broad consensus across borders that we must bring transparency and lower risk through regulation of the global derivatives marketplace. Therefore the time has come to bring comprehensive regulation to the derivatives marketplace. We must ensure a transparent, fair and open market just as earlier generations did in the securities and futures markets.*

In response to calls for action, the G-20 leaders at the Washington Summit on Financial Markets and the World Economy in September 2008 launched a broad process of dialogue on financial regulation and reform. The world's leading financial services firms also launched new initiatives to improve risk management and governance in the companies. In London in April 2009, the G-20 leaders went further and agreed to create the Financial Stability Board (FSB) to address vulnerabilities and to develop and implement strong regulatory, supervisory and other policies in the interest of financial stability.[46] Specifically, the FSB was asked to:

a) assess vulnerabilities affecting the global financial system and identify and review on a timely and ongoing basis the regulatory, supervisory and related actions needed to address them, and their outcomes;
b) promote coordination and information exchange among authorities responsible for financial stability;
c) monitor and advise on market developments and their implications for regulatory policy;
d) advise on and monitor best practice in meeting regulatory standards;
e) undertake joint strategic reviews of the policy development work of the international standard-setting bodies to ensure their work is timely, coordinated, focused on priorities and addressing gaps;
f) set guidelines for and support the establishment of supervisory colleges;
g) support contingency planning for cross-border crisis management, particularly with respect to systemically important firms;

[46] Financial Stability Board, http://www.financialstabilityboard.org/publications/ r_090925d.pdf.

h) collaborate with the International Monetary Fund (IMF) to conduct Early Warning Exercises; and
i) undertake any other tasks agreed by its Members in the course of its activities and within the framework of this Charter.

Ultimately all of these steps would be critical to prevent another crisis. However, for the purpose of this chapter, we focus on the issues of regulation and, in particular, the regulation of the OTC derivatives markets. The crisis exposed fundamental weaknesses in the structure of over-the-counter derivatives markets that had contributed to the build-up of systemic risk across continents, markets and financial instruments. The trading of OTC derivatives had linked and contaminated 'No Street' corn, soybean and wheat farmers and consumers with international markets such as the Chicago Board of Trade and other renowned financial houses in an unprecedented way. While OTC derivatives had been the subject of much debate prior to the financial crisis in academic, regulatory and financial institutions, they were rarely the subject of broad conversation in earlier years (Petzel, 1995; Romano, 1996). In fact, in 1994 after a number of highly publicized losses by some users of OTC derivatives, Congress requested that the GAO conduct a study of OTC derivatives (GAO, 1998). However, the regulation of these markets remained very weak. Developing country financial market regulators on their part rarely or never focused on these markets.

The FSB at the Pittsburgh G-20 summit in 2009 was asked to specifically look into the weaknesses in the infrastructure of the OTC derivatives. In Toronto in June 2010, the G-20 leaders once again focused on this issue and agreed that all OTC derivative contracts should be traded on exchanges or electronic trading platforms, where appropriate, and cleared through central counterparties (CCPs) by the end of 2012. They also agreed that OTC derivatives contracts should be reported to trade repositories.[47] The G-20 Leaders' commitments concerning standardization, central clearing, exchange or electronic platform trading, and reporting of OTC derivatives transactions to trade repositories, are an important step, critical to improving transparency of the commodity trading system.

On the agriculture front in Africa, the response to the food crisis has been to help countries improve their production and productivity as well as to put in place safety net systems to support the most vulnerable. Efforts to secure stocks for humanitarian assistance are also underway. However, what is clear today is that the market for agriculture commodities is clearly linked to the financial markets, and as developing countries increase production and productivity and try to diversify their markets they will become increasingly connected to global market logistics and trading systems.

Following the crisis there has been a move to improve the commodity trading infrastructure in Africa, and much discussion has occurred regarding the need for improved market transparency, standardization in order to command scale and liquidity, and continued furtherance of the link with international markets. Some countries like Ethiopia have developed commodity exchanges, while countries like Tanzania, Ghana, Uganda,

[47] See June 2010 Toronto Summit Declaration, paragraph 19. In addition, Annex II to the Declaration provides: 'We pledged to work in a coordinated manner to accelerate the implementation of over-the-counter (OTC) derivatives regulation and supervision and to increase transparency and standardisation. We reaffirm our commitment to trade all standardised OTC derivatives contracts on exchanges or electronic trading platforms, where appropriate, and clear through central counterparties (CCPs) by end-2012 at the latest. OTC derivative contracts should be reported to trade repositories (TRs). We will work toward the establishment of CCPs and TRs in line with global standards and ensure that national regulators and supervisors have access to all relevant information.'

Zambia, Kenya and UMOA (Monetary Union of West Africa) either have nascent commodity exchange platforms or are looking to create one. The development of these exchanges must now be consistent with FSB requirements. In the US, the Dodd-Frank law, the most comprehensive financial regulation in 30 years, has outlined a framework which should be analyzed and understood by developing countries seeking to develop commodity trading platforms. Over time, as African countries develop, exchange trading platforms for commodity and derivative trading will be critical to ensure that the lessons from the 2008 financial crisis are learned. Korea, Japan and the EU are also developing policies to deal with OTC derivative trading, but none is as comprehensive as the Dodd-Frank Law.

African countries must not be left on the sidelines as new financial market regulations are put into place. It is important that African countries are consulted and are part of these discussions and endorse the recommendations of the FSB. In this regard, the G-20 leaders should also ensure that there is adequate support provided to these countries to help enforce the recommendations suggested by the FSB.

The financial crisis was not a failure of markets but a failure of systems and institutions that regulate markets. So, any reversals from market principles must be limited in scope, justified and time bound. Poorly regulated markets in developed countries can devastate markets everywhere. We must also not ignore market failures that leave the poor behind. The policies adopted to restore growth must also build trust in the system. Restoring market confidence would be the single most challenging task of leaders post-crisis. As developing countries reform and improve their agriculture sectors, the need to develop effective markets must be the central focus of the debate.

Innovation would be an important component in the development of the agriculture sector in Africa. Innovation is critical for markets to function and for growth. The introduction of electronic trading platforms should improve market infrastructure, link farmers to the value chain more effectively and provide added liquidity for growth. It would be easy to conclude that derivatives and the innovative financial products bundled and sold as secure assets caused the crisis. But this would be misleading. It is the lack of transparency related to asset valuation and product bundling that regulation should address, as the FSB is now doing.

Today the developing world and SSA in particular need to address the underlying problems of rural poverty and poor farm production and productivity. Many of the African countries that grew rapidly before the crisis need to renew and expand their infrastructure. These countries need access to financial products, and investors need and continue to design instruments to hedge against risks. Even as the debate on financial regulation is ongoing, many financial institutions are building new insurance instruments to help developing country governments and farmers manage the next crisis. There is a new industry of financial innovation around agriculture and climate change products that will directly affect developing country policy makers and farmers. Therefore any new financial regulations must take into account the impact and applicability to developing country markets.

This means the new system must be inclusive and transparent. First, FSB recommendations should be discussed at a broader level, beyond the G-20 alone. Second, the regulatory framework and agency-monitoring system of the FSP should as a matter of course be mandated to investigate and highlight risks and implications to developing countries of financial activities in other markets or systemically important financial institutions in all reports. Third, the capacity of national regulatory agencies should be assessed and provisions made to strengthen them. In the presence of globalized markets, regulation of financial products should be comprehensive and integrated so that interdependencies are transparent and arbitrage is minimized or eliminated. A key role of FSB in this case would be to highlight emerging gaps in the system and propose remedies, including those that relate to developing countries. Finally, regulators must acknowledge the truly global nature of financial markets and instruments. These markets must be treated as parts of one whole. Any monitoring systems for risk mitigation must be comprehensive and cover the entirety of the market.

References

Bank For International Settlements. (2010) International Banking and Financial Market Developments. *BIS Quarterly Review,* March 2010.

Bank For International Settlements. (2011) Table 23A: Derivative financial instruments traded on organized exchanges. *BIS Quarterly Review,* March 2011.

Benson, T. (2008) An assessment of the likely impact of rising global food prices on Ugandan households. IFPRI, Washington, DC.

Bureau of Economic Analysis. (2007) Survey of Current Business. Available at: www.bea.gov/scb/pdf/2007/.

Commodity Futures Trading Commission (CFTC). (2008) CFTC Releases Staff Report on Swap Dealers and Index Traders. Available at: http://www.cftc.gov/PressRoom/PressReleases/pr5542-08.html.

CFTC. (2010) Commodity Index Trader Supplement Statistics. Available at: http://www.cftc.gov/

Currie, A. and Cox, R. (2009) Bank Branches Slow to Vanish. *New York Times.* Available at: http://www.nytimes.com/2009/08/17/business/17views.html.

Dell'Ariccia, G., Igan, D. and Laeven, L. (2008) Credit Booms and Lending Standards: Evidence from the Subprime Mortgage Market. IMF Working Paper 08/106, International Monetary Fund, Washington, DC.

FAO (2009a) FAOSTAT. Available at: http://faostat.fao.org/.

FAO (2009b) Economic crises: impacts and lessons learned. *The State of Food Insecurity in the World 2009.* FAO and WFP, Rome. Available at: ftp://ftp.fao.org/docrep/fao/012/i0876e/i0876e.pdf.

FAO (2010) Addressing food insecurity in protracted crises. *The State of Food Insecurity in the World 2010.* FAO and WFP, Rome. Available at: http://www.fao.org/docrep/013/i1683e/i1683e.pdf

Federal Housing Finance Agency. (2011) News Release: FHFA Seasonally Adjusted Housing Price Index for USA. Washington, DC, February 24. Federal Reserve Interest Data. Available at: http://www.federalreserve.gov.

Fender, I. and Scheicher, M. (2008) The ABX: How Do the Markets Price Subprime Mortgage Risk? *BIS Quarterly Review,* July, 67–81.

Financial Stability Board. (2009) Financial Stability Board Charter. Available at: http://www.financialstabilityboard.org/publications/ r_090925d.pdf.

G-20 Toronto. (2010) The G-20 Toronto Summit Declaration. Available at: http://canadainternational.gc.ca/g20/assets/pdfs/g20_declaration_en.pdf.

Government Accountability Office (GAO). (1998) OTC Derivatives: Additional Oversight Could Reduce Costly Sales Practice Disputes. Available at: http://www.gao.gov/archive/1998/gg98005.pdf.

GAO (2009) Characteristics and Performance of Nonprime Mortgages. GAO-09-848R. Available at: http://www.gao.gov/new.items/d09848r.pdf.

Gensler, G. (2010) Remarks as Chairman, Commodity Futures Trading Commission, Panel to Discuss Financial Reform. April 12, Columbia University, New York.

Global Development Finance. (2007) The Globalization of Corporate Finance in Developing Countries. World Bank, Washington, DC. Available at: http://econ.worldbank.org/website/external/extdec/extdecprospects/extgdf/extgdf2007/0,menuPK:3763156~pagePK:64167702~piPK:64167676~theSitePK:3763080,00.html.

Global Development Finance. (2008) The Role of International Banking. World Bank, Washington, D.C. Available at: http://siteresources.worldbank.org/INTGDF2008/Resources/gdf_complete_web-appended-6-12.pdf

IMF (2008a) Food and Fuel Prices—Recent Developments, Macroeconomic Impact, and Policy Responses. Available at: http://www.imf.org/external/np/pp/eng/2008/063008.pdf.

IMF (2008b) Fuel and Food Price Subsidies: Issues and Reform Options. Available at: http://www.imf.org/external/np/pp/eng/2008/090808a.pdf

IMF (2009) IMF primary commodity prices. Available at: http://www.imf.org/external/np/res/commod/index.asp

IMF (2010a) IMF primary commodity prices. Available at: http://www.imf.org/external/np/res/commod/index.asp

IMF (2010b) Rebalancing Growth. World Economic Outlook April 2010. Available at: http://www.imf.org/external/pubs/ft/weo/2010/01/pdf/text.pdf

Minot, N. (2010) Transmission of World Food Price Changes to African Markets and its Effect on Household Welfare. Comesa-MSU-IFPRI African Agricultural Markets Project (AAMP).

Mitchell, D. (2008) A note on rising food prices. Policy Research Working Paper No. 4682. World Bank, Washington, DC.

Mortgages Bankers Association. Available at: mbaa.org.

New York Times. (2009) "Citi and BofA Post Losses and Big Changes." New York, January 9.

Petzel, T. (1995) Derivatives: Market and Regulatory Dynamics. 21 J. Corp. L. 95, 96.

Prakash, A. (2011) Safe Guarding Food Security in Volatile Markets. FAO, Rome.

Renewable Fuels Association (2011). Building bridges to a more sustainable future. *Ethanol Industry Outlook 2011*. Available at: http://ethanolrfa.3cdn.net/1ace47565fabba5d3f_ifm6iskwq.pdf

Romano, R. (1996) A Thumbnail Sketch of Derivatives Securities and Their Regulation, 55 *Maryland Law Review,* 1, 8.

Sala-i-Martin, X. and Pinkovskiy, M. (2010) African Poverty is Falling…Much Faster than YouThink! NBER Working Paper, No. 15775.

Shiller, R.J. (2008) *The Subprime Solution: How Today's Global Financial Crisis Happened and What to Do about It.* Princeton University Press, Princeton, New Jersey.

Timmer, P. (2009) Did Speculation Affect World Rice Prices? Center for Global Development, ESA Working Paper No. 09-07. Available at: www.fao.org/es/esa.

UN (2009) 2008 International Trade Statistics Yearbook, Volume I. New York.

United States Department of the Treasury *(nd)* Interest Rate Statistics. Available at: http://www.treasury.gov/resource-center/data-chart-center/interest-rates.

von Braun, J. (2007) The World Food Situation: New Driving Forces and Required Actions. Food Policy Report, IFPRI, Washington, DC, December.

Wallison, P.J. (2008) Cause and Effect: Government Policies and the Financial Crisis. *AEI Financial Services Outlook,* November 2008.
Wisner, R. (2009) Ethanol Economic Crisis: Potential Impact on Corn Use & Ethanol Production vs. Mandated Ethanol Use. *AgMRC Renewable Energy Newsletter,* February.
World Bank. (2002) WITS Trade Database. Available at: http://wits.worldbank.org/wits/.
World Bank. (2008a) Double Jeopardy: Responding to High Food and Fuel Prices. Memo of the World Bank to the G8 Summit in Hokkaido, Toyako. World Bank, Washington, DC.
World Bank. (2008b) World Development Report 2008. *Agriculture for Development.* World Bank, Washington, DC.
World Bank. (2008c) Rising Food Prices and Fuel Prices: Addressing the Risks to Future Generations. World Bank, Washington, DC.
World Bank. (2009) World Economic Indicators 2009. World Bank, Washington, DC.
World Bank. (2009a) Global Economic Prospects. *Commodities at the Crossroads.* World Bank, Washington, DC
World Bank. (2010a) World Economic Indicators 2010. World Bank, Washington, DC.
World Bank. (2010b). Global Monitoring Report. World Bank, Washington, DC.

Chapter 7

Agricultural Productivity in Sub-Saharan Africa

Keith O. Fuglie
Economic Research Service, USDA

Abstract

Agricultural productivity in sub-Saharan Africa remains low and is falling further behind the rest of the world. Nevertheless, agricultural output growth for the region accelerated in the 1990s and if sustained could spur economic development and poverty reduction. This chapter combines production function and index number approaches while incorporating natural resource quality variables to explore patterns of agricultural productivity growth in sub-Saharan Africa between 1961 and 2008. The results indicate that most of the recent rise in agricultural productivity has been due to resource expansion that can be explained in part by improved macroeconomic and political environments. The rise in global commodity prices since 2006 has also improved agriculture's terms of trade. In addition, there is evidence that total factor productivity growth improved in some countries. This chapter explores possible reasons why some African countries have apparently been able to accelerate agricultural productivity growth and whether this can be sustained.

Introduction

Poverty and food insecurity are pervasive in sub-Saharan Africa (SSA); it is the one major world region where such conditions have not seen much improvement over the past several decades. A key, if not the principal, factor behind this disappointing record has been a lack of robust growth in agriculture. This is the sector from which the majority of the region's population draws its livelihood. For the past several decades the rate of increase in food production has not kept pace with population growth, leading to rising food-import dependence and little or no improvement in reducing poverty and malnutrition. The food and financial crises that have affected the global economy beginning in 2006 have refocused attention on sub-Saharan Africa, both for the crises' impacts on the region's poor and on the potential of the region to become a new source of agricultural surplus. But if agriculture is to become an engine of economic growth, its productivity will need to dramatically improve. The focus of this chapter is on the constraints to expanding agricultural productivity as a means of expanding agricultural supply and farm income in sub-Saharan Africa.

From the policy side, for the first two to three decades of the post-1960 (post-independence) period, farmers in much of SSA suffered from heavy direct or indirect taxation, such as overvalued exchange rates (Delgado, 1995). But recent years have witnessed improved macroeconomic conditions and a renewed interest on the part of governments in promoting agriculture. In a wide-ranging review of the prospects for agricultural and rural development in SSA, Binswanger-Mkhize and McCalla (2009) cite the reduction of armed conflict, improved macroeconomic management, the spread of democratic and civil society institutions, stronger regional organizations, and growing volumes of foreign aid as cause for renewed optimism. In fact, the rate of growth in agriculture (and in the economies generally) of the SSA region saw improvement in the 1990s and early 2000s compared with previous decades. However, if this renewed agricultural growth is primarily *resource-led*, that is, brought about by expanding cropland, or if it is driven by cyclically high commodity prices such as during the 2007–2008 food-price crisis, then the prospects for sustained growth are likely to be inherently limited. Ultimately it is productivity that will need to grow if African agriculture is to supply both profitable and low-cost food, so that poverty and malnutrition can be reduced.

The reasons productivity in African agriculture has remained low historically are succinctly summarized in a paper by Binswanger and Townsend (2000). They note that both adverse resource endowments and poor governing institutions and policies prevented African agriculture from accumulating sufficient capital to grow fast enough to be an engine of economic growth and poverty reduction. But they give greater explanatory weight to institutional and policy factors over adverse resource endowments, and they were generally optimistic that the political and policy reforms achieved in the region since the mid-1980s would improve agricultural growth. It is worth noting that Binswanger and Townsend (2000) did not include cultural endowments as an impediment to growth, and there is ample historical evidence that farmers in sub-Saharan Africa vigorously and successfully mobilize resources to expand production when new profitable opportunities arise (Hill, 1970).

Globally, what has distinguished countries that have been most successful in agricultural development is that they were able to raise their growth rates by enhancing the productivity of resources, rather than simply mobilizing new resources for production (Hayami and Ruttan, 1985). But raising agricultural productivity requires national institutions that are capable of delivering improved technologies and farming methods (Evenson and Fuglie, 2010). Among SSA countries, the evidence on agricultural productivity performance is ambiguous. Block (1995), comparing agricultural growth among 39 SSA countries between 1963 and 1988, found evidence that productivity growth 'increased dramatically' in the mid-1980s compared with previous years. He attributed the productivity growth to technical change brought about from past investments in agricultural research and to policy reforms, such as real exchange rate depreciation that shifted relative prices in favour of producers of tradable goods. However, Block (1995) also noted that gains from policy reform might prove to be a one-time effect and that maintaining long-run growth would require greater investment in agricultural research in order to broaden and sustain technical change. Nin-Pratt and Yu (2008), who offer probably the most comprehensive assessment of agricultural productivity change in SSA countries to date, show that growth performance across a broad set of countries was significantly correlated with the pace and timing of macroeconomic and agricultural policy changes made since 1984. However, their evidence also demonstrates that much of the higher productivity growth rates achieved since the mid-1980s was merely making up for productivity *regressions* that took place in the 1960s and 1970s: the total factor productivity *level* for SSA was hardly better in 2003 than it was in 1961 (and actually lower for the SSA region as a whole if Nigeria is excluded from the aggregate).

The evidence on the payoffs from agricultural research in Africa is also mixed. Frisvold and Ingram (1995), who examined sources of agricultural growth for a set of SSA countries between 1973 and 1985, found that improved export competitiveness accounted for a significant share of growth but did not find research-induced technical change to have significant explanatory power. Studies by Lusigi and Thirtle (1997) and Alene and Coulibaly (2009) did find a significant correlation between African countries' investments in research and agricultural productivity growth, but these studies included North African countries and/or South Africa, which generally have much greater research capacities and better growth performance than the poorer African countries. It seems likely that the significant effect of research on agricultural productivity found in these studies occurred in the middle-income, subtropical countries in their samples, and not the poor, tropical countries of Africa. Alene and Coulibaly's (2009) measure of agricultural productivity (agricultural GDP per worker) also confounds productivity improvements and terms of trade effects, since (inflation-adjusted) agricultural prices were also rising in many SSA countries over the period of their study (Anderson and Masters, 2009).

The aim of this chapter is to provide a new set of measures of agricultural productivity growth for sub-Saharan African countries in light of the commodity price and financial shocks that have in recent years affected the global economy. This chapter examines the performance of 48 sub-Saharan countries over the 1961–2008 period, paying particular attention to 2006–2008, which includes the recent 'food-price crisis' years.[48] I measure productivity both in terms of partial indices of output per unit of land and labor, and in terms of growth in total factor productivity (TFP) of all resources employed in farm production. I use a parametric (production function estimation) approach to aggregate the effects of measurable resources (land, labor, livestock, machinery and fertilizer inputs) on output and then attribute residual growth to changes in TFP. I also critically assess the quality of the FAO's FAO data series for agricultural output and inputs in Africa and propose some modifications to some of these measures. Unlike previous studies (Block, 1995; Nin-Pratt and Yu, 2008), I do not find evidence of a marked increase in productivity growth in recent decades, with the notable exception of some West African countries. By far the most important factor accounting for growth in agricultural output since 1961 has been the expansion of cropland harvested, which in turn is closely correlated with population growth. However, I do find evidence of deteriorating input intensity, or fewer inputs applied per crop area harvested, which has suppressed crop yield. It is important to keep in mind that while the structural adjustment policies introduced beginning in the mid-1980s did improve agricultural terms of trade, they also reduced development assistance and state investments in agriculture and raised farm prices of fertilizer relative to crops (World Bank, 2007).

In the next section of the chapter I provide a brief overview of economic and agricultural development indicators for the sub-Saharan Africa region as a whole and describe long-run trends in agricultural land and labor productivity. I also describe in this

---

[48] In order to maintain a continuous time series, data for Ethiopia and Eritrea are aggregated together for the years after their political separation in 1993. Throughout the chapter the Republic of South Africa, which is far more industrialized than the other countries in sub-Saharan Africa, is excluded from regional aggregates unless otherwise noted.

section some of the problems encountered in using agricultural data from the region and suggest some modifications to improve measures of resource use and productivity. The third section describes the methodology for modeling growth in total factor productivity. My approach is to estimate an agricultural production function for the panel of SSA countries and use the estimated production elasticities as weights for creating an index of aggregate resource (input) utilization. Then I use growth accounting methods to derive an agricultural TFP index for each country. The econometric results as well as the estimated TFP indexes are presented in the following section. Here, I also decompose output growth for the region as a whole into crop area, input intensity and TFP components. The chapter's final section concludes with a discussion of why some countries appear to be performing better than others in raising agricultural productivity, and hence, farm income and affordable food supply.

Agriculture in Africa's Economic Development

This section looks briefly at agriculture's place in the overall economic development of sub-Saharan Africa and reviews agricultural production changes over the past half-century. We also compare the trends in agricultural land and labor productivity in SSA with other world regions. A comprehensive assessment of the economic performance of SSA economies over this period is provided by Ndulu *et al.* (2007), and the interested reader is encouraged to consult this reference for more depth on the topic. Many of the observations in the Ndulu *et al.* (2007) study are especially pertinent to the agriculture sector. One observation is that while SSA countries have had relatively low levels of investment, it has been the slower growth of productivity that more sharply distinguishes African growth performance from the rest of the world. The Ndulo report confirms the 'centerpiece' role of the agricultural sector if SSA countries are to make significant progress toward rapid economic growth, poverty reduction and improved food security.

Table 7.1 presents some basic indicators for the SSA region by decade since the 1960s and also breaks out the performance immediately prior to and during the food/financial crisis years of 2006–2008. Population was still growing by about 2.5 percent per year during the 2000–2010 decade, nearly the same as it had been in the 1960s, but slightly lower than the peak of 2.9 percent in the 1980s. The delayed demographic transition of SSA countries has meant that the proportion of young in the population, and therefore the dependency ratio (the ratio of the working to the nonworking population), has remained relatively high. In fact, this factor alone accounts for most of the lower household savings rates observed in SSA compared with other developing regions (Ndulu *et al.*, 2007). By 2006–2008, although agriculture comprised only 14 percent of GDP (World Bank), about 60 percent of the labor force was employed in agriculture. Average GDP per capita in 2006–2008 (in constant 2005 purchasing power parity dollars) was $1,871 and growing by 3.7 percent per year, one of the best performances of the past half-century. But African economies were still making up for lost ground during the 1980s and 1990s when GDP per capita declined from the historical peak achieved in the 1970s. The higher economic growth of the 2000s enabled poverty rates to decline, but only back to their 1980s level. Average life expectancy, another key indicator of well-being, saw some gradual improvement between the 1960s and 1980s but has stagnated at about 50 years of age since then. In some countries, high HIV/AIDS infection rates have caused life expectancy to fall. Regarding educational achievement, adult literacy appears to have improved somewhat between the 1980s and 2000s, with about six out of ten adults obtaining basic literacy skills. Literacy rates are generally a better indicator of rural education levels than average years of schooling since most individuals with post-primary schooling leave agriculture.

Table 7.1. Development Indicators for sub-Saharan Africa

	1961-1970	1971-1980	1981-1990	1991-2000	2001-2005	2006-2008
Population, total (millions)	263	342	455	599	725	800
Population growth (annual %)	2.54	2.81	2.89	2.70	2.53	2.49
Regional GDP (billions of constant 2005 PPP $)	n.a.	n.a.	734	899	1,181	1,498
Industry, value added (% of GDP)	31	33	34	29	30	32
Manufacturing, value added (% of GDP)	17	17	17	16	14	13
Services, etc., value added (% of GDP)	48	48	48	52	52	54
Agriculture, value added (% of GDP)	21	20	18	18	18	14
Trade (% of GDP)	48	55	53	57	64	71
Share of labor force employed in agriculture (% of total)	80	75	70	65	62	60
GDP per capita (constant 2005 PPP $)	n.a.	n.a.	1,616	1,501	1,626	1,871
GDP per capita growth (annual %)	n.a.	n.a.	-1.07	-0.30	2.43	3.71
Percent of population living on less than $2/day (constant PPP$)	n.a.	n.a.	75	77	74	n.a.
Life expectancy at birth (years)	44	47	49	50	51	52
Adult literacy (% of population age 15 and over)	n.a.	n.a.	n.a.	57	n.a.	63

n.a. not available. Figures include South Africa.
Source: World Bank (2008), except for share of labor force in agriculture, which is from FAO (2009).

Some basic trends in agricultural production and resource use are given in Table 7.2. These figures cover all 48 countries in sub-Saharan Africa but exclude South Africa, which is considerably more developed than the rest of the sub-continent. Gross agricultural output, measured in constant 2000 US dollars,[49] grew at 2.5–3.5 percent per year on average each decade except in the 1970s, when growth averaged just over 1 percent annually. Agricultural GDP (in constant dollars), on the other hand, grew at over 2 percent per year each decade since the 1970s, and averaged over 3.3 percent growth during 2001–2008. The difference between growth in real output and real GDP is primarily in terms of trade effect: changes in real value added are due to 1) changes in the quantity of output and 2) changes in (inflation-adjusted) domestic prices, or the terms of trade between agricultural and non-agricultural goods. Thus, changes in the growth rates between agricultural output and agricultural GDP reflect the changes in agricultural prices relative to a general price index. Agriculture experienced an increasing terms-of-trade (rising real

[49] Real agricultural output is based on the FAO gross agricultural production series. The FAO has developed a global set of representative prices, measured in constant 1999-2001 US$, for aggregating 142 categories of crop outputs and 30 categories of animal outputs into the total.

prices) during the 1970s and again in the present decade, but experienced a declining terms-of-trade in the 1980s and 1990s.

Table 7.2. Agricultural Indicators for sub-Saharan Africa

	1961-1970	1971-1980	1981-1990	1991-2000	2001-2005	2006-2008
Gross agricultural output (billions of US$)	33.7	41.3	49.6	0.1	86.7	97.6
Crop share of agricultural output (% of total)	76.7	76.1	74.4	77.6	77.7	78.0
Livestock share of agricultural output (% of total)	23.3	23.9	25.6	22.4	22.3	22.0
Growth in real agricultural output (average annual %)	3.02	1.17	2.88	3.16	3.47	2.43
Growth in real agricultural GDP (average annual %)	n.a.	3.02	2.15	2.95	3.19	3.52
Crop area harvested (million Ha)	92.7	99.8	109.7	147.2	169.0	186.5
Food crop share of total area harvested (% of total)	83.5	84.1	85.5	87.6	87.7	87.8
Cash crop share of total area harvested (% of total) [a]	16.5	15.9	14.5	12.4	12.3	12.2
Area in permanent crops (perennials) (million Ha)	12.6	14.9	17.2	18.8	20.4	21.9
Land in permanent pasture (million Ha)	704.4	707.7	714.4	731.5	745.0	748.1
Agricultural labor force (millions)	80.6	96.5	118.4	148.8	174.3	189.3
Agricultural output per worker (US$ per worker)	417.5	428.6	418.3	463.9	497.4	515.8
Growth in agricultural output per worker (average annual %)	1.56	-0.98	0.55	0.96	1.38	0.39
Crop output per ha harvested (US$ per Ha)	278.4	315.2	336.3	363.5	399.0	408.3
Growth in crop yield (average annual %)	1.26	0.77	0.81	1.14	0.27	1.38
Head of livestock (millions of cattle equivalents)	171.6	206.1	240.9	283.3	339.1	374.3
Ruminant livestock (% of total)	97.4	96.8	96.2	95.8	95.4	95.3
Non-ruminant livestock (% of total)	2.6	3.2	3.8	4.2	4.6	4.7
Animal output per head of cattle-equivalent (US$ per animal)	41.5	43.9	48.5	50.5	53.2	53.6
Growth in livestock yield (average annual %)	0.31	1.04	0.47	0.34	0.79	-0.36
Area harvested per worker (hectares)	1.15	1.04	0.93	0.99	0.97	0.99
Irrigated cropland (% of area harvested)	3.1	3.5	3.9	3.5	3.3	3.0
Fertilizer per area harvested (kg per hectare)	3.0	7.1	10.0	8.5	7.9	7.0
Tractors per area harvested (units per 1000 hectares)	0.7	0.9	1.0	0.9	0.9	0.9

Monetary values in constant US$ for the year 2000. Figures are aggregated for all countries in sub-Saharan Africa except South Africa. ha = hectares.
[a] Cash crops include cotton and other fibre crops, cocoa, coffee, tea, oil palm, rubber, tobacco and sugar cane.
Source: FAO, except growth in agricultural GDP (value-added), which is from the World Bank.

These estimates of agricultural production are based largely on FAO data, which in turn are either provided by national statistical authorities or estimated by FAO. The accuracy of the commodity production data, however, varies considerably from country to country and by commodity. It is generally better for widely traded commodities like cereal grains, oil-crops, and tropical perennials than for crops that are consumed locally, such as roots and tubers, vegetables and fruits. The only independent source of global agricultural statistics other than FAO is the Foreign Agricultural Service of the US Department of Agriculture (USDA) through its Production, Supply and Distribution (PSD) Online data set. The PSD estimates are compiled by the Agricultural Attachés assigned to US embassies and are based partly on official statistics and partly on expert opinion. However, the coverage of USDA's PSD is less comprehensive than FAOSTAT, providing information on production and area planted only for major cereals, oil-seeds, cotton, sugar, peanuts, and a few other internationally-traded commodities. Nonetheless, the USDA data at least provide a 'check' on the reliability of some of FAO's production figures.

The challenge in assessing agricultural trends in SSA can be illustrated by the case of Nigeria, the largest agricultural producer on the continent. FAO data show very little growth in agricultural output between 1961 and the mid-1980s, but then show output growing by an average of over 5 percent per year since then, with production increasing for a broad range of cereal grains, oil-seeds, and root and tuber crops. For cereal grains, USDA data confirm that production rose from about 9 million metric tons (mmt) per year in the mid-1980s to 24 mmt per year by the early 2000s. Field studies have also documented rapid growth in cereal production due to technical change and other factors, such as for maize in northern Nigeria (Smith *et al.,* 1994). For oil-crops, USDA and FAO production data track fairly closely until the 1990s and then diverge, with USDA data showing less than half the growth rate in vegetable oil production that FAO's data show since 1991. But the performance of Nigeria's agriculture since the mid-1980s is most affected by claims about the growth in root and tuber (mainly cassava and yam) production, which by the early 2000s accounted for 40 percent of FAO's gross value of Nigeria's agricultural output. Production of root and tuber crops is particularly difficult to measure because they are often grown as part of inter-cropping systems, a large share is for home consumption, and they are often harvested piecemeal (Norton, 1988). FAO data show annual production of root and tuber crops in Nigeria rising at an astounding rate from 17 mmt in 1981–1985 to 74 mmt in 2001–2005, or by nearly 9 percent per year. Although there is some field evidence of significant growth in the production of cassava *(Manihot esculenta)* caused by technical improvements and growth in commercial demand for processed *gari* (Nweke, 2004), there is virtually no evidence to corroborate the reported growth in output of yams *(Dioscorea spp.),* the principal root and tuber crop of Nigeria. In fact, in a review of constraints to yam production in Nigeria, Chukwu and Ikwelle (2000) predicted the crop's eventual demise due to its high demands on labor and fertile soil, little technical improvement, and competition from lower-cost foodstuffs. A new data set on crop production in Nigeria over the 1994–2005 period compiled by the International Institute for Tropical Agriculture (described in Oni *et al.,* 2009) confirms a divergence between cassava and yam crop performance in Nigeria—it has cassava production growing over these years at about the same rate as reported by FAO but shows yam production remaining essentially flat at about 25 mmt per annum since 1994.

On the input side, there is also considerable uncertainty regarding trends in agricultural employment in SSA. According to FAO, the number of people in SSA economically active in agriculture more than doubled between the 1960s and the 2000s (Table 7.2). The FAO figures refer to the stock of potential agricultural labor and not to actual hours worked in agricultural activities and are derived from UN projections of the total population, the labor force participation rate, and the share of the labor force employed in agriculture (based on national population censuses and labor force surveys). The FAO data indicate that the share of total labor employed in agriculture is falling over time and in a few cases—Nigeria in particular—the decline is quite significant. Again, one can question the assumptions upon which such a trend is based. Nigeria's last officially recognized population census dates from 1963. Censuses conducted in 1973 and 1991 were not considered to be reliable, although preliminary figures released from the 2006 census are considered plausible (Yin, 2007). FAO's estimates (2008 revision) of Nigeria's population are considerably lower than the 1963 census figure (48.2 million versus 55.7 million in the 1963 census) but are slightly higher than the 2006 census estimate (144.2 million versus 140.0 million in the 2006 census). More importantly for our purposes, FAO assumes that agriculture's share of the labor force in Nigeria fell from 72.4 percent in 1963 to 28.0 percent in 2006. Not only did the agricultural share of the total labor force fall precipitously, according to FAO, but farm labor has been falling in absolute numbers since 1970. It is rare to observe countries making such a labor force transition without major sustained gains in per capita GDP brought about from growth in industrial employment and urban wages (Johnston and Kilby, 1975; Dovring, 1978), neither of which appears to have occurred in Nigeria (Iyoha, 2007). In addition, the FAO figures imply that agricultural area harvested per worker in Nigeria more than doubled between the 1960s and early 2000s despite only very small gains in farm mechanization, although the use of animal plowing did expand in some northern tsetse-free areas of the country (Pingali, Bigot and Binswanger, 1987). Finally, the FAO figures appear to be at odds with the International Labour Organization's LABORSTA estimates, drawn from labor force surveys. The LABORSTA estimates, available for 1963 and 1986, show a much slower rate of decline in the agricultural labor share, from 56 percent to 43 percent, and imply that agricultural employment in absolute numbers of persons was still rising in the mid-1980s (LABORSTA). The pattern of a sharply declining employment share in agriculture extends to a few other small states in SSA (Gabon and Congo in Central Africa, and Namibia, Botswana, Lesotho and Swaziland in Southern Africa) but appears most difficult to reconcile with other evidence in the case of Nigeria, the most populous country in Africa.

The uncertainties regarding the FAO estimates of Nigeria's agricultural output and employment suggest the use of alternative data for these series. For output, this analysis uses USDA data for the production of grains, oil-seeds and major export crops; for root crops and grain legumes since 1994, I use Oni *et al.* (2009), and FAO for the other commodities or years. For agricultural labor, I assume a growth rate of 2 percent per year since 1961, using the LABORSTA estimates for 1963 to base the projection. According to this alternative measure, Nigeria's agricultural labor force grew from 9.5 million in 1961 to 24.1 million in 2006, while agriculture's share of the total labor force fell from 55.7 percent to 51.4 percent. The alternative series show slower output growth and more rapid input growth, and thus lower productivity growth, than the FAO data. Comparing the two estimates may provide a plausible range of measured changes in Nigeria's agricultural productivity; in the results section, both are reported.

Another source of uncertainty lies in the FAO figures for African cropland. FAO provides an estimate of 'arable land' (land cultivated in annual crops or in temporary fallow of one to two years) and area under 'permanent crops,' or perennials. However, one can also derive an estimate of cropland by summing up area harvested over all crop commodities.[50] Normally, we would expect the series on total cropland (arable land plus permanent crop land) and total area harvested to track each other or reflect the changing intensity of land use. But area harvested for SSA shows substantially more growth than the FAO cropland series, even though there is scant evidence that land cropping intensity has increased. While long fallows associated with swidden agricultural systems in SSA have almost certainly declined (Pingali, Bigot and Binswanger, 1987), the FAO cropland estimates by definition do not include land in long-term fallow. Furthermore, irrigated area, which could allow greater cropping intensity, has remained at only 3 to 4 percent of total cropland in SSA since the 1960s. I suspect that at least for some countries the FAO cropland data substantially underestimate the growth in actual area under cultivation. Nigeria, for example, increased its area harvested from 30 million hectares (mHa) to 41.9 mHa between 1961 and 2003, but the FAO cropland shows a change from 28.8 mHa to only 30.4 mHa over this period. Consequently, using the FAO cropland series would overstate productivity growth by attributing more of the observed increase in output to yield rather than area expansion. Therefore, I have chosen to use crop area harvested to indicate agricultural land area in the analysis of productivity trends (and reported in Table 7.2), unless otherwise noted. These data show that total crop area harvested in SSA increased from about 93 mHa in the 1960s to 186 mHa in 2006–2008 (Table 7.2). The share of cropland devoted to food crops slowly drifted upward from about 84 percent in the 1960s to 88 percent in the 2000s, with a declining share of land resources devoted to cash (export-oriented) crops.

Using the area harvested measure, average crop yield (in constant 2000 US$ per hectare) rose from $278/Ha in the 1960s to $408/Ha during 2006–2008 (Table 7.2). Trends in crop yield are difficult to discern both due to underlying problems regarding output and cropland data, and year-to-year variation due to weather. Between 1960 and 2000 the average annual rate of crop yield growth was only about 1 percent, far below the global average. It fell to 0.3 percent/year during 2001–2005 before recovering to 1.4 percent/year during 2006–2008. Animal yield, measured as $1000 of meat, milk, and egg output per head of livestock capital,[51] showed a small gain from $42/head in the 1960s to $54/head during 2006–2008. Not included in this measure is the insurance or manure value of livestock. Insurance is an important component of livestock value, especially in drought-prone areas (Binswanger and McIntire, 1987).

Two important forms of agricultural capital formation in SSA are the establishment of tree crop plantations (primarily in forest zones) and the building up of livestock herds (mainly in tsetse-free savannas and highlands). For tree capital, area planted expanded from 16.1 mHa

[50] Measuring area harvested in intercropping systems can be problematic and is often inferred from estimates of total production and average yield. Yield estimates may be derived from small plot samples and extrapolated based on assumptions about standard plant or tree density under monoculture. Thus, area harvested estimates for a commodity generally are designed to avoid counting areas multiple times when crops are grown simultaneously on the same field in intercropping systems.

[51] Livestock capital is measured in terms of 'cattle equivalents,' where each species is weighted by its size relative to cattle. I use the size weights suggested by Hayami and Ruttan (1985): camels=1.38, buffalo and horses=1.23, cattle and other equine species=1.00, pigs=0.25, sheep and goats=0.13, and poultry=0.0125. I have excluded the value of game meat from the measure of value of output per head of stock. In some countries, game meat accounts for more than half of the total value of animal output.

in the 1960s to 21.9 mHa in 2006–2008. About 60 percent of SSA's tree crop area lies in West Africa, where cocoa and oil palm are the predominant perennial commodities. Farm holdings of livestock capital increased from 172 million head in the 1960s to 374 million head in 2006–2008, with ruminant species making up over 95 percent of the total. The dominance of ruminants implies a reliance on pastures for feed with relatively little crop production diverted as feed for animals. FAO reports there are more than 700 mHa in permanent pastures in SSA, about four times the crop area. Most of the pastures are unimproved and lie in arid, semi-arid and savanna zones. Transhumance and nomadic pastoralism are common practices to address seasonal availability of green pastures, and access to these pasture lands and water are typically governed through historical claims by kinship groups. In some areas, encroachment of cultivators on nomadic grazing lands is a recurring source of conflict (Oba and Lusigi, 1987). However, McIntire, Bourzat and Pingali (1992) show that integrated crop-livestock farming has increased in relation to human population density on agricultural land. Cropland expansion, deforestation and removal of wildlife hosts reduce tsetse infestation and have enabled livestock husbandry to become more established in some areas, such as the sub-humid savanna belt of Nigeria (Bourn and Wint, 1994).

Land and labor productivity in SSA are compared with global trends in Figure 7.1. The figures are based on FAO data for agricultural output per hectare of crop and pasture land (on the Y-axis) and agricultural output per agricultural worker (on the X-Axis), aggregated for major world regions. Output is measured (in log scale) by applying the same set of prices in 2000 US$ to crop and livestock production in all countries. The horizontal dashed lines show the ratio of agricultural land to labor. Trends are estimated for each region taking five-year averages and plotting each average from 1961–1965 through 2006–2008.

The developed country regions show the highest levels of land and labor productivity having shifted their 'technology frontier' steadily outward over time. Similar rates of productivity growth were achieved in industrialized countries with very different relative land-to-labor resource endowments, represented at one extreme by Japan-Korea with only about 1 ha of agricultural land per worker and at another extreme by Australia-New Zealand with an average of 1000 ha per worker. Sub-Saharan Africa has shown relatively small gains in output per area and virtually no gains in output per worker over this 40-year period, and in fact has fallen further behind not only developed countries but also other developing regions. Note that Figure 7.1 shows that agricultural land per worker in the SSA region fell from 9 hectares to just under 5 hectares between 1961–1965 and 2001–2005. The area classified as permanent pasture by FAO (about 80 percent of total agricultural land in the region in 2005) has not changed appreciably over time, while cropland expanded roughly in parallel with agricultural population.

Measuring Total Factor Productivity

The trends in land and labor productivity described in the previous section are useful for indicating factor-saving biases in technical change but are likely to overstate the overall improvement in technology and production efficiency because they do not account for changes in other input use. For example, rising output per worker may follow from adoption of farm machinery, and higher crop yield may be due to application of more fertilizer. For this reason, a measure of total factor productivity (TFP) relating output to all of the inputs used in production gives a superior indicator of a sector's technological or efficiency improvement than indices of partial productivity.

Figure 7.1. International comparisons of agricultural land and labor productivity, 1961–1965 to 2006–2008

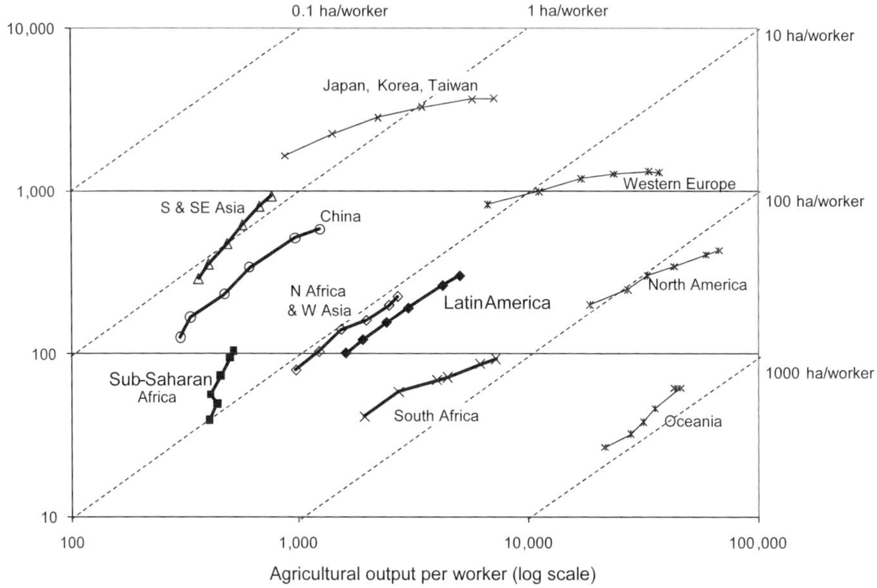

Notes: Ha = hectare. Agricultural output is measured as gross crop and livestock production valued at constant 2000 prices in US$. The curves show the progression in land and labor productivity for different global regions over time. Each hash-mark shows the output/worker and output/hectare combination (averaged over five-year periods) from 1961–1965, 1966–1970, ...2001–2005 and finally for 2006–2008. The dashed line shows the average agricultural area per worker. Agricultural area includes cropland and permanent pasture.
Source: derived from FAO data.

Attempts at measuring trends in TFP for agriculture in sub-Saharan Africa have been hampered by the lack of representative price data for farm inputs. Without reliable data on farm input costs, it is difficult to form an aggregate measure of input use, which is necessary for applying growth-accounting methods like that developed by Ball *et al.* (1985) for the United States. Instead, previous studies of total factor productivity in SSA agriculture have used either parametric estimation of production functions or nonparametric estimation of a Malmquist index. In the nonparametric approach, a solution to a linear program is found which measures each observation's distance from a technology frontier, the frontier being defined by those observations achieving the highest output level for a similar bundle of inputs. Lusigi and Thirtle (1997), Fulginiti, Perrin and Yu (2004), and Nin-Pratt and Yu (2008) all derived Malmquist indices in their studies of agricultural productivity in SSA countries. No assumptions about farmer behaviour, market structure or functional form are imposed on the model. An additional feature of this method is that one can decompose efficiency changes over time into the part due to shifts in the frontier (technical change) and the part due to moving closer to (or farther from) the frontier (efficiency change). The solution to the model also provides estimates of shadow prices for the production inputs. But results from this method are sensitive to dimensionality, or the number of countries and number of outputs and inputs included in the model (Coelli and Rao, 2005). Nin-Pratt and Yu (2008) have also pointed out that estimation often results in an implausibly large number of zero values for input shadow prices, implying, for example, that land and labor employed in agriculture have no opportunity cost. Results can also give TFP growth figures that seem implausibly negative or large (Lusigi and Thirtle, 1997).

Parametric approaches to productivity analysis usually involve choosing a functional form to link agricultural output to a set of production inputs and other factors. Applications of this approach to agriculture in SSA include the studies by Block (1995) and Frisvold and Ingram (1995). By making some basic assumptions about producer behavior and market structure, it is possible to draw inferences from these estimates about the level and direction of total factor productivity. Although this approach involves stronger technical and economic assumptions than nonparametric methods, it has the advantage of imposing more structure on the data. When the underlying data have a high degree of measurement error, this added structure can help produce more plausible results. In essence, economic theory is used to partially compensate for poor data.

The analysis in this chapter employs a parametric approach to examining agricultural productivity in SSA countries. One limitation of previous studies using parametric methods is that they are subject to simultaneous equations bias (the right-hand side explanatory variables—agricultural inputs—are endogenous choice variables). I employ an instrumental variables approach to estimate a Cobb-Douglas production function for a panel of SSA countries. Aggregate crop and livestock output is measured as a function of agricultural labor, non-agricultural labor, land, livestock (traditional farm-supplied inputs), machinery, inorganic fertilizer (modern, industrial inputs), and natural resource quality. The Cobb-Douglas functional form has the convenience of being linear in logs with parameters equal to production elasticities.[52]

Let Y represent output and X_i be input i, with subscript c indicating country and t time; then the Cobb-Douglas production function in log form is given by:

Equation 1:

$$\ln(Y_{ct}) = \ln(A_{ct}) + \sum_{i=1}^{n} \alpha_i \ln(X_{i,ct})$$

where the α_i's are production elasticities for n inputs and the A_{ct}'s are intercept terms (representing resource quality and technology differences over time and space) to be estimated. Factor-neutral improvements in technology or production efficiency over time imply more output is forthcoming from the same bundle of inputs. This would shift the production function upward and be seen as an increase in the value of intercept A_{ct}.

[52] The Cobb-Douglas form of the production function imposes the property that inputs have unitary elasticity of substitution, although intuitively we may think of machinery inputs as substituting more strongly for labor and fertilizer inputs more strongly for land. Hayami and Ruttan (1985) tested this assumption for a sample of developed and developing countries and found that the elasticity of substitution between labor and non-labor inputs in agricultural production was not significantly different from 1.00 (they lacked, however, sufficient price data to conduct multiple input substitution tests). They also found that agriculture in developing countries exhibited constant returns to scale and concluded there was no strong prima facie evidence against the use of the Cobb-Douglas form for estimating an agricultural production function with country-level data.

Differences in resource quality (some of which are observed) would also shift A_{ct}. These 'production function shifters' are modeled as follows:
Equation 2:

$$\ln(A_{ct}) = TFP_{ct} + \eta_c + \sum_{j=1}^{m} \beta_j Z_{j,ct} + \varepsilon_{ct} .$$

The first term, TFP_{ct}, is a country-specific index of technological change. The next two terms represent resource quality differences between countries, some of which may change over time: η_c is an unobserved and random country-specific effect, while the $Z_{j,ct}$s are observed differences in resource quality (their effect on output is given by the coefficients β_j). $Z_{j,ct}$ may change over time due to natural resource degradation or improvement, or may remain constant. The last term, ε_{ct}, is a purely random component capturing pure noise or measurement error. The random components of the model η_c and ε_{ct} are assumed to be independently distributed with zero means and positive variances σ_η^2 and σ_ε^2, respectively.

An index of TFP is given by the change in A_{ct} over time. Substituting Equation 2 into Equation 1 and taking the derivative with respect to time expresses output growth in terms of percentage changes in the variables:

Equation 3:

$$\frac{\partial \ln(Y_{ct})}{\partial t} = \frac{\partial TFP_{ct}}{\partial t} + \sum_{j=1}^{m} \beta_j \frac{\partial Z_{j,ct}}{\partial t} + \sum_{i=1}^{n} \alpha_i \frac{\partial \ln(X_{i,ct})}{\partial t} + \frac{\partial \varepsilon_{ct}}{\partial t} .$$

Solving for TFP_{ct} (and dropping the last term which due to the independence assumption on the random error terms has an expectation of zero) gives:

Equation 4:

$$\dot{TFP}_{ct} = \dot{Y}_{ct} - \sum_i \alpha_i \dot{X}_{i,ct} - \sum_j \beta_j \dot{Z}_{j,ct} \overline{Z}_{j,ct} .$$

where the dot above a variable signifies its growth rate and the bar its mean. Thus, the growth in TFP is just the difference between the growth in aggregate output and growth in aggregate input (where aggregate input growth is found by summing the growth rate of each input weighted by its production elasticity) minus the effects of any changes in resource quality.

Under certain economic assumptions, the production elasticities α_i's can be interpreted as cost shares, or the share of output that each input receives in payment for its services. Suppose the production function exhibits constant returns to scale, producers are price-takers for inputs and outputs, and they employ inputs up to the point where the value of their marginal product equals their price or opportunity cost, such that $P_Y \, \partial Y / \partial X_i = P_i$ for each X_i (where P_Y and P_i are prices or opportunity costs of output and input X_i, respectively). Multiplying both sides of this expression by Xi/Y gives $\frac{\partial Y}{\partial X_i}\frac{X_i}{Y} = \frac{P_i X_i}{P_Y Y}$, or $\alpha_i = S_i$, where S_i is the factor share of input X_i (constant returns to scale assures that the cost shares sum to one, so that total revenue equals total cost). In other words, the α_i's should all have values between 0 and 1 and their values indicate how output is distributed as payments to the inputs. In the case where labor, land and livestock capital are owned by the farmer, the factor share of these inputs is the return (share of revenue) a producer receives for supplying these inputs, while the factor shares of machinery and fertilizer are payments to industrial manufacturers. If wage labor is employed on farms or if land or livestock are held in tenancy, then the factor shares indicate the payments that the owners of these resources receive when inputs are paid their value-marginal products.

Once estimates of the α_i*'s (or* S_i*'s)* and β_j*'s* are available, it is straightforward to construct an index of TFP for each country from Equation 4. These parameter estimates are found by estimating Equation 1 from the panel data from SSA countries over the 1961–2006 period. To reduce the multicollinearity problem, the output and inputs are divided by input X_1 (or equivalently, $ln(X_{1,ct})$ is subtracted from each side of the equation). The resulting estimation model is then:

Equation 5:

$$\ln\left(\frac{Y_{ct}}{X_{1,ct}}\right) = A + \sum_{i=2}^{n}\alpha_i \ln\left(\frac{X_{i,ct}}{X_{1,ct}}\right) + \sum_{j=1}^{m}\beta_j Z_{j,ct} + \eta_c + \varepsilon_{ct}.$$

(An intercept A term is included to assure that the expected mean of η_c is zero). Because returns to scale are assumed to be constant, the coefficient on X_1 can easily be recovered from the parameter estimates by $\hat{\alpha}_1 = 1 - \sum_{i=2}^{n}\hat{\alpha}_i$.

The econometric procedure used to estimate Equation 5 is a random effects model with instrumental variables. I estimate two sets of regressions, one with all 48 countries of SSA, which includes South Africa and a number of small continental and island states. The second set of regressions omits South Africa, 15 small countries with a 2004 population of under 2 million (this excludes all of the island states as well as eight small continental countries), and four countries with particularly unreliable data (Angola, the Democratic Republic of Congo, Nigeria, and Somalia). Once the production elasticities in Equation 5 are estimated, these are used to aggregate inputs and construct TFP indexes for each country and region in SSA. The SSA countries and their regional groupings are shown in Table 7.3. Due to its size, I consider Nigeria as its own region.

Instruments are used for (potentially) endogenous X and Z variables in Equation 5 in order to avoid potential endogeneity bias in the estimates. Since producers decide how much to allocate to production inputs and invest in resource improvements, these variables may be correlated with the unobserved error term ε_{ct}. For example, farmers with relatively good soil and climate conditions may use fertilizer more intensively and obtain higher average yields than farmers in a more arid region. But the higher yields are only partly due to fertilizer; the resource quality conditions also contribute independently to yield. But as environmental factors are not fully observed in the model, the error term ε_{ct} may be correlated with the X and Z variables.

For instruments I use a measure of population pressure on cropland (explained below), indexes of global agricultural output and input prices, and lagged values of the X and Z variables to capture unobserved country-specific factors. Boserup (1965) hypothesized that input intensity would rise with population pressure on agricultural land, so we can expect input use to be influenced by land scarcity and relative prices. However, simple measures of a country's population density can significantly misrepresent actual land scarcity if soil quality and climate are not considered (Binswanger and Pingali, 1988).

Table 7.3. Countries Included in Productivity Analysis

Regions						
Nigeria	**Western**	**Sahel**	**Central**	**Eastern**	**Horn**	**Southern**
Nigeria	Benin	Burkina Faso	Cameroon	Burundi	Ethiopia & Eritrea[a]	Angola
	Côte d'Ivoire	Chad	Cent. African Rep.	Kenya	Somalia	Madagascar
	Ghana	Mali	Congo	Rwanda	Sudan	Malawi
	Guinea	Mauritania	DRC	Tanzania	Djibouti [s]	Mozambique
	Liberia	Niger	Eq. Guinea [s]	Uganda		Zambia
	Sierra Leone	Senegal	Gabon [s]	Seychelles [s]		Zimbabwe
	Togo	Cape Verde [s]	Sao Tome & Principe [s]			Botswana [s]
	Guinea-Bissau [s]	Gambia [s]				Comoros [s]
						Lesotho [s]
						Mauritius [s]
						Namibia [s]
						Réunion [s]
						Swaziland [s]

[s] = small state with total population under 2 million in 2004.
[a] To maintain a consistent historical time series, agricultural output and input data for Ethiopia and Eritrea are aggregated in the analysis.

To account for population pressure on agricultural land, I use Higgins *et al.*'s (1983) measure of *agroclimatic population density* as an instrument for input use in Equation 5. To derive this measure Higgins *et al.* (1983) estimated the potential population carrying capacity of each country (assuming three levels of technology—low, intermediate and high) given a country's endowments of land area, soil quality, rainfall, and irrigation as of 1975. I divide the FAO estimate of each country's population in year *t* with the population-carrying capacity using intermediate technology as an index of population pressure on land in year *t*. For the influence of prices on input use, I construct global price indexes for agricultural output, fertilizer and farm machinery. For output, I divide the Grilli-Yang agricultural commodity price index (Pfaffenzeller, Newbold, and Rayner, 2007) by the IMF's MUV price index to capture trends in the terms of trade between agricultural and manufactured goods. For fertilizer input, I use the US fertilizer price index (Economic Research Service), and for farm machinery I derive a tractor export price index from FAO tractor export quantities and value series for major tractor-exporting nations. Both the fertilizer and machinery price indexes are divided by the Grilli-Yang commodity price index to reflect trends in input prices relative to output prices. For other country-specific factors (like policy and infrastructure that influence divergence between global and domestic prices), I include four lagged values of the X and Z variables as instruments (I also include current and lagged variables of the population density and price instruments). Since data for all variables in the model cover the 1961–2008 period, with four lags included as instruments, the model is estimated over 1965–2008. The STATA *xtivreg* procedure was used for the estimation of the random effects with the instrumental variables model.

The data for estimating Equation 5 are from FAO, with the following modifications. For output, I use the FAO gross agricultural output series.[53] The econometric model is estimated using these data, but for constructing TFP indexes I smoothed the output series for each country using the Hodrick-Prescott filter, choosing a *lambda* value of 6.25 as is recommended for annual observations (Ravn and Uhlig, 2002). Smoothing the output series helps to isolate long-term trends in output and productivity from short-run fluctuations due to weather and other shocks.

The production inputs X included in the model are agricultural labor, cropland harvested, number of livestock (representing farm-supplied inputs), the number of tractors in use, and the quantity of inorganic fertilizers applied (representing modern industrial inputs). Labor is chosen to be X_1 in Equation 4, so that the Y and other X variables are measured as output and input per worker and the labor variable itself is omitted from the regression.

For agricultural labor I use the FAO estimates of the number of economically active males and females employed in agriculture for all countries except Nigeria, where I experiment with two values—the FAO estimate and my own estimate described in the previous section. For agricultural land I use the FAO estimate of crop area harvested rather than the FAO cropland series for reasons discussed previously. I have not included pasture area because I assume that from a farmer's perspective this is seen as a fixed resource (and the data show very little variability at the national level over time). Rather, the producer decision to increase animal output rests with expanding the herd. Livestock (in cattle equivalents) as well as the number of tractors in use are from FAO. For fertilizer consumption I use the more up-to-date annual data available from the International Fertilizer Association's IFADATA database for the 12 largest fertilizer users in SSA and FAO for the other countries. These 12 countries account for about 85 percent of fertilizer use in the region.

The natural resource quality variables (vector Z) in Equation 5 are based on the farming systems typology developed by the International Food Policy Research Institute (IFPRI) as reported in Sebastian (2007). The typology classifies agricultural land into the share that is either irrigated,[54] in good rain-fed areas, or in less favourable rain-fed areas. The shares of total cropland in each of these categories are derived from the Agro-ecological Zones (AEZ) methodology developed by FAO and the International Institute for Applied Systems Analysis. Their methodology provides a standardized framework for incorporating climate, soil and terrain conditions relevant to agricultural production. Good rain-fed areas are defined as agricultural lands[55] with a growing season of at least 150 days

---

[53] The FAO output series is calculated from a set of reference prices for crop and livestock commodities valued in constant 2000 US dollars using prices from the 1999–2001 period. FAO derives these prices using the Geary-Khamis method, in which each commodity price is calculated by dividing the total value of output of the commodity across all countries, converted to international dollars at purchasing power parity, by the total quantity produced of the commodity (Rao, 1993).

[54] FAO data actually refer to areas 'equipped for irrigation' which is generally larger than actual area receiving irrigation. However, estimates of irrigated area may differ depending on definitions used. FAO irrigation data appears to include area served by public irrigation schemes, private or community tubewell, weir, and shaduf irrigation, as well as areas equipped for spate irrigation. It does not appear to include the large areas under *fadama* farming, or controlled lowland flooding. For example, irrigated area for Nigeria is reported by FAO to be 245,000 hectares in 2000, which would exclude an estimated 724,000 hectares under fadama farming (International Commission on Irrigation and Drainage).

[55] Agricultural areas, or the 'global extent of agriculture' is determined from satellite imagery and climate data. It is defined as all areas with 10 percent or greater cropland, grazing land, or irrigated area net of areas with a growing period of zero days (Sebastian, 2007).

per year and with relatively flat terrain. Less favourable rain-fed areas are agricultural lands with a growing season of less than 150 days per year or with relatively hilly or rough terrain. The data describe agricultural land qualities as they existed around the year 2000. To derive a time series of land qualities, which may change due to investments in irrigation, I assume that irrigated areas in SSA lie primarily in regions that would otherwise be less-favourable rain-fed areas. I calculate the share of cropland harvested that is irrigated for each year and country from FAO. An increase (decrease) in the share of irrigated cropland is then treated as a decrease (increase) in the share of less-favourable cropland. The share of cropland in good rain-fed areas is assumed to remain constant over time. The rationale for this assumption is based on the observation that most irrigated areas in sub-Saharan Africa fall within arid or semi-arid areas (with growing seasons in the absence of irrigation of less than 150 days). Major irrigated areas include the Nile diversion schemes in the Sudan, the inland delta of the Niger River in Mali, the Senegal River irrigation schemes on the Senegal-Mauritania border, the weir diversion projects along the rivers flowing through northern Nigeria, Somalia, Kenya, and South Africa, and the irrigated rice schemes of northern and central Madagascar. All of these areas, with the possible exception of Madagascar, lie in semi-arid or arid zones. Irrigation depends on highly seasonal river flows and the cropping intensity of areas equipped for irrigation is usually substantially below 1.00.

Sources of Agricultural Growth

Production Function Estimates

Table 7.4 presents the estimates of the agricultural production function for SSA countries. The table also shows the production elasticity for labor implied by constant returns to scale. The first column of estimates shows the results for the random effects with the instrumental variables (REIV) model, first for the full sample of 48 countries and then for a selected sample of 28 countries, which excludes 15 small states with populations under 2 million, South Africa, and four other states with questionable data quality (Angola, Democratic Republic of Congo, Nigeria, and Somalia). The estimation procedure for this model requires that the variance-covariance matrix be homoskedastic (constant variance across all observations). However, if the variance is non-constant the consequence is that the estimated standard errors could be low, exaggerating the level of statistical significance (the coefficient estimates, however, would still be unbiased). I also estimated a random effects (RE) model allowing for heteroskedasticity using the Huber-White sandwich estimator. This model provides more reliable standard errors but does not have the instrumental variables procedure to control for possible endogeneity of the explanatory variables.

For the full sample of countries, the estimated production elasticities are all highly significant and economically plausible (Table 7.4a). In addition, the two estimation methods give similar results, including the estimates of standard errors. The fact that instrumental variables did not significantly change the parameter values suggests that endogeneity is not a serious problem and the assumption of homoskedastic structure for the variance-covariance matrix may be innocuous. The overall R^2's from the REIV model indicates that the input variables plus country-specific effects explain about 70 percent of the variation in output within countries as well as the variation in output across countries.

The estimated variances ($\sigma_{\eta}^{2} = 0.392$ for cross-country effects and $\sigma_{\varepsilon}^{2} = 0.130$ for other random effects) indicate that unspecified country differences are the largest component of residual error in the model.

The regression estimates for the sample of 28 large developing countries (Table 7.4b) are also all statistically significant. The estimated production elasticity of labor is about twice the value, and the elasticity for farm machinery about half the value of the estimates from the full sample of countries. Several of the countries omitted from this model (such as South Africa, Mauritius, Reunion, Namibia, and Botswana) have relative high per capita income and farm mechanization levels. It is not surprising, then, that excluding these countries from the regression implies higher factor payments for labor and a smaller role for machinery.

Table 7.4. Regression Estimates of an Agricultural Production Function for SSA

7.4a. Full sample of 48 countries

Model	**Random Effects with Inst. Var.** [a]		**Random Effects**	
Number of observations	2016		2208	
Number of countries	48		48	
Obs per country	42		46	
VC matrix estimation [b]	Homoskedasticity assumed		Huber-White sandwich estimator [c]	
Variable	**Prod. elasticity**	**Std. Error *****	**Prod. elasticity**	**Std. Error *****
Production function variables				
Labor [d]	0.121		0.130	
Crop area harvested	0.415	0.013	0.428	0.013
Animal stocks	0.375	0.011	0.373	0.011
Tractor machinery	0.051	0.007	0.037	0.006
Fertilizers	0.039	0.004	0.032	0.004
Resource quality variables				
Irrigated cropland (%)	0.854	0.131	0.807	0.217
High rainfall cropland (%)	0.970	0.122	0.989	0.081
R^2 within	0.706		0.692	
R^2 between	0.700		0.970	
R^2 overall	0.700		0.672	
Wald $chi^2(4)$	4518.01		14525.31	
Prob > chi^2	0.00		0.00	
σ_η (inter-country effects)	0.392		0.390	
σ_ε (purely random effects)	0.130		0.135	

7.4b. Selected sample of 28 countries

Model	**Random Effects with Inst. Var.** [a]		**Random Effects**	
Number of observations	1176		1288	
Number of countries	28		28	
Obs per country	42		46	
VC matrix estimation [b]	Homoskedasticity assumed		Huber-White sandwich estimator [c]	
Variable	**Prod. elasticity**	**Std. Error *****	**Prod. elasticity**	**Std. Error *****
Production function variables				
Labor [d]	0.248		0.216	
Crop area harvested	0.315	0.021	0.358	0.020
Animal stocks	0.357	0.026	0.360	0.014
Tractor machinery	0.024	0.007	0.024	0.006
Fertilizers	0.055	0.005	0.042	0.004
Variable	**Prod. elasticity**	**Std. Error *****	**Prod. elasticity**	**Std. Error *****
Resource quality variables				
Irrigated cropland (%)	0.680	0.137	0.782	0.080
High rainfall cropland (%)	1.245	0.134	1.242	0.211
R^2 within	0.520		0.549	
R^2 between	0.451		0.445	
R^2 overall	0.456		0.455	
Wald $chi^2(4)$	1119.76		11771.72	
Prob > chi^2	0.00		0.00	
σ_η (inter-country effects)	0.297		0.296	
σ_ε (purely random effects)	0.112		0.112	

*** All estimated coefficients are significantly different from 0 at the 1% significance level
[a] South Africa, Nigeria, Congo DR, Angola, Somalia and 15 small countries omitted.
[b] Instrumental variables include current and four lagged values of a measure of population pressure on cropland, indexes of real global fertilizer, tractor and agricultural commodity prices, and four lagged values of explanatory variables (see text).
[c] The Huber-White sandwich estimators provides heteroskedasticity-consistent standard errors.
[d] The production elasticity of labor is estimated as a residual assuming constant returns to scale, so that the sum of elasticities = 1.00.
Source: Author's estimates.

The natural resource quality variables are significant and the coefficient values similar across the models. Under the model assumptions, the coefficients indicate the productivity of irrigated and high rainfall cropland relative to less favourable cropland. For the REIV model estimated with the full set of countries, one hectare of irrigated land had on average 85 percent higher output and high-rainfall land 97 percent higher yield compared to less favourable cropland. In other words, equipping less favourable land with irrigation raised its productivity to almost that of high-rainfall areas. These productivity improvements are often achieved by switching to higher-valued crops like cotton, sugar cane, or rice, which could not otherwise be profitably grown in these areas. The fact that few irrigated hectares in SSA are double-cropped lends plausibility to these parameter estimates having similar values.

For the purposes of agricultural TFP estimation, I chose to represent production elasticities or factor shares by the estimates of the REIV model for the set of 28 large countries in Table 7.4b. These are probably more representative of the large developing countries in the SSA region, although the estimates from all of the models are close enough to yield similar trends in TFP. These estimates give the production elasticity of labor a value of 0.25, for land a value of 0.32, and for livestock 0.36. In other words, a 10 percent increase in one of these inputs (holding other inputs constant) would raise aggregate output by about 3 percent. The elasticities on the modern inputs of fertilizer and farm machinery are considerably smaller—only 0.06 for fertilizer and 0.02 for tractors. A 10 percent increase in fertilizer use would raise output only by 0.6 percent. Getting a more powerful supply response from large increases in fertilizer use would likely require complementary investment in irrigation, adoption of better soil and water management practices and access to improved crop varieties (Morris *et al.*, 2007).

It is possible to get a sense of the plausibility of these estimates by comparing them with similar estimates from other developing countries. Fuglie (2008) compared factor share estimates from India, Indonesia, China and Brazil for the same five classes of inputs used in this study (land, labor, livestock-related inputs, farm machinery, and agricultural chemicals), and found general similarity in shares across these four large developing countries. The land-cost share for these four countries ranged from 0.22 to 0.30, and the land production elasticity estimated for sub-Saharan Africa falls within this range. The labor share among the four countries was somewhat higher than in SSA (ranging from 0.37 to 0.46, compared with 0.28 for SSA) and the livestock share somewhat lower (ranging from 0.15 to 0.29, compared with 0.33 in SSA). The production elasticities estimated for sub-Saharan Africa fit the general pattern of input cost shares found for the other four countries, with labor, land and livestock accounting for about 90 percent and modern inputs only about 10 percent of production costs.

Indexes of Total Factor Productivity

Agricultural TFP indexes for the entire sub-continent as well as regions are given in Figure 7.2. The indexes are set to 100 for 1961 for each region, so changes to the index reflect changes in TFP relative to 1961. During the first two and a half decades of the post-independence period, agricultural TFP grew very slowly in SSA as a whole (only 0.2 percent per annum between 1961 and 1984), and this growth was dominated by productivity improvement in eastern and southern African countries. Between 1985 and 2008, there was a noticeable increase in the rate of TFP growth in SSA, to 1.3 percent per year, and now the leading regions were western Africa and Nigeria. Using the revised estimates for agricultural labor in Nigeria significantly reduced its TFP growth rate, although TFP growth was still substantially better than elsewhere in SSA (and measured 1.1 percent per year for the SSA region during 1985–2008 using the revised data for Nigeria). Since the 1990s there has also been TFP growth in southern Africa (led principally by Mozambique and Angola as peace was restored in these countries), the Horn of Africa (Ethiopia and Sudan) and the Sahel.

There is a growing body of evidence from field studies on the impact of agricultural technology diffusion that lends support to the TFP growth patterns observed in Figure 7.2.

During the 1970s and 1980s, there were significant improvements in maize productivity in several eastern and southern African countries led by the adoption of improved varieties and supportive government policies (Byerlee and Eicher, 1997). Maize is the dominant crop in this part of Africa, and growth in maize productivity could explain the better-than-average agricultural TFP growth observed in eastern and southern Africa during these decades. However, the maize success story was not sustained when government support waned in the 1990s (Smale and Jayne, 2003); this is consistent with the lower TFP growth observed for these regions in Figure 7.2. In West Africa (including Nigeria), three well-documented cases of successful technological innovations include maize (Smith *et al.*, 1994), cassava (Nweke, 2004) and rice (Dalton and Guei, 2003). All three are major crops in the region, and the timing of the diffusion of productivity-enhancing innovations (after 1980) corresponds with the increase in TFP growth observed for western Africa and Nigeria in Figure 7.2.

Figure 7.2a. Agricultural TFP indexes for SSA regions, 1961-2008 (Index, 1961=100)

7.2a. Sahel, Horn, and Central Africa

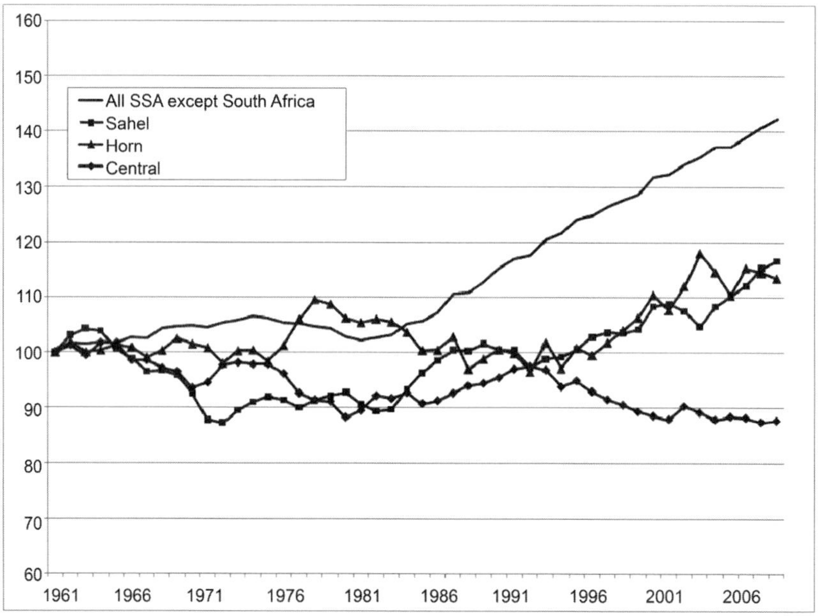

Source for Figures 7.2a, b, and c: Author's estimates.

In the 1990s, further technological improvements in sorghum production occurred in the Sahel-Sudan belt, where sorghum is a major food staple (Deb and Bantilan, 2003). This is again consistent with the TFP patterns observed for these regions in the figure, although this could also be influenced by a favourable weather trend in the Sahel (Olsson, Eklundh and Ardö, 2005). Agricultural productivity in the Sahel and Guinea savanna has also benefitted from gradual diffusion of animal traction (Smith *et al.*, 1994; Starkey, 2000) and improved natural resource management (Reij, Tappan and Smale, 2009).

Figure 7.2b. Western Africa and Nigeria

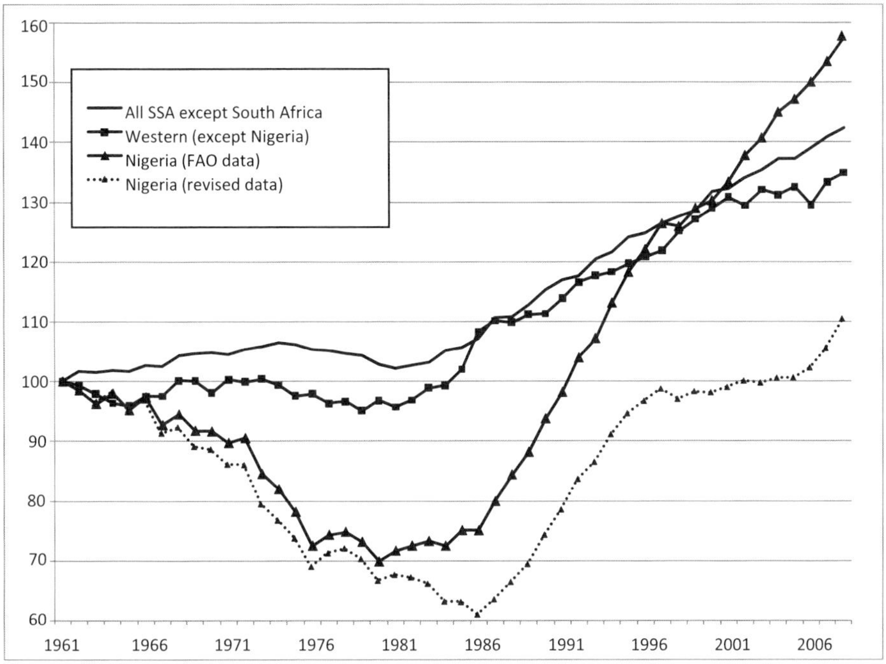

Figure 7.2c. Southern and Eastern Africa

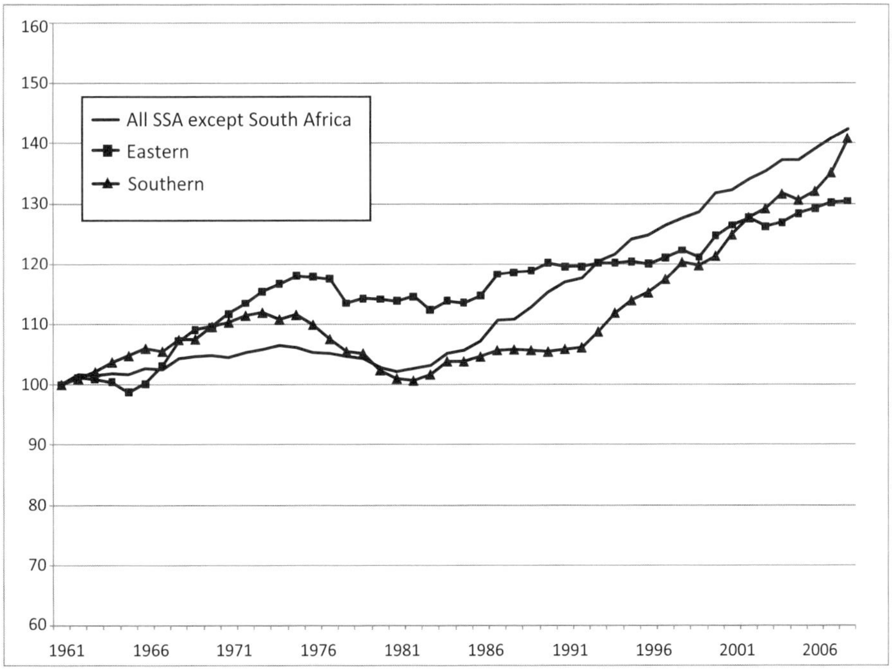

Indexes of agricultural output and total factor productivity for each SSA country and region are given in Table 7.5. For SSA countries as a whole, agricultural output grew by 241 percent (229 percent using revised data for Nigeria) between 1961 and 2008 (from an index value of 100 to 341), while TFP grew by 34 percent (26 percent with the revised data). The difference between output and TFP growth is the rate of growth in aggregate inputs (land, labor, livestock, machinery and fertilizer). Growth in these conventional factors of production accounted for 86 percent of total output growth over the entire period. This is a far larger share than for most developing countries. A recent study by Fuglie (2008) found that for developing countries as a whole, growth in inputs accounted for about 40 percent of the increase in agricultural output between 1961 and 2006, with TFP improvements responsible for the other 60 percent, and with the TFP share of output growth rising over time.

Among individual SSA countries, only a few appear to have been able to achieve sustained growth in TFP over a long period, and several have shown productivity regressions. Kenya and Swaziland are two countries in SSA (other than South Africa) that have had sustained, long-term growth in agricultural TFP since the 1960s. Kenya's agricultural TFP increased by 67 percent between 1961 and 2008, meaning that a given bundle of agricultural resources (land, labor, capital, materials, etc.) produced 67 percent more crops and livestock in 2008 than in 1961. A few other countries appeared to enter a sustained agricultural TFP growth path in the 1980s and 1990s. These include Benin, Ghana, Malawi, and Zambia. Each of these countries increased its TFP by at least 30 percent between 1980 and 2008. A few countries appeared to be on a sustained TFP growth path but then saw productivity stagnate or decline. Cote d'Ivoire and Zimbabwe had positive TFP growth beginning in the 1960s, but Zimbabwe went into sharp productivity regression beginning around 1997, while Cote D'Ivoire's productivity stagnated after 2000. In both countries, these reversals in TFP growth correlated with periods of political instability and/or poor macroeconomic management. Another set of countries, notably Mozambique and Angola after 1991, showed strong TFP growth (or TFP recovery) following periods of productivity regression that took place during times of prolonged war or civil unrest. Finally, a number of countries in SSA have shown no significant change in agricultural TFP over the past 50 years. Countries in Central Africa, the Horn of Africa, most small island states, and scattered other countries fall into this 'no growth' category. The outcome for Nigeria—the largest state in SSA, accounting for about one-fourth of the region's agricultural output—is uncertain. Using FAO's data, Nigeria appears to be a star performer, increasing its agricultural TFP by 54 percent over 1961–2008. But with the revised data for Nigeria's agricultural output and labor force growth, the change in TFP measures is only 8 percent over these years.

While declining rates of agricultural productivity can sometimes be directly linked to periods of political unrest or poor governance, another source of productivity regression may be natural resource degradation. Stoorvogel and Smaling (1990) and Henao and Baanante (2006) found that soil nutrient balances in most SSA countries have been negative since at least the 1980s (meaning that more nutrients were being removed from soil than were being replenished from inorganic and organic sources). However, negative nutrient balances are not atypical of areas where swidden agriculture is commonly practiced, as in much of SSA. Moreover, the data used to estimate soil nutrient balances are of varying degrees of quality (data on inorganic fertilizer use, for example, is available only at the national level).

Table 7.5. Agricultural Output and TFP Indexes for Countries and Regions in sub-Saharan Africa

	Avg Output	Gross Agricultural Output Index						Agricultural Total Factor Productivity Index					
	2006-2008	(1961=100)						(1961=100)					
	(bil. US$)	1971	1981	1991	2001	2005	2008	1971	1981	1991	2001	2005	2008
Central Africa	**6.53**	**129**	**156**	**200**	**206**	**215**	**220**	**93**	**87**	**94**	**85**	**85**	**85**
Cameroon	2.61	151	178	213	294	326	332	103	95	103	115	118	121
Cent. Afr. Rep.	0.67	136	172	208	296	314	336	91	84	94	111	112	110
Congo	0.24	121	138	158	203	231	248	83	89	85	92	126	115
Congo, DR	2.76	121	147	199	157	155	157	88	89	94	89	94	81
Gabon	0.20	119	163	208	242	245	250	108	89	91	103	94	93
Eastern Africa	**16.63**	**151**	**177**	**232**	**284**	**321**	**342**	**110**	**112**	**116**	**122**	**123**	**125**
Burundi	0.71	122	135	174	160	170	172	85	88	90	88	82	78
Kenya	4.80	135	195	292	350	408	446	101	122	132	144	155	167
Rwanda	1.45	146	216	246	272	317	341	95	113	99	106	96	81
Tanzania	4.78	140	198	242	301	368	403	100	112	118	128	131	139
Uganda	4.88	177	152	200	263	273	277	128	129	129	127	121	107
Horn	**13.92**	**128**	**156**	**166**	**240**	**274**	**291**	**98**	**102**	**97**	**101**	**101**	**105**
Ethiopia, former	6.45	120	137	146	198	241	272	87	98	90	92	97	102
Somalia	1.23	142	185	180	204	211	209	109	111	114	126	120	125
Sudan	6.19	134	173	187	307	338	342	93	87	88	100	100	104
Sahel	**8.74**	**138**	**145**	**165**	**214**	**232**	**252**	**107**	**98**	**102**	**119**	**123**	**132**
Burkina Faso	1.80	129	158	289	436	525	557	86	79	95	121	104	105
Chad	1.13	104	111	147	215	233	237	85	91	93	97	96	93
Gambia	0.10	126	107	100	140	144	140	84	60	47	54	46	43
Mali	2.01	124	167	225	299	349	394	78	93	109	113	115	120
Mauritania	0.34	109	121	141	169	183	189	89	96	94	96	98	99
Niger	2.30	123	159	181	297	368	478	76	67	75	82	91	100
Senegal	1.02	95	101	115	131	134	158	73	72	73	68	67	72
Southern Africa	**10.62**	**113**	**134**	**175**	**246**	**284**	**323**	**87**	**89**	**94**	**100**	**101**	**106**
Angola	1.55	136	95	106	180	235	268	79	55	57	82	92	93
Botswana	0.17	145	150	170	158	169	176	126	108	134	105	117	114
Lesotho	0.09	112	122	125	143	135	123	87	92	93	82	89	80
Madagascar	2.19	129	148	173	179	198	210	100	96	102	103	103	108
Malawi	2.06	151	210	240	406	458	597	106	109	106	162	158	208
Mauritius	0.18	119	123	136	147	150	145	111	115	116	116	120	113
Mozambique	1.53	138	121	107	186	209	220	103	76	76	88	97	95
Namibia	0.29	148	128	136	131	130	134	131	118	114	95	80	96
Swaziland	0.19	152	218	261	243	263	267	143	180	193	209	216	227
Zambia	0.92	144	166	237	286	347	372	105	110	119	138	160	162
Zimbabwe	1.27	148	172	204	254	208	191	106	109	116	127	118	107
Western Africa	**13.34**	**136**	**162**	**234**	**348**	**390**	**423**	**99**	**94**	**110**	**126**	**127**	**129**
Benin	1.39	126	155	272	479	511	496	91	96	122	150	172	160
Côte d'Ivoire	4.52	162	254	352	484	509	543	101	105	108	133	128	134
Ghana	4.49	131	111	185	316	377	422	88	63	93	115	124	129
Guinea	1.36	119	138	184	257	296	338	100	107	117	108	109	110
Guinea-Bissau	0.19	76	105	143	201	224	243	78	69	91	87	95	96
Liberia	0.26	148	186	144	201	213	237	97	94	97	108	108	103
Sierra Leone	0.54	132	149	174	160	242	300	100	90	90	90	102	111
Togo	0.58	125	140	198	277	286	297	91	83	75	84	79	78

	Avg Output 2006-2008 (bil. US$)	Gross Agricultural Output Index (1961=100) 1971	1981	1991	2001	2005	2008	Agricultural Total Factor Productivity Index (1961=100) 1971	1981	1991	2001	2005	2008
Nigeria	**27.85**	**132**	**124**	**238**	**361**	**426**	**467**	**89**	**73**	**97**	**131**	**144**	**154**
Nigeria (revised*)	23.61	129	125	215	319	354	405	85	69	77	97	98	108
All SSA	97.61	134	150	204	278	315	341	102	101	113	126	129	134
All SSA (revised*)	93.37	133	150	199	269	301	329	102	100	108	119	121	126
South Africa	**9.28**	**134**	**167**	**181**	**211**	**226**	**244**	**101**	**106**	**134**	**177**	**206**	**215**

* Revised data for Nigeria uses alternative measure of output and agricultural labor. Output data uses USDA data for grains, oilseed and cash crops, national data on roots & tubers and legumes (reported in Oni *et al.*, 2009) since 1994, and FAO data otherwise. The agricultural labor series uses FAO data for 1961 and assumes 2% annual growth for subsequent years, about the same rate of growth as the total labor force.
Source: Author's estimates.

The actual prevalence of significant, long-term land degradation is unknown, but the (albeit slow) increases in TFP reported in Table 7.5 for most regions does not suggest that long-term land degradation is pervasive in the sub-continent. Declining land quality is likely to be of greatest concern in regions of high population density and fragile soils, such as the Lake Victoria basin and Central African and Ethiopian highlands.

Decomposing Sources of Growth

Another way of portraying sources of agricultural growth is to decompose growth into 'extensification,' or land expansion, and 'intensification,' or yield growth. A schematic of this decomposition is shown in Figure 7.3. In the figure, growth in the value of output or sector GDP is first decomposed into changes due to terms-of-trade effects and changes due to growth in production, or real output. Growth in production is then further decomposed into growth due to expanding agricultural land and the growth in output per unit of area, or yield. Finally, yield growth is decomposed into the shares due to input intensification (i.e., more capital, labor, and fertilizer per hectare of land), and TFP, where TFP reflects the overall efficiency with which the inputs are used, including the effects of technical change. Decomposing yield growth in this way is intuitively appealing and has some direct relevance for policy as well: input intensification is strongly influenced by changes in resource endowments and relative prices. Increases in population density or higher crop prices can induce more intensive use of existing farmland and investments in land improvement (Boserup, 1965), but in the short run the ability to raise yields through intensification is largely confined to existing technology. Changes in TFP, on the other hand, are driven by changes in technology and allocative efficiency. The rate of TFP growth will be more influenced by investments in agricultural research, extension, and rural schooling. Market liberalization and increased commercialization can also be sources of TFP growth as producers shift resources to produce commodities in which they have a comparative advantage.

Figure 7.3. Decomposing agricultural growth

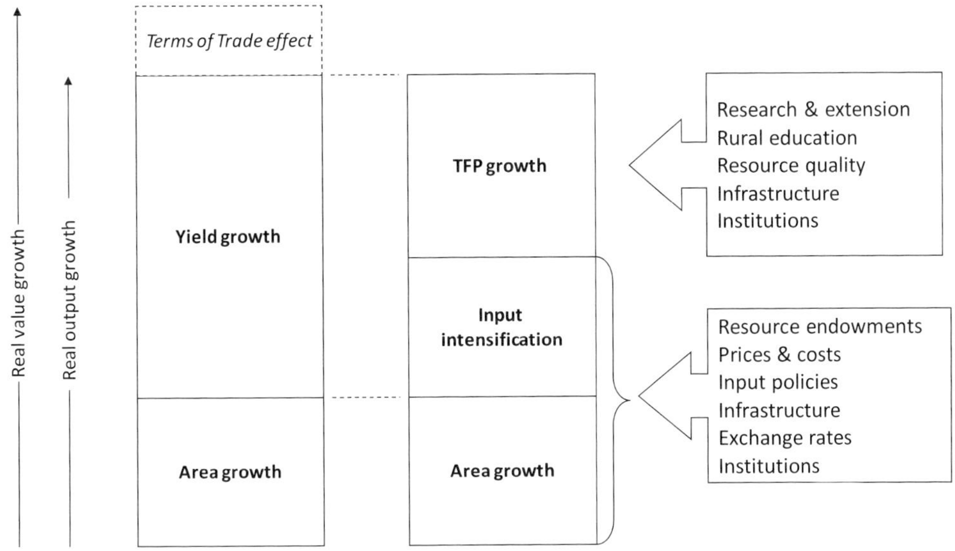

Table 7.6 shows the results of this decomposition of real output growth for the SSA region as a whole by decade since 1961 and breaks out the current decade into the pre- and post-crisis years. In each decade, inflation-adjusted agricultural GDP growth averaged at least 2 percent per year, with growth in the current decade accelerating to over 3 percent per year. However, the acceleration in agricultural GDP growth since 2006 is almost entirely a terms-of-trade effect, reflecting the surging prices of agricultural commodities. Growth in gross agricultural output actually fell slightly in 2006–2008 from previous periods to only about 2.5 percent per year. Just over 30 percent of the growth in agricultural GDP during 2006–2008 was due to higher prices (terms of trade) and the rest to rising real output. Resource expansion (increases in agricultural land and input intensification) accounted for 42 percent of total GDP growth, with improvements to TFP accounting for the remaining 27 percent. Given the cyclical behavior of commodity prices, current rates of agricultural GDP are unlikely to be maintained or even regress. Since around the 1980s there has been some improvement in the rate of TFP growth, from under 0.5 percent per year to about 1 percent per year, but this improvement has been partially offset by a decline in the rate of input intensification. Thus, yield growth has not picked up; it has averaged less than 2 percent per year every decade since the 1960s. Sustaining agricultural growth over the long run will likely require both greater input intensification and that growth in TFP dramatically improve.

Explaining the Past and Future Prospects

The results from this analysis generally agree with other recent studies that there has been an acceleration of agricultural growth in sub-Saharan Africa since the 1980s. But most of this improved growth performance has been resource-led. Since 2006, improved terms of trade has also contributed to growth in agricultural GDP. Growth in total factor productivity, which is a broad measure encompassing the effects of improved technology as well as improved production efficiency, remains far below the global average. To achieve and maintain a high rate of growth in the sector, and especially to raise agricultural output per capita, will increasingly depend on raising the underlying productivity of agricultural resources, in other words, on improving TFP.

Table 7.6. Sources of Agricultural Growth in sub-Saharan Africa

	Real Agricultural GDP	Terms of Trade	Gross Agricultural Output	Agricultural Land Area	Yield	Inputs/ Area	Total Factor Productivity
	A = B + C	B	C = D + E	D	E = F + G	F	G
			(average annual growth rate)				
1961-70	n.a.	n.a.	3.02	2.12	0.90	0.60	0.30
1971-80	3.02	1.85	1.17	-0.44	1.61	1.75	-0.14
1981-90	2.15	-0.73	2.88	2.14	0.74	-0.21	0.95
1991-00	2.95	-0.21	3.16	2.13	1.03	-0.14	1.17
2001-05	3.19	-0.28	3.47	3.11	0.36	-0.59	0.96
2006-08	3.52	1.09	2.43	0.82	1.60	0.66	0.94
1961-08	n.a.	n.a.	2.61	1.60	1.01	0.39	0.62

n.a. not available.
Estimates are for all countries in SSA except South Africa and use FAO agricultural output and input data for Nigeria.
Sources: Real agricultural GDP from World Bank; Gross agricultural output and inputs from FAO; Agricultural land area includes cropland harvested, permanent pasture, and irrigated cropland weighted by relatively quality; TFP is author's estimate.

Comparing the agricultural growth experience across different SSA countries and regions reveals a range of performance over space and time. While most areas have not been able to sustain productivity growth for any lengthy period, there appear to be a few countries that have successfully sustained TFP growth over the past several decades. Several countries in western Africa have emerged as regional drivers of SSA agricultural productivity growth, in particular Ghana, Benin, and possibly Nigeria (data quality issues yield uncertain results for this important country). These countries appear to have sustained average agricultural TFP growth rates of at least 1.5 percent per year since 1980. In eastern Africa, Kenya has maintained fairly steady TFP improvement since the 1960s, which has resulted in an improvement in its agricultural TFP of 67 percent between 1961 and 2008. A key driver of higher TFP growth appears to be the diffusion of improved agricultural technologies, especially food crop varieties. Another important element has been macroeconomic management and political stability. Indeed, observed growth patterns in agricultural TFP can often be traced directly to political events in those countries, such as civil war.

Sustaining and accelerating agricultural productivity growth in SSA will depend largely on the degree to which public policies and governance institutions can be strengthened. Two main policy tools for increasing TFP growth in agriculture are

1) liberalizing markets so that producers have an incentive to specialize in their comparative advantage and 2) providing support for agricultural technology development and dissemination. Market liberalization includes not only reducing tariffs and improving terms of trade but also developing rural infrastructure and marketing services to reduce transportation and market transaction costs. The general processes and efficiency gains from agricultural commercialization and specialization are described in Pingali and Rosegrant (1995). The extent to which market liberalization benefits (or hurts) small-holder agricultural producers in developing countries is controversial, but a review by Binswanger and von Braun (1991) found that agricultural commercialization largely stimulates growth and employment and expands the food supply, which are all central to the alleviation of poverty. There is considerable scope in many parts of Africa to expand agricultural production, such as in the Guinea savanna. The World Bank estimates that 400 million hectares of the Guinea savanna could be farmed, although only about 10 percent of this is currently cultivated (World Bank, 2009).

Policies to enhance technology development and dissemination include government support for agricultural higher education, research and extension, provision of rural schooling, and a regulatory environment that encourages the private sector to invest in agricultural innovation and technology transfer. However, indicators of government priorities on these matters in SSA countries show a poor record. Expenditures by national governments on agricultural research amounted to only 0.7 percent of agricultural GDP in 2000 and by this measure have fallen each decade since 1980 (Pardey *et al.*, 2006). Further, agricultural higher education and research systems in several African countries have sharply contracted or collapsed (Eicher, 1990, 2009; Pardey, Roseboom and Beintema, 1997). While international agricultural research centers supported by the Consultative Group on International Agricultural Research (CGIAR) have increased their investments in agricultural research in SSA, a declining share of this investment is being allocated to crop improvement (CGIAR, 2008) despite the evidence that returns on CGIAR crop improvement research in SSA have been larger than returns on natural resource or livestock research (Mywish and Raitzer, 2006). The private sector does not perform much agricultural research in sub-Saharan Africa (Pray and Umali-Deininger, 1998) and has been discouraged from developing agricultural biotechnology for the region by government policies (Paarlberg, 2008). Government regulations may also discourage private companies from supplying a range of farm inputs like seed, fertilizer, pesticides, and machinery, for reasons that go beyond the need to address externalities (Tripp and Gisselquist, 1996; Gisselquist, Nash and Pray, 2002).

Finally, there is a pressing need to strengthen agricultural statistics in SSA countries. This chapter addresses some of the shortcomings and inconsistencies in current statistics on agricultural production and input use and the difficulties this poses for assessing sector performance. More accurate and timely data will greatly improve our ability to understand trends in agricultural productivity and the influences of policies on these trends.

Note and Acknowledgments

The views expressed in this paper are the author's own and do not necessarily reflect those of the US Department of Agriculture. The comments and suggestions of Hans Binswanger, Derek Byerlee, Philip DeCosse, Paul Heisey, Pat Sullivan and the seminar participants at Cornell University and the Economic Research Service are gratefully acknowledged.

References

Alene, A.D. and Coulibaly, O. (2009) The impact of agricultural research on productivity and poverty in sub-Saharan Africa. *Food Policy* 24, 198–209.

Anderson, K. and Masters, W.A. (eds.) (2009) *Distortions to Agricultural Incentives in Africa*. World Bank, Washington, DC.

Ball, V.E. (1985) Output, input and productivity measurement in U.S. agriculture, 1948–79. *American Journal of Agricultural Economics* 76 (3), 475–86.

Binswanger-Mkhize, H.P. and McCalla, A. (2009) *The Changing Context and Prospects for African Agricultural Development*. International Fund for Agricultural Development and African Development Bank, Rome.

Binswanger, H.P. and McIntire, J. (1987) Behavior and material determinants of production relations in land-abundant tropical agriculture. *Economic Development and Cultural Change* 36 (1), 73–99.

Binswanger, H.P. and Pingali, P. (1988) Technology priorities for farming in sub-Saharan Africa. *World Bank Research Observer* 3 (1), 81–98.

Binswanger, H.P. and Townsend, R.F. (2000) The growth performance of agriculture in sub-Saharan Africa. *American Journal of Agricultural Economics* 85 (2), 1075–1986.

Binswanger, H.P. and von Braun, J. (1991) Technological change and commercialization in agriculture: The effect on the poor. *World Bank Research Observer* 6 (1), 57–80.

Block, S.A. (1995) The recovery of agricultural productivity in sub-Saharan Africa. *Food Policy* 20 (5), 385–405.

Boserup, E. (1965) *Conditions of Agricultural Growth: The Economics of Agrarian Change Under Population Pressure*. New York: Aldine Publishing, New York, NY.

Bourn, D. and Wint, W. (1994) Livestock, land use and agricultural intensification in sub-Saharan Africa. ODI Network Paper No. 37a. Overseas Development Institute, London.

Byerlee, D. and Eicher, C.K., eds. (1997) *Africa's Emerging Maize Revolution*. Lynne Publishers, Boulder, CO.

CGIAR (2008) *CGIAR Financial Report 2007*. Consultative Group on International Agricultural Research, Washington, DC.

Chukwu, G.O. and Ikwelle, M.C. (2000) Yam: Threats to its sustainability in Nigeria. *Palawija News* 17 (1), 1–7. The CGPRT Center, Bogor, Indonesia.

Coelli, T.J. and Rao, D.S.P. (2005) Total factor productivity growth in agriculture: A Malmquist index analysis of 93 Countries, 1980–2000. *Agricultural Economics* 32, 115–134.

Dalton, T.J. and Guei, R.G. (2003) Ecological diversity and rice varietal improvement in West Africa. In: Evenson, R.E. and Gollin, D. (eds.) *Crop Variety Improvement and its Effects on Productivity*. CABI Publishing, Wallingford, UK, pp. 109–134.

Deb, U.K. and Bantilan, M.S.C. (2003) Impacts of genetic improvement in sorghum. In: Evenson, R.E. and Gollin, D. (eds.) *Crop Variety Improvement and its Effects on Productivity*. CABI Publishing, Wallingford, UK, pp. 183–214.

Delgado, C.L. (1995) Africa's changing agricultural development strategies: Past and present paradigms as a guide to the future. IFPRI Discussion Paper 3. International Food Policy Research Institute, Washington, DC.

Dovring, F. (1978) The share of agriculture in a growing population. In: *FAO Studies in Agricultural Economics and Statistics, 1952–1977*. Food and Agriculture Organization, Rome, pp. 186–96.

Economic Research Service. U.S. fertilizer use and price. U.S. Department of Agriculture, Washington, DC. Available as Table 8 at http://www.ers.usda.gov/Data/FertilizerUse/ (accessed 10 January 2009).

Eicher, C. (1990) Building African scientific capacity for agricultural development. *Agricultural Economics* 4, 117–143.

Eicher, C. (2009) Rebuilding Africa's scientific capacity in food and agriculture. Background Paper No. 4, InterAcademy Council (IAC) Study Panel on Science and Technology Strategies for Improving Agricultural Productivity and Food Security in Africa, Amsterdam.

Evenson, R.E. and Fuglie, K.O. (2010) Technology capital: The price of admission to the growth club. *Journal of Productivity Analysis* 33, 173–190.

FAO. FAOSTAT Database. Food and Agricultural Organization, Rome. Available at http://faostat.fao.org/ (accessed 1 April 2009).

Frisvold, G. and Ingram, K. (1995) Sources of agricultural productivity growth and stagnation in sub-Saharan Africa. *Agricultural Economics* 13, 51–61.

Fuglie, K.O. (2008) Is a slowdown in agricultural productivity growth contributing to the rise in commodity prices? *Agricultural Economics* 39 (supplement), 431–441.

Fulginiti, L.E., Perrin, R.K. and Yu, B. (2004) Institutions and agricultural productivity in sub-Saharan Africa. *Agricultural Economics* 31, 169–180.

Gisselquist, D., Nash, J. and Pray, C. (2002) Deregulating the transfer of agricultural technology: Lessons from Bangladesh, India, Turkey and Zimbabwe. *World Bank Research Observer* 17 (2), 237–265.

Henao, J. and Baanante, C. (2006) Agricultural production and soil nutrient mining in Africa: Implications for resource conservation and policy development, summary. Report prepared for the IFDC—An International Center for Soil Fertility and Agricultural Development, Muscle Shoals, Alabama.

Hayami, Y. and Ruttan, V.W. (1985) *Agricultural Development: An International Perspective*. Johns Hopkins University Press, Baltimore, MD.

Higgins, G.M., Kassam, A.H., Naiken, L., Fischer, G. and Shah, M.M. (1983) Potential population supporting capacities of land in the developing world. Technical Report INT/75/P13, Food and Agricultural Organization, Rome.

Hill, P. (1970) *Studies in Rural Capitalism in West Africa*. Cambridge University Press, Cambridge, UK.

International Fertilizer Association. IFADATA Statistics, International Fertilizer Association, Paris, France. Available at: http://www.fertilizer.org/ifa/ifadata/search (accessed 1 July 2008).

International Commission on Irrigation and Drainage (undated). Nigeria, Country Profile. National Committees, New Delhi, India. Available at: http://www.icid.org/index_e.html.

International Labour Organization. LABORSTA Database. Bureau of Statistics, International Labor Organization, Geneva, Switzerland. Available at: http://lborsta.ilo.org/ (accessed 1 February 2009).

Iyoha, M. (2007) Leadership, policy-making and economic growth in African countries: The case of Nigeria. Working Paper No. 17. Commission on Growth and Development, World Bank, Washington, DC.

Johnston, B. and Kilby, P. (1975) *Agriculture and Structural Transformation: Economic Strategies in Late-Developing Countries.* Oxford University Press, New York, NY.

Lusigi, A. and Thirtle, C. (1997). Total factor productivity and the effects of R&D in African agriculture. *Journal of International Development* 9 (4), 529–538.

McIntire, J., Bourzat, D. and Pingali, P. (1992) *Crop-livestock Interaction in sub-Saharan Africa.* World Bank, Washington, DC.

Morris, M., Kelly, V.A., Kopicki, R.J. and Byerlee, D. (2007) *Fertilizer Use in African Agriculture.* World Bank, Washington, DC.

Mywish, K.M. and Raitzer, D.A. (2006) CGIAR and NARS partner research in sub-Saharan Africa: Evidence of impact to date. Commissioned Paper, CGIAR Science Council, Rome.

Ndulu, B.J., Chakraborti, L., Lijane, L., Ramachandran, V. and Wolgin, J. (2007) *Challenges of African Growth: Opportunities, Constraints and Strategic Directions.* Washington, DC: World Bank.

Nin-Pratt, A. and Yu, B. (2008) An updated look at recovery of agricultural productivity in sub-Saharan Africa. IFPRI Discussion Paper 00787, International Food Policy Research Institute, Washington, DC.

Norton, D. (1988) *Underground Crops: Long-term Trends in Production of Roots and Tubers.* Winrock International, Morrilton, AR.

Nweke, F. (2004) New challenges in cassava transformation in Nigeria and Ghana. EPTD Discussion Paper No. 118, International Food Policy Research Institute, Washington, DC.

Oba, G. and Lusigi, W.J. (1987) An overview of drought strategies and land use in African pastoral systems. ODI Network Paper No. 23a. Overseas Development Institute, London.

Olsson, L., Eklundh, L. and Ardö, J. (2005) A recent greening of the Sahel—Trends, patterns and potential causes. *Journal of Arid Environments* 63, 556–566.

Oni, O., Nkonya, E., Pender, J., Phillips, D. and Kato, E. (2009) Trends and drivers of agricultural productivity in Nigeria. Nigeria Strategy Support Program Report 001, International Food Policy Research Center, Washington, DC.

Paarlberg, R. (2008) *Starved for Science: How Biotechnology is Being Kept Out of Africa.* Harvard University Press, Cambridge, MA.

Pardey, P.G., Beintema, N.M., Dehmer, S. and Wood, S. (2006) Agricultural research: A growing global divide? Food Policy Report. International Food Policy Research Center, Washington, DC.

Pardey, P.G., Roseboom, J. and Beintema, N.M. (1997) Investments in African agricultural research. *World Development* 25 (3), 409–423.

Pfaffenzeller, S., Newbold, P. and Rayner, A. (2007) A short note on updating the Grilli and Yang commodity price index. *The World Bank Economic Review 21*(1), 151–163.

Pingali, P. and Rosegrant, M. (1995) Agricultural commercialization and diversification: Processes and policies. *Food Policy* (20) 3, 171–185.

Pingali, P., Bigot, Y. and Binswanger, H.P. (1987) *Agricultural Mechanization and the Evolution of Farming Systems in sub-Saharan Africa.* Johns Hopkins University Press, Baltimore, MD.
Pray, C. and Umali-Deininger, D. (1998) The private sector in agricultural research systems: Will it fill the gap? *World Development* 26 (6), 1127–1148.
U.S. Department of Agriculture. PSD Online: Production, supply and distribution database. Foreign Agricultural Service, Washington, DC. Available at: http://www.fas.usda.gov/psdonline/psdHome.aspx (accessed 15 July 2009).
Rao, D.S.P. (1993) Intercountry comparisons of agricultural output and productivity. FAO Economic and Social Development Paper, Food and Agricultural Organization, Rome.
Ravn, M.O. and Uhlig, H. (2002) On adjusting the Hodrick-Prescott Filter for the frequency of observations. *Review of Economics and Statistics* 84 (2), 371–376.
Reij, C., Tappan, G. and Smale, M. (2009) Agroenvironmental transformation in the Sahel: Another kind of 'Green Revoluion.' Discussion Paper 00914, International Food Policy Research Institute, Washington, DC, November.
Sebastian, K. (2007) GIS/spatial analysis contribution to 2008 WDR: Technical notes on data & methodologies. Background Paper for the World Development Report 2008, World Bank, Washington, DC.
Smale, M. and Jayne, T. (2003) Maize in Eastern and Southern Africa: 'Seeds' of success in retrospect. EPTD Discussion Paper No. 97, International Food Policy Research Institute, Washington, DC.
Smith, J., Barau, A.D., Goldman, A. and Mareck, J.H. (1994) The role of technology in agricultural intensification: The evolution of maize production in the Northern Guinea Savanna of Nigeria. *Economic Development and Cultural Change* 42 (3), 537–554.
Starkey, P. (2000) The history of working animals in Africa. In: Blench, R.M. and MacDonald, K. (eds.) *The Origins and Development of African Livestock: Archaeology, Genetics, Linguistics and Ethnography.* University College London Press, UK, pp. 478–502.
Stoorvogel, J.J. and Smaling, E.M.A. (1990) Assessment of soil nutrient depletion in sub-Saharan Africa: 1983–2000. Report no. 28. Vol. 1–4. Winand Staring Center, Wageningen, The Netherlands.
Tripp, R. and Gisselquist, D. (1996) A fresh look at agricultural input regulation. Natural Resource Perspectives Number 8. Overseas Development Institute, London.
World Bank. World Development Indicators Database, World Bank, Washington, DC. Available at: http://publications.worldbank.org/WDI/ (accessed 1 October 2008).
World Bank. (2007) *World Bank Development Report 2008.* World Bank, Washington, DC.
World Bank. (2009) *Awakening Africa's Sleeping Giant: Prospects for Commercial Agriculture in the Guinea Savannah Zone and Beyond.* Agricultural and Rural Development Unit, Sustainable Development Network, Africa Regional Office, World Bank, Washington, DC.
Yin, S. (2007) In the news: Results trickle out from the Nigerian Census. Population Reference Bureau, Washington, DC, January.

Chapter 8

Are Staple Foods Becoming More Expensive for Urban Consumers in Eastern and Southern Africa? Trends in Food Prices, Marketing Margins and Wage Rates in Kenya, Malawi, Mozambique, and Zambia

Nicole M. Mason, T.S. Jayne, Cynthia Donovan and Antony Chapoto
Department of Agricultural, Food and Resource Economics, Michigan State University, East Lansing, Michigan, USA

Abstract

The world food and financial crises have threatened to undermine the real incomes of urban consumers in eastern and southern Africa (ESA). This study investigates patterns in staple food prices, wage rates, and marketing margins for urban consumers in Kenya, Malawi, Mozambique, and Zambia between the mid-1990s and 2009. We find that formal sector wages rose at a faster rate than retail maize meal and bread prices in urban Kenya and Zambia over this period. High prices during the crisis were a major shock to urban consumers but did not push formal sector wage earners' staple food purchasing power to unprecedentedly low levels. The quantities of staple foods affordable per daily wage in urban Kenya and Zambia at the peak of the food price crisis were still roughly double the levels of the mid-1990s. The national minimum wage in Mozambique also grew more rapidly than rice and wheat flour prices in Maputo from the mid-1990s through the mid-2000s. Maputo minimum wage earners' purchasing power declined during the food price crisis, while purchasing power for rice and wheat at the peak of the crisis was still higher than in the mid-1990s. These findings obtain for formal sector wage earners in Kenya and Zambia and for (formal sector) minimum wage earners in Mozambique; however, the majority of the urban poor in these countries are employed in the informal sector. The general conclusion of improving food purchasing power in the decade before the food price crisis may or may not hold for a significant percentage of the urban poor, who are most vulnerable to food price spikes. Maize marketing margins trended downward between 1994 and 2004 in urban Kenya, Malawi, and Zambia, while wheat marketing margins declined only in Kenya and Zambia. For the public sector, important strategies for moderating food price increases for consumers include strengthening the capacity for forecasting crop production and import needs, facilitating imports in a timely manner, and ensuring the continued availability of low-cost staple food options for urban consumers.

Figure 8.1. Urban centers in Kenya, Malawi, Mozambique, and Zambia used in the analysis

Introduction

The food price crisis of 2007/2008 and the global financial crisis that followed thereafter strained economies around the world, including those in eastern and southern Africa (ESA). Although world commodity prices began to decline in mid-2008, domestic staple food prices in several ESA countries remained high throughout 2008 before finally peaking in early 2009. ESA countries are urbanizing rapidly and the urban poor are particularly vulnerable to food and financial crises: high food prices decrease their purchasing power, as most urban consumers rely on markets to access food, and reductions in employment and wages as a result of financial and economic crises can further undermine their real incomes (Baker, 2008).

Social unrest in more than 30 countries during the 2007/2008 food crisis underscores the importance of effective government, donor, and civil society responses to mitigate the impacts of such shocks on urban populations (von Braun *et al.*, 2008). This chapter investigates historical patterns in staple food prices, wage rates, and marketing margins for urban consumers in Kenya, Malawi, Mozambique, and Zambia, with a special focus on the 2007/2008 food crisis, and discusses the implications of the empirical findings for policy options to shield the urban poor from the potential adverse effects of future staple food price increases.

An important determinant of how food price increases affect urban consumers in ESA is the extent to which formal and informal sector wages adjust to compensate for higher food prices. Therefore, the first (two-part) objective of this chapter is to determine, for urban centers in Kenya, Mozambique and Zambia, whether key staple foods were becoming more or less expensive for urban wage earners *prior to* the food price crisis, and then to determine the extent to which their purchasing power declined *during* the food price crisis. We do this by tracking movements in the retail prices of rice along with prices of maize, wheat, and cassava products relative to wage rates between the mid-1990s and 2009. A key limitation of this part of our analysis is that, due to data constraints, we are only able to track staple food prices relative to national minimum wage rates in Mozambique and relative to formal sector wages in Zambia and Kenya. No wage rate time series is available for Malawi, and informal sector wage data are not available for any of the four countries. Our analysis, therefore, does not capture the subset of the labor force that earns wages in the informal sector or workers whose livelihoods depend on informal business activities.[56]

Our second objective in this chapter is to determine whether vertical marketing margins for maize and wheat products have declined in the various urban centers. The vertical marketing margin is the price difference for a given commodity between two different stages of the value chain (but at the same location), with quantities expressed in comparable units, e.g., the *wholesale maize grain* to *retail maize meal* marketing margin. Reducing vertical marketing margins through increased competition and efficiency can be a major means of improving the affordability of food for urban consumers. While this was a

[56] In sub-Saharan Africa and developing countries in general, the majority of the poor rely on informal sector wage employment or business activities to earn a living (Guha-Khasnobis and Kanbur, 2006). However, in Zambia and Kenya, a non-trivial percentage of urban workers, including the poor, are employed in the formal sector. In Zambia as of 2004, the formal sector was the main sector of employment for 43 percent of urban workers overall and for 38 percent of relatively poor workers (CSO, 2005). In Kenya as of 1997, the percentage of urban workers with formal sector employment was 64 percent overall and 32 percent for the relatively poor (Odhiambo and Manda, 2003). And in Mozambique as of 2003, 28 percent of the active urban labour force was employed in the formal sector (CTA, 2004).

major objective of market reforms and liberalization, there has been very little empirical investigation of this issue across countries in the region.

The third and final objective of the chapter is to use the empirical findings to identify policy tools to protect urban consumers from future dramatic surges in food prices. The specific urban centers on which we focus are the capital cities of Kenya, Malawi, Mozambique, and Zambia—Nairobi, Lilongwe, Maputo and Lusaka, respectively—as well as Nampula in Northern Mozambique, Kitwe on the Zambian Copperbelt, and Mansa, a northern town in Zambia (see Figure 8.1). These urban centers account for a significant proportion of the total urban populations in the respective countries (Potts, 2006; Brinkhoff, n.d.).

The chapter is organized as follows: in the second section, we provide background information on urban staple food consumption patterns and sources of urban staple food supplies in the four case study countries. The third section details the methods and data used in the analysis. The fourth and fifth sections present the results. The sixth section outlines strategies that governments in ESA could use to keep staple food prices at moderate levels for urban consumers. The final section discusses the conclusions that emerge from the empirical findings.

Background

Staple Food Consumption Patterns

The four staple food commodities for which prices are analyzed in this chapter are maize, wheat, rice, and cassava. These items were selected because they account for a large proportion of households' overall food and staple food budgets in key urban centers in Kenya, Malawi, Mozambique and Zambia. The share of maize, wheat, rice and cassava in urban households' total value of food consumption ranges from 19.5 percent in Lusaka to 47.5 percent in urban Northern Mozambique including Nampula city (Table 8.1). The most recently available urban consumption survey data indicate that budget shares for wheat exceed those for maize in Nairobi, Maputo, Lusaka and Kitwe (Table 8.1). Wheat has become a more important staple food budget item in the region since the mid-1990s, yet maize is still the major staple among the urban poor (Muyanga *et al.*, 2005; Tschirley *et al.*, 2006; Mason and Jayne, 2009). In Mansa, Zambia, maize has the largest staple food budget share, but wheat and cassava are also important. And among urban consumers in Northern Mozambique, cassava and potatoes represent the largest staple food expenditure category. Information on staple food budget shares for urban consumers in Malawi is not available, but among all consumers (urban and rural) in that country, maize is by far the most dominant staple food budget item.

Sources of Urban Staple Food Supplies

Supplies of maize, wheat and rice products to urban consumers in Kenya, Malawi, Mozambique and Zambia come from both domestic production and imports. Domestic cassava production is sufficient to satisfy local demand in Malawi, Mozambique and Zambia. Of all the marketed maize in Kenya, evidence suggests that approximately one half is from domestic production, while the other half is from Tanzania and Uganda. In years of large production shortfalls, the international market becomes more important and may account for up to 25 percent of total marketed supplies. Wheat is produced in Kenya on large farms and meets about 50 percent of the country's wheat consumption needs; wheat is imported to fulfil the remaining needs, and most rice consumed in Kenya is imported.

Table 8.1. Staple Food Budget Shares, Urban Centers in Kenya, Malawi, Mozambique and Zambia

		Percentage share of food group in total value of consumption of main staples[a]				Percentage share of main staples in total value of food consumption
Urban center/country	Year	Maize	Wheat	Rice	Cassava	
Nairobi, Kenya	1995	42.4	35.3	22.4	0.0	--
	2003	33.7	45.3	21.0	0.0	28.4
Malawi (urban & rural)	2004/05	83.1	5.0	5.5	6.4	42.1
Urban Maputo Province	1996	2.6	50.7	35.0	11.7	42.8
	2002	8.9	57.4	28.9	4.8	27.0
Urban Northern Mozambique (includes Nampula city)	2002	32.6	8.2	14.7	44.4[b]	47.5
Lusaka, Zambia[c]	2007/08	39.0	49.4	10.7	0.9	19.5
Kitwe, Zambia[c]	2007/08	42.5	45.3	10.3	2.0	23.2
Mansa, Zambia[c]	2007/08	45.8	28.2	10.0	16.0	23.8

Sources: Muyanga *et al.*, 2005; Ayieko *et al.*, 2005; Tschirley *et al.*, 2006; Zanias and Gunjal, 2007; Barslund, 2007; Mason and Jayne, 2009.
Notes: [a]Main staples refers to maize, wheat, rice, and cassava. Budget shares of these four staple foods sum to 100 percent (+/- 0.1 percent). Shares for Nairobi and Northern Mozambique are percentage of total food purchases. [b]Cassava share is for cassava and potatoes (separate figure for cassava only not available). [c]Excludes foods purchased and consumed away from home. -- = information not available.

In Malawi, about 50 percent and 10 percent of marketed maize supplies come from domestic smallholder and estate farms, respectively; the remaining 40 percent is imported mainly from Mozambique but also from Tanzania and Zambia. In drought years, maize is also imported from South Africa, but informal regional trade is almost always the largest source of imported maize. Almost all wheat and rice consumed in Malawi is imported.

For Mozambique, almost all wheat is imported, although a wheat production promotion program is currently underway. There is substantial rice production in Mozambique, but most is consumed by producing households, leaving very little marketed surplus. For urban markets, the major source of rice is imports. Maize is mainly produced in the Northern and Center Regions[57] of the country. Production from the North supplies Nampula city and is also exported to Malawi. Maize supplies in Maputo come from domestic production in the Center region of the country and also from imports from South Africa.

---

[57] These are officially defined governmental regions of the country.

In Zambia, marketed maize from domestic production is from both smallholder and large-scale commercial farms. Smallholder maize accounts for approximately 80 percent of total marketed maize supplies. Maize is both imported and exported in most years, and in good production years, exports exceed imports. In drought years, large quantities of imported maize are necessary to meet domestic consumption requirements. South Africa is the main source of imports, but imports from Tanzania and, historically, Zimbabwe, are also important (Jayne *et al.*, 2006). Most rice in Zambia comes from domestic production, although small quantities are imported in most years. Wheat is grown on commercial farms in Zambia, and production levels have increased dramatically over the past decade. Wheat imports were substantial from the mid-1990s to early 2000s, but the country is now nearing wheat self-sufficiency.

Methods and Data

Methods

Quantities of Staple Foods Affordable per Daily Wage

Our first objective is to determine whether key staple foods were becoming more or less expensive in the various ESA urban centers prior to the food price crisis and then to determine the extent to which urban wage earners' staple food purchasing power declined during the crisis. To address these objectives, we divide the average daily wage of workers in a given country by the nominal retail prices of maize grain, maize meal, bread or wheat flour, cassava flour and rice in each month from January 1993 through January 2009.[58] This gives us the physical quantity of each staple food affordable per the daily wage. (Details on the specific wage and price data used in each country/urban center are provided in the Data section that follows.) To determine whether there have been trends over time in the quantity of each staple affordable per daily wage, we graph these variables over time and look for patterns and use econometric analysis to test for statistically significant trends. We also compare wage earners' staple food purchasing power at the height of the food price crisis to levels over the previous 15 or so years.

In the econometric analysis, we estimate two models for the *quantity affordable per daily wage* (QAPDW) for each staple food and urban center: one where the QAPDW (the dependent variable) is in levels and another where the QAPDW is in first differences (i.e., the QAPDW in month t minus the QAPDW in month t-1). In the first model, the monthly QAPDW in levels is regressed on a constant, a time trend, and 11 monthly dummy variables. (The monthly dummies are included to control for seasonality.) This model is estimated using the Cochrane-Orcutt iterative procedure with heteroskedasticity-robust standard errors. The coefficient on the time trend is the main result of interest; it indicates the expected month-to-month change in the QAPDW, controlling for seasonality. If this coefficient is positive and statistically significant (at say, the ten percent level or lower), this would indicate a positive trend in the QAPDW, i.e., that the formal sector wage earners' purchasing power for that staple food and location improved over time.

This specification of the model assumes that the QAPDW time series is covariance-stationary, i.e., its mean and variance are constant over time and the covariance is the same

[58] Some data series begin later than January 1993. See Notes on Data Sources at the end of this chapter.

for all pairs of time periods that are the same number of months apart. Diagnostic tests are inconclusive with respect to the stationarity of many of the QAPDW time series, so we also estimate a second model for each QAPDW variable that relaxes the stationarity assumption.[59]

In the second model specification, we regress the monthly first difference of the quantity affordable per daily wage on a constant and 11 monthly dummy variables. The model is estimated using ordinary least squares (OLS) with heteroskedasticity-robust standard errors. Here the main result of interest is the coefficient on the constant. Similar to the coefficient on the time trend in the first model described above, the coefficient on the constant in the second model is the expected month-to-month change in the QAPDW, controlling for seasonality. A statistically significant and positive coefficient would indicate a positive trend in QAPDW. Due to space constraints, we only report the results based on the regressions where the QAPDW is in levels but briefly discuss the results based on the regressions where the QAPDW is in first differences.

Marketing Margins

Our second objective in this study is to determine whether vertical marketing margins for maize and wheat products have declined over time. Wholesale maize grain to retail maize meal marketing margins are calculated as follows. The nominal price spread between retail maize meal and wholesale maize grain (*maizeMM*) is computed as:

$$(1)\ maizeMM_{k,t} = pmeal_{k,t} - (z_k \times pgrain_t) + [(z_k - 1) \times pbyproduct_t]$$

where *pmeal* is the retail maize meal price per kilogram; z_k is the extraction rate, i.e., the average number of kilograms of maize grain required to produce one kilogram of type *k* maize meal; *pgrain* is the wholesale maize grain price[60]; *pbyproduct* is the per kilogram price of the milling by-product (about which we will say more below); *t* indexes the month; and *k* indexes the type of maize meal. The specification of Equation 1 follows Traub and Jayne (2008). Following Jayne and Argwings-Kodhek (1997), and due to the lack of by-product price data, we estimate $pbyproduct_t$ as 40 percent of *pgrain*.[61]

Different types of maize meal (*k*) are examined for different urban centers. For Zambia, we look at margins for breakfast meal and for roller meal. Both are commercially manufactured maize meals, but breakfast meal is more highly refined than roller meal. For Mozambique, we analyze margins for high quality maize meal (roughly comparable to breakfast meal) and roller meal. The extraction rate z_k is set equal to 1.54 for breakfast meal/high quality maize meal and 1.18 for roller meal, per Mwiinga *et al.* (2002). For

---

[59] Each QAPDW variable was tested for unit roots using various specifications of the Augmented Dickey-Fuller, Phillips-Perron, and Kwiatkowski, Phillips, Schmidt and Shin tests. The test results are inconclusive for several QAPDW time series: some tests suggest stationarity but others indicate unit root behavior. Failure to reject the null hypotheses of the various tests could be due to their notoriously low power and/or to failure to model structural breaks (Perron, 1989).

[60] For Lilongwe, Kitwe and Kasama, only retail (and no wholesale) maize grain price data are available. For these cities, the margin is computed between retail maize meal and retail maize grain prices; for Nairobi, Maputo, Nampula and Lusaka, the margin is computed between retail maize meal and wholesale maize grain prices.

[61] Traub and Jayne (2008) conducted sensitivity analyses and found that their results for trends in marketing margins were not sensitive to differing assumptions about extraction rates and the value of the milling by-product. We varied the value of by-product from 40 percent (per Jayne and Argwings-Kodhek [1997]) to 70 percent (per Traub and Jayne [2008]) of the maize grain price; inferences about trends in marketing margins are not sensitive to such changes.

Lilongwe and Nairobi, the retail maize meal prices are average prices across all types of maize meal. We set z equal to 1.33 and 1.25 for maize meal in Lilongwe and Nairobi, respectively, because, on average, maize meal is more refined in Lilongwe than in Nairobi.

Because of general inflation over time, nominal maize marketing margins also increase over time. To control for this, we use two different approaches. In one approach, we calculate the nominal *maize meal–maize grain* price spread (*maizeMM*) as a percentage of the retail maize meal price and refer to this as the *percentage marketing margin.* In the second approach, we deflate the nominal maize meal–maize grain price spread by the Consumer Price Index (CPI) and refer to this as the *real marketing margin.* We compute the marketing margins in both real and percentage terms to test the robustness of trends in the marketing margins to alternative definitions of the margin. However, the CPIs used to calculate the real marketing margins are based on both food and non-food prices. (Non-food CPIs were not available for all countries.) Given that staple foods are important items in the basket of goods used to calculate the CPI, marketing margins deflated by the total CPI may be over- or underestimated in some periods. Therefore, we focus our discussion of the results mainly on the percentage marketing margins, which do not require adjustment for inflation, but also briefly mention the findings based on the real marketing margins.

For wheat products (bread in Zambia, Kenya, and Malawi, and wheat flour in Mozambique), we first compute the nominal spread between the retail wheat product price and the world wheat price (*wheatMM*):

(2) $wheatMM_{j,t} = pwheatprod_{j,t} - (v_j \times pwwheat_t)$

where *pwheatprod* is the retail price per loaf of bread or per kilogram of wheat flour; *pwwheat* is the price in local currency units per kilogram of No.1 hard red winter wheat (ordinary protein, FOB Gulf of Mexico—e.g., the *world wheat price*); v_j is the average number of kilograms of wheat required to produce one 700-gram loaf of bread (v_1=0.649) or one kilogram of wheat flour (v_2=1.282); and j indexes the wheat product (j = bread or wheat flour). The v_1 figure was obtained via interviews with millers and bakers in Lusaka; the v_2 figure is from Muendane *et al.* (2000).[62] We focus on the margin between retail wheat products and the world wheat price due to the unavailability of domestic wholesale or producer level wheat price data and to the importance of wheat imports during the period of analysis in all four countries as discussed above. We adjust the nominal wheat marketing margin (*wheatMM*) by the retail wheat product price to obtain the percentage wheat marketing margin, and by the CPI to obtain the real wheat marketing margin.

To determine whether there have been trends over time in the various marketing margins, we use graphical and econometric analyses analogous to those described above for the time series of quantities affordable per daily wage. The weight of the evidence from diagnostic tests suggests that the marketing margin time series are covariance-stationary, so the models are estimated in levels as described above for the first set of regressions for quantities affordable per daily wage.

Table 8.2 summarizes the staple food price series and marketing margins studied in each urban center for the two different objectives and associated sets of methods described above. Data limitations prevent us from doing some aspects of the analysis for certain commodity/city pairs.

---

[62] A 'typical' loaf of bread weighs approximately 700 grams in Zambia and Malawi, and 400 grams in Kenya; we adjust the v_1 for Kenya accordingly.

Table 8.2. Staple Food Price Series and Marketing Margins Analyzed for Each Urban Center

	Quantities affordable per daily wage						Marketing margins		
Urban center	Maize grain	Maize meal	Bread	Wheat flour	Cassava flour	Rice	Retail maize meal/ maize grain	Retail bread/ world wheat	Retail wheat flour/ world wheat
Nairobi	X[a]	X					X		
Urban Kenya			X					X	
Lilongwe							X[b]	X	
Maputo	X	X		X		X	X		X
Nampula	X	X		X	X	X	X		X
Lusaka	X	X	X				X	X	
Kitwe	X	X					X[b]		
Mansa	X	X			X		X[b]		

Notes: X indicates that the analysis was done for the particular urban center/country.
[a]No retail maize grain prices available; wholesale maize grain prices used in the analysis. [b]Margin is between retail maize grain and retail maize meal prices (no wholesale maize grain prices available); maize marketing margins in other urban centers are between wholesale maize grain and retail maize meal prices.

Data

Data sources and the price series used in the analysis for the various urban centers are summarized in the Data Source Notes at the end of this chapter. We analyze trends in wheat flour prices in Maputo and Nampula (Mozambique) instead of bread prices because bread prices in Mozambique are administratively determined.[63] Market wage rates for Mozambique are not available and the official minimum wage rates for formal non-agricultural and agricultural sector employment are usually adjusted once per year, loosely based on the consumer price index and cost of a basic consumption basket. We use the non-agricultural formal sector minimum wage in the analysis of the quantities of staple foods affordable per daily wage in Maputo and Nampula.

Formal sector wages for a number of employment sectors are available for both Kenya (public and private sector, which are further subdivided into 12 total sectors) and Zambia (central government, local government, parastatals, and private sector). The various wage series in Kenya and Zambia are highly correlated within each country, and these correlations are all statistically significant at the five percent level or lower. For the Kenya wage series, all pair-wise correlation coefficients are greater than or equal to 0.96 except for those involving local government; the correlations between local government wages and wages in the other 11 employment sectors range from 0.63 to 0.78. For the Zambia wage series, pair-wise correlations range from 0.89 to 0.98. In our analysis of the quantities of various commodities affordable per daily wage, we use a weighted average daily wage across all employment sectors in each country, where the weights correspond to the share

[63] Bread prices are set in coordination with the Ministry of Commerce and Tourism in Mozambique, and bakeries may change the size of the loaf or the quality rather than the price in order to reflect higher or lower costs. Data are not available on monthly changes in flour used per loaf of bread. Bread prices are not controlled in Kenya or Zambia.

of total employment attributed to a given sector.[64] However, as a robustness check, we examine trends in the kilograms of maize grain affordable per daily wage for each of the four wage series in Zambia and for the average public sector and average private sector wage series in Kenya.

A final note on the data used in the analysis concerns the bread prices for Lusaka, Kenya and Lilongwe. These price data are per loaf of bread, but the weight per loaf was not collected; we also do not have information on the ingredients used and how relative proportions of those ingredients may have changed over time. Therefore, results for the loaves of bread affordable per daily wage and for retail bread to world wheat marketing margins must be interpreted with this caveat in mind.

Results: Trends in the Quantities of Staple Foods Affordable per Daily Wage

We begin this section with a brief description of the econometric results. The remainder of the section discusses the graphical analysis.

Regression Results

Table 8.3 (columns A to D) summarizes the regression results for trends in the quantities of maize grain, maize meal, bread/wheat flour, rice and cassava flour affordable per daily wage in the various urban centers based on the models where the dependent variable is in levels. For 17 of the 23 QAPDW variables, there is a statistically significant ($p<0.05$) positive trend, indicating that the affordability of these 17 staple foods improved between the mid-1990s and January 2009 (Table 8.3, columns A and B). Despite the fact that food prices were very high during the food price crisis at the end of this period, there is still a statistically significant positive trend in most of the QAPDW variables. If we limit the regression analysis to observations through May 2007 only (i.e., the period before the food price crisis), the econometric evidence of positive trends in staple food purchasing power over the last decade or so is even stronger: 21 of 23 QAPDW variables have statistically significant positive trends, and the magnitude of the month-to-month increase is greater for most variables than when all observations are used (see Table 8.3, columns C and D and compare the coefficients in columns A and C). As expected, the improvement in purchasing power over time is greater when observations from June 2007 through January 2009 are excluded since food prices spiked dramatically during those months.

The regression results from models where the dependent variable is in first differences are similar to those from models where the dependent variable is in levels in that the estimated trend in almost all QAPDW variables is positive (21 of 23 are positive when all observations are used and 22 of 23 are positive when only observations through May 2007

[64] Formal sector wage data for Zambia were missing for some quarters and the most recently available wage data at the time of writing were through the fourth quarter of 2007. Fitted values from a regression of the available wage data on a cubic function of time trends were used to approximate the missing wage data points. Daily wage rates for formal sector workers in Kenya were only available for June of each year, and the last year of data available at the time of writing was 2007. Estimates of these wages in months other than June and for July 2007 through January 2009 were calculated by regressing the wages on a fifth degree polynomial function of time trends, and using the fitted values from the regression as the approximate daily wage rate for each month in the period of analysis.

Table 8.3. Summary of Results: Trends over Time in Quantities of Staple Foods Affordable per Daily Wage

Urban center	Quantity affordable per daily wage (QAPDW) variable (units)	Regression results: Estimated month-to-month change in QAPDW: All observations: Coef.	p-value	Observations through May 2007: Coef.	p-value	Summary statistics: Average QAPDW during each agricultural marketing year[a]: 1995/96	2000/01	2006/07	2007/08	2008/09[b]	Obs.
		(A)	(B)	(C)	(D)	(E)	(F)	(G)	(H)	(I)	(J)
Nairobi	Maize grain (kg)	0.287**	<0.001	0.362**	<0.001	25.2	32.3	71.3	75.8	48.6	181
	Maize meal (kg)	0.009	0.961	0.420**	0.001	14.1	18.8	43.2	41.4	23.1	180
Urban Kenya	Bread (loaves)	0.051	0.528	0.191**	<0.001	15.9	28.2	41.1	37.4	36.6	164
Maputo	Maize grain (kg)	0.026**	<0.001	0.033**	<0.001	2.2	6.9	7.9	7.6	5.9	192
	Maize meal (kg)	0.004	0.427	0.006	0.425	1.4	4.0	3.3	3.2	3.2	153
	Wheat flour (kg)	0.013*	0.012	0.019**	<0.001	1.2	2.7	3.9	3.2	2.7	190
	Rice (kg)	0.012	0.232	0.024**	<0.001	1.2	3.7	4.1	4.2	3.3	192
Nampula	Maize grain (kg)	0.028	0.127	0.049**	0.008	4.3	13.5	12.2	10.4	7.4	190
	Maize meal (kg)	0.021	0.125	0.052**	0.010	--	5.4	4.6	4.8	4.2	97
	Wheat flour (kg)	0.018**	<0.001	0.024**	<0.001	1.1	3.1	4.2	3.7	3.6	174
	Rice (kg)	0.017**	0.004	0.026**	<0.001	1.1	3.1	4.4	3.9	2.7	192
	Cassava flour (kg)	0.042**	<0.001	0.048**	<0.001	2.4	4.8	7.0	8.1	7.9	193
Lusaka	Maize grain (kg)	0.243**	0.001	0.258**	0.005	20.0	33.3	50.0	67.7	61.4	173
	Breakfast meal (kg)	0.198**	<0.001	0.187**	0.001	10.0	17.2	32.7	43.3	36.5	181
	Roller meal (kg)	0.255**	<0.001	0.228**	0.003	11.9	23.0	48.7	58.7	48.2	181
	Bread (loaves)	0.104**	<0.001	0.089**	<0.001	6.8	9.2	17.3	22.5	22.0	181
Kitwe	Maize grain (kg)	0.311**	<0.001	0.339**	<0.001	23.1	33.0	64.9	74.3	64.0	174
	Breakfast meal (kg)	0.180**	<0.001	0.262**	0.003	9.7	17.4	34.3	42.8	35.5	189
	Roller meal (kg)	0.250**	0.005	0.244**	0.006	11.2	21.2	49.3	60.2	48.5	185
Mansa	Maize grain (kg)	0.288**	<0.001	0.262**	0.001	26.2	37.4	64.1	67.6	69.6	178
	Breakfast meal (kg)	0.169**	<0.001	0.183**	<0.001	9.7	17.2	29.9	39.4	34.4	187
	Roller meal (kg)	0.245**	0.001	0.327*	0.015	11.8	19.4	40.7	53.9	47.8	186
	Cassava flour (kg)	0.233*	0.043	0.233	0.388	--	11.3	42.4	37.2	45.6	82

Source: Authors' calculations.

Notes: [a]The agricultural marketing year is July through June in Kenya and May through April in Mozambique and Zambia. [b]Through November/December 2008 or January 2009. **, *, + significant at the 1, 5, and 10 percent levels, respectively. -- = no observations.

are used). However, very few of the estimated trends are statistically significant at the 10 percent level or higher in this set of results (only 2 of 23 are statistically significant when all observations are used and 5 of 23 are statistically significant when only observations through May 2007 are used). None of the estimated trends from the regression models in levels or first differences is negative or statistically significant, which would have indicated that staple foods became more expensive for formal sector wage earners over the study period. In general, then, the econometric results suggest that the purchasing power of formal sector workers (and of workers whose wages are positively correlated with those of formal sector workers) for staple foods improved between the mid-1990s and January 2009, and especially in the period prior to the food price and financial crises in 2007 to 2009.

Comparisons of Wheat Product Affordability in Urban Kenya, Maputo, and Lusaka

Figure 8.2 depicts the loaves of bread affordable per daily wage in urban Kenya and Lusaka, and the kilograms of wheat flour affordable per daily wage in Maputo. (Note that the *y*-axis for Maputo wheat flour is on the right.) The purchasing power for wheat increased in all three locations between the mid-1990s and 2006/2007. Some of this increase in all three countries can be attributed to increases in the quantity of world wheat affordable per daily wage (i.e., wages divided by the world price of wheat in local currency units). Declining real retail bread to world wheat marketing margins in urban Kenya and Lusaka may have also contributed to improving purchasing power for bread prior to the food price crisis (see the results on trends in marketing margins later in the chapter). While bread and wheat flour purchasing power declined sharply in 2007 in urban Kenya and Maputo, respectively, bread purchasing power in Lusaka between mid-2007 and January 2009 was relatively flat. Bread purchasing power in Lusaka may have been relatively stable during the food price crisis because Zambia is nearly self-sufficient in wheat production. Mozambique and Kenya, on the other hand, rely more heavily on wheat imports and so would have been more exposed to shocks to world wheat prices during the crisis.

At the height of the food price crisis in 2008/2009, bread purchasing power in urban Kenya was comparable to levels last seen in 2005, while wheat flour purchasing power for Maputo minimum wage earners was comparable to levels in 2000. These results suggest that high food prices during the food crisis partially reversed or stalled improvements in bread and wheat flour purchasing power in urban Kenya, Lusaka and Maputo but did not drive wheat product affordability to unprecedentedly low levels. Results for the other staple foods and urban centers generally support this point as well.

Trends in Staple Foods Affordable per Daily Wage in Urban Kenya, Zambia and Mozambique

Figures 8.3, 8.4 and 8.7 show the quantities affordable per daily wage for various staple foods in urban Kenya, Lusaka and Maputo, respectively, each month between the early 1990s and 2008/2009. Columns E through I in Table 8.3 show the average quantities affordable per daily wage during five different agricultural marketing years over the sample period for all of the staple foods and urban centers included in the analysis. (The agricultural marketing year is from July through June in Kenya and from May through April in Zambia and Mozambique.) Increases over time in staple food purchasing power are clearly evident for maize grain, maize meal and bread in urban Kenya and Lusaka

(Figures 8.3 and 8.4). For all of the staple foods and urban centers in Kenya and Zambia that were analyzed, the average quantity affordable per daily wage was higher in the 2000/2001 marketing year than in 1995/1996, and higher still in 2006/2007 than in 2000/2001 (Table 8.3, columns E, F, and G). Staple food purchasing power for formal sector workers in 2006/2007 (i.e., just before the food price crisis) was 2.4 to 4.4 times greater than it was in 1995/1996.

Figure 8.2. Loaves of bread affordable per daily wage in urban Kenya and Lusaka, and kilograms of wheat flour affordable per daily wage in Maputo January 1994–January 2009

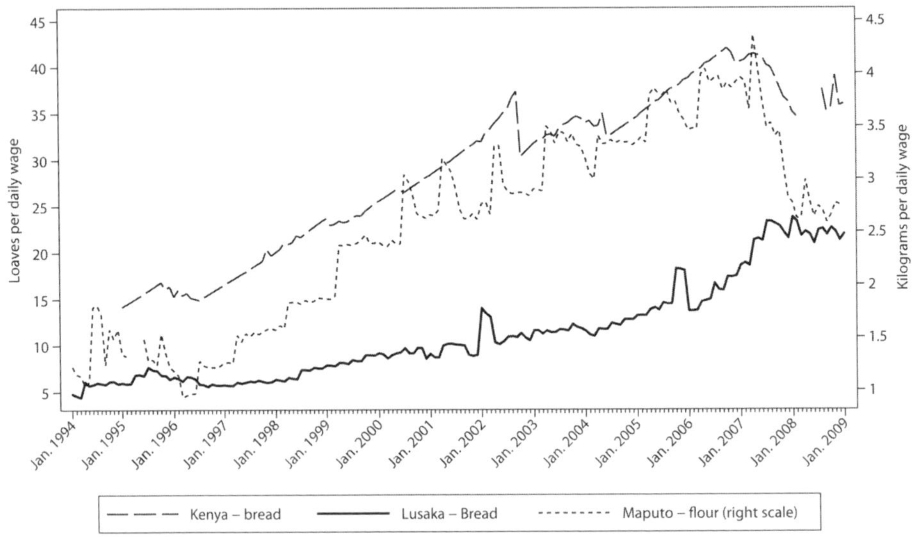

Sources: Kenya Ministry of Trade & Industry (MTI), Kenya National Bureau of Statistics (KNBS), Zambia Central Statistical Office (CSO), Mozambique Agricultural Market Information System (SIMA), Government of Mozambique Monthly Bulletins (GRM)
Notes: Average formal sector daily wage used for urban Kenya and Lusaka; formal sector worker daily minimum wage used for Maputo.

Figures 8.3 and 8.4 also reveal a sharp decline in maize and maize meal affordability in Lusaka and Nairobi and in bread purchasing power in urban Kenya when prices soared during the food price crisis. The average quantities of maize meal and bread affordable per daily wage in urban Kenya were, respectively, 47 percent and 11 percent lower in the 2008/2009 marketing year than in 2006/2007 (Table 8.3, columns G and I). In the Zambian urban centers, formal sector wage earners' maize meal purchasing power was 11 percent to 19 percent lower in 2008–2009 than in 2007/2008 (Table 8.3, columns H and I). The food price crisis was clearly a major shock to urban consumers in these locations. However, gains in staple food purchasing power (at least for formal sector workers) over the preceding decade were sufficiently large that the food crisis did not push staple food affordability to historically low levels. Despite high food prices, purchasing power for maize grain, maize meal and bread in urban Kenya was still higher in 2008/2009 than it had been in the mid-1990s and early 2000s. In urban Zambia, the food price crisis only turned back gains in purchasing power by a year or two, as the quantities affordable per daily wage in 2008/2009 were comparable to or greater than levels in 2006/2007.

Figure 8.3. Kilograms of maize meal and maize grain affordable per daily wage in Nairobi, and loaves of bread affordable per daily wage in urban Kenya January 1994–January 2009

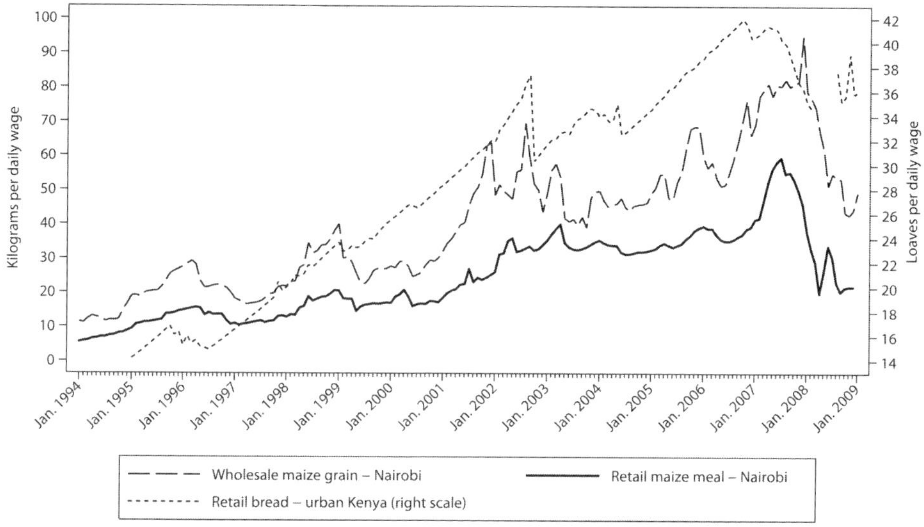

Sources: Kenya Market Information Center, Ministry of Agriculture (MIC), MTI, KNBS

The preceding discussions of trends in staple food affordability in urban Kenya and Zambia are based on a weighted average daily wage across all (formal) sectors in each country, where the weights correspond to the share of total employment attributed to a given sector. As a robustness check, we examine trends in the kilograms of maize grain affordable per daily wage for each of the four wage series in Zambia (central government, local government, parastatals, and private sector) and for the average public sector and average private sector wage series in Kenya. For Kenya, the quantity of maize grain affordable per daily wage for the average public sector worker and the average private sector worker tracked very closely between January 1994 and January 2004 (Figure 8.5). Since then, private sector workers' purchasing power has been somewhat greater than that of public sector workers. In Zambia, trends in maize purchasing power are similar for workers in central government, local government, and the private sector, but purchasing power rose much more rapidly for parastatal employees; however, parastatal employees accounted for only 5 percent to 8 percent of total formal sector employees in Zambia in 2007 (CSO, 2007) (Figure 8.6).

Figure 8.4. Kilograms of maize grain and maize meal and loaves of bread affordable per daily wage: Lusaka, Zambia, January 1994–January 2009

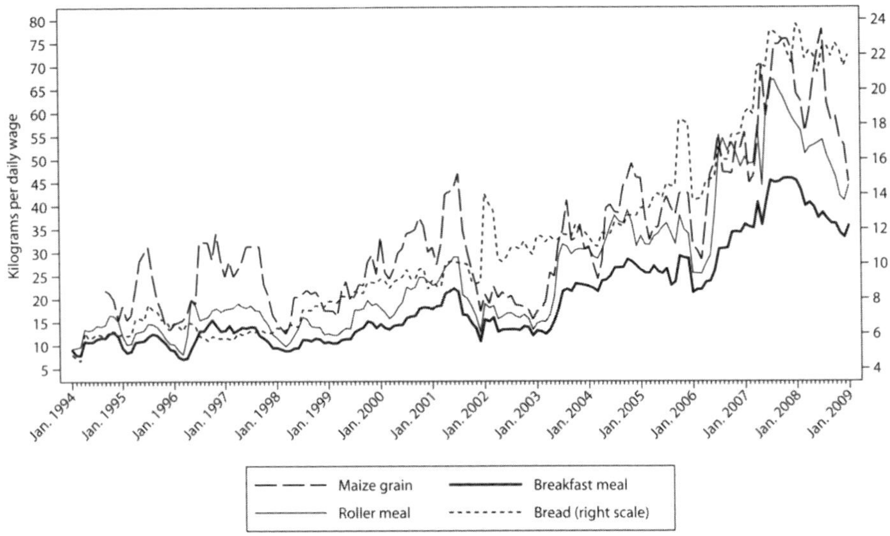

Source: CSO

Figure 8.5. Kilograms of wholesale maize grain affordable per daily wage for workers in the public sector and private sector: Nairobi, Kenya January 1994–December 2008

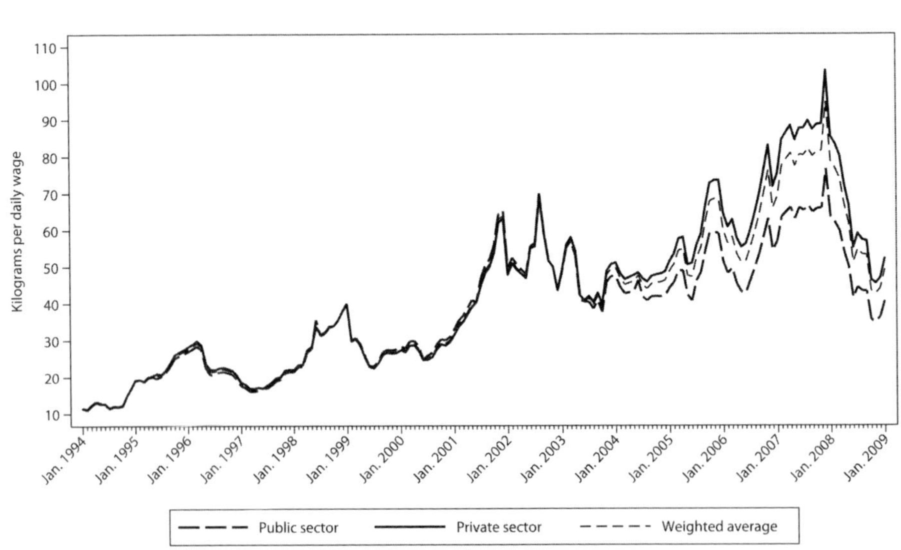

Source: CSO

Minimum wage earners in Maputo and Nampula saw some gains in their staple food purchasing power in the decade or so prior to the food price crisis (Figure 8.7 and Table 8.3).[65] The average quantities of maize grain, maize meal, wheat flour, rice and cassava that these workers could buy with a day's minimum wage in 2006/2007 were 2.4 to 3.8 times higher than in 1995/1996 (Table 8.3, columns E and G). Figure 8.7 indicates that Maputo minimum wage earners' purchasing power for maize grain, wheat flour and rice declined during the food price crisis between 2007 and 2009. The quantities of these foods affordable per daily minimum wage in Maputo in 2008/2009 (during the food price crisis) were 20 percent to 31 percent lower than in 2006/2007 (before the food price crisis); in Nampula, the declines in affordability ranged from 14 percent to 39 percent (Table 8.3, columns G and I). Nonetheless, Maputo and Nampula minimum wage earners' purchasing power for staple foods during the food price crisis was not pushed to all-time low levels (see Figure 8.7 and Table 8.3).

Figure 8.6. Kilograms of retail maize grain affordable per daily wage for workers in the central government, local government, parastatals and private sectors: Lusaka, Zambia, September 1994–January 2009

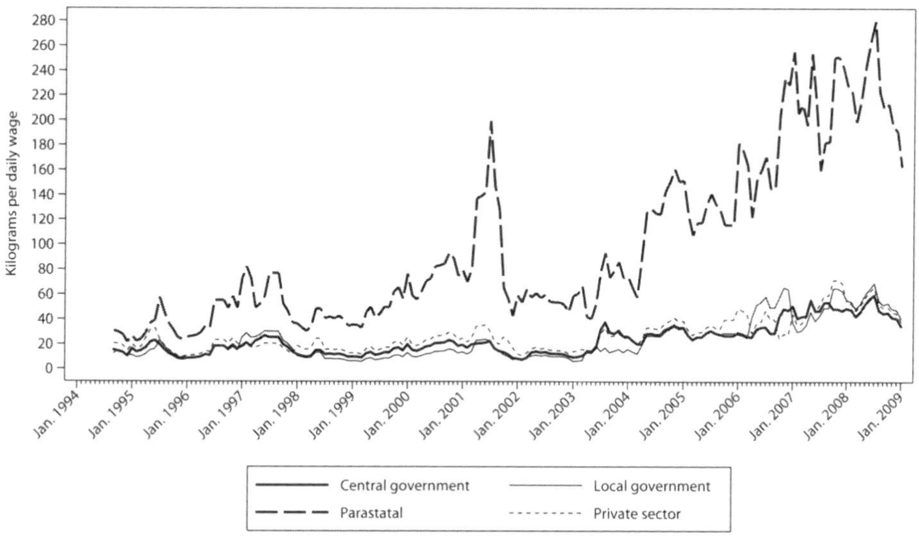

Source: CSO

Records of the number of persons employed in the formal sectors in Kenya and Zambia can shed some light on the finding of increased purchasing power among formal sector workers in those countries. The number of formal sector employees in Kenya grew each year between 1993 and 2007, the most recent year for which data are available (KNBS, various years). In Zambia, there were fewer formal sector employees in 1997–1998 than in 1992–1995 (CSO, various years). Employment level information is not

[65] The sharp drop in maize and maize meal purchasing power in Maputo around January 2006 was due to spikes in both commodity prices at that time. National maize production for 2005 was substantially overestimated and there was a shortage of maize instead of the predicted surplus, resulting in high maize grain and maize meal prices.

available for 1999 through 2005, but the number of persons employed in the formal sector in 2006 was similar to the number employed in 1997/1998, and employment levels began to increase in 2007 (CSO, various years). The number of formal sector employees did not grow as rapidly as either the total or urban populations in either Kenya or Zambia between 1993 and 2007 (KNBS, various years; UNPD, 2007; CSO, various years).[66] The share of informal sector employment in total employment and the total number of informal sector employees grew significantly in both countries over the study period.

Figure 8.7. Kilograms of maize meal, maize grain, wheat flour, and rice affordable per daily wage: Maputo, Mozambique, January 1993–December 2008

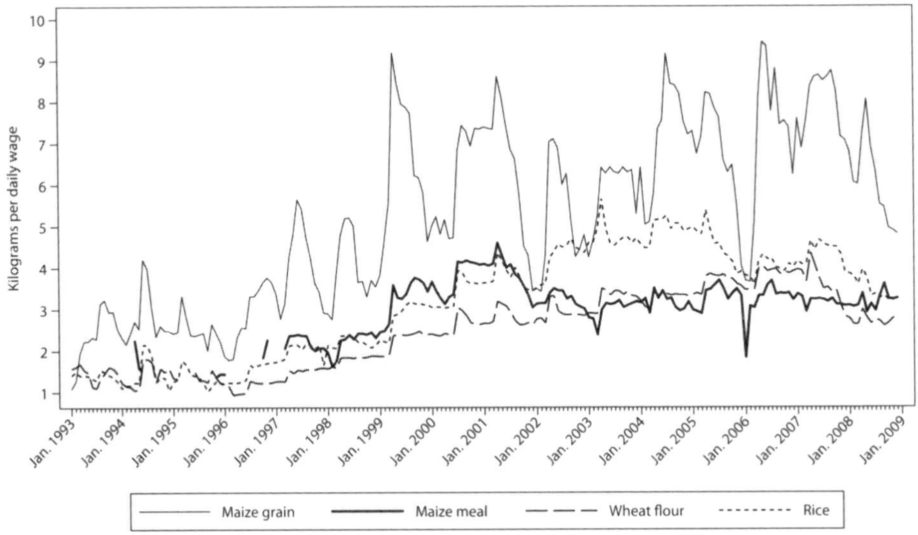

Sources: SIMA, GRM

It is important to bear in mind that the findings of positive trends in the quantities of staple foods affordable per daily wage highlighted here hold for formal sector workers in Kenya and Zambia and for minimum wage earners in Mozambique (and for workers whose wages are positively correlated with these formal sector or minimum wages). Time series data on informal sector wages and returns to formal/informal business activities are not available, so we cannot speak to trends in purchasing power for staple foods for urban consumers who rely on these types of earnings for their livelihoods. Informal sector wages and business returns may be positively correlated with formal sector wages; however, this is ultimately an empirical question, and one that cannot be answered for Kenya, Zambia or Mozambique given the lack of data on informal sector wages and business returns.

[66] Between the early 1990s and 2007 in both Kenya and Zambia, private sector employees made up an increasing share of total formal sector employees (KNBS, various years; CSO, various years).

Results: Trends in Marketing Margins for Maize and Wheat Products

Kenya

Figure 8.8 indicates that the retail maize meal to wholesale maize grain percentage marketing margin in Nairobi generally declined between 1994 and late 2003 but trended upward between 2004 and late 2008. A significant downward trend is evident even between 1994 and 2006 but is broken by events in 2007 and 2008. Previous research suggests that the decline in maize marketing margins in Kenya is due to intense competition in the milling sector following market liberalization and to related milling efficiency gains associated with competitive pressures to cut costs (Jayne and Argwings-Kodhek, 1997; Jayne and Jones, 1997; Muyanga *et al.*, 2005; Jayne and Chapoto, 2006; Ariga and Jayne, 2010). The reduction in maize marketing margins between 1994 and 2006 was likely a key driver of the positive trend in purchasing power for maize meal among formal sector wage earners in Kenya over the same period. Maize marketing margins rose sharply in 2008. As a result, the linear trends in the real and percentage maize grain/maize meal marketing margins in Nairobi over the entire 1994 to 2009 study period are not statistically significant (Table 8.4, columns A and B).

Figure 8.8. Nairobi retail maize meal / wholesale maize grain price spread as a percentage of the retail maize meal price, and urban Kenya retail bread / world wheat price spread as a percentage of the retail bread price: January 1994–December 2008

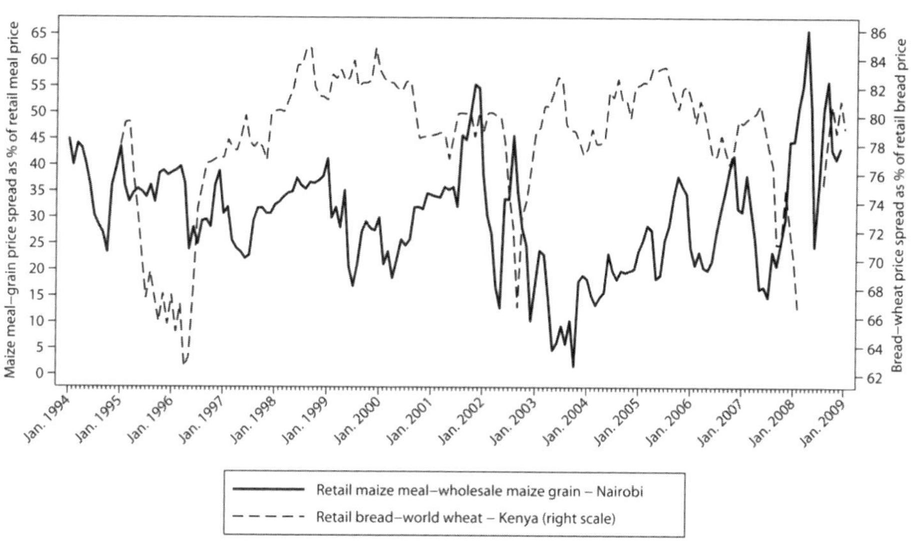

Sources: MIC, MTI, IMF, KNBS

The reasons for the dramatic rise in maize meal to maize grain marketing margins in 2008 are not entirely clear, but post-election violence, poor weather and delayed imports may have been factors. In response to a national maize production shortfall in 2007/2008 (not in response to the global food price crisis), the Kenyan government arranged to import

Table 8.4. Summary: Trends over Time in Marketing Margins for Maize and Wheat Products

Urban center	Products	Marketing margin definition	--Regression results-- Estimated change in margin from month-to-month Coef. (A)	p-value (B)
Nairobi	Retail maize meal / wholesale maize grain	Price spread as % of meal price	-0.003	0.956
		Real price spread (Ksh/kg, 2007=1)	-0.029	0.288
Urban Kenya	Retail bread / world wheat	Price spread as % of bread price	-0.004	0.953
		Real price spread (Ksh/loaf, 2007=1)	-0.041+	0.055
Lilongwe	Retail maize meal / retail maize grain	Price spread as % of meal price	-0.173**	<0.001
		Real price spread (MWK/kg, 2007=1)	-0.109	0.376
	Retail bread / world wheat	Price spread as % of bread price	-0.058	0.331
		Real price spread (MWK/loaf, 2007=1)	0.074*	0.014
Maputo	Retail breakfast meal / wholesale maize grain	Price spread as % of meal price	0.061	0.652
		Real price spread (MTN/kg, 2004=1)	0.032**	0.003
	Retail flour / world wheat	Price spread as % of flour price	-0.007	0.933
		Real price spread (MTN/kg, 2004=1)	0.002	0.912
Nampula	Retail roller meal / wholesale maize grain	Price spread as % of meal price	-0.019	0.892
		Real price spread (MTN/kg, 2004=1)	-0.009	0.613
	Retail flour / world wheat	Price spread as % of flour price	-0.047	0.631
		Real price spread (MTN/kg, 2004=1)	-0.013	0.420
Lusaka	Retail breakfast meal / wholesale maize grain	Price spread as % of meal price	-0.110+	0.073
		Real price spread (ZMK/kg, 2007=1)	-7.047**	<0.001
	Retail roller meal / wholesale maize grain	Price spread as % of meal price	-0.158**	0.003
		Real price spread (ZMK/kg, 2007=1)	-6.082**	<0.001
	Retail bread / world wheat	Price spread as % of bread price	-0.026	0.409
		Real price spread (ZMK/loaf, 2007=1)	-14.194**	<0.001
Kitwe	Retail breakfast meal / retail maize grain	Price spread as % of meal price	-0.022	0.544
		Real price spread (ZMK/kg, 2007=1)	-3.150**	0.002
	Retail roller meal / retail maize grain	Price spread as % of meal price	-0.087**	0.008
		Real price spread (ZMK/kg, 2007=1)	-3.561**	<0.001
Mansa	Retail breakfast meal / retail maize grain	Price spread as % of meal price	-0.032	0.405
		Real price spread (ZMK/kg, 2007=1)	-4.249**	<0.001
	Retail roller meal / retail maize grain	Price spread as % of meal price	-0.113*	0.017
		Real price spread (ZMK/kg, 2007=1)	-5.736**	<0.001

Table 8.4 continued

------------------------Summary statistics------------------------

Average margin during each agricultural marketing year[a]

1995/96 (C)	2000/01 (D)	2006/07 (E)	2007/08 (F)	2008/09[b] (G)	All (H)	Obs. (I)
35.3	32.5	30.6	37.6	45.1	30.2	180
12.8	14.7	8.2	11.4	19.1	12.1	180
66.3	79.3	78.9	72.5	78.9	78.4	164
21.3	23.8	20.9	20.8	20.3	24.2	164
75.2	74.5	58.6	54.3	43.2	64.8	146
74.6	43.2	40.0	38.7	36.4	54.2	146
72.9	77.0	74.6	65.2	--	77.0	168
42.9	42.8	55.4	49.5	--	47.5	168
--	22.7	50.2	46.5	25.0	34.4	123
--	1.7	6.1	6.2	3.6	4.0	123
45.8	60.9	47.3	42.0	61.9	55.3	190
6.8	6.9	4.9	5.6	10.3	6.8	190
--	65.2	62.8	52.6	41.1	49.6	94
--	3.7	5.7	4.7	4.4	4.6	94
50.2	55.5	43.8	34.3	48.4	54.9	174
8.5	5.5	4.3	4.1	6.0	6.8	174
43.4	61.2	44.6	38.2	27.8	40.3	176
1596.4	1260.9	692.0	554.0	474.5	984.0	176
43.8	57.1	31.3	29.9	21.2	35.8	176
1326.9	882.5	337.5	328.8	275.5	707.7	176
76.8	80.0	81.1	72.2	78.8	80.4	181
4042.8	3001.7	2330.3	1998.7	2268.4	3253.1	181
39.2	28.5	30.0	22.8	25.7	24.8	173
1425.4	577.6	445.9	329.8	453.5	595.8	173
42.4	28.1	15.9	10.4	15.8	21.6	173
1337.4	459.4	176.7	110.7	204.0	446.5	173
43.2	36.2	31.7	18.0	32.4	30.7	175
1568.9	773.7	559.6	282.5	585.2	768.9	175
42.1	39.9	22.4	6.8	21.6	29.6	175
1354.2	744.3	299.2	74.8	276.5	665.8	175

Source: Authors' calculations.

Notes: [a]The agricultural marketing year is from July through June in Kenya and from May through April in Malawi, Mozambique, and Zambia. [b]Through November/December 2008 or January 2009. **, *, + significant at the 1, 5, and 10 percent levels, respectively. -- = no observations.

200,000 MT of maize through the National Cereals and Produce Board (NCPB) in August 2008. When these imports finally arrived in Kenya in late 2008 (the actual quantity imported was less than 200,000 MT), the NCPB sold the maize to selected local firms at a subsidized price (approximately two-thirds of import parity). The firms were to sell the maize to selected millers at a subsidized price, and millers were expected to pass along the savings to consumers. These subsidies may have given millers room to substantially widen their margins.

The percentage marketing margin between retail bread prices in Kenya and world wheat prices was lower in 1995/1996 than in the latter 1990s and most of the 2000s (Figure 8.8 and Table 8.4, columns C to G). On average, the marketing margin was 78 percent of the retail bread price (Table 8.4, column H). There is no statistically significant linear trend in this marketing margin in percentage terms, but in real terms the bread/world wheat marketing margin declined over time (Table 8.4, columns A and B). The decrease in real bread/world wheat marketing margins likely contributed to improvements in purchasing power for bread among Kenyan formal sector workers between the mid-1990s and the food price crisis.

Lilongwe, Malawi

Retail maize meal/retail maize grain percentage marketing margins are highly volatile in Lilongwe; this percentage marketing margin ranges from 16 percent to 88 percent and appears to have declined somewhat between 2004 and 2008 (Figure 8.9).

Figure 8.9. Lilongwe retail maize meal/retail maize grain price spread as a percentage of retail maize meal price; retail bread/world wheat price spread as a percentage of the retail bread price: January 1996–July 2008

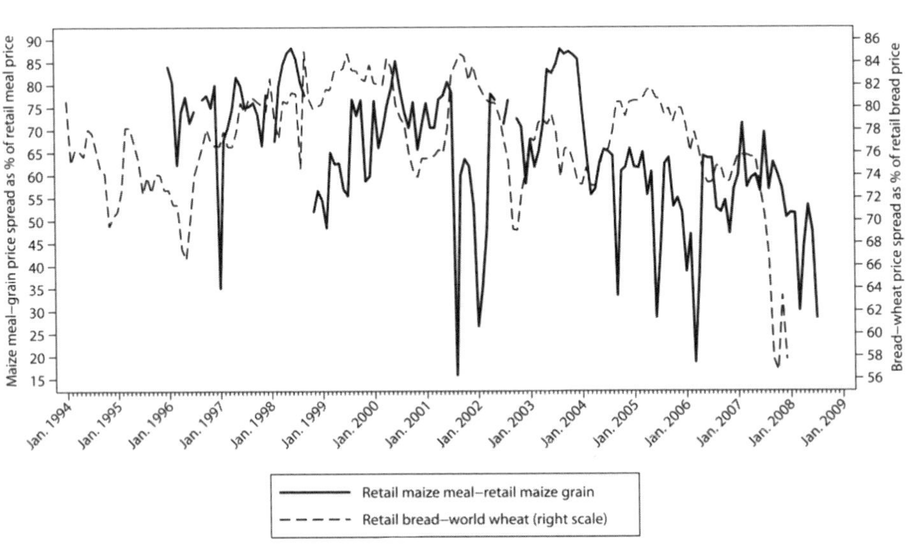

Sources: MAFS, NSO, IMF

Comparing average maize marketing margins (in percentage and real terms) across several marketing years, the margins were lower in 2008/2009 than in 1995/1996, 2000/2001, 2006/2007, and 2007/2008 (Table 8.4, columns C to G).[67] Regression results indicate a statistically significant ($p \leq 0.01$) negative trend in the maize meal/maize grain percentage marketing margin in Lilongwe (Table 8.4, columns A and B). The parameter estimate indicates a 0.17 percentage point decrease in the marketing margin from month-to-month; this corresponds to a yearly decrease in the margin of approximately 2.0 percentage points.

The percentage marketing margin between retail bread prices in Lilongwe and world wheat prices was slightly lower in the 2007/2008 marketing year (65.2 percent) than it was in 1995/1996, 2000/2001, and 2006/2007, when it ranged from 72.9 percent to 77.0 percent (Table 8.4, columns C to F). (The most recent bread prices available at the time of writing were for December 2007.) The bread/wheat percentage marketing margin during the last months of 2007 was substantially lower than it was during any other month in the period of analysis (Figure 8.9). More recent data are needed to determine whether these lower marketing margins persisted and why. One possible explanation is that the period in which the Lilongwe bread/wheat percentage marketing margin plummeted is also the period in the early months of the food price crisis when world wheat prices spiked dramatically. A lag between the time when world prices rose sharply and when bread prices in Lilongwe increased would explain the lower retail bread to world wheat percentage marketing margins in late 2007. There is no statistically significant linear trend in the bread/wheat margin in percentage terms, but in real terms, there is a statistically significant monthly increase of 0.07 real MWK (2007=100) in the margin (Table 8.4, columns A and B).

Mozambique

Retail maize meal/wholesale maize grain percentage marketing margins were quite volatile during the period of analysis in Maputo, showing dramatic seasonal movements (Figure 8.10). There was no statistically significant linear trend in the maize grain/maize meal marketing margin in percentage terms in Maputo or Nampula, but the real marketing margin in Maputo has a statistically significant, positive trend (Table 8.4, columns A and B). This finding is consistent with earlier work on marketing margins in Mozambique, which also indicates a positive trend in maize marketing margins in Maputo (Abdula, 2005).

Percentage retail wheat flour/world wheat marketing margins increased from 1996 and peaked in 1998/1999 in both Maputo and Nampula (Figure 8.10). Between 2003 and 2007, monetized food-aid wheat delivered to millers represented about 20 percent of total supplies (Emerging Markets Group, 2008) and may have contributed to the relatively lower wheat flour/world wheat margins during the period. There were no statistically significant linear trends in the wheat flour/world wheat margins for either city during the period of analysis (Table 8.4, columns A and B).

Zambia

The clearest pattern of trends in maize marketing margins emerges for urban centers in Zambia. The regression analysis indicates statistically significant negative trends in roller

---

[67] The agricultural marketing year in Malawi is from May through April.

meal/maize grain marketing margins in both percentage and real terms in Lusaka, Kitwe and Mansa (Table 8.4, columns A and B). There were also statistically significant negative trends in breakfast meal/maize grain margins in all three cities in real terms, but in percentage terms, the negative trend was only statistically significant in Lusaka. Graphical analysis of the maize marketing margins in Lusaka reveals that these margins declined between 1994 and 2003 and were relatively flat between 2004 and 2008 (Figure 8.11). The average breakfast meal/maize grain percentage margin in the 2008/2009 marketing year in Lusaka was 27.8 percent compared to 43.4 percent in 1995/1996; for roller meal, the percentage margin averaged 21.2 percent in 2008/2009 and 43.8 percent in 1995/1996 (Table 8.4, columns C and G). Similar patterns hold in Kitwe and Mansa.

Figure 8.10. Maputo retail maize meal/wholesale maize grain price spread as a percentage of retail maize meal price; retail wheat flour / world wheat price spread as a percentage of the retail flour price: January 1993–December 2008

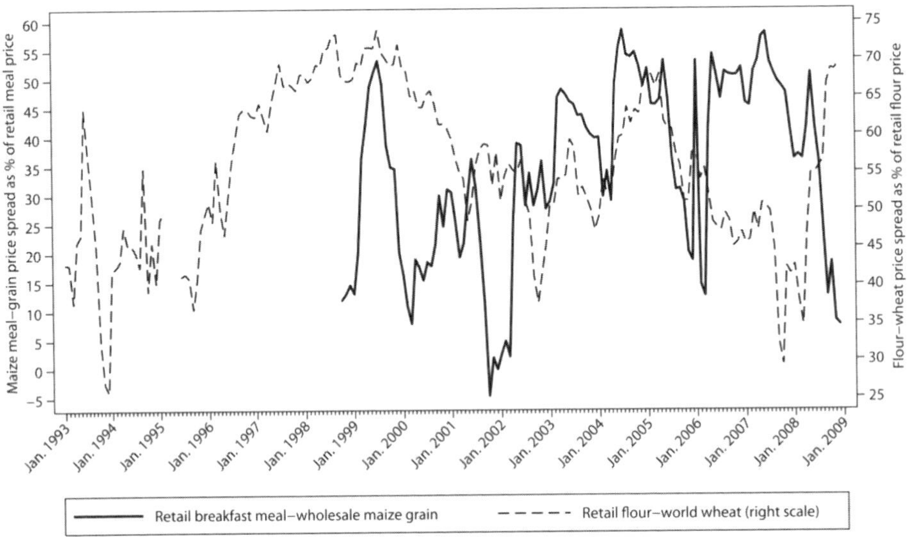

Source: SIMA, IMF, BDM

The finding of declines in *maize meal/maize grain* marketing margins in Zambia is consistent with previous evidence from Zambia (Chapoto and Jayne, 2006). Following liberalization of private maize trade and of the maize processing industry in Zambia, the number of small- to medium-scale millers and retailers expanded rapidly. Large-scale millers who had a *de facto* oligopoly on maize milling prior to market reforms were forced to lower their prices to maintain market share. At the same time, the increasing availability of hammer mills in urban areas gave urban consumers the (cheaper) option of buying (or producing) grain and having it custom-milled (Chapoto and Jayne, 2006). It is less likely that milling efficiency gains contributed to the declining marketing margins, as established large-scale millers have made few investments in improved milling technology over the last decade. Declining maize marketing margins are likely to have been a key driver of improving maize meal purchasing power among formal sector wage earnings in Zambia.

Retail bread/world wheat percentage marketing margins in Lusaka ranged from 63 percent to 87 percent. There is not much variation in the average bread/wheat percentage marketing margin across the five marketing years analyzed (Table 8.4, columns C to G). Regression analysis indicates that there was no statistically significant linear trend in the bread/wheat marketing margin in percentage terms but that the real marketing margin had a significant, negative trend (Table 8.4, columns A and B). Improving bread purchasing power over time in Lusaka may have been driven in part by the lower real bread/world wheat marketing margins.

Figure 8.11. Lusaka retail maize meal / wholesale maize grain price spread as a percentage of the retail maize meal price; retail bread / world wheat price spread as a percentage of the retail bread price: January 1994–January 2009

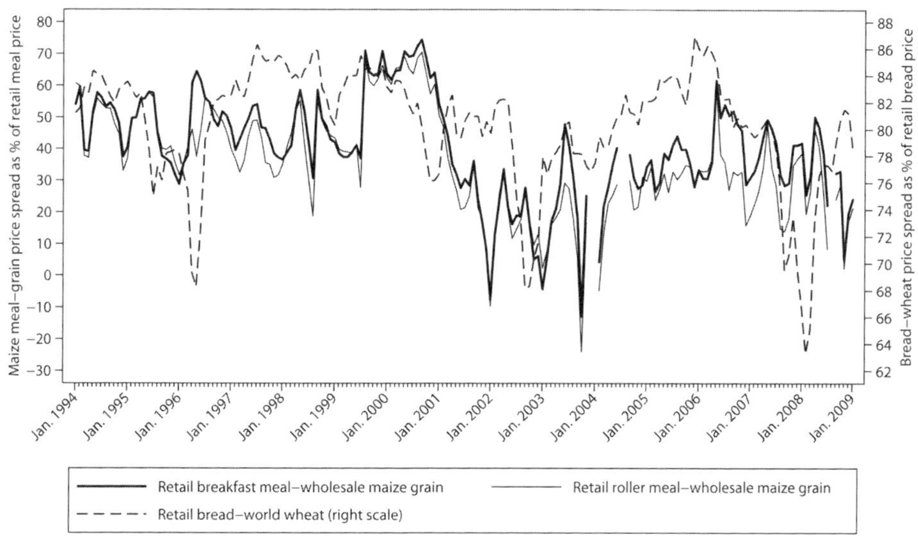

Sources: Zambia Agricultural Marketing Information Center (AMIC), CSO, IMF, Bank of Zambia (BOZ)

Potential Strategies to Moderate Increases in Staple Food Prices for Urban Consumers

The analysis in this chapter shows that in ESA, urban consumers' staple food purchasing power was hard-hit during the food price crisis. What are some potential food marketing policies and strategies that governments in the region can use to keep staple food prices at moderate or tolerable levels for urban consumers during times of high prices? First, ensuring that maize grain is available in public markets, especially during the lean season, keeps pressure on large-scale millers to maintain low maize meal prices and margins in order to compete with smaller-scale millers. When grain is in public markets, consumers have a variety of options for acquiring maize meal, including the relatively inexpensive one of buying grain in the market and having it milled for a fee by a local miller. However, when grain supplies in public markets dwindle due to poor harvests—

while at the same time import licenses are issued only to selected large millers or high duties are imposed on grain imports for direct sales—the entire milling and retail market structure changes. In Mozambique, this has meant a decline in small-scale milling facilities since the early 2000s. Commercially manufactured meal becomes the only source of maize meal and the large millers enjoy much lower levels of competition, which may lead to higher vertical marketing margins and maize meal prices for consumers. In recent years of poor maize harvests, the Zambian and Kenyan governments have imported maize and channeled it to large-scale millers at highly subsidized prices. Not only does this not improve maize availability in public markets, but it also reduces incentives to private sector actors to import maize and sell it at market prices, further exacerbating price spikes in deficit years.

Second, ensuring a broad range of food products in local markets (maize grain and otherwise) facilitates consumer substitution among staple foods, which may help mitigate the effects of food price spikes on urban consumers. When the prices of the main tradable staples rise, as they did during the food price crisis, assuming a positive cross-price elasticity of demand, urban consumers would be expected to switch to cheaper staple foods in order to maintain overall consumption levels. For example, commercially-milled maize meal prices appear to have increased more during the food price crisis than did bread prices in urban Kenya and Zambia, and maize grain prices increased less than maize meal prices. Cassava is generally an inexpensive staple substitute. Urban consumers in Kenya and Zambia would therefore be expected to demand less commercially-milled maize meal and more bread, cassava and/or custom-milled maize meal when commercially-milled maize meal prices rise. Expanding the staple food options available to urban consumers, e.g., by keeping maize grain available in public markets, and by promoting urban agriculture and the marketing of staple substitutes such as cassava and sweet potatoes, could help facilitate such substitution and buffer consumers against food price spikes. The importance of ensuring a broad range of food products in public markets is reinforced by the finding that more than half of the pair-wise correlations of first differenced retail prices in the various urban centers examined are statistically significant and positive (see Table 8.5), indicating that consumer substitution among staple foods may help to mitigate the effects of retail price increases.

Third, timely and accurate crop production and market information systems are needed to identify well in advance whether imports are needed, and if so, how much is needed to stabilize food prices during tight market situations. Both the public and private sectors have the problem of assessing import demand; inaccurate crop forecasts hamper public sector planning and responses and constrain the private sector's ability to program commercial activities in a timely fashion for greatest profitability. The private sector is also strongly affected by the lack of accurate forecasts as it cannot predict price movements and domestic supply availability for purchasing of commodities. Accurate crop forecasts are also critical, *inter alia*, for decision-making by public and private sector actors regarding crop exports and for the World Food Programme to respond to food emergencies and to work with partners planning local crop purchases.

It is becoming increasingly clear that national crop estimates in some countries in the region are unreliable. An example of how inaccurate crop production estimates can exacerbate food insecurity is the case of Malawi in 2007/2008. On the basis of the government's forecast of a record maize harvest in 2007 and a projected maize surplus of 1.2 million tons over national consumption requirements, the government contracted with other states in the region to export over 400,000 tons of maize. However, the government was only able to source some 300,000 tons and this sent the price of maize rocketing to levels seen only in the most severe drought years. In hindsight, it is widely believed that the 2007 Malawi harvest was overestimated by roughly 25 percent (Dorward *et al.*, 2008).

Table 8.5. Pair-wise Correlation Coefficients for First-differenced Nominal Retail Staple Prices: Key Urban Centers in Kenya, Malawi, Mozambique and Zambia

Price series	Nairobi[a]	Lilongwe	Maputo[b]	Nampula	Lusaka	Kitwe	Mansa
Maize grain, breakfast meal	--	--	0.022	--	0.276**	0.442**	0.342**
Maize grain, roller meal	--	--	--	0.252*	0.277**	0.409**	0.240**
Maize grain, maize meal	0.100	0.113	--	--	--	--	--
Maize grain, bread	0.100	0.188*	--	--	0.057	--	--
Maize grain, wheat flour	--	--	0.091	0.208**	--	--	--
Maize grain, cassava flour	--	--	--	0.277**	--	--	0.106
Maize grain, rice	--	--	0.171*	0.108	--	--	--
Breakfast meal, roller meal	--	--	--	--	0.790**	0.791**	0.613**
Breakfast meal, bread	--	--	--	--	0.124+	--	--
Breakfast meal, wheat flour	--	--	0.028	--	--	--	--
Breakfast meal, cassava flour	--	--	--	--	--	--	0.031
Breakfast meal, rice	--	--	0.002	--	--	--	--
Roller meal, bread	--	--	--	--	0.107	--	--
Roller meal, wheat flour	--	--	--	0.177+	--	--	--
Roller meal, cassava flour	--	--	--	0.160	--	--	0.051
Roller meal, rice	--	--	--	-0.015	--	--	--
Maize meal, bread	0.317**	0.050	--	--	--	--	--
Wheat flour, rice	--	--	0.285**	0.182*	--	--	--
Wheat flour, cassava flour	--	--	--	0.121	--	--	--
Rice, cassava flour	--	-	--	-0.047	--	--	--

Source: Authors' calculations.

Notes: + significant at 10 percent level; * significant at 5 percent level; ** significant at 1 percent level. – = not applicable or data not available. [a]Wholesale maize grain prices used as proxy for retail maize grain prices in Nairobi; bread price is average for urban Kenya. [b]Breakfast meal refers to high quality maize flour (e.g., Top Score brand).

If the government had been able to produce a more accurate estimate of crop production, it might not have arranged to export maize, which in turn might have avoided the late 2007/early 2008 price surge that caused such hardship for maize-buying households. Problems of overestimated crop forecasts have been noted elsewhere in the region, especially where improved food self-sufficiency has become a key litmus test of politicians' effectiveness and governments' popularity.

Fourth, if accurate crop forecasts indicate that imports are required, making early arrangements for importation is another high-priority step for moderating food price increases during years of tight market conditions. In 2008, relatively timely early warning analysis reported that maize imports would be required in several countries of the region to keep food prices from spiking above import parity in early 2009. However, imports were both late and insufficient to prevent maize prices from rising over US$400 per ton in Kenya and Zambia, and over US$500 per ton in parts of Malawi in late 2008 and early 2009, despite the fact that world market prices declined back to the range of US$150 to US$180 per ton by November 2008. Had import arrangements been made earlier, maize prices in these countries would likely not have risen above import parity.

A fifth and related point is that removing import tariffs on maize and other staple commodities well in advance of the time when large quantities of imports are needed will help prevent the clogging of port and road infrastructure. For example, late removal of import tariffs by the Kenyan government likely exacerbated the spike in maize prices in 2008/2009. Despite early warnings that 2007/2008 maize production was one million MT short of national requirements, the government was slow to arrange imports in 2008 and ultimately imported less than 200,000 MT. High maize tariffs of 50 percent through the port of Mombasa discouraged private sector imports. When the tariff was finally removed in late January 2009 (private traders and millers had been calling for its removal since early 2008), the private sector was quick to arrange for 700,000 MT to be imported. However, port and road infrastructure capacity was insufficient to quickly absorb this large quantity of maize and move it to deficit areas, so prices continued to soar for several months after private sector imports arrived in Mombasa. Had the import tariff been removed much earlier in the season, the private sector would have been able to import earlier and space out (temporally) the arrival of imported grain at the ports and its transport to retail markets.

Beyond these strategies, governments in Kenya and Zambia should also reconsider their policies of buying maize at pan-territorial, typically above-market prices from farmers, as such policies put upward pressure on maize prices. The Malawian governments' restriction of private sector maize trade in recent years has likely had similar effects on maize prices. The National Cereals and Produce Board (NCPB) in Kenya and the Food Reserve Agency (FRA) in Zambia, both parastatals, have increased their direct involvement in maize marketing in recent years (Jayne *et al.*, 2007). For example, the FRA has purchased more than 50 percent of Zambian smallholders' marketed maize in three of five recent years (2006/2007–2010/2011 marketing years), including 2007/2008 during the food price crisis. Between its establishment in 1996 and the 2005/2006 marketing year, the FRA's maize purchases were much lower (from zero to 38 percent). In Kenya, the NCPB's activities effectively raised average wholesale maize prices by 20 percent between 1995 and 2004 (Jayne *et al.*, 2008a), and the FRA's activities are likely to have had similar effects on maize market prices in Zambia.

As currently structured, NCPB and FRA operations are a major drain on the national treasuries, the resources used to fund them have a high opportunity cost, and the policies benefit very few households. Maize sales in Kenya and Zambia are highly concentrated among a small number of large-scale farmers and better-capitalized smallholders. Such households benefit from the higher maize prices that result from NCPB and FRA policies. However, the majority (or near majority) of households in both countries are net-buyers of maize: urban and smallholder rural households that buy more maize than they sell. Net-buyers of maize are harmed, not helped, by policies that raise maize prices, such as those of the NCPB and FRA. In Malawi in recent years (including in 2008 during the food price crisis) the government has occasionally banned or otherwise restricted the private sector maize trade and granted a legal monopoly on maize trading to the Agricultural Development and Marketing Corporation (ADMARC) (Minot, 2010). This has likely resulted in upward pressure on maize prices as well.

In the longer run, there are many elements to a comprehensive strategy for moderating food prices for urban consumers, many of which derive from promoting on-farm productivity gains and cost reductions in the marketing system. First, investments in agricultural public goods such as research and extension, market information systems, and infrastructure have the potential to stimulate supply response and productivity growth in agriculture (Baker, 2008; Jayne *et al.*, 2008b; von Braun *et al.*, 2008; World Bank, 2008). Increasing agricultural productivity is one way to address the 'food price dilemma' and keep food prices for consumers at tolerable levels without undermining farmers' production incentives.

Second, facilitating regional trade of staple commodities by keeping borders open and lowering taxes and tariffs can help contain staple food prices within import-export parity price bands and prevent food staple prices from surging above import parity in years of national production shortfalls (FAO, 2008; IMF, 2008; von Braun *et al.*, 2008; World Bank, 2008; Dorosh *et al.*, 2009). For example, Dorosh *et al.* (2009) show that a drought in Zambia (modeled as a 30 percent reduction in national maize production) results in a 163 percent increase in domestic maize prices if the borders are closed but only a 36 percent increase if private sector imports are unrestricted. The negative impact of the drought on the urban poor is greatly buffered by regional trade: their maize consumption declines by 25 percent when borders are closed but by only 8 percent when private sector imports are allowed and the domestic maize price is capped at import parity.

Third, improving incentives for staple food imports by the private sector, including engendering mutual trust between the public and private sectors, can also help moderate staple food prices for urban consumers (Nijhoff *et al.*, 2002; Mwanaumo *et al.*, 2005; Chapoto *et al.*, 2008; Dorosh *et al.*, 2009; Tschirley and Jayne, 2010). Even if borders are ostensibly 'open' in years of maize production deficits, private traders may not be willing to take on the risk of importing maize and selling it at commercial prices if the policy environment is too uncertain. Governments often interpret the private sector's reluctance to import in such circumstances as evidence that the private sector cannot be relied upon to import sufficient maize when domestic production falls short of national consumption requirements. This is used as justification for government-arranged imports, which could further undermine incentives for private imports and sales at commercial prices. And so the vicious cycle goes.

'Credible commitments' by both government and private sector actors (Tschirley and Jayne, 2010) and predictable, transparent and consistent government policies are essential to incentivize private sector grain imports—and private sector participation and investments in food marketing more broadly—and to give governments the confidence to maintain open borders (Dorosh *et al.*, 2009). Unpredictable government maize marketing policies, related to both domestic and external trade, contributed to retail maize prices shooting above import parity in Malawi and Zambia on multiple occasions over the past decade (Tschirley and Jayne, 2010). Highly discretionary government maize marketing policies also contribute to higher maize price volatility and price uncertainty in Malawi and Zambia compared to countries such as Kenya and Mozambique, where maize marketing policies are more predictable and open (Chapoto and Jayne, 2009). More rules-based maize marketing policies—for example, with government interventions triggered by specific market conditions announced in advance—have the potential to reduce policy-induced maize price volatility, unpredictability, and price spikes above import parity (Chapoto and Jayne, 2009; Abbink *et al.*, forthcoming).

Finally, expanding, strengthening, and improving the targeting of safety net programs, and improving social protection more broadly—including conditional cash transfers, food vouchers and school feeding programs—are essential to protect the urban poor's access to food when staple food prices soar (Baker, 2008; FAO, 2008; IMF, 2008; von Braun *et al.*, 2008; World Bank, 2009). Even if the policies and strategies outlined above are adopted, there will still be households with insufficient effective demand to meet their staple food and other consumption requirements. In Mozambique, for example, a social safety net program in urban areas currently focused on the elderly and highly vulnerable children may need to be expanded to vulnerable households in general when staple food prices rise sharply. The design and targeting of social protection programs are essential to ensure that intended beneficiaries are reached, to minimize leakage to non-targeted groups, and to minimize distortion of incentives for private sector involvement in staple food production and marketing (FAO, 2008).

Conclusions

In this chapter, we have examined trends since the 1990s in formal sector wage earners' staple food purchasing power and maize and wheat marketing margins in key urban centers in Kenya, Malawi, Mozambique, and Zambia. The chapter highlights five key findings. First, formal sector wages rose at a faster rate than retail maize meal and bread prices in urban Kenya and Zambia between the mid-1990s and 2007. The quantities of these staple foods affordable per daily wage were 2.4 to 4.4 times greater in the 2006/2007 marketing year than in 1995/1996. By reducing retail maize meal to wholesale maize grain marketing margins in both countries, maize market and pricing reforms in the late 1980s and early 1990s are likely to have been key drivers of improvements in formal sector workers' maize meal purchasing power in the decade or so before the food price crisis.

Second, soaring food prices during the 2007/2008 food crisis resulted in a significant decline in formal sector workers' purchasing power for staple foods in urban Kenya and Zambia as wages failed to rise in step; nonetheless, increases in the affordability of staple foods over the 10 to 13 years prior to the food price crisis were large enough that the spike in prices during the crisis did not push purchasing power to unprecedentedly low levels. In urban Zambia, formal sector workers' purchasing power for bread and maize meal declined by 2 percent and 16 percent, respectively, between 2007/2008 when affordability peaked and 2008/2009 when food prices soared. In urban Kenya, formal sector workers' purchasing power for bread and maize meal in 2008/2009 was 11 percent and 47 percent lower, respectively, than in 2006/2007 when affordability was at its highest point. However, even at the peak of the food price crisis in 2008/2009, the quantities of staple foods affordable per daily wage in urban Kenya and Zambia were still roughly double their levels of the mid-1990s.

Third, the staple food purchasing power of minimum wage earners in Maputo and Nampula, Mozambique increased from the mid-1990s into the 2000s, and although high prices during the recent food crisis were a significant shock to urban consumers, they did not push staple food affordability for these workers to all-time low levels. In Maputo, the quantities of rice and wheat affordable per daily minimum wage approximately tripled between the mid-1990s and the 2006/2007 marketing year. As a result of high prices during the food crisis, rice and wheat purchasing power in Maputo in 2008/2009 was 20 percent and 31 percent lower, respectively, in 2008/2009 than in 2006/2007. Despite these declines, Maputo minimum wage earners' rice and wheat flour purchasing power in 2008/2009 was still higher than in the mid-1990s and roughly similar to levels at the turn of the millennium.

The results above hold for formal sector wage earners in urban Kenya and Zambia and for (formal sector) minimum wage earners in Maputo and Nampula. However, the urban poor in these three countries are employed predominantly in the informal sector, and time series data on informal sector wages are not available. The general conclusion of improving staple food purchasing power over the decade or so before the food price crisis may or may not hold for informal sector workers. Efforts to establish a system for collecting and disseminating informal wage rate movements over time would be an important step in improving governments' ability to monitor trends and potential abrupt changes in food affordability among low-income households.

Our fourth key finding is that maize meal to maize grain marketing margins trended downward during most of the period of analysis in urban Kenya, Malawi, and Zambia. Maize marketing margins in Maputo actually increased between 2000 and the 2006/2007 marketing year. Declining maize marketing margins in urban Kenya and Zambia are due, at least in part, to increased competition and efficiency gains in the milling industries of both countries following market liberalization in the early 1990s; improvements in milling technology may have also contributed to the lower margins (Jayne and Argwings-Kodhek, 1997; Jayne and Jones, 1997; Muyanga *et al.*, 2005; Jayne and Chapoto, 2006; Ariga and Jayne, 2010). Lower marketing margins and consumer prices for maize grain and maize meal since the mid-1990s are two key outcomes of maize market and pricing reforms implemented in eastern and southern Africa in the late 1980s and early 1990s (Kherallah *et al.*, 2002).

The fifth main finding is that real retail bread to world wheat marketing margins trended negatively in Lusaka and urban Kenya but positively in Lilongwe. Further research is necessary to determine what is driving these trends; however, anecdotal evidence from Zambia suggests that wheat is more profitable than maize for millers and that bakers and millers may be trying to induce a consumption shift to bread by keeping bread prices low relative to maize meal prices.

The analysis in this chapter demonstrates that the global food price crisis of 2007/2008 negatively affected the purchasing power for staple foods of formal sector workers in urban Kenya and Zambia and of minimum wage earners in urban Mozambique. In the decade or so before the crisis, their staple food purchasing power was on the rise. The food price crisis turned back the clock on improvements in staple food affordability in eastern and southern Africa but did not completely erase the progress made over the previous decade. As the economic and financial crisis has continued, the data may subsequently show that cuts in formal sector wages and/or employment levels may have further undermined workers' staple food purchasing power. With fewer jobs in the formal sector, the labor supply in the informal sector is likely to increase, putting downward pressure on informal sector wages and negatively affecting informal sector workers' staple food purchasing power as well.

As discussed in detail in the previous section, there are various potential food marketing policies and strategies that governments in ESA can use to moderate staple food prices for urban consumers. These include: 1) ensuring that maize grain is available in public markets to expand consumers' maize meal options and to keep competitive pressure on large-scale millers to maintain low maize meal prices and margins; 2) promoting the availability of a wide range of staple food products (maize and otherwise) in local markets to facilitate consumer substitution among staple foods, a strategy that can help attenuate the negative effects of food price spikes on urban consumers; 3) improving the timeliness and accuracy of crop forecasts to promote more effective public- and private-sector responses to national production shortfalls (and surpluses); 4) making timely arrangements for imports when they are deemed necessary; 5) removing import tariffs early in the marketing year when large import volumes are required so that the arrival of imports can be spaced out over time to minimize port and road infrastructure bottlenecks; and 6) facilitating regional trade and private sector participation and investment in staple food markets by maintaining open borders, reducing taxes and tariffs on exports and imports, building mutual trust between the public and private sectors, and increasing the predictability and transparency of government grain marketing policies. In addition to these food marketing-related strategies, investments in agricultural public goods such as research and extension, market information systems, and infrastructure can help promote increases in agricultural productivity, thereby maintaining farmers' production incentives while keeping food prices at tolerable levels for consumers. Finally, safety net and other social protection programs may need to be strengthened and expanded in order to protect vulnerable urban households' access to food during periods of soaring food prices.

Acknowledgments

We wish to acknowledge the role of the national statistical offices and food market price information systems in Kenya, Mozambique, Malawi, and Zambia, and the various agencies involved in building their capacity in making this study possible. The authors also acknowledge financial support from USAID missions in Kenya, Mozambique, Malawi, and Zambia, as well as from the Bill and Melinda Gates Foundation. We appreciate the helpful comments from David Lee and other participants in the May 2009 Cornell University Institute for African Development symposium, 'Food and Financial Crises and their Impacts on Achievement of the Millennium Development Goals in Africa.' We are also grateful to Steve Longabaugh for creating the map included in this chapter.

The views expressed herein do not necessarily reflect the opinions of Michigan State University, USAID, the Bill and Melinda Gates Foundation, or any other organization.

Note on Data Sources

The data series analyzed in this study and their sources are as follows:

Kenya: Retail bread prices (monthly, 1/95-1/09) from MTI and FEWS; average formal sector daily wage (annual, 2003-2007), consumer price index (monthly, 1/94-12/08), and exchange rate (monthly, 1/94-12/08) from KNBS.

Nairobi: Wholesale maize grain prices (monthly, 1/94-12/08) from MIC; retail maize meal prices (monthly 1/94-12/08) from MTI.

Malawi: Consumer price index and exchange rate (monthly, 1/94-12/08) from NSO.

Lilongwe: Retail maize grain prices (monthly, 1/94-12/08) from MAFS; retail maize meal prices (1/96-7/08) and retail bread prices (monthly, 1/94-12/07) from NSO.

Mozambique: Minimum wage (annually adjusted, 12/92-12/08) from GRM; consumer price index (1/93-12/08) from INE; exchange rate (monthly, 1/93-12/08) from BDM.

Maputo: Wholesale maize grain prices (weekly, 10/98-1/09), retail maize meal prices (weekly, 1/94-12/08), and retail prices for maize grain, wheat flour, and rice (all weekly, 1/93-12/08), from SIMA.

Nampula: Wholesale maize grain prices (weekly*, 10/98-1/09), retail maize meal prices (weekly*, 4/01-12/08), retail cassava flour prices (weekly*, 4/91-1/09), and retail prices for maize grain, wheat flour and rice (weekly*, 1/93-12/08), from SIMA. *weekly aggregated to monthly.

Zambia: Formal sector ave. monthly wages (quarterly, Q1/93-Q4/07), and consumer price index (monthly, 1/94-1/09) from CSO; exchange rate (monthly, 1/94-1/09) from BOZ.

Lusaka: Wholesale maize grain prices (monthly, 1/94-1/09) from AMIC; retail maize grain prices (monthly, 9/94-1/09), and retail prices for breakfast meal, roller meal and bread (all monthly, 1/94-1/09) from CSO.

Kitwe: Retail maize grain prices (monthly, 2/94-11/08), and retail prices for breakfast meal and roller meal (both monthly, 1/93-11/08) from CSO.

Mansa: Retail maize grain prices (monthly, 11/93-1/09), retail cassava flour prices (monthly, 9/00-1/09) and retail prices for breakfast meal and roller meal (both monthly, 2/93-1/09), from CSO.

World wheat: No. 1 hard red winter wheat prices (monthly, 1/93-1/09, FOB Gulf of Mexico) from IMF.

Sources: MIC = Kenya Market Information Center, Ministry of Agriculture; MTI = Kenya Ministry of Trade & Industry; FEWS = Famine Early Warning Systems Network; KNBS = Kenya National Bureau of Statistics; MAFS = Malawi Ministry of Agriculture & Food Security; NSO = Malawi National Statistical Office; SIMA = Mozambique Agricultural Market Information System; GRM = Government of Mozambique Monthly Bulletins; INE = *Mozambique Instituto Nacional de Estatistica*; BDM = *Banco de Mocambique*; AMIC = Zambia Agricultural Marketing Information Center; CSO = Zambia Central Statistical Office; BOZ = Bank of Zambia; IMF = International Monetary Fund Primary Commodity Prices database.

References

Abbink, K., Jayne, T.S. and Moller, L. (Forthcoming) The relevance of a rules-based maize marketing policy: an experimental case study of Zambia. *Journal of Development Studies.*

Abdula, D. (2005) Maize marketing and trade policies to promote household food security in southern Mozambique. MSc thesis. Michigan State University (MSU), East Lansing, Michigan.

Ariga, J. and Jayne, T.S. (2010) Maize trade and marketing policy interventions in Kenya. In: Sarris, A. and Morrison, J. (eds.) *Food Security in Africa: Market and Trade Policy for Staple Foods in Eastern and Southern Africa.* Food and Agriculture Organization of the United Nations, Northampton, Massachusetts, pp. 221-251.

Ayieko, M., Tschirley, D. and Mathenge, M. (2005) Fresh fruit and vegetable consumption patterns and supply chain systems in urban Kenya: implications for policy and investment priorities. Working Paper No. 19. Tegemeo Institute for Agricultural Policy and Development, Nairobi, Kenya.

Baker, J.L. (2008) Impact of financial, food, and fuel crisis on urban poor: directions in urban development. The World Bank, Urban Development Unit, Washington, D.C.

Barslund, M. (2007) Regional differences in food consumption in urban Mozambique: a censored demand system approach. Discussion Paper No. 07-15. University of Copenhagen, Copenhagen, Denmark.

Brinkhoff, T. (no date) City population. Available at: http://www.citypopulation.de/index.html (accessed 30 March 2009).

Chapoto, A. and Jayne, T.S. (2006) Trends in breakfast meal and maize marketing margins in Zambia. Policy Synthesis No. 14. Food Security Research Project, Lusaka, Zambia.

Chapoto, A. and Jayne, T.S. (2009) The impacts of trade barriers and market interventions on maize price predictability: evidence from eastern and southern Africa. International Development Working Paper No. 102, MSU, East Lansing, Michigan.

Chapoto, A., Haggblade, S., Shawa, J., Jayne, T.S. and Weber, M.T. (2008) Marketing policy options for consumer price mitigation actions in the 2008/2009 maize marketing season in Zambia. Policy Synthesis No. 31. Food Security Research Project, Lusaka, Zambia.

CSO. (Zambia Central Statistical Office). (2005) *Living Conditions Monitoring Survey Report, 2004.* CSO, Lusaka, Zambia.

CSO. (2007). *Quarterly Employment and Earnings Inquiry Report, 2007.* CSO, Lusaka, Zambia.

CSO. (Various years) *Quarterly Employment and Earnings Summary Report.* CSO, Lusaka, Zambia.

CTA (*Confederação das Associações Económicas de Moçambique*). (2004) *Reflexão sobre o salário mínimo para 2004 na República de Moçambique.* Paper presented at the 1st Ordinary Session of the Consultative Labor Commission, Maputo, Mozambique, 19 March 2004.

Dorosh, P.A., Dradri, S. and Haggblade, S. (2009) Regional trade, government policy and food security: recent evidence from Zambia. *Food Policy* 34, 350-366.

Dorward, A., Chirwa, C., Kelly, V., Jayne, T.S., Slater, R. and Boughton, D. (2008) Evaluation of the 2006/2007 Agricultural Input Subsidy Programme, Malawi. Final Report for the Malawi Ministry of Agriculture and Food Security, Lilongwe, Malawi.

Emerging Markets Group. (2008) Mozambique: FY08-12 Bellmon monetization and distribution analysis. Emerging Markets Group, Maputo, Mozambique.

FAO (Food and Agriculture Organization of the United Nations). (2008) FAO's Initiative on Soaring Food Prices: guide for immediate country level action. FAO, Rome, Italy.

Guha-Khasnobis, B. and Kanbur, R. (2006) Introduction: informal labor markets and development. In: Guha-Khasnobis, B. and Kanbur, R. (eds.) *Informal Labor Markets and Development.* Palgrave MacMillan, New York, New York, pp. 1-6.

Haggblade, S., Nielson, H., Govereh, J. and Dorosh, P. (2008) Potential consequences of intra-regional trade in short-term food security crises in southeastern Africa. Report No. 2 prepared by Michigan State University for the World Bank. MSU, East Lansing, Michigan.

IMF (International Monetary Fund). (2008) Food and fuel prices: recent developments, macroeconomic impact, and policy responses. IMF, Washington, D.C.

Jayne, T.S. and Argwings-Kodhek, G. (1997) Consumer response to maize market liberalization in urban Kenya. *Food Policy* 22, 447-58.

Jayne, T.S. and Chapoto, A. (2006) Emerging structural maize deficits in eastern and southern Africa: implications for national agricultural strategies. Policy Synthesis No. 16. Food Security Research Project, Lusaka, Zambia.

Jayne, T.S. and Jones, S. (1997) Food marketing and pricing policy in eastern and southern Africa: a survey. *World Development* 25, 1505-1527.

Jayne, T.S., Chapoto, A., Zulu, B., Haggblade, S., Shaffer, J., Shawa, J. and Haantuba, H. (2006) Zambia's maize value chain: toward national and regional food security. Draft Working Paper. Food Security Research Project, Lusaka, Zambia.

Jayne, T.S., Chapoto, A. and Govereh, J. (2007). Grain marketing policy at the crossroads: challenges for eastern and southern Africa. Paper presented at the FAO workshop on Staple Food Trade and Market Policy Options for Promoting Developing in Eastern and Southern Africa, Rome, Italy, 1-2 March 2007.

Jayne, T.S., Nyoro, J.K. and Myers, R.J. (2008a) The effects of NCPB marketing policies on maize market prices in Kenya. *Agricultural Economics* 38, 313-325.

Jayne, T.S., Chapoto, A., Minde, I. and Donovan, C. (2008b) The 2008/2009 food price and food security situation in eastern and southern Africa: implications for immediate and longer run responses. International Development Working Paper No. 97. Michigan State University, East Lansing, Michigan.

KNBS (Kenya National Bureau of Statistics). (Various years) *Statistical Abstract.* KNBS, Nairobi, Kenya.

Kherallah, M., Delgado, C., Gabre-Madhin, E., Minot, N. and Johnson, M. (2002) *Reforming Agricultural Markets in Africa.* Johns Hopkins University Press, Baltimore, Maryland.

Mason, N. and Jayne, T.S. (2009) Staple food consumption patterns in urban Zambia: results from the 2007/2008 Urban Consumption Survey. Working Paper No. 42. Food Security Research Project, Lusaka, Zambia.

Minot, N. (2010) Food price stabilization: lessons from eastern and southern Africa. Paper presented at the 4th African Agricultural Markets Program policy symposium, Agricultural Risks Management in Africa: Taking Stock of What Has and Hasn't Worked, Lilongwe, Malawi, 6-10 September, 2010.

Muendane, C., Zandamela, C. and Schalke, A. (2000) Os mercados de arroz e de trigo em Moçambique. Nota de Pesquisa da DNCI No. 14. Ministério da Industria e Comércio, Direcção Nacional do Comércio Interno, Maputo, Mozambique.

Muyanga, M., Jayne, T.S., Argwings-Kodhek, G. and Ariga, J. (2005) Staple food consumption patterns in urban Kenya: trends and policy implications. Working Paper No. 16. Tegemeo Institute for Agricultural Policy and Development, Nairobi, Kenya.

Mwanaumo, A., Jayne, T.S., Zulu, B., Shawa, J., Mbozi, G., Haggblade, S. and Nyembe, M. (2005) Zambia's 2005 maize import and marketing experiences: lessons and implications. Policy Synthesis No. 11. Food Security Research Project, Lusaka, Zambia.

Mwiinga, B., Nijhoff, J.J., Jayne, T.S., Tembo, G. and Shaffer, J. (2002) The role of mugaiwa in promoting household food security: why it matters and who gets access to government maize imports. Policy Synthesis No. 5. Food Security Research Project, Lusaka, Zambia.

Nijhoff, J.J., Jayne, T.S., Mwiinga, B. and Shaffer, J. (2002) Markets need predictable government actions to function effectively: the case of importing maize in times of deficit. Policy Synthesis No. 6. Food Security Research Project, Lusaka, Zambia.

Odhiambo, W. and Manda, D.K. (2003) Urban poverty and labor force participation in Kenya. Paper presented at the World Bank Urban Research Symposium. Washington, D.C., 15-17 December 2003.

Perron, P. (1989) The Great Crash, the oil price shock, and the unit root hypothesis. *Econometrica* 57, 1361–1401.

Potts, D. (2006) Urban growth and urban economies in eastern and southern Africa: trends and prospects. In: Bryceson, D.F. and Potts, D. (eds.) *African Urban Economies: Viability, Vitality or Vitiation?* Palgrave MacMillan, New York, New York, pp. 67-104.

Traub, L.N. and Jayne, T.S. (2008) The effects of price deregulation on maize marketing margins in South Africa. *Food Policy* 33, 224-36.

Tschirley, D., Abdula, D. and Weber, M.T. (2006) Toward improved maize marketing and trade policies to promote household food security in Central and Southern Mozambique. Research Paper Series No. 60E. Ministry of Agriculture, Directorate of Economics, Maputo, Mozambique.

Tschirley, D. and Jayne, T.S. (2010) Exploring the logic behind southern Africa's food crises. *World Development* 38, 76-87.

UNPD (United Nations Population Division). (2007) World urbanization prospects: the 2007 Revision Population Database. Available at: http://esa.un.org/unup/index.asp?panel=1(accessed 20 March 2009).

von Braun, J., Ahmed, A., Asenso-Okyere, K., Fan, S., Gulati, A., Hoddinott, J., Pandya-Lorch, R., Rosegrant, M.W., Ruel, M., Torero, M., van Rheenen, T. and von Grebmer, K. (2008) High food prices: the what, who, and how of proposed policy actions. Policy Brief. International Food Policy Research Institute, Washington, D.C.

World Bank. (2008) Rising food prices: policy options and World Bank response. Background Note. The World Bank, Washington, D.C.

World Bank. (2009) Swimming against the tide: how developing countries are coping with the global crisis. Background Paper prepared by World Bank Staff for the G-20 Finance Ministers and Central Bank Governors Meeting, Horsham, UK, 13-14 March, 2009.

Zanias, G.P. and Gunjal, K. (2007) *Food Demand Analysis and Food Aid Requirements*. Food and Agriculture Organization of the United Nations, New York, New York.

Chapter 9

The Short-term Impact of the 2008 Food Price Shock on Poverty in Uganda

Kenneth R. Simler
World Bank

Abstract

World prices for staple foods began increasing in 2006 and accelerated sharply in 2008. The impact on the poor in developing countries was severe. In Uganda, initial analysis indicated that the adverse effects of higher food prices were likely to be small because of the diversity of its staple foods, high level of food self-sufficiency, and weak links with world markets. This paper extends the previous analyses, disaggregating by regions and individual food items, using more recent price data, and estimating the impact on consumption poverty. We find that poor households in Uganda tend to be net buyers of food staples and therefore suffer welfare losses when food prices increase. This is most pronounced in urban areas, but holds true for most rural households as well. The diversity of staple foods has not been an effective buffer to price increases because these increases occur across a range of staple foods. We estimate that both the incidence and depth of poverty increased—at least in the short run—as a result of higher food prices in 2008, by 2.6 and 2.2 percentage points, respectively. This implies an additional 700,000 Ugandans living below the poverty line, and a reduction in the average income of the poor from 72 percent of the poverty line to only 68 percent of the poverty line. The increase in poverty is highest in the Northern region, which is already the poorest in Uganda. The resulting need for mitigating social protection measures appears to be greater than previously recognized. Not only are the negative impacts larger, but they are also much more widespread geographically. This suggests the need for continued close monitoring of the situation, expansion of existing safety nets and feeding programs, and contingency planning for new safety net programs to reach those threatened by high food prices.

Introduction

During 2007–2008 world prices of cereals increased dramatically. International wheat prices more than doubled between March 2007 and March 2008, rising from $200 to $440 per ton. Rice prices in international markets nearly tripled in the four months from January to

April 2008, rising to more than $900 per ton. Maize prices increased from $150 per ton to nearly $300 per ton between July 2007 and June 2008 (World Bank, 2008a). Prices of oilseeds also increased rapidly over this period. The impact on consumers in developing countries was profound, with an estimated 100 million people pushed into poverty (Ivanic and Martin, 2008), and an even larger impact on the estimated 1.4 billion people who were already living on less than $1 per day before the food price shock (Dessus *et al.,* 2008).

This spike in world food prices has been attributed to several factors, most prominently increased diversion of food grain and oilseeds to biofuels production, a weak US dollar, increased food production costs from higher energy and fertilizer prices, and adverse policy responses to the initial shock, which pushed prices even higher (Mitchell, 2008). Although prices have since subsided from their peaks in the first half of 2008, they still remain above early 2006 levels, especially in sub-Saharan Africa, as the result of another rapid increase that began in the latter half of 2010.

The impact of higher food prices was greatest in low- and middle-income countries, where more than half of the household budget typically goes to basic food items. Uganda had made significant progress in reducing absolute poverty over the past two decades, and higher food prices have threatened to stall, or even reverse, these gains. Moreover, the impacts within Uganda are likely to be distributed very unevenly. In general, the worst impact is suffered in areas with the steepest price increases and by those for whom market purchases of staple foods represent a large share of total consumption. Subsistence-oriented rural households that produce most of their staple food needs are partially buffered from the food price shocks, as are those whose main staples are foods that have not increased in price. Finally, rural households that produce marketable surpluses may potentially benefit from higher crop prices, although that benefit may be partially offset by higher production costs.

Uganda has a relatively diverse mix of staple foods, including maize, cassava, sweet potatoes, and *matooke* (plantains or cooking bananas). Benson *et al.* (2008) concluded that the likely impact of rising food prices on Ugandan households would be modest for several reasons, most notably Uganda's relative isolation from global food markets, the large share of food staples that are not traded internationally, and the high levels of auto-consumption among rural Ugandan households. That said, Benson *et al.* (2008) also identified three groups that consume most of their calories from maize and are likely to be adversely affected by higher maize prices: the urban poor, residents of internally displaced persons (IDP) camps, and residents of institutions such as schools, prisons, hospitals, and military bases. Benson *et al.* (2008) also noted the need for continued monitoring of the situation, especially the possibility of persistently high maize prices and increasing prices of other staple foods.

This paper extends the analysis by Benson *et al.* (2008) in three important directions. First, it uses a continuous measure—the net benefit ratio (NBR)—rather than discrete categories to assess the impact of higher food prices on household well-being. A continuous measure is advantageous because it captures the important differences in impact between households that are marginally net buyers or sellers and those who depend on food markets for most of their consumption (net buyers) or income (net sellers). Another advantage of the NBR is that it measures the impact of higher food prices relative to a household's overall expenditure level. Second, this paper disaggregates the food price data using region-specific prices for five staple food crops in the calculation of the NBR. This disaggregation is critical because of strong evidence of large regional variations in staple food prices in Uganda. It also has the advantage of using more recent price data, covering the period through October 2008 for most crops. Third, this paper estimates the short-run change in poverty in Uganda as a result of higher food prices. We estimate both the incidence (headcount) and depth (average poverty gap) of poverty, disaggregating by region and rural/urban area of residence.

We estimate an increase in the poverty headcount ratio of approximately 2.6 percentage points in the short term (that is, until the next harvest season) as a result of the recent food price increases. This is equivalent to an additional 700,000 Ugandans living below the poverty line. Even more significant is the increased depth of poverty, with the poverty gap index increasing by 2.2 percentage points, which is a 25 percent increase over the most recently available estimates. Despite the perception that Uganda is relatively insulated from distant world markets, food prices increased sharply in 2008 not only for cereals like maize and rice, which are traded on world markets, but also for less widely traded substitutes such as cassava and *matooke*. As noted by Benson *et al.* (2008), increased demand from regional trading partners such as Kenya and southern Sudan has exerted upward pressure on food prices in Uganda. Although prices dipped somewhat following the harvest in mid-2008, in 2009 prices for staple foods in Uganda returned to levels approaching the 2008 peak. Prices fell to pre-crisis levels in late 2009 and early 2010, but rose again sharply in the second half of 2010.

This chapter is organized as follows. The introduction is followed by background information on staple food consumption patterns in Uganda, and on the magnitude and timing of food price increases. Next, the third section (Methods and Data) describes the calculation of the net benefit ratio (NBR), the analytical methods used to estimate changes in poverty, and the underlying household survey data. The fourth section presents results on which income groups and regions are most affected by food price increases, while the fifth reports the impact of food price increases on poverty levels in Uganda. The final section summarizes and offers concluding remarks.

Background

Uganda is a predominantly rural country, with only 15 percent of its 27 million inhabitants living in urban areas (Uganda Bureau of Statistics [UBOS], 2006). Almost three-quarters (73 percent) of the country's work force is employed in agriculture (UBOS 2006), which accounts for 29 percent of GDP (World Bank, 2008b). Although most rural households are engaged in food crop production, most (57 percent) are also net buyers of staple foods; in urban areas 92 percent of households are net buyers of staple foods (Benson *et al.*, 2008).

Unlike many countries in Asia or southern Africa, where a single commodity is the dominant food energy source (rice and maize, respectively), Uganda has a relatively diverse mix of staple foods, including maize, cassava, sweet potatoes, and *matooke*. Table 9.1 shows the average budget shares in Uganda, disaggregated by region and rural/urban area of residence. The primary staple has a pronounced regional pattern, corresponding with production environments. *Matooke* figures prominently in Central and Western regions, while maize and cassava are the dominant staples in the Eastern and Northern regions. On average, slightly more than half of the household budget goes to food in Uganda (including valuation of home-produced food).

As a landlocked country, Uganda is not well-integrated with international markets, especially for low value commodities such as cereals. Thus price trends within Uganda deviate somewhat from global price trends, because local market conditions figure more prominently in the determination of staple food prices in Uganda. Particularly prominent in late 2007 and early 2008 was the civil unrest in neighbouring Kenya, which is the conduit for Uganda's fuel supplies and also a large importer of Ugandan maize. Another significant factor was the sharply increased demand for Ugandan roots and tubers by southern Sudan following the peace accords in that country (Benson *et al.,* 2008). Figure 9.1 plots price indices in Uganda for maize, rice, cassava, and *matooke* for 2003–2008, with May 2003 as the base (1.00). Maize prices had been fluctuating around the same level from 2003 through 2007, and then doubled between January and April, 2008. Although maize prices fell slightly in August–September, they increased again in October, 2008. The prices of *matooke*, cassava, and rice had been rising steadily from 2004 through 2007, and then increased rapidly in 2008. Note that Figure 9.1 illustrates national average prices in Uganda, and that in some regions and markets the increase in food prices has been even more pronounced. For example, the rapid increase in cassava prices in 2008 was entirely due to increases in the Northern region, driven in part by rising demand from southern Sudan. Similarly, although the national average sweet potato price in 2008 was still near 2003 levels, prices for sweet potatoes in the Northern region rose sharply in 2008. Sub-national price trends are discussed further in the section on Poverty Impact of Food Price Increases.

Figure 9.1. Average staple food prices in Uganda, 2003–08

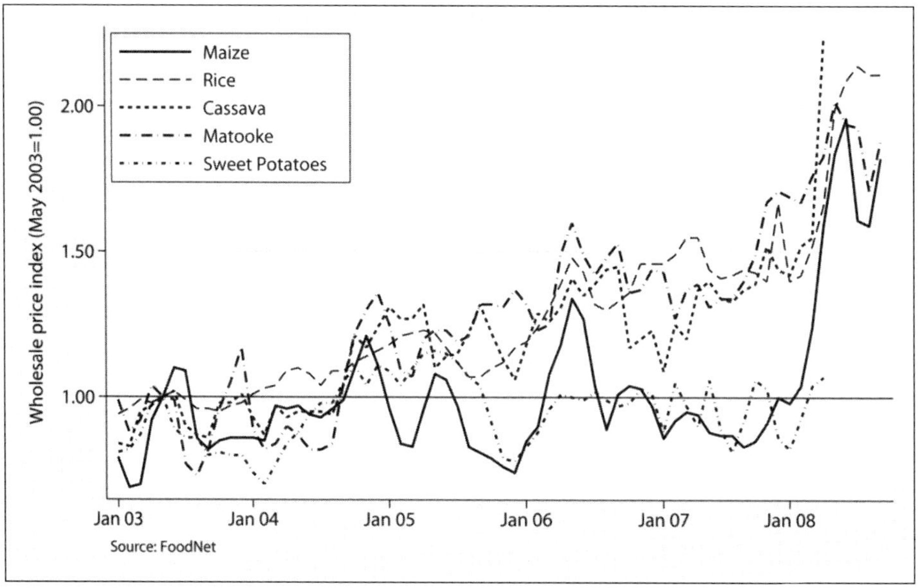

Methods and Data

The impact of rising food prices on poverty in an individual country depends on several factors including: 1) the magnitude of the price increase (which is affected by local market forces and the extent to which world market prices are passed through to domestic prices), 2) the initial poverty level and number of people clustered around the poverty line, 3) the number of net buyers or net sellers of the food commodities in question, 4) the share of poor people's budgets devoted to food overall and key staples in particular, 5) the extent of own-consumption relative to market purchases, and 6) the effect of food price increases on real wages of poor people.

Table 9.1. Average Budget Shares by Region and Rural/Urban Area of Residence

Table 9.1. Average Budget Shares by Region and Rural/Urban Area of Residence

	Rural					Urban					All				
	Central	Eastern	Northern*	Western	Total	Central	Eastern	Northern*	Western	Total	Central	Eastern	Northern*	Western	Total
Matooke	7.0	3.7	0.3	12.2	6.2	4.4	2.3	0.2	7.6	3.8	6.3	3.6	0.3	11.9	5.9
Maize	5.8	7.5	7.2	4.3	6.1	2.8	5.8	6.1	2.7	3.8	4.9	7.4	7.0	4.2	5.8
Cassava	4.3	6.2	9.1	5.0	6.0	1.0	2.5	5.6	2.9	2.3	3.3	5.9	8.6	4.9	5.4
Sweet potato	6.1	8.6	3.5	4.8	5.9	1.8	2.5	2.3	2.8	2.1	4.8	8.1	3.3	4.7	5.3
Beans	3.8	2.6	6.7	6.3	4.8	1.7	2.3	5.0	3.9	2.7	3.2	2.5	6.5	6.1	4.4
Millet & Sorghum	0.2	2.0	3.3	2.4	1.9	0.1	1.1	1.5	0.8	0.6	0.2	1.9	3.1	2.2	1.7
Rice	1.1	1.5	0.2	0.6	0.9	1.9	3.0	0.7	1.1	1.7	1.3	1.6	0.3	0.7	1.0
Meat & Fish	5.9	7.1	6.1	5.9	6.3	4.7	6.8	7.1	5.2	5.5	5.5	7.1	6.3	5.9	6.2
Fruit & vegetables	5.1	6.6	5.3	3.4	5.1	2.9	4.8	4.6	3.1	3.5	4.5	6.4	5.2	3.4	4.8
Milk & eggs	2.5	1.9	0.7	1.8	1.8	2.0	1.8	0.6	2.1	1.7	2.3	1.9	0.7	1.8	1.8
Fats & oils	1.0	1.4	2.9	0.7	1.4	1.0	1.5	2.4	0.9	1.3	1.0	1.4	2.8	0.8	1.4
Sugar	3.1	3.3	1.9	1.4	2.5	2.8	3.3	2.9	2.1	2.8	3.0	3.3	2.1	1.5	2.5
Beverages	1.9	2.2	3.6	2.3	2.4	3.0	2.5	3.7	2.9	3.0	2.2	2.2	3.6	2.4	2.5
Other food	5.8	4.6	7.7	5.6	5.8	9.7	8.3	6.4	8.2	8.7	7.0	4.9	7.5	5.8	6.2
Nonfood	46.4	41.0	41.4	43.1	43.0	60.1	51.4	50.6	53.7	56.4	50.4	41.8	42.7	44.0	45.1

Source: Author's calculations from 2005–06 UNHS

Note: *=includes IDP

Deaton (1989, 1997) provides a straightforward approach for estimating the short-run impact of an increase in food prices on household welfare. The impact on a household can be measured by the net benefit ratio (NBR). The NBR is the value of net food sales (total food production minus total food consumption) divided by total household consumption. It captures the positive or negative impact on household welfare by measuring the change in real income arising from changes in food prices as a proportion of total consumption.

Ravallion (1990) extended Deaton's model to incorporate wage effects of higher food prices. Higher producer prices increase the derived demand for agricultural labor and likely increase the wages of agricultural laborers, with a possible ripple effect for labor in other sectors. Where agricultural wage labor is an important income component, the positive wage effect may significantly offset the negative price effect for net buyers. Wage responses may also occur in other sectors as workers negotiate for higher wages to compensate for higher food prices. The Deaton model, with or without the Ravallion labor extension, has been widely used to assess the first-order welfare effects of a food price increase (Budd, 1993; Barrett and Dorosh, 1996; Loening and Oseni, 2007; Vu and Glewwe, 2008; Wodon and Zaman, 2008).

The basic model is:

$$\Delta w_{irc} = \Delta p_{rc}\left[\left(PR_{irc} - CR_{irc}\right) + \eta L_{ir}\right]$$

where

Δw_{irc}	=	change in welfare for household i in region r arising from a change in the price of commodity c, expressed as a percentage of total expenditures of household i,
Δp_{rc}	=	percentage change in the price of commodity c in region r,
PR_{irc}	=	food production ratio,
CR_{irc}	=	food consumption ratio,
η	=	wage rate elasticity with respect to food price change, and
L_{ir}	=	wage labor share in household income.[68]

The food production ratio (PR) is the value of the food commodity produced by household i divided by total household food and non-food consumption. Analogously, the food consumption ratio (CR) is the value of the food commodity consumed divided by total household food and non-food consumption. Food consumed includes food purchased, produced at home, received as an exchange in kind, or received for free. The net benefit ratio, NBR, is ($PR_i - CR_i$). The NBR can be interpreted as the elasticity of real income to changes in the price of the food commodity. The total welfare change for household i from the price changes of several commodities is obtained by summing Δw_{irc} over all commodities c. It bears noting that the ratios are expressed in value terms. Therefore, a household that sells a given quantity of food at harvest time and buys the exact same quantity later at a

[68] The wage response is not considered in the empirical analysis that follows. In their study of food price inflation in Ethiopia, Loening and Oseni (2007) found the wage effect response to be small because of the low wage elasticity to food prices and the small share of wage labor income among Ethiopian households. It is expected that the wage elasticity and wage labor share are similarly small in Uganda, so that the exclusion of the wage effect will not distort the results appreciably.

higher price is considered a net buyer, because their expenditures on the food item exceed their receipts from sales of the item.

The basic model involves four simplifying assumptions that should be highlighted. First, it only captures the short-run impact and does not take into account the possibility of consumers shifting their consumption patterns in response to higher prices. Normally, one would expect that over time consumers would substitute away from the foods whose relative prices are increasing. As a result, the model overestimates the negative impact of higher prices on net buyers of a commodity. While common sense and economic theory dictate that consumers will shift to less expensive staples, the magnitude of that substitution is a matter of some debate. In the short run, substitution will be constrained by available supplies from that year's harvest or imports. Thus substitution will push up prices for these other staples, as appears to be the case in Uganda. Recent econometric estimates by Ulimwengu and Ramadan (2009), using 2005–2006 Uganda National Household Survey (UNHS) data, indicate a remarkably low degree of substitutability between staples for consumers. They estimate Hicksian (compensated) cross-price elasticities of 0.05 and 0.04 for the food groups 'cereals' and 'roots' and 'plantains.' This implies that a 10 percent increase in the price of cereals would increase demand for roots and plantains by only 0.5 percent if the consumers' real incomes were not affected by the cereal price increase. Similarly, a 10 percent increase in the price of roots and plantains would increase cereal demand by only 0.4 percent. Of course, real incomes are affected by the staple food price increases, which is why Ulimwengu and Ramadan's (2009) estimated Marshallian (uncompensated) cross-price elasticities for these food groups are negative, indicating that an increase in cereals' prices would lead to a small *reduction* in the demand for roots and plantains, and vice versa.

Second, the analysis assumes that the increase in the producer price is the same as the increase in the consumer price, i.e., sellers capture the full benefits of the price increase. In practice this margin could be diminished by higher margins for middlemen and/or higher production costs, such as the increased costs of transportation or fertilizer. This assumption likely overestimates the positive impact of higher food prices on net sellers of a commodity. This is especially germane in Uganda, where much of the staple food price increase appears to have been driven by increases in transportation costs arising from disruptions in the supply of fuel because of post-election conflict in Kenya that began in late 2007 and extended well into 2008.

Third, the model does not allow for second-round effects as producers adjust their price expectations when making planting decisions for the subsequent season. If producers, including net buyers, believe the price increase will be sustained, they would most likely increase production, which would relieve at least some of the upward pressure on staple food prices as well as increase income from staple food production. The multi-market analysis by Ulimwengu and Ramadan (2009) shows that in Uganda these second-round effects dampen the adverse welfare effects of the price shock, but do not completely counteract them.

Finally, the analysis does not incorporate possible mitigating measures, such as food subsidies that might be established, or increased, to dampen the impact of the food price shock.

The primary data source for the present analysis is the Uganda National Household Survey (UNHS) 2005–2006. The Uganda Bureau of Statistics, which conducted the survey, interviewed over 7,400 households throughout Uganda between May 2005 and April 2006, inclusive. This comprehensive living standards survey is the source of information about household expenditure patterns and total consumption. At the time of the 2008 food price shock it was the most recent national household survey in Uganda, but it has the limitation of not capturing many of the improvements in well-being that occurred in northern Uganda following the peace settlement in 2008. Information on food prices comes from FoodNet, a multi-agency agricultural research network operating in several east African countries. The price data were collected for numerous food items in ten agricultural markets spread across Uganda, with weekly observations covering the period from January 2003 to October 2008.

The welfare change in equation 1 will vary for each household depending on the value of net purchases or sales as a fraction of total household consumption (and the share of wage income in total household income, which is not considered here). The impact will also vary by the magnitude of the price increase, which varies by region. To illustrate how the NBR varies by household expenditure (income) level and region, we estimate a series of non-parametric regressions, which trace the relationship of the NBR against total consumption, showing how the average impact of the food price increases varies by income level.

To estimate the short-run impact of higher food prices on absolute poverty, the change in total expenditure in real terms is simulated for each household using the calculated NBR for each household and the observed price change in the relevant region. The simulated total consumption is then compared to the poverty line calculated from the UNHS (Uganda Bureau of Statistics, 2006). Results are presented for the poverty headcount ratio and the poverty gap in the section on poverty impact of food price increases.

Net Benefit Ratios by Region and Rural/Urban

Who are the net buyers and net sellers of major food staples in Uganda? Figures 9.2–9.6 present the results of this analysis. Each graph shows how the NBR (on the vertical axis) varies with household consumption per adult equivalent (AE) on the horizontal axis. The vertical reference line at approximately 21,000 Ugandan shillings per month is the national poverty line: households to the left are below the poverty line and those to the right are above the poverty line. There is also a horizontal reference line at zero: households below zero are net buyers and those above zero are net sellers. The value on the vertical axis is the average value of net purchases or sales for that commodity, expressed as a proportion of household consumption. To facilitate comparison of results across regions and food items, the axis scales are identical for all of the non-parametric regression plots in Figures 9.2–9.6. The top graph in each figure shows results separately for rural households, urban households, and households in internally displaced persons' (IDP) camps.[69] The next graphs show results by region, in urban and rural zones, respectively. Both disaggregations are relevant as net benefit ratios are significantly different for most crops by location and income.

For most crops, the poor are more vulnerable to food price increases primarily because net food purchases are a larger share in total consumption. Maize (Figure 9.2) is the staple food for which purchases account for the highest share of total calories on average (Benson *et al.*, 2008). Among rural households (dashed line in the top graph of Figure 9.2), the poorest spend an average of approximately 7 percent of their total budget including auto-

[69] The UNHS 2005–2006 sample includes 300 households residing in IDP camps. All of them are in the Northern region, and 290 of them are in rural areas.

consumption on net purchases of maize.[70] Thus a doubling of maize prices would be equivalent to a real income loss of 7 percent. Poor urban households (dotted line) have a greater dependence on net purchases of maize, with average net maize purchases reaching as much as 12 percent of total consumption for the poorest urban households, and about 5 percent for urban residents living near the poverty line. The importance of net maize purchases in total consumption diminishes at higher income levels, although even urban households with monthly consumption up to 100,000 shillings per AE, which is more than quadruple the poverty line, are net buyers on average. However, at incomes greater than 50,000 shillings per AE per month, average net sales or purchases of maize are an insignificantly small share of total household consumption, so the impact on household welfare is small.

Households living in IDP camps (solid line in the top graph of Figure 9.2) appear to be relatively unaffected by the increase in maize prices, but the reality is more complex. At the time of the 2005–2006 UNHS, over 90 percent of the maize consumed by IDP camp residents was received free of charge as food aid. Like auto-consumption, receipt of free food aid is not a market transaction, and the increase in the market price of maize has no effect at that level of the distribution chain. However, those in IDP camps could suffer welfare losses if higher maize prices impeded the ability of the World Food Programme and other organizations to procure and distribute food aid. Unfortunately, the data needed to explore this question in greater depth are not available.

The middle graph in Figure 9.2 shows that, on average, urban households whose monthly consumption per AE is less than 100,000 shillings are net buyers of maize in each of the four regions. Among the urban poor, net maize purchases average from 5 to 16 percent of total consumption, with that proportion highest in the Eastern region (short dashed line). In the bottom panel of Figure 9.2 we see that even in rural areas, poor households tend to be net buyers of maize, with net maize purchases averaging more than 10 percent of consumption in the poorest households in the Central region, compared to about 5 percent for poor households in other regions. Among higher-income rural households, only those in the Eastern region tend to be net sellers of maize. In the Eastern region the average NBR reaches approximately 7 percent in the richest households, meaning that a doubling of maize prices would increase household income by 7 percent.

Figure 9.3 shows a similar analysis for rice, which has also experienced large price increases, but only plays a minor role in Ugandan diets. On average, net sales or purchases of rice are an insignificant share of household consumption in urban and rural areas of almost all regions. Therefore even a large increase in rice prices would not have a major impact on household welfare for most Ugandan households. The only exception is poor households in the urban Central region, whose net rice purchases average 3 to 8 percent of total consumption (dotted line in the middle graph of Figure 9.4).

---

[70] Note that the nonparametric regression lines represent the weighted mean of the NBR at different levels of total consumption, and that there is often considerable dispersion around this mean, especially at the tails of the regression lines.

Figure 9.2. Net benefit ratios for maize

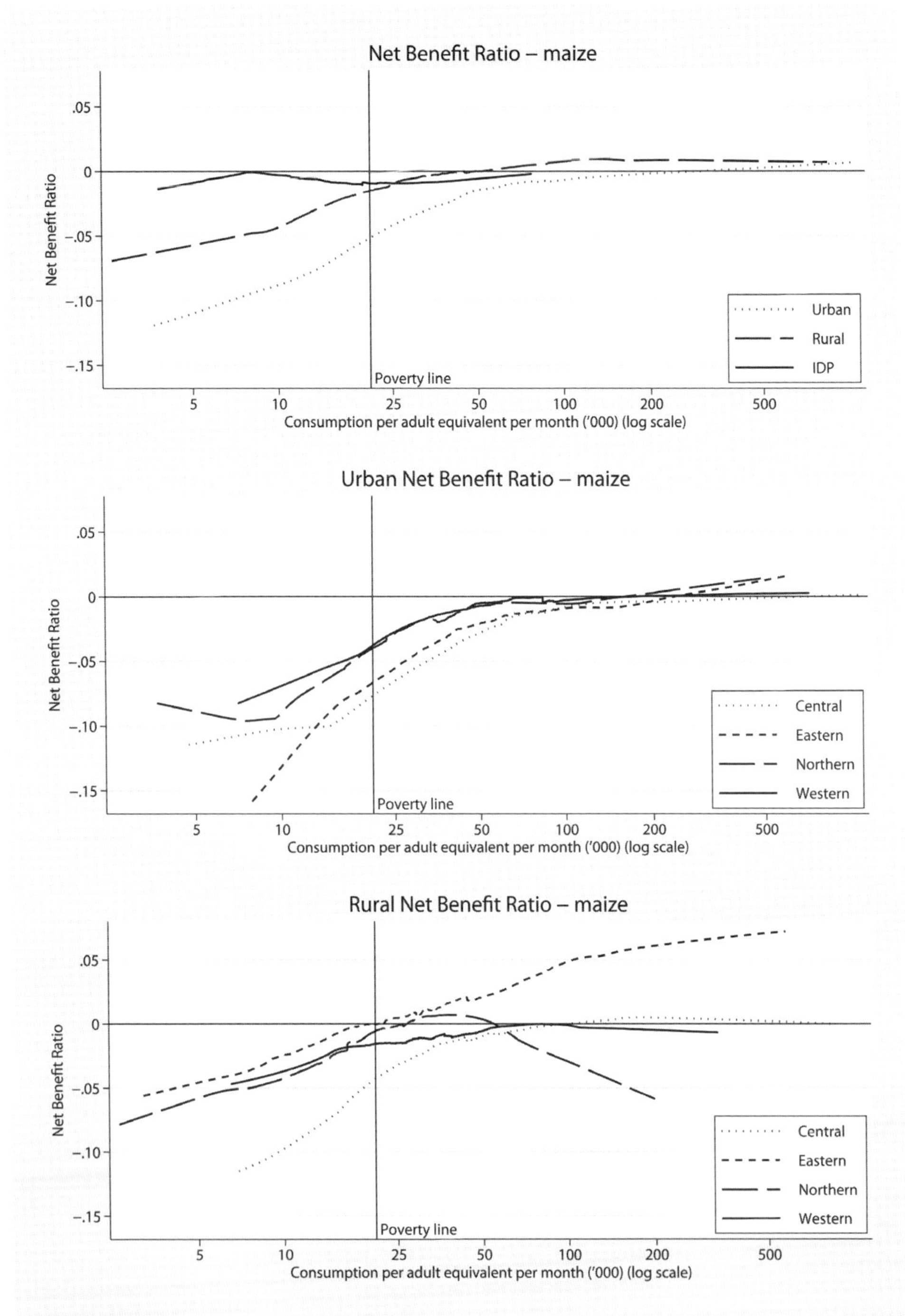

Figure 9.3. Net benefit ratios for rice

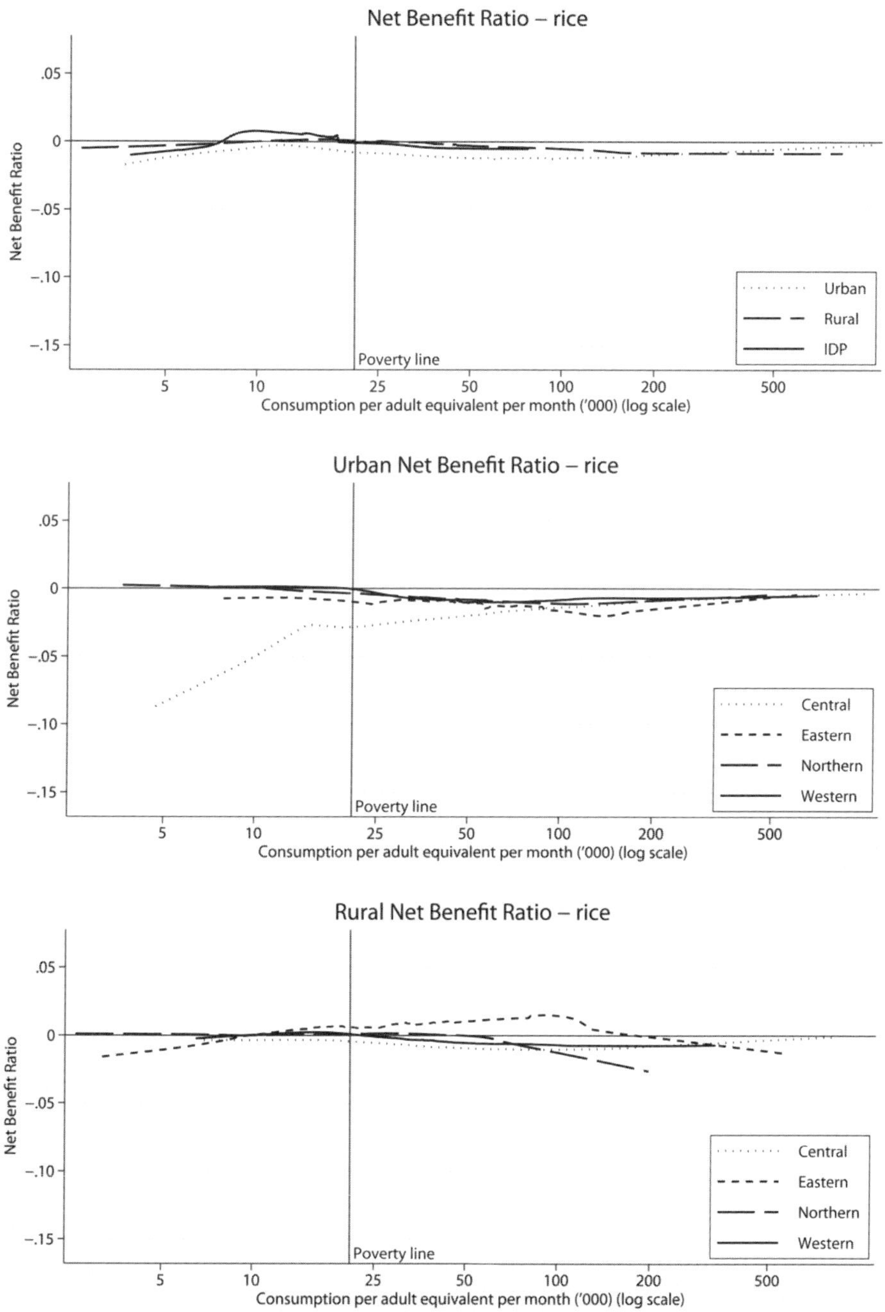

Figures 9.4, 9.5, and 9.6 present analogous results for *matooke*, cassava, and sweet potato, respectively. Turning first to *matooke* (Figure 9.4), we see that most households in the Central, Eastern, and Western regions are net buyers. The share of total consumption is relatively small except in the Western region, where net purchases of *matooke* average 5 to 13 percent of total consumption for poor urban households (solid line in the middle graph of Figure 9.4). In rural areas of the Central, Eastern, and Northern regions, the poor tend to be net sellers of *matooke*. In the Northern region average net sales and purchases of *matooke* are nearly zero across all income levels, in both urban and rural areas.

Most of the poor in both urban and rural areas are net buyers of cassava, with the exception of the poorest households in the urban Northern region (Figure 9.5). Net purchases of cassava as a proportion of total consumption are large in the urban Central region, and to a lesser extent in the rural Northern region. Figure 9.6 shows the net buyer/seller results for sweet potatoes. On average most households in the Central, Eastern, and Western regions are net buyers of sweet potatoes, while average net purchases and sales in the Northern region are negligible for all income groups. Net purchases of sweet potato are more important as a share of total consumption for poor households than for non-poor households, especially in rural areas. Only in the rural Eastern region do households tend to be net sellers of sweet potatoes.

Poverty Impact of Food Price Increases

The NBR analysis above has shown that poor households in Uganda tend to be net purchasers of staple food commodities, even in rural areas. Because of the multiplicity of staple foods, the net buyer or seller status of individual households is more complex than is the case in countries with only one or two major staples. Analysis of the 2005–2006 UNH Survey reveals that in rural areas, 63 percent of households are net sellers of at least one staple food, but 87 percent are also net buyers of at least one staple food. Net buyers of staples typically do not sell any of that staple, as opposed to selling at harvest time and buying in the market later in the year. Net purchases are financed by household income from other sources, including sale of other agricultural products (such as cash crops like coffee), non-farm enterprises, wage income, and remittances. The finding that most rural farm households are net food buyers is consistent with other studies in Uganda (Benson *et al.,* 2008) and elsewhere in sub-Saharan Africa (Minten and Barrett, 2008; Poulton *et al.,* 2006; Jayne and Chisvo, 1991). Therefore food price increases are likely to deepen their poverty, especially in the short term. In addition, those slightly above the poverty line tend to be marginal net purchasers (i.e., on average they are net buyers, but the purchases represent a small share of total consumption). Staple food price increases are likely to push some of these households into poverty.

Changes in welfare and poverty depend on the size of the price increase as well as the net benefit ratio for a given household. We estimate the change in household welfare (consumption per adult equivalent) by multiplying the household-level NBRs calculated in the preceding section by the actual price changes that occurred in Uganda from 2007 to 2008. From the price data in Figure 9.1, one may observe a seasonal pattern in food prices, with prices tending to be lower in January than at other times of the year. To control for these seasonal effects we use the price changes during the most recent 12 months for which data are available, which should purge the seasonal component from the price changes. To facilitate comparison with the previous analysis of Benson *et al.* (2008), price data were drawn from the same set of six markets used in that study.

Figure 9.4. Net benefit ratios for matooke

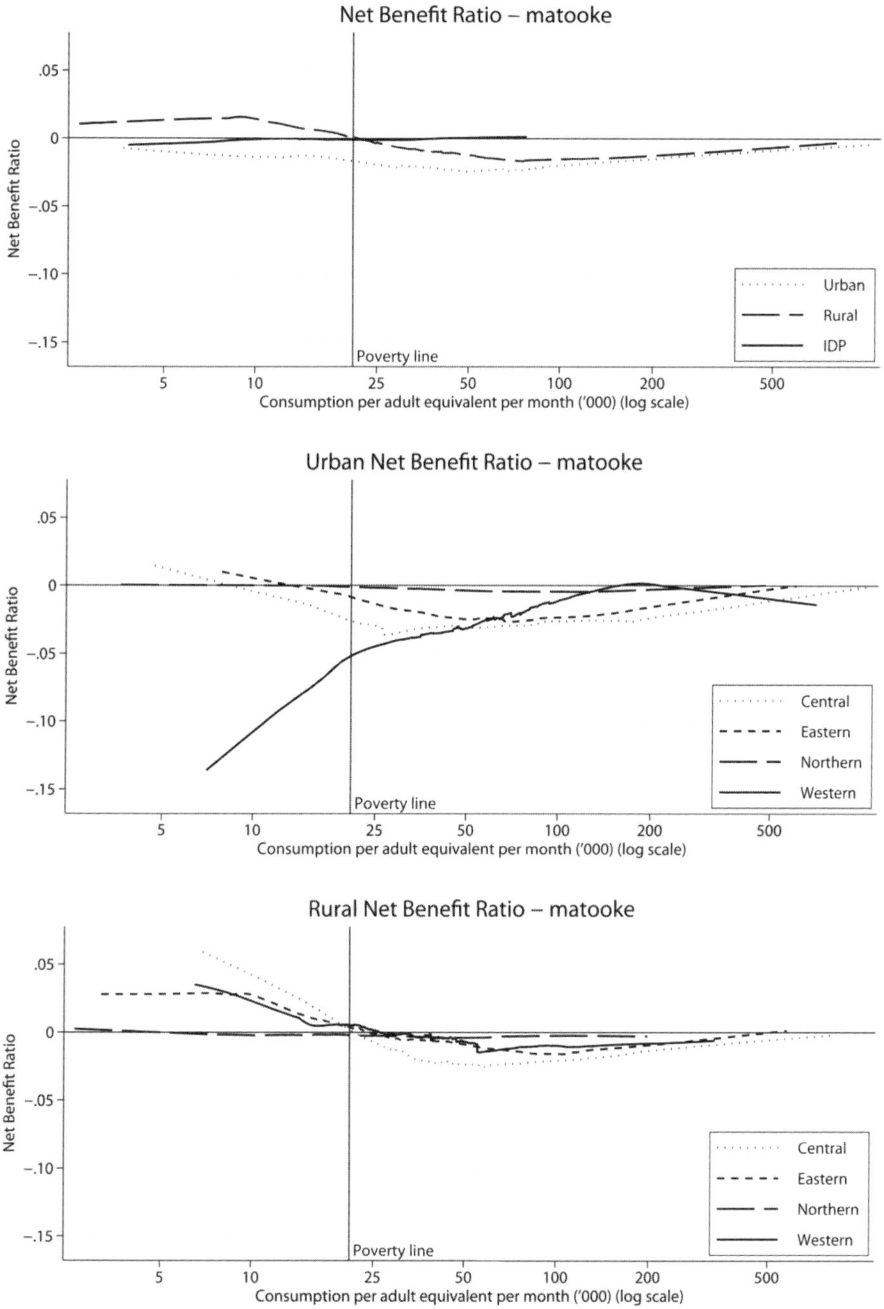

Figure 9.5. Net benefit ratios for cassava

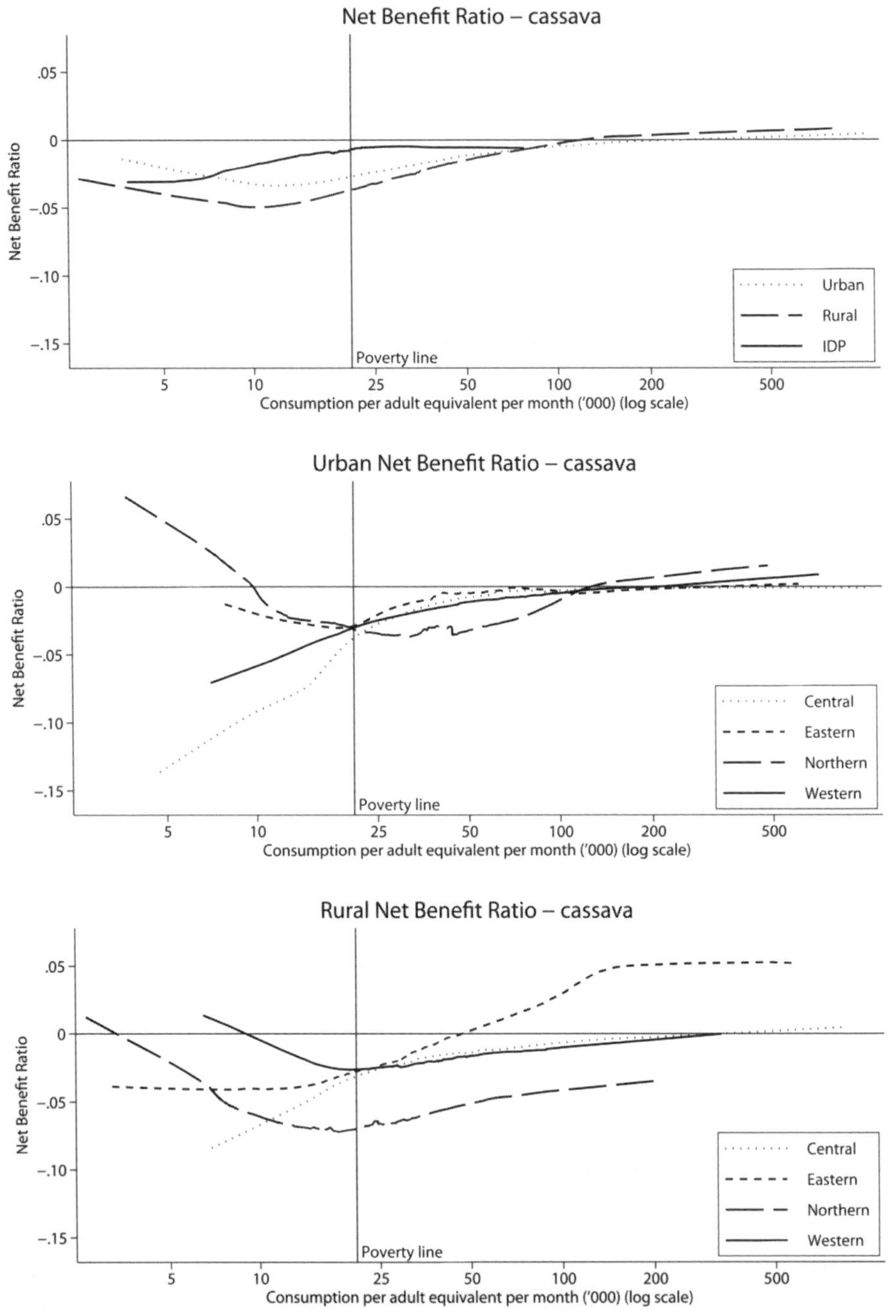

Figure 9.6. Net benefit ratios for sweet potato

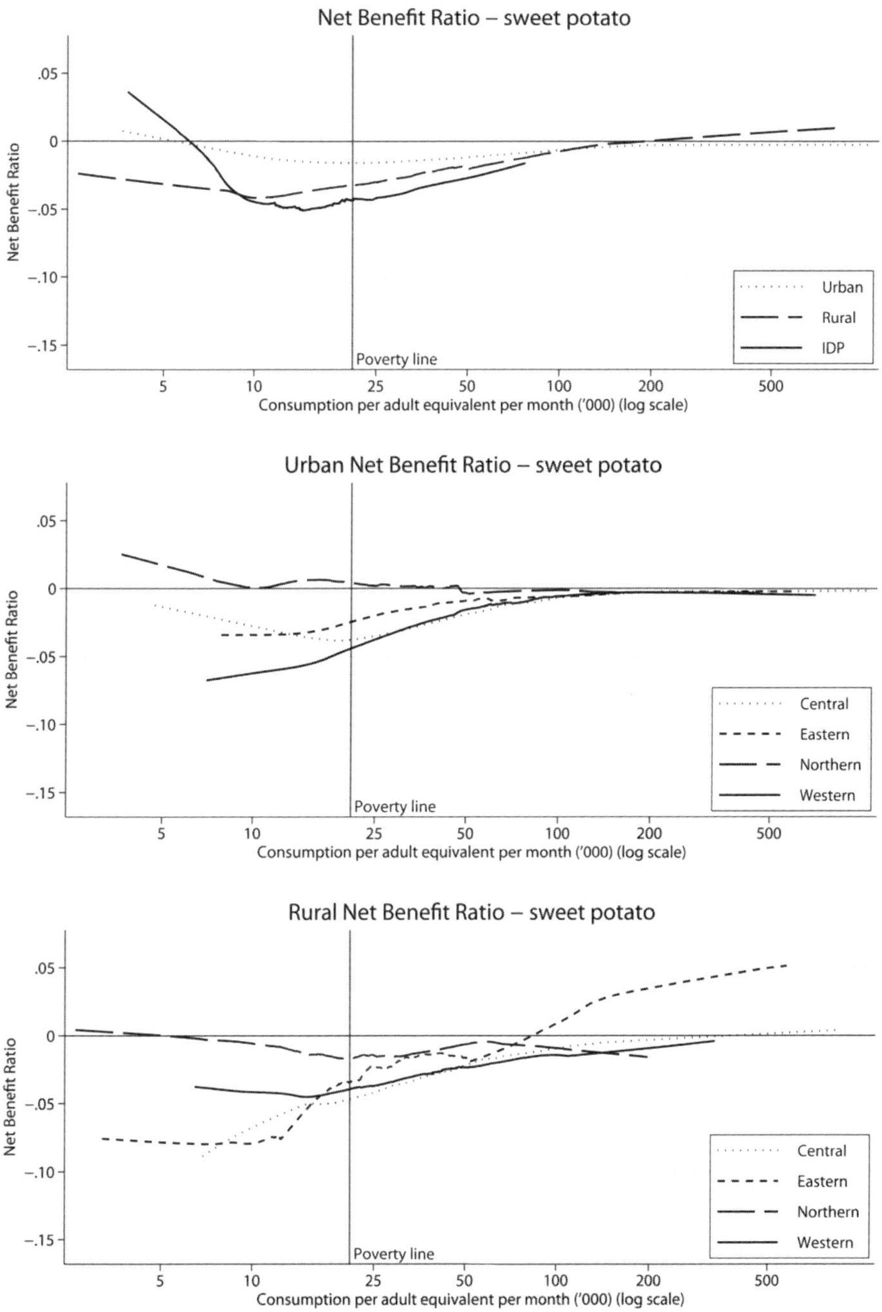

The region-specific price data from FoodNet are shown in Table 9.2. As seen in the table, the price data are not complete for cassava and sweet potatoes. First, cassava and sweet potato prices are only available through May 2008. Therefore, for cassava and sweet potatoes we use the observed price increases for May 2007 to May 2008 instead of October to October. The incomplete price information that is available for cassava roots and cassava flour indicates that the percentage change from May 2007 to May 2008 is a close approximation of the increase from October 2007 to October 2008, including the sharp increase in cassava prices in the Northern region in mid-2008. Second, there are no cassava or sweet potato price data more recent than April 2007 for the Eastern region. This is a major gap, especially because the average budget shares of these foods in the Eastern region are 6 percent and 8 percent, respectively (see Table 9.1). In the absence of better information, we close this gap in the data by using the simple average of the percentage price changes in the Central and Western regions. This assumes that the large cassava and sweet potato prices observed in the Northern region did not occur in the Eastern region, and is thus a conservative estimate of the change in prices for these foods in the Eastern region.

One of the more striking observations from Table 9.2 is enormous heterogeneity of price changes by region and commodity. As noted earlier, Uganda is not tightly integrated with world food markets, in large part because of its landlocked status and poor infrastructure. These conditions also contribute considerably to poor integration in Uganda's internal markets.

Table 9.2. Staple Food Prices by Region, 2007–08 (Uganda shillings per kg)

		Central	Eastern	Northern	Western
Maize	October 2007	267	220	327	292
	October 2008	690	495	450	613
	Percentage change	159	125	38	110
Matooke	October 2007	234	325	617	209
	October 2008	315	400	950	268
	Percentage change	35	23	54	28
Cassava	May 2007	205	–	383[a]	92
	May 2008	185	–	1000	105
	Percentage change	-10	2[b]	161	14
Sweet Potato	May 2007	275	–	381[a]	280
	May 2008	200	–	550	130
	Percentage change	-27	-40[b]	44	-54
Rice	October 2007	970	967	1400	1350
	October 2008	1625	1450	2150	1750
	Percentage change	68	50	54	30

Source: FoodNet

Notes: Prices are wholesale prices, calculated from weekly data collected in the following markets: Owino (Central), Tororo (Eastern), Arua (Northern), and the average of Mbarara, Kabale, and Kasese (Western).

[a] May 2007 prices are not available in the Northern market for cassava and sweet potatoes, so a linear interpolation of the April and June prices is used.

[b] Because cassava and sweet potato price data are not available for Eastern region, the simple average of the percentage price changes recorded in Central and Western regions is used for the simulations.

The short-run impact of higher food prices on the poverty headcount ratio (i.e., the percentage of the population below the poverty line) is shown in Table 9.3. The figures in the Base column are the actual estimates from the 2005–2006 UNH Survey, which is the most recent source of poverty estimates for Uganda. The second column, labelled 'All 5 foods,' shows the combined impact of higher prices for all five food items in the table, and the remaining columns show the impact of higher prices for each of the five individual food commodities. At the national level, higher food prices are estimated to increase the headcount ratio by 2.6 percentage points in the months immediately following the price increase. Taking the 2005–2006 survey as a base, this 2.6 percentage point increase would be equivalent to increasing the number of Ugandans living below the poverty line from 8.4 to 9.1 million. The 2.6 percentage point increase is slightly smaller than estimates of the poverty impact of higher food prices globally (Ivanic and Martin, 2008) and in west and central Africa (Wodon *et al.,* 2008).

Table 9.3. Estimated Impact of Food Price Increases on Poverty Headcount Ratio

		Impact of observed price increases (percentage point change in poverty headcount ratio)					
	Base (2005–06)	All 5 foods	Maize	Matooke	Cassava	Sweet potato	Rice
National*	31.1	2.6	1.7	0.1	0.9	-0.7	-0.1
Urban*	13.7	3.6	2.5	-0.1	0.9	0.0	0.4
Rural*	34.2	2.4	1.6	0.1	0.9	-0.8	-0.2
Central	16.4	3.2	3.1	-0.1	-0.4	-0.9	0.1
Eastern	35.9	1.0	1.4	-0.2	-0.1	-1.7	-0.2
Northern*	60.7	5.9	0.5	0.0	5.2	0.7	0.0
Western	20.5	0.9	1.4	0.7	0.1	-0.6	-0.2
Central urban	5.5	3.0	2.5	0.0	0.0	-0.2	0.6
Eastern urban	16.9	6.4	6.4	0.0	0.0	0.6	0.2
Northern urban	38.3	6.0	0.9	0.0	5.0	0.7	0.3
Western urban	9.3	0.6	0.6	-0.4	0.0	-0.9	0.0
Central rural	20.9	3.3	3.3	-0.2	-0.6	-1.2	-0.1
Eastern rural	37.5	0.5	1.0	-0.2	-0.1	-1.9	-0.2
Northern rural	57.6	8.3	0.6	0.0	7.7	0.8	0.0
Western rural	21.4	1.0	1.4	0.8	0.1	-0.6	-0.2
IDP	77.9	0.9	0.1	0.0	-0.2	0.6	-0.4

Source: Author's simulations based on 2005–06 UNHS
Note: * = includes IDP camps

This is a larger poverty impact than other studies in Uganda would suggest, and further inspection of Table 9.3 helps identify the drivers of the estimated impact on the poverty headcount. As expected, the increase in the poverty headcount ratio is greater in urban areas, increasing by 3.6 percentage points in urban areas and 2.4 percentage points in rural areas. In both rural and urban areas it is maize price increases that account for most of the poverty increases, followed by cassava. Recall that the cassava price data are only available through May 2008, when it was at its highest level up to that time. World prices of other food commodities eased slightly in the second half of 2008, and if cassava prices in Uganda also fell, then using the May cassava price data may be slightly exaggerating the poverty impact. At the national level, the observed price increases for *matooke* and rice have no appreciable impact on the poverty headcount. In rural areas, falling sweet potato prices actually helped cushion the poverty impact of rising prices of other foods.

At the regional level, the largest impact was in the poorest region (the North), with the poverty headcount increasing by almost six percentage points. The poverty increase in the Northern region was driven mostly by increases in cassava prices in both rural and urban areas. The impact of cassava in the Northern region was influenced in large part by the magnitude of the cassava price increase (161 percent); here again, the caveats about the incomplete cassava price series and the improvements in the North following the peace settlement should be noted.

The Central region, which is the least poor, is estimated to have had the second highest increase in the poverty headcount as a result of increases in staple food prices. The poverty headcount ratio in the Central region is estimated to have increased by 3.2 percentage points, with approximately equal increases in rural and urban areas. Most of the higher poverty rates in the Central region are attributable to maize, which increased in price by 159 percent in the Central region between October 2007 and October 2008.

The poverty headcount measure tells us how many poor there are, but it tells us nothing about *how poor* they are. The poverty gap measure provides information about the depth of poverty, detecting increases or decreases in the consumption levels of poor households even if they do not reach the poverty line. Table 9.4 presents simulation results for changes in the poverty gap measure arising from food price increases. It shows a very large increase in the national poverty gap of 2.2 percentage points, which is a 25 percent increase over the 8.7 percent recorded by the 2005–2006 UNHS. Unlike the poverty headcount ratio, the estimated poverty gap increase is larger in rural areas (2.3 percentage points) than in urban areas (1.6 percentage points). Maize and cassava price increases were the main contributors to the increased poverty gap in both rural and urban areas.

Regional disaggregation of the poverty gap reveals that the sharpest increase is in the Northern region, whose increase of nearly 6 percentage points far exceeds that of the Central (1.9), Eastern (1.4), or Western (0.4) regions. Most of the poverty gap increase in the Northern region comes from cassava price increases. The increase in the poverty gap is largest in rural Northern region, but also very high in urban areas of the Northern region.

Closely related to the poverty gap measure is the concept of the poverty deficit. The poverty deficit is the amount of money required to lift all of the poor exactly to the poverty line. One can think of it as the cost of a perfectly targeted transfer that would eliminate poverty as defined by the consumption poverty line used in Uganda. It is calculated as the poverty gap index multiplied by the poverty line and the country's population. From the results of the 2005–2006 UNHS, the aggregate poverty deficit may be calculated as approximately 49 billion Ugandan shillings per month (8.7 percent x 21,000 Ugandan shillings x 27 million Ugandans), which is equal to approximately 3.7 percent of Uganda's GDP. Based on the estimates in Table 9.4, that amount would increase by about 25 percent to 62 billion Ugandan shillings per month, or 4.7 percent of GDP.

Table 9.4. Estimated Impact of Food Price Increases on Poverty Gap

		Impact of observed price increases (percentage point change in poverty gap index)					
	Base	All 5 foods	Maize	Matooke	Cassava	Sweet potato	Rice
National*	8.7	2.2	1.3	0.0	1.0	-0.2	0.0
Urban*	3.5	1.6	0.9	0.0	0.5	0.0	0.1
Rural*	9.7	2.3	1.4	0.0	1.1	-0.2	0.0
Central	3.6	1.9	2.1	0.0	0.0	-0.2	0.1
Eastern	9.1	1.4	1.8	0.0	0.0	-0.4	0.0
Northern*	20.7	5.9	0.3	0.0	5.1	0.4	0.0
Western	5.1	0.4	0.7	0.1	0.1	-0.4	0.0
Central urban	1.1	1.1	0.9	0.0	0.0	0.0	0.2
Eastern urban	4.4	2.0	1.9	0.0	0.0	-0.1	0.1
Northern urban	11.4	3.7	0.6	0.0	3.0	0.0	0.0
Western urban	2.0	0.3	0.3	0.1	0.1	-0.2	0.0
Central rural	4.7	2.3	2.5	0.0	-0.1	-0.2	0.0
Eastern rural	9.5	1.4	1.8	0.0	0.0	-0.4	0.0
Northern rural	18.8	8.1	0.3	0.1	7.5	0.2	0.0
Western rural	5.4	0.5	0.7	0.1	0.1	-0.4	0.0
IDP	29.2	2.2	0.2	0.0	1.0	1.1	-0.1

Source: Author's simulations based on 2005–06 UNHS
Note: * = includes IDP camps

How much of the increase in the poverty deficit is caused by the increased number of poor people, and how much by the increased depth of poverty among those who were already poor before the food price increases? Based on the simulations reported here, the 2.6 percentage point increase in the poverty headcount ratio due to increased food prices is the net result of 4.9 percent of the population that was initially non-poor moving into poverty and 2.3 percent of the population that was initially poor moving out of poverty (i.e., net staple food sellers who were initially below the poverty line). Thus, 28.8 percent of the population was below the poverty line both before and after the food price shock, and most of them are pushed further into poverty by the shock. Approximately 72 percent of the increase in the aggregate poverty deficit stems from welfare losses among those who were below the poverty line both before and after the rise in food prices increased the poverty deficit, with the remaining 28 percent accounted for by net changes among those who moved into or out of poverty. To frame the increase in the poverty gap a little differently, before the price shock the average consumption among poor households amounted to 72 percent of the poverty line, and after the price shock that average is estimated to have fallen to only 68 percent of the poverty line (the latter figure includes those who were pushed into poverty by the food price shock).

Conclusions

There are many good reasons for expecting a country like Uganda to be relatively unaffected by increases in the world prices of staple cereals. As a landlocked country with high transportation costs, its trade volumes of low value-per-weight staple crops are relatively small. Uganda's population is overwhelmingly rural and most—although certainly not all—households produce a substantial share of their staple food needs. Ugandan households also consume an unusually wide variety of staple foods, so they are less vulnerable to a maize price shock than southern African countries, or to a rice price shock than East Asian countries. Ugandan staples include foods that are not widely available on international markets, such as cooking bananas, cassava, and sweet potatoes.

Nevertheless, the data presented here demonstrate that staple food prices in Uganda increased dramatically in early 2008, most likely through a combination of price increases on world markets and local conditions such as sharply higher fuel costs and increases in demand for staple food imports by Uganda's regional trading partners. Our analysis shows that Uganda was vulnerable to these price increases and likely suffered significant welfare losses, including increases in the incidence and depth of absolute poverty. Based on the analysis presented, three factors stand out as the most important contributors to the short-term increase in poverty following the food price shock in 2008.

The first was the magnitude of the maize price increase. Maize, an important staple in Eastern and Northern Uganda as well as urban areas, more than doubled in price between October 2007 and October 2008. As described by Benson *et al.* (2008), much of the upward pressure on maize prices was a result of increased demand from Kenya, which experienced a production shortfall following the civil unrest in December 2007 and early 2008. Kenya is expected to remain a significant source of demand for Ugandan maize.

The second major factor was the large increase in the prices of other staples. Prices of cassava, *matooke*, and rice had been trending upward in Uganda since 2004–2005 and accelerated rapidly in 2008, presumably from increased demand as consumers substituted away from maize. There are also indications that increased demand from southern Sudan for roots and tubers was an important contributor to higher prices, especially for cassava. Like maize prices, the higher prices for *matooke* persisted at least through 2008 and into 2009.

The third key factor was that most of the poor are net buyers of staple foods, even in rural areas. As shown in the NBR analysis, the poor tend to be net buyers of maize, cassava, and sweet potatoes. Thus the incidence of the food price shock is highest on those households that are least equipped to deal with it. This is also observed at the sub-national level, as the poverty impacts are highest in the Northern region, which was already the poorest region before the food price shock. Contrast this with the impact in West Africa, where the adverse impact of higher food prices was much less in poorer areas than in richer areas (Wodon and Zaman, 2008; Coulombe and Wodon, 2008).

Although increased demand from regional trading partners is one of the proximate causes of food price increases in Uganda, it would be a mistake to inhibit this trade in an effort to bring food prices down. In this context, it is important not to blunt the price signals that can help spur agricultural investment and production. Uganda has invested heavily in its Plan for the Modernization of Agriculture, aiming for improvements in agricultural productivity and marketing efficiency. If it succeeds, Uganda will be well placed to supply regional markets as well as its own rapidly growing population. The rural poor can benefit if they are able to become net sellers of these foods. However, it should also be recognized that a large part of the staple food price increases in Uganda was likely caused by higher production and marketing costs, especially higher fuel prices. Moves to stabilize input costs and improve marketing efficiency will be important for enabling a supply response by staple food producers, be they net buyers or net sellers.

That said, the need for mitigating social protection measures appears to be greater than was initially recognized. Not only are the negative impacts larger, but they are also much more widespread geographically. For example, in the worst affected area, the Northern region, most of the welfare losses appear to have occurred among those living outside IDP camps, encompassing both rural and urban areas. Urban areas of the Eastern region were also badly affected, as were poor households in both rural and urban areas of the Central region. This suggests the need for continued close monitoring of the situation, continuation and possible expansion of existing safety net and feeding programs in the hard-hit Northern districts, and contingency planning for national safety net programs to reach those threatened by high food prices. The Northern Uganda Social Action Fund is an example of an existing safety net program that can be scaled up in northern Uganda, and lessons from its successes can be applied to developing similar programs elsewhere in Uganda.

Acknowledgments

The author thanks Rui Benfica, Todd Benson, Louise Cord, Louise Fox, Madhur Gautam, Jesko Hentschel, Kathie Krumm, Varun Kshirsagar, Albert Musisi, Willie Odwongo, Paul Okwi, Ana Revenga, Bob Rijkers, Johan Swinnen, Hassan Zaman, and conference participants at the University of Oxford and Cornell University for helpful comments on earlier versions of this paper. The author is solely responsible for any remaining errors. This paper has not undergone the review accorded to official World Bank publications. The findings, interpretations, and conclusions expressed herein are those of the author and do not necessarily reflect the views of the International Bank for Reconstruction and Development / The World Bank and its affiliated organizations, or those of the Executive Directors of The World Bank or the governments they represent.

References

Barrett, C.B. and Dorosh, P.A.. (1996) 'Farmers' welfare and changing food prices: Nonparametric evidence from rice in Madagascar.' *American Journal of Agricultural Economics* 78(3): 656–669.

Benson, T., Mugarura, S. and Wanda, K. (2008) 'Impacts in Uganda of rising global food prices: the role of diversified staples and limited price transmission.' *Agricultural Economics* 39(s1): 513–524.

Budd, J.W. (1993) 'Changing food prices and rural welfare: A nonparametric examination of Côte d'Ivoire.' *Economic Development and Cultural Change* 41(3): 587–603.

Coulombe, H. and Wodon, Q. (2008) 'Assessing the geographic impact of higher food prices in Guinea.' Policy Research Working Paper 4743. World Bank, Washington, DC.

Deaton, A. (1989) 'Rice prices and income distribution in Thailand: A non-parametric analysis.' *Economic Journal* 99(395): 1–37.

Deaton, A. (1997) *The Analysis of Household Surveys: A Microeconometric Approach to Development.* World Bank and The Johns Hopkins University Press, Washington, DC.

Dessus, S., Herrera, S. and de Hoyos, R. (2008) 'The impact of food inflation on urban poverty and its monetary cost: Some back-of-the-envelope calculations.' Policy Research Working Paper 4666. World Bank, Washington, DC.

FoodNet. (n.d.) FootNet Project: Marketing and Postharvest Research in Eastern and Central Africa. Association for Strengthening Agricultural Research in Eastern and Central Africa. Kampala, Uganda. Available at: www.foodnet.cgiar.org.

Ivanic, M. and Martin, W. (2008) 'Implications of higher global food prices for poverty in low-income countries.' Policy Research Working Paper 4594. World Bank, Washington, DC.

Jayne, T. and Chisvo, M. (1991) 'Unraveling Zimbabwe's food insecurity paradox: Implications for grain market reform in southern Africa.' *Food Policy* 16(4): 319–329.

Loening, J. and Oseni, G. (2007) 'Approximating rural and urban welfare effects of food price inflation in Ethiopia.' World Bank, Washington, DC. Mimeo.

Minten, B. and Barrett, C.B. (2008) 'Agricultural technology, productivity, and poverty in Madagascar.' *World Development* 36(5): 797–822.

Mitchell, D. 2008. 'A note on rising food prices.' Policy Research Working Paper 4682. World Bank, Washington, DC.

Poulton, C., Kydd, J., Wiggins, S. and Dorward, A. (2006) 'State intervention for food price stabilization in Africa: Can it work?' *Food Policy* 31(4): 342–356.

Ravallion, M. (1990) 'Rural welfare effects of food price changes under induced wage responses: Theory and evidence for Bangladesh.' *Oxford Economic Papers* 42(3): 574–585.

Uganda Bureau of Statistics (UBOS). (2006) 'Uganda National Household Survey 2005/2006: Report on the socioeconomic module.' Uganda Bureau of Statisics, Kampala.

Ulimwengu, J. and Ramadan, R. (2009) 'How does food price increase affect Ugandan households? An augmented multimarket approach.' IFPRI Discussion Paper No. 00884. International Food Policy Research Institute, Washington, DC.

Vu, L. and Glewwe, P. (2008) 'Impacts of rising food prices on poverty and welfare in Vietnam.' Department of Applied Economics, University of Minnesota. Mimeo.

Wodon, Q., Tsimpo, C., Backiny-Yetna, P., Joseph, G., Adoho, F. and Coulombe, H. (2008) 'Potential impact of higher food prices on poverty: Summary estimates for a dozen west and central African countries.' Mimeo. World Bank, Washington, DC.

Wodon, Q. and Zaman, H. (2008) 'Rising food prices in sub-Saharan Africa: Poverty impact and policy responses.' Policy Research Working Paper 4738. World Bank, Washington, DC.

World Bank. (2008a) *Global Economic Prospects 2009: Commodity Markets at the Crossroads.* World Bank, Washington, DC.

World Bank. (2008b) World Development Indicators database. World Bank, Washington, DC.

Chapter 10

The Likely Impacts of Food Price Increases on Nutritionally Vulnerable Households in South Africa

Hettie C. Schönfeldt, Nicolette Gibson and Hester Vermeulen

Abstract

The intake of food is a basic human physiological need that is essential for survival, growth, health and general well-being. Without an adequate supply of food a human being cannot sustain life, grow or develop optimally, nor utilize energy. Such lack of access implies food insecurity. South Africa (SA) is classified as a developing country, with developing countries representing a third of the world's population. Increased food prices in 2007–2008 were a worldwide phenomenon; it is argued that this case study presents insights that apply more broadly than to one country alone. About 35 percent of the SA population was food insecure and categorized as being poor in 2005. With the food price crisis of 2007–2008 and the global economic crisis which followed soon thereafter, most households needed to employ food coping strategies to survive. Strategies such as skipping meals, reduction of dietary diversity and reducing portion sizes of staple foods consumed are discussed in this chapter along with the costs of a balanced varied diet compared to average household income. Of the coping strategies documented here, some have had significant negative impacts on individuals' often already deprived nutritional status. The likely impacts of the 2007–2008 food price crisis and the continuing effects of food price inflation on the nutritional status of vulnerable households highlight the prevailing inadequate nutritional situation facing poor households in South Africa. This chapter addresses these issues as well as proposing possible solutions to the problems.

Introduction

It is well recognized that food is a basic human physiological need that is essential for survival, growth in children, health and general well-being. Humans cannot grow and develop optimally, nor utilize energy for sustained livelihoods, without access to an adequate supply of nutritious food. The absence of this access implies food insecurity. South Africa is a developing country and grouped as one of the countries with the highest rate of income inequality in the world, with the poorest 20 percent of the population accounting for less than 1.5 percent of total household income in the country in 2005–2006 (Statistics South Africa, 2008; Altman *et al.,* 2009). According to South Africa's Bureau of Market Research, in the period 2007 to 2008, 51 percent of households in South Africa acquired only 11 percent of national income (Masemola and De Jongh, 2009). In the period from 2008 to 2009, a similar scenario was reported, with 50 percent of households acquiring 10.7 percent of national household income (Masemola *et al.,* 2010).

Similar to many developing countries, there are no precise figures on household food security status in South Africa due to the lack of a national monitoring program, and published figures are often extrapolated from different scenarios. However, there is general consensus that a large portion of South African households are increasingly food insecure (Altman *et al.,* 2009; Badham, 2009). This is consistent with the wide consensus that reported figures in developing countries are often greatly underestimated (Svedberg, 2002). According to South Africa's National Food Consumption Survey (NFCS), 52 percent of households experienced hunger in 2005 prior to the food price crisis of 2007–2008; in roughly the same period more than 14 million, or about 35 percent, of the South African population was recorded as food insecure and categorized as poor (De Klerk *et al.*, 2004, Lemke, 2005). In November 2010, the Bureau of Market Research published a report stating that in 2010, 75 percent of South Africa's adult population had a marginal income of less than ZAR 50,000 (approximately US$7,000) per person per annum. Low personal income growth rates (in nominal terms) were experienced by adults in all the lower income groups. This could be due to the after-effects of the recession on personal income growth in South Africa (Van Aardt and Coetzee, 2010). Furthermore, the higher income groups in South Africa experienced much higher levels of income growth than the middle and lower income groups in 2009–2010, demonstrating that the recession had a particularly severe impact on the growth of the emerging middle class in South Africa (Van Aardt and Coetzee, 2010).

Food price inflation is a global phenomenon and was reflected in South Africa in the form of severe inflation rates in 2007–2008. Moreover, over the period 2006 to 2009, the rate of food price increases was consistently higher than the general rate of inflation as measured by the Consumer Price Index (CPI). This is illustrated in Table 10.1.

Table 10.1. A Comparison of General Inflation and Food Inflation Based on Consumer Price Index (CPI) Figures, 2006–2009

Year	Average monthly change:	
	CPI (general)[a]	CPI (food and non-alcoholic beverages)[b]
2006	4.6%	6.1%
2007	7.3%	9.5%
2008	11.5%	15.3%
2009	7.1%	9.7%

[a] Statistics South Africa, 2011
[b] South African Reserve Bank, 2011

The global food supply system is facing challenges from economic and related crises along with climate changes, all directly affecting the nutritional well-being of the poor and most vulnerable population groups by reducing their access to nutritious foods (Bloem *et al.,* 2010). Increases in agricultural commodity prices along with exponential increases in crude oil prices translate into increasing costs of food production, processing, transportation and distribution (OECD Outlook, 2008). In the 2008 Income and Expenditure Survey conducted by Statistics South Africa, during 2005–2006 (just before the period of high inflation) almost half of the South African population had incomes of no more than ZAR 800 (US$118.52) per household per month, of which up to an estimated 70 percent was used for food purchases (Statistics South Africa, 2008). Such a high proportion of household income being spent on food even before the crisis indicates the severe potential impact of the 2007–2008 period of high inflation and the continuing increases in food prices on the purchasing and consumption patterns of vulnerable households, especially among the poorest groups in society. The objective of this chapter is to explore the likely nutritional implications of food price inflation in South Africa, particularly on very poor households which experience the highest levels of nutritional vulnerability in the country.

South African Incomes and Demographics

South Africa is a diverse country with more than 49 million inhabitants, 11 official languages, and a variety of different income groups and living standards (Statistics South Africa, 2008). While more than 75 percent of South Africa's population comprises black Africans, this category is neither culturally, linguistically nor financially homogenous. The Bureau of Market Research (2010) indicated that, in the period 2008–2009, 79 percent of households in the highest income group (annual household income of more than ZAR 750,000 (approximately $US90,000) belonged to the white population. The black African population showed gains with respect to this high income group from 2008 to 2009; African households within the lowest income group (annual household income of less than ZAR 50,000 (about US$6,000) declined from 61.5 percent in 2008 to 60.2 percent in 2009 (Euromonitor International, 2008; Masemola *et al.,* 2010). Of the Indian households, 50 percent fell in the highest income group, while at least four in every five Indian households fell in or above the middle income group (more than ZAR 300,000 or US$35,000) per annum (Statistics South Africa, 2008),

The unequal income distribution in South Africa is illustrated by the fact that the wealthiest 10 percent of income earners accrued almost 50 percent of total income in 2005–2006 (Statistics South Africa, 2008). Furthermore the fortification baseline of the 2005 National Food Consumption Survey (NFCS-FB-1) reported that 55 percent of South African households earned a nominal monthly income of between R1 (US$0.14) and R1,000 (US$140) per month in 2005 (NFCS-FB-1, 2008). Similarly, Prahalad and Hart (2006) reported that almost half of the 10 to 11 million households in South Africa could be classified as very low income, with a nominal monthly income of less than ZAR 800 (US$126) per month in 2005.

On average, these poor households consisted of five members (Amuli, 2006; Oldewage-Theron *et al.,* 2006), which translates into an average nominal household income in 2005 of ZAR 5.33 (US$0.84) per person per day to meet all needs. Even prior to the financial crises, in 2007–2008, the amount of available money was substantially lower than the international poverty line indicator of US$1.25 per day (ZAR 8.44) (IDA14, 2004, 2006).

The Burden of Malnutrition in South Africa

As previously mentioned, different reference sources publish different estimates of undernutrition and poverty, especially in developing countries (Masset, 2010; Cafiero and Gennari, 2011), with South Africa being no exception. It was reported in 2002 that up to 43 percent of South African households suffered from food poverty (Rose and Charlton, 2002). Two years later, in 2004, it was estimated that approximately 25 percent of the population was vulnerable to food poverty, with 25 percent of children under the age of six exhibiting stunted growth because of malnutrition (Human Sciences Research Council [HSRC], 2004). Food poverty can be defined as a state where physiological human needs are not adequately met as the available amount of money is not enough to purchase a basic nutritionally balanced diet providing minimum dietary energy requirements (De Rose *et al.*, 1998; Sibrian, 2009). The majority of South African households consume a limited variety of foods (mainly staples) available in the home (NFCS, 1999). In 2003, one out of two children had an energy intake providing less than two-thirds of their energy needs, and a great number of children consumed a diet with poor nutrient density not meeting their daily (macro- and micro-) nutrient requirements (South African Demographic and Health Survey [SADHS], 2003). Even before the 2007–2008 economic crises, constantly rising food prices and increasing poverty threatened household food security by reducing the resources available for purchasing food (Hendriks, 2005), which has resulted in a constant increase in the number of hungry people (Badham, 2009).

According to the NFCS in 1999, one in ten children between the ages of one and nine years were underweight, and just more than one in five were stunted. Four years later, children's mean intakes of calcium, iron, zinc, vitamins A, D, E, C, B6, B2 and niacin were all recorded as low in comparison with the 2003 recommended dietary allowances (RDAs) (SADHS, 2003). Even after the implementation of the mandatory South African food fortification program in 2003, the NFCS-FB-1 still found that as of 2005 two out of three children and one out of four women had a poor vitamin A status, one out of five women and one out of seven children had poor iron status, and 45 percent of children had an inadequate zinc status (NFCS-FB-1, 2008). These national food intake surveys were done prior to the food price crises in 2007–2008 but already indicated increased deficiencies when compared with previous nutritional data, in spite of mandatory fortification of staple foods.

Effect of Malnutrition on Livelihoods

Chastre *et al.* (2007) point out that nutritional deficiencies experienced by children before the age of 24 to 36 months are virtually irreversible. Undernourished children are affected for the rest of their lives, as those who do not achieve their optimum heights (stunted) or consistently experience bouts of weight loss during their childhoods seldom reach optimum size as adults, have lower mental capacity and have greater risks of infections. Other long-term consequences of chronic malnutrition are that a ten percent increase in stunting rates is estimated to be associated with an eight percent decrease in children reaching the final grade at school (Chastre *et al.*, 2007). All these factors translate into significant potential economic losses for a country.

In 2005–2006, approximately 11 percent of the South African population suffered from HIV/AIDS (Statistics South Africa, 2008). In 2009, an estimated 552,000 people in South Africa (1.1 percent of the population) were diagnosed with HIV/AIDS by a medical practitioner or nurse (GHS, 2009). As stated by Chastre *et al.* (2007), malnutrition can be particularly profound in those individuals who are affected as opportunistic infections interact with poor nutritional status in a vicious cycle.

Low intake levels of essential micronutrients also have significant effects on health and well-being in all age groups. Iron deficiency affects performance in school and work, iodine deficiency can result in goiter—and in severe cases in cretinism, and vitamin A deficiency results in blindness. Apart from being a significant contributing factor to morbidity, malnutrition is the single biggest contributor to childhood mortality (Chastre *et al.,* 2007). Population groups that are already vulnerable to food insecurity have little resistance to further possible shocks and stresses, such as price increases, that add to hunger and malnutrition (Hendriks, 2005).

Consumer Food Purchasing Behaviour

The South African Advertising Research Foundation (SAARF) has developed a market segmentation tool to profile the South African consumer market, namely the Living Standards Measurement (LSM).[71] The SAARF LSM's market segmentation is based on consumers' living standards using a variety of criteria such as degree of urbanization and ownership of household assets and major appliances; SAARF divides the population into 10 LSM groups from the lowest status (LSM 1) to the highest status (LSM 10) (SAARF, 2006).

According to estimates by the Bureau of Market Research (Martins, 2006), a household classified as LSM 1 would typically have spent about 71 percent of its average monthly household income on food in 2005, with this proportion decreasing to less than 5 percent of household income for the wealthiest socioeconomic subgroups (LSM 9 and 10). Furthermore, the limited amount of income available to spend on food for the lower LSM groups has resulted in a very limited food basket (Golden, 2000; SAARF, 2006; Oldewage-Theron *et al.*, 2006). Figure 10.1 presents an overview of the food expenditure patterns of the various LSM groups during 2005–2006 (Statistics South Africa, 2008). According to the 2005 data, the lowest socioeconomic groups (LSM 1 to 3) spent almost one third of their total food cash expenditures on bread and cereals, dominated by maize meal, followed by bread (Figure 10.1). As incomes increase, a lower percentage of income is spent on the bread and cereal group and more on the meat/meat alternative and dairy and egg groups. This is part of the widely recognized trend that as income increases in developing countries, the per capita consumption of animal products increases. Dietary simplification by lower socioeconomic groups, in contrast to dietary diversity, has negative impacts on food security, nutrition and health (FAO, 2010). This low dietary diversity in the period prior to a period of major food price increases indicates the potential risk for worsening of nutritional status of this already vulnerable population group, particularly as related to micronutrient deficiencies (Thorne-Lyman *et al.,* 2009).

Urbanization is a growing trend in South Africa, with people continually moving from rural areas into urban settlements in search of better work opportunities and income generation potential. A subset of characteristics that define urban livelihoods and the ways in which the urban poor achieve household and individual food security was reported by Ruel *et al.* (2009). These include: 1) a greater reliance on cash income; 2) a limited access to urban agriculture or to land in rural areas; 3) greater participation of women in the labor

---

[71] This is distinct from the World Bank's Living Standards Measurement Survey (LSMS).

force outside the home, with potential consequences for child care; 4) greater availability of services but larger inequality in access; and 5) changes in lifestyle and consumption patterns associated with the nutrition transition.

Figure 10.1. Estimated food expenditure patterns on the dominant food groups of three general LSM consumer groups

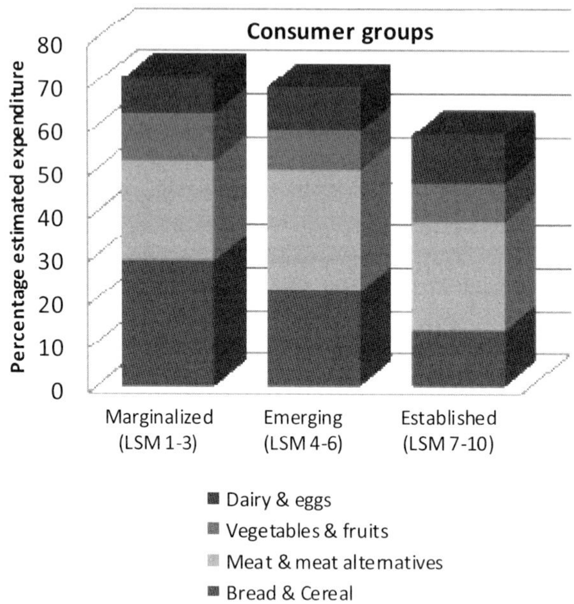

Calculations based on food expenditure data published by the Bureau of Market Research, Martins, 2006.

Although the vulnerability of the urban poor to the food price crises has been widely acknowledged (Ruel *et al.,* 2009), the impact of inflation on the rural poor should not be ignored. In South Africa, a significant difference in nutrient intake is seen between rural and urban areas and between different living standards within the same area. In 1998, the South African Demographic and Health Survey reported mortality rates in rural areas as high as 7.12 percent, compared to a 4.32 percent rate in urban areas (SADHS, 1998). Stunting rates are also consistently higher for children living in rural areas and on commercial farms. Although rural populations often have access to agricultural land and consequently may have the option to harvest cultivated or wild foods, food prices are often higher in rural areas due to limited access and market competition. Over the years, food prices in rural areas have been increasingly higher than in urban areas in South Africa. In January 2009, rural consumers paid ZAR 9.75 (US$1.16) more for a list of ten food products monitored by the National Agricultural Marketing Council (NAMC) Food Price Monitor than did urban consumers. The price difference for this food basket in rural versus urban areas increased to ZAR 17.49 (US$2.40) by January 2010, with the difference fueled mainly by price increases for rice, maize meal and sugar (NAMC, 2010).

A study done in 2005 in urbanized informal settlements found that the majority of these households (60 percent) had a monthly income of less than ZAR 500/month (approximately US$80). Of the amount available to these households, up to 71 percent was allocated to the purchasing of food, which consisted mainly of maize meal (Amuli, 2006). The maize porridge consumption by this population group in 2005 amounted to approximately 532g/day (made up, according to meal times, as 345g of stiff maize porridge plus 124g of soft maize porridge plus 63g of crumbly maize porridge), eaten over two or three meals, and representing 66 percent of the total energy intake per day (Oldewage-Theron *et al.,* 2006; Duvenage and Schönfeldt, 2007). The 532g/person/day daily maize portions consumed in these settlements were significantly smaller than those reported in the South African food consumption studies done amongst different population groups between 1983 and 2002 (Nel and Steyn, 2002). These food consumption studies listed maize as the most commonly eaten food consumed by 78 percent of the population, with an average portion size of 848g/person/day (Nel and Steyn, 2002). The discrepancies in estimated portion sizes could be attributed to different sampling populations used by the various studies, which would also result in differences in income, eating culture, availability of food, etc. In most regional studies, only specific rural or urban populations were investigated, while the National Food Consumption Surveys (NFCS) aimed at representing the full diversity of the national population. For this case study, the 2006 food intake survey done in urbanized informal settlements (Duvenage and Schönfeldt, 2007), with available data on household income, was selected as the most accurate assumption of food consumption for this specifically vulnerable population group. The obvious limitations resulting from the lack of national food intake data differentiating between urban and rural population groups should be kept in mind (Van Heerden and Schönfeldt, 2011).

However, it may be worth noting that South Africa experiences a double burden of disease in the forms of both under- and overnutrition. The 2003 Demographic and Health Survey (DHS) of the South African Department of Health reported a total of 21.1 percent of South African men over the age of 15 years to be overweight, and 8.7 percent to be obese. For women over the age of 15 years, the corresponding numbers were 29 percent overweight and 23 percent obese, indicating that over 40 percent of South African adults are either overweight or obese (SADHS, 2003). Large portion sizes of staple foods contribute to obesity especially in the low LSM groups, with obesity incidence increasing constantly. Although it was not measured, the population group studied by Duvenage and Schönfeldt (2007) did not reflect national obesity incidence, and members of the households were described as undernourished based on visual appraisal. Although many factors could have affected intake, the most probable reason was the lack of access to food (severe poverty).

The most commonly consumed foods in South Africa, as reported by the 2003 South African Demographic and Health Survey, are maize meal porridge, government brown bread, full cream fresh milk, white sugar and tea (SADHS, 2003). In Table 10.2, the average portions of these commonly consumed foods as recorded by various consumption surveys over the years are presented. As tea is measured differently (sometimes as diluted, sometimes as dry leaves) and has a low macro- and micronutrient contribution, it was excluded from the data. It can be seen that the portion sizes of all foods listed (maize meal porridge, brown bread, milk and sugar) differ significantly among the different studies. The two most recent studies, done for marginalized consumer groups, reported the lowest intake of these staples foods, with the most significant difference seen for maize meal porridge. Daily maize meal porridge portions decreased from more than 800g per daily portion recorded in studies reported in the 1990s to 532g recorded in 2005 (Duvenage and Schönfeldt, 2007).

Table 10.2. Portion Sizes Reported from Various Food Consumption Surveys in Low Income Populations over Time

Surveys done on food intake in low income populations	Ethnic Groups	Average daily portion consumed (g)			
		Maize	Bread	Milk	Sugar
Adult Food Consumption studies, 1983 – 2002[a]	All	848	165	204	27
Lebowa Study, 1991[a]	Black, rural, 10yrs+	858	153	41	20
Dikgale study, 1998[a]	Black, rural, 19yrs+	891	121	121	27
THUSA Bana Study, 1996–1998[a]	Black, urban + rural, 10yrs+	532	115	72	21
Duvenage Study, 2005[b]	Black, informal urban, 20yrs+	532	150	56	22

[a] Nel and Steyn, 2002
[b] Duvenage and Schönfeldt, 2007

During the period 2007–2008 South Africa experienced significant increases in the prices of a wide range of prominent food types. From January 2007 to January 2008, many food products experienced year-to-year price increases above the overall CPI-based inflation rate of 9.3 percent, including white bread (19.9 percent), brown bread (16.2 percent), special maize meal (28.0 percent), fresh full cream milk (37.1 percent), potatoes (47.1 percent) and apples (22.7 percent) (NAMC, 2008).

Such increases in food prices and other forms of stress exerted on very low income consumers can have severe impacts on their consumption behaviour in terms of both food basket composition and consumption quantities. In order for vulnerable households to survive, they employ various food-coping strategies (FCS); depending on the severity of food shortages and resulting household food insecurity, those affected may employ a single, or various combinations, of FCS. Unfortunately, many of these strategies have increasingly negative consequences on the nutritional status of household members. Common FCS include: 1) eating less-preferred, cheaper, foods; 2) gathering wild foods; 3) consuming seed stock; 4) limiting portion sizes; 5) buying food on credit; 6) restricting adult consumption in favour of children; 7) borrowing money or food; 8) sending household members to eat elsewhere; 9) sending family members to beg; 10) feeding working members of the household at the expense of non-working members; 11) rationing money to buy ready-to-eat food, and 12) going the entire day without meals (Maxwell *et al.*, 2003; Kruger *et al.*, 2008). Demographic factors also play a role in the FCS employed in the case of food crises—i.e., urban individuals are not able to gather wild foods due to their lack of access to open lands, whereas rural individuals may not be able to buy food on credit or to buy ready-to-eat foods. According to Ortiz *et al.* (2011), poor households around the globe have since 2008 exhausted many of their coping strategies—for example, eating fewer meals, increasing household debt and working longer hours—in the relentless aim to cope with high food costs. Tiwari and Zaman (2010) estimated that the 2008 food price spike had increased undernourishment by nearly 7 percent worldwide. The most severely affected were those who were already facing high pre-existing levels of malnutrition (Ortiz *et al.*, 2011).

South African Experience with Staple Food Fortification

With food and nutrition regarded as being of fundamental importance to public health, there is a general consensus that obtaining and maintaining a desirable nutritional state demands concerted holistic and multisectoral approaches. One key area to addressing the double burden of malnutrition and disease in South Africa lies in the development of sound educational programs teaching people how to select a more healthy diet. To this purpose, eleven Food-Based Dietary Guidelines (FBDGs) were developed in 1998 through a scientifically based process recommended by a joint FAO/WHO expert consultation (Vorster *et al.,* 2001). Implementation of the FBDGs started in mid-2004 with the training of health care workers (INP, 2004). The FBDGs were developed based on prevailing eating patterns and diet-related health criteria, isolated from the 1999 NFCS which revealed various areas of nutritional requirements that needed to be addressed.

The high incidence of micronutrient deficiencies in South Africa prompted the Department of Health to implement various other mandatory programs to combat this situation, including the food fortification program, targeted micronutrient supplementation, dietary diversification and other public health measures including parasite control (Witten *et al.,* 2003). The mandatory food fortification programs in South Africa started with the iodization of salt (1995), followed by extensive fortification of staple foods including maize meal and bread flour (2003). In October 2003, mandatory fortification became legally applicable and the compulsory addition of eight micronutrients—vitamin A, thiamine, riboflavin, niacin, vitamin B6, folic acid, iron and zinc—to all maize meal and wheat flours in the country was implemented (*Training Manual: Food Fortification for Environment Health Practitioners*, 2004). The fortification composition and addition rates were based on food consumption patterns observed from the NFCS of 1999 and the South African Vitamin A Consultancy Group (SAVACG) study of 1994. In Table 10.3 the percentages of the micronutrients in selected fortified foodstuffs are presented compared to the current RDAs for people over the age of five years. It is evident that most nutrients are added so as to contribute 25 percent or more of the recommended dietary requirements for each specific nutrient, assuming 200g raw weight of maize meal or wheat flour is consumed daily. This amount translates to approximately 370g of baked brown bread and is dependent on the consistency of cooked maize porridge—between 530g (hard porridge) and 1450g (soft porridge)—that should be consumed in order to obtain these contributions to the RDAs.

Table 10.3. Average Percentage RDA in 200g Fortified Maize Meal or Wheat Flour

Micronutrient	Maize meal (% per 200g raw)	Wheat flour (% per 200g raw)
Vitamin A	25	25
Thiamin	25	25
Riboflavin	17	20
Niacin	25	25
Vitamin B6	25	25
Folic acid	50	50
Iron	25	25
Zinc	20	20

Source: Training Manual: Food Fortification for Environment Health Practitioners, 2004

As stated previously, based on their 2005 study, Duvenage and Schönfeldt (2007) reported the average daily intake of maize porridge to be 532g, which is in line with the quantities required for stiff maize porridge, while daily bread intake was reported to be much lower than the required amounts at around 150g/day. With the effect of food price increases likely resulting in households coping through the consumption of even smaller food portions, it can be presumed that daily intake could be even less than what was recorded in 2005. These presumptions are confirmed by the 2005 NFCS-FB-1, which reported an increase in vitamin A deficiency as well as an increase in iron deficiency in children, in spite of mandatory fortification of staple foods since 2003 (NFCS-FB-1, 2008).

The Potential Impact of Inflation on the Nutritional Status of Poor Households in South Africa

The 2007–2008 food crises demonstrated that soaring food prices, both nationally and internationally, can have serious consequences for developing countries. Most recently, the international price index for basic foodstuffs rose sharply at the end of 2010, and according to Ortiz *et al.* (2011), has recently exceeded the peak levels of the 2007–2008 crises. Severe food price inflation is particularly problematic in Africa, since according to the United Nations Food and Agriculture Organization, 21 of the 36 countries around the globe which experienced a food price crisis in 2007–2008 were in Africa. The countries relying on imports of basic staple grains such as maize, rice and wheat were particularly vulnerable in this regard (World Bank, 2008; Ortiz *et al.*, 2011).

After an 18-month period of relative stability in prices following a decline in the global food price index in late 2008, food prices increased dramatically—by 33 percent between January 2010 and January 2011 (on a month-to-month basis) (NAMC, 2011). According to Kirsten (2011, personal communication), South Africa is experiencing a situation of 'déjà vu' with 20 to 25 percent nominal food price increases within a short period of time. From 1991–1992 to 2002–2003, food price increases of 20 to 25 percent were reported over an eleven-year period. Since 2002–2003, the same percent increase in nominal prices was seen within a period of six years (e.g., by 2008–2009). This same range of food price increase (20 to 25 percent) has been experienced again, this time after only a little over two years, between 2008 and 2010–2011.

Despite South Africa's being a surplus producer of maize, the impact of global agricultural commodity price increases and rising input costs has translated into increasing costs of food production, processing, transportation and distribution. The domestic commodity market has been affected by increased food price volatility, particularly among staple food goods. For example, in nominal terms, the average retail price for a five-kilogram bag of maize meal fell 3 percent from December 2004 to December 2005, but rose nearly 23 percent from December 2006 to December 2007 (Figure 10.2).

As discussed earlier in this chapter (Table 10.1), food price increases (based on the CPI for food and non-alcoholic beverages) were consistently higher than general inflation (measured by the general CPI) for the years 2006 to 2009. To further explore the impacts of inflationary trends during this period, Table 10.4 presents data comparing increases in food prices and general inflation for selected one-year periods in order to better capture developments during the relevant time frame. The differences between the figures in Table 10.1 and Table 10.4 are explained by the more detailed price fluctuations captured in Table 10.4, while Table 10.1 is based on monthly averages. Positive increases in real food prices (e.g., food prices relative to overall inflation) have clearly prevailed during the 2005–2008 period. Alternatively, the disposable incomes of the poorest 30 percent of households in South Africa should have been at least 22 percent higher in October 2008 than in April 2007 if they were to maintain their food purchasing power (NAMC, 2008). More recently, the renewed food price increases of 2010–2011 resulted in the cost of the basic food basket of ten items monitored by the South African National Agricultural Marketing Council (expressed as a share of average monthly income of the poorest 30 percent of the population) increasing from 33.2 percent in January 2009 to 33.4 percent in January 2010, and to 33.9 percent in January 2011.

Table 10.4. Trends in Food Prices and Overall Inflation, April 2005 to Early 2008

Period	Nominal food price increases (%)	Overall inflation rate (CPI-based) (%)
April 2005 to April 2006	5.7	3.3
July 2005 to July 2006	6.0	5.0
October 2005 to October 2006	7.3	5.4
December 2005 to December 2006	7.9	5.8
March 2006 to March 2007	7.6	6.1
July 2006 to July 2007	13.8	7.0
January 2007 to January 2008	13.4	9.3

Source: NAMC, 2007, 2008

The Cost of a Balanced Diet

According to the World Health Organization (WHO), a diet is considered acceptable for an individual if it covers both the micro- and macronutrient requirements, and often dietary tools are developed in order to ensure such intakes. The South African FBDGs have only been in existence since 2010. Established with the assistance of FAO, they are being developed into a food guide to be used as a quantifiable reference for a healthy balanced diet. No quantifiable national reference was available when the case study reported below was done; South Africa also lacked a specific selection of foods within the official national food price monitoring systems to represent a balanced diet. In fact, there is a great need for these references be standardized in South Africa as they are in many other countries, and for the components of the market basket, their prices, and the standards against which they are applied to be carefully determined and monitored over time.

Many countries have quantifiable nutrition education guidelines and tools available to enable consumers to plan their daily eating patterns, such as MyPyramid from the US Department of Agriculture (USDA). The Canadian Food Guide recommends proportional consumption of five basic food groups, the specific amounts depending on age and gender, corresponding in principle with the eleven South African Food-Based Dietary Guidelines. As a result the Canadian Food Guide is selected here as an example of recommendations for a healthy, balanced South African diet. For an adult between 19 and 50 years of age, the Canadian Food Guide recommends seven to ten portions of fruits and vegetables, six to eight portions of starch, two to three portions of meat and two portions of dairy products per person per day in order to ensure the optimal intake of all essential macro- and micronutrients.

Figure 10.2. South African retail prices of selected maize meal products

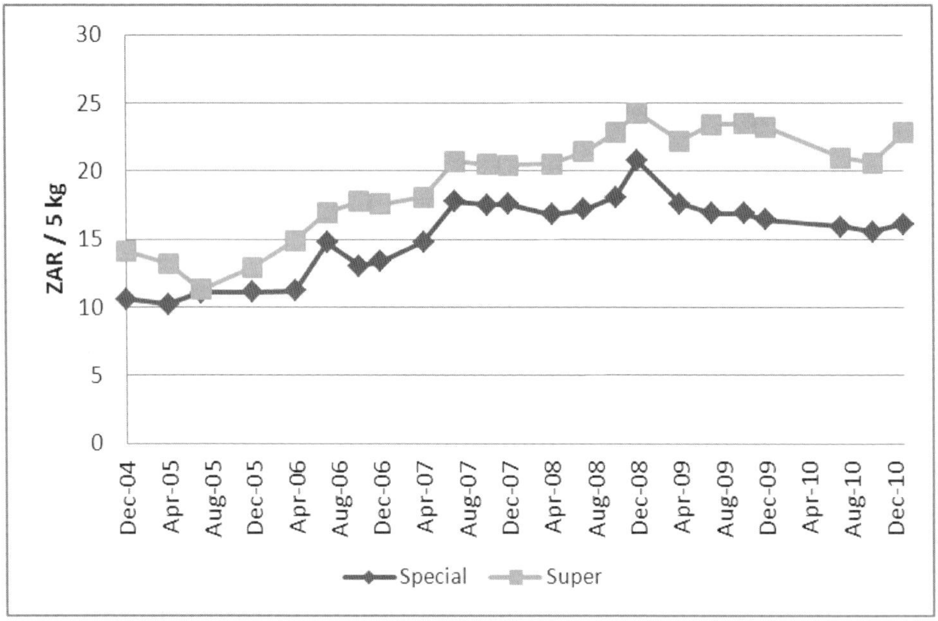

Note: Constructed from maize meal price data from Statistics South Africa, as reported by Vermeulen *et al.*, 2008.

As a practical example, to give insight into the effects of food price increases from a nutritional perspective, the cost of a nutritionally balanced food basket purchased by poor consumers was estimated based on a snapshot of retail food prices at a specific prominent South African retail outlet in July 2008. The most affordable and regularly consumed foods were included so as to represent the balanced diet recommended by the Canadian Food Guide, screened for the poor consumer. The price observations were used as an example of the approximate cost of a nutritionally balanced diet for poor urban consumers in South Africa. This was done for two reasons. First, the official food price monitoring mechanisms employed in South Africa do not include all the products present in this hypothetical affordable nutritionally balanced food basket, e.g., they exclude products such as bananas, oranges, spinach and soup bones. Second, the food products monitored for official inflation measurement purposes in South Africa are usually for pre-packaged fresh produce (e.g., a 1kg bag of potatoes) being sold in large volumes. Since very poor consumers have a limited amount of cash available on a daily basis, the prices observed in-store were rather based on 'loose-sell' fresh produce (i.e., non-packaged fruit displayed and sold by weight in retail outlets). This was done as these consumers often cannot afford to purchase a packet of apples, for example, despite that fact that it is often more economical in the long run to purchase fresh produce in bulk packaged form.

The food basket purchased consisted of fruit and vegetables, staple foods and meat. Eight different fruits and vegetables were purchased out-of-pack. Government-subsidized brown bread and a 5kg bag of maize meal were purchased, as these are most often purchased by poor households. The prices for bread and maize meal were estimated proportionately in order to represent eight portions of starch as recommended in the Canadian guide. Soup bones (the most affordable animal protein available in the supermarket) were purchased and represented the two required portions of meat, while a 500ml carton of *maas* (cultured milk), a cultural favourite of various African consumers, represented the two portions of dairy products recommended. In this particular example, the recommended balanced diet, although not representative of the complete market, amounted to a nominal cost of ZAR 22.31 (US$2.71) per person per day in July 2008, which is far beyond the estimated ZAR 5.33 (US$0.65) available to individuals within the vulnerable groups (Statistics South Africa, 2008). Thus, the consumption of an adequate and balanced diet was evidently far out of reach for a majority of poor households in South Africa.

The Effect of High Food Prices on Dietary Diversity

One of the main coping mechanisms to counter rising food costs at the household level is altering consumption patterns. According to Ortiz *et al.* (2011), at the height of the 2007–2008 food price crisis, poor households frequently ate cheaper foods with lower nutritional value, consumed less food per meal (reduced portion sizes), or skipped meals entirely. To highlight the cost of introducing diversity into a poor consumer's food basket, the results of the analysis indicated that the starch-based staple foods (maize meal and bread) cost only ZAR 1.38 (US$0.17) out of the total cost of ZAR 22.31 (US$2.71), or 6.7 percent of the cost of the food basket, while the remaining expenses went towards providing dietary diversity. This staple food portion amounts to about 48.7 percent of the energy provided by the food basket, 43.9 percent of the protein provided, 52.4 percent of iron (fortified), but only 6.8 percent of total vitamin A. The role of dietary diversity is further highlighted by the fact that the price of one apple was similar to the total price of all the daily recommended starch portions (bread and maize).

It comes as no surprise, then, that global low consumption of fruits and vegetables in developing countries is a widespread response to the food crisis, encouraged by continually increasing food prices. As stated by the WHO technical report on *Diet, Nutrition and the Prevention of Chronic Diseases* (2003), only a minority of the global population consumes the generally recommended intake of fruits and vegetables. Similarly, in South Africa, the NFCS (1999) showed that low income households consume a monotonous diet consisting mainly of staple starches with very few fruits and vegetables, supporting the hypothesis that fruits and vegetables are the first to be omitted from the diets of low-income consumers.

The Likely Effects of Food Price Increases on Portion Sizes

As mentioned, poor consumers employ various food coping strategies in order to manage food crises. In many cases, they first consume cheaper foods with lower nutritional value, then reduce portion size, and then skip meals. In this scenario, the consumption of cheaper foods for very low-income consumers is not possible as they already consume subsidized staple foods (maize meal and bread). Reduction in portion sizes remains one of the simplest and least severe FCS strategies employed frequently by individuals in times of food crisis (Kruger *et al.,* 2008). It is estimated that many South African households employed this strategy during the food crisis prior to skipping meals altogether. When smaller portions of food are consumed, smaller quantities of macro- and micronutrients are obtained. The fortification of staple foods assumes a minimum consumption of 530g/person/per day for maize and 370g/person/day for bread. If actual consumption is at quantities below the amounts considered as 'basic portions,' fortification will contribute significantly less to improved nutritional status than originally intended by the program. Some of the poorest South African households also incorporate coping strategies wherein children or unemployed members of the household are excluded from mealtimes in order to feed the working household members; this strategy results in an even greater detrimental effect on these vulnerable groups, often already suffering from deprived nutritional status (Kruger *et al.*, 2008).

The estimated effects of price increases on the portion sizes of the main staple foods consumed—namely, of maize meal, bread, full cream fresh milk and sugar—are presented in Table 10.5. The 28 percent price change for maize meal between June 2006 and June 2007 would have resulted in the same portion costing ZAR 0.80 (US$0.13) in 2005 compared to ZAR 0.85 (US$0.12) in 2007, and to ZAR 0.88 (US$0.11) in June 2008. The same portion of bread would have increased in price from ZAR 0.97 (US$0.15) in 2005 to ZAR 1.44 (US$0.18) in 2008, and the same portion of milk from ZAR 0.29 (US$0.04) in 2005 to ZAR 0.43 (US$0.05) in 2008. Although these food price increases might be only marginal to higher income consumers, even the smallest changes in food prices affect the food purchasing behaviour of poor consumers. If a household is unable to generate more income, reduction of portion sizes would be the least severe, and most likely, FCS to be employed. The estimated reductions in portion sizes for the main staple foods consumed as a result of increased nominal food prices from 2005 to 2009 are also presented in Table 10.5.

The 1994 South African Vitamin A Consultancy Group Survey (SAVACG) among children 6 to 71 months of age found that 33 percent of South African children were vitamin A deficient (as indicated by serum retinol <20μg/dL). A 21 percent anemia prevalence, 10 percent prevalence of iron deficiency, and 5 percent prevalence of iron deficiency anemia were also observed (INP, 2004). Five years later in 1999, the NFCS reported that one in two children consumed less than half the recommended levels of vitamin A, riboflavin, niacin, vitamin B6, folic acid, calcium, iron and zinc. The portions of food consumed during these earlier years were substantially higher than the amounts recorded in 2005, and with the likely reduction in portion sizes in response to food price increases (see Table 10.1), the nutritional situation is in all likelihood worse.

The likely effects of reduced portion sizes for the most commonly consumed foods (maize meal, bread, sugar and milk) on the intakes of selected nutrients are presented in Table 10.6. The poorest consumers, consuming little more than the basic staple foods (maize meal and bread, along with a little tea with milk and sugar), already had a limited intake of energy and other essential nutrients, as observed in 2005. With a reduction in portions consumed in attempting to cope with increased food prices, these intakes would likely have decreased even more. According to Table 10.6, the energy intakes of the poorest consumers were likely to decrease significantly, from an already marginal 44.7 percent of the recommended daily energy requirements to 30 percent, or approximately 3048kg/person/day. Iron intakes would have decreased in individuals employing this strategy from 93.3 percent of daily requirements in 2005 to 61.3 percent by 2009, vitamin A from 81.5 percent to 53.5 percent, and protein from 53.1 percent to only 34.9 percent of the recommended daily amounts (RDAs).

Table 10.5. Estimated Effects of Food Price Increases on Portion Sizes and Nutrient Intakes

Scenario	Rate of price increase	Typical portion size (g)	Ave. price in time period	Est. cost of reduced portion	Est. cost of regular portion	Energy value of portion (kJ) [1,2,3]
Maize Meal		**ZAR/5kg**				
As consumed 2005[4]		532	16.43	0.70	0.70	2420
June 2006 to June 2007	28%	381	20.00	0.61	0.85	1737
June 2007 to June 2008	5%	361	20.63	0.60	0.88	1643
June 2008 to June 2009	3%	349	21.29	0.60	0.91	1590
Bread			**ZAR/700g**			
As consumed 2005[4]		150	4.51	0.97	0.97	1545
June 2006 to June 2007	10%	108	5.06	0.78	1.08	1396
June 2007 to June 2008	24%	102	6.74	0.98	1.44	1061
June 2008 to June 2009	0%	99	6.76	0.95	1.45	1058
Full cream fresh milk			**ZAR/2L**			
As consumed 2005[4]		56	10.13	0.29	0.29	164
June 2006 to June 2007	5%	40	12.73	0.26	0.37	156
June 2007 to June 2008	29%	38	14.78	0.29	0.43	111
June 2008 to June 2009	9%	36	16.08	0.31	0.47	101
White sugar			**ZAR/kg**			
As consumed 2005[4]		22	13.20	0.12	0.12	341
June 2006 to June 2007	6%	15	13.92	0.09	0.12	321
June 2007 to June 2008	4%	14	14.56	0.09	0.13	307
June 2008 to June 2009	3%	15	14.97	0.09	0.13	299

[1] Wolmarans *et al.*, 2005
[2] Danster *et al.*, 2008
[3] Medical Research Council of South Africa: Food Composition Tables 1991
[4] Duvenage and Schönfeldt, 2007

Apart from the obvious consequences of undernutrition, the hidden hunger caused by the high cost of a varied diet and deficiencies resulting from low fruit and vegetable intake, as well as low intake of essential micronutrients, results in a decreased work force and increased health care costs, creating a severe economic strain on the government. Implementing nutrient fortification of staple foods has not succeeded in breaking this chain of causality as increased food prices have prevented poor consumers from adequately addressing micronutrient deficiencies in their diets.

Table 10.6. Estimated Effects of Food Price Increases on Intakes of Energy, Protein, Iron and Vitamin A

Intake of certain essential nutrients	Maize Meal	Bread	Milk	Sugar	Total Intake	RDA (%)
Energy (RDA 10,000kJ/day)[1,2,3]						
As consumed 2005[4]	2420	1545	164	340	4470	44.7
June 2006 to June 2007	1736	1395	156	320	3609	36.1
June 2007 to June 2008	1643	1061	110	307	3122	31.2
June 2008 to June 2009	1590	1058	100	298	3048	30.5
Protein (RDA 56g/day)[1,2,3]						
As consumed 2005[4]	14.4	13.5	1.85	-	29.7	53.1
June 2006 to June 2007	10.3	9.69	1.33	-	21.3	38.1
June 2007 to June 2008	9.75	9.16	1.25	-	20.2	36.0
June 2008 to June 2009	9.44	8.87	1.21	-	19.5	34.9
Iron (RDA 14mg/day)[1,2,3]						
As consumed 2005[4]	6.92	6.15	-	-	13.1	93.3
June 2006 to June 2007	4.96	4.41	-	-	9.37	70.0
June 2007 to June 2008	4.69	4.17	-	-	8.87	63.4
June 2008 to June 2009	4.54	4.04	-	-	8.58	61.3
Vitamin A (RDA 400mcgRE/day)[1,2,3]						
As consumed 2005[4]	180.9	126	19.0	-	326	81.5
June 2006 to June 2007	129.8	90.4	13.7	-	234	58.5
June 2007 to June 2008	122.8	85.5	12.9	-	221	55.3
June 2008 to June 2009	118.8	82.8	12.5	-	214	53.5

[1] Wolmarans *et al.*, 2005
[2] Danster *et al.*, 2008
[3] Medical Research Council of South Africa: Food Composition Tables 1991
[4] Duvenage and Schönfeldt, 2007

Conclusions and Recommendations

With the continued increases in food prices characterizing the 2007–2008 global food price crisis, it is almost inevitable that low income households in South Africa would need to consume smaller amounts of staple foods and reduce variety in their daily diets. Without intervention, continuing food price increases will validate the many predictions that malnutrition will increase, instead of decreasing, by 2015 (Chastre *et al.*, 2007). If the current run-up in food prices for 2010–2011 continues and results in further reductions in food intake, it seems inevitable that South Africa will move still further away from Millennium Development Goal 1 (MDG1) as established in 2000: reducing the proportion of the population living on less than US$1.25 (roughly ZAR 8.79) per day and reducing the proportion of the under-five population that is underweight (Chastre *et al.*, 2007). In South Africa, as is projected to be the case in many developing countries, although the proportion of hungry people is decreasing, the number of hungry people is consistently increasing (Badham, 2009; Ortiz, Chai and Cummins, 2011).

The objective of this chapter has been to explore the likely implications of food price increases in South Africa on the nutritionally vulnerable population, particularly on the very poor households that experience the highest levels of malnutrition in the country. Policy makers are interested in understanding the projected impacts of high food prices on poor and vulnerable populations as this provides insights into how to combat worsening malnutrition—especially since there is currently no nationally representative monitoring system in place in South Africa to formally measure the changing nutritional status in all population groups. This is also the case in many other developing countries. Evidence about the negative epidemiological and economic consequences of consuming unhealthy diets is increasing over time. If suitable attention is not given to combatting these outcomes, global gains in health brought about by declines in infectious diseases will be eroded by the rapid emergence of chronic diseases (Yach, 2008).

Considering the results presented in this chapter, the efforts by the South African government to fortify staple foods based on 2003 quantities of micronutrient additions should be reconsidered. The portion sizes of foods that are consumed by the most marginalized consumers were recorded to be much less in 2005 than the average amounts used for calculating fortification levels. The likely further impact of the 2008–2009 financial crisis and continually increasing food prices on portion sizes means that vulnerable consumers are probably consuming significantly lower quantities of these staple foods than before. Consequently, the fortification cocktail can be expected to contribute significantly less to the RDAs of those nutrients. The South African government, through the Department of Health, is actively engaging stakeholders to revisit the nutritional situation. They are revisiting the fortification program, fortification levels, the bio-availability of the fortificants, and exploring additional mechanisms for improving nutrition.

As stated by Yach *et al.* (2010), to be successful in combating malnutrition, efforts must be sustained by multiple stakeholders from various sectors. Government intervention to aid in the increased consumption of a variety of foods—apart from the staples obtained from the starch group—would help in the elimination of hidden hunger and the associated costs. Towards this end, South Africa specifically requires further research into potential policy interventions to increase food affordability to poor consumers. The South African Price Monitoring Committee has been appointed to protect vulnerable consumers, including those in rural areas with limited access to work or income. The findings of this Committee are widely disseminated to reveal inequalities and to facilitate the use of public pressure to align food prices. The committee previously focused on retail prices in supermarkets, but more recently has included spot-checks in rural areas; this effort has revealed that prices in these rural areas are often significantly higher than in urban areas. Other national interventions include price subsidies on brown bread and value-added tax exemption on fresh produce, as well as social assistance transfers which are funded from general revenues through the National Department of Social Development. These transfers are for old-age, disability, child-support, foster-care, dependent care and war-veterans' grants, and for temporary grant-in-aid relief. Although these social assistance cash grants aim to provide targeted income support to those whose livelihoods are most at risk, the money which one individual obtains is often the only or major source of household income and is used to support all members of the family.

Many food industries also have the resources and the ability to make products and conduct their business in ways that benefit consumers. Globally, health concerns such as obesity have emerged as major drivers of nutritional concerns. Many NGOs, legislators and consumers demand and seek authentication that companies are responding to the needs of the changing market. The same approach should be followed within a developing country context, with industry sharing some of the responsibility within undernourished communities. The food industry has a vital role to play alongside governments, NGOs and academics in addressing the malnutrition situation, and the notion of private-public partnerships in health should be more broadly implemented and accepted. Sustainable approaches from industry could include, but are not limited to: 1) investing in agriculture, especially local smallholders; 2) expanding the use of corporate distribution and quality control capabilities; 3) greater support for the fortification of staples and commonly consumed nutritious foods and beverages; 4) innovation and expansion of efforts for complementary feeding to address acute and chronic undernutrition; 5) increasing investments in the development of nutritional science capacity in developing nations; 6) product reformulations for low-cost nutritious foods for all markets; and 7) advocacy for nutrition-friendly trade policy (Yach *et al.*, 2010).

References

Altman, M., Hart, T.G.B. and Jacobs, P.T. (2009) Household food security status in South Africa. *Agrikon,* 48(4) 345–361.

American Dietetic Association: Position Paper. (2006) Position of the American Dietetic Association: food insecurity and hunger in the United States. *Journal of the American Dietetic Association*. 106: 446–458.

Amuli, DJ. (2006) Purchasing patterns of major plant staples in low-income households in the Vaal Triangle. MTech dissertation. Vaal University of Technology, Vanderbijlpark, South Africa.

Badham, J. (2009) Have we taken our eyes off the real public health issues? *South African Food Review*, 36(1), 24–27.

Bloem, M.W., Semba, R.D. and Kraemer, K. (2010) An Introduction to the Impact of Climate Change, the Economic Crisis, and the Increase in the Food Prices on Malnutrition. *Journal of Nutrition* 140(1): 132S–135S.

Cafiero, C. and Gennari, P. (2011) The FAO indicator of the prevalence of undernourishment. Incomplete draft, 11 February 2011. Food and Agriculture Organization, Rome.

Canada's Food Guide. (2008) Accessed on 19 August 2008. Available online: http://www.hc-sc.gc.ca/fn-an/food-guide-aliment/index-eng.php

Chastre, C., Duffield, A., Kindness, H., LeJeune, S. and Taylor, A. (2007) The minimum cost of a healthy diet: Findings from piloting a new methodology in four locations: Bangladesh, Myanmar, Ethiopia, Tanzania. Save the Children Fund, United Kingdom.

Danster, N., Wolmarans, P., Buitendag, C.S. and de Jager, A. (2008) *Energy and nutrient composition of South African wheat, wheat flour and bread.* Technical Report. Medical Research Council, Cape Town, South Africa.

De Klerk, M., Drimie, S., Aliber, M., Mini, S., Mokoena, R., Randela, R., Modiselle, S., Roberts, B., Vogel, C., de Swardt, C. and Kirsten, J. (2004) *Food Security in South*

Africa: Key Policy Issues for the Medium Term. Human Science Research Center, Pretoria, South Africa.

De Rose, L., Messer, E. and Millmann, S. (1998) *Who is hungry? And how do we know? Food shortage, poverty and Deprivation*. United Nations University, Tokyo.

Duvenage, S.S. and Schönfeldt, H.C. (2007) Impact of South African fortification legislation on product formulation for low-income households. *Journal of Food Composition and Analysis* 20: 688–95.

Euromonitor International. (2008) Accessed on 22 August 2008. Available online at www.euromritor.com/factfile.aspx?country=za.

FAO (2010) Biodiversity in Sustainable Diets. Technical Workshop Report. Rome, 31 May–1 June.

General Household Survey (GHS). (2009) Statistical Release P0318. Statistics, South Africa.

Golden, M.H.N. (2000) Famine relief. Section 4, nr 32. In: Garrow, J.S., James, W.P.T., Ralph, A. (eds.) *Human Nutrition and Dietetics*. Churchill Livingstone, London, UK, 501–13.

Hendriks, S.L. (2005) The challenges facing empirical estimation of household food (in)security in South Africa. *Development Southern Africa*, 22(1), 103–123.

Human Science Research Council (HSRC). (2004) Integration of rural and regional development. Food security in South Africa: key policy issues for the medium term. http://www.sarpn.org.za. Accessed July 2009.

IDA14. (2004) Global data monitoring information system. Proportion of the population below US$1/day poverty line. The World Bank Group, Washington, DC.

IDA14. (2006) Global data monitoring information system, sub-Saharan Africa. The World Bank Group, Washington, DC.

Integrated Nutrition Programme: a foundation for life (INP). (2004) South African Department of Health, Issue 4. Pretoria, South Africa.

Kruger, R., Schönfeldt, H.C. and Owen, J.H. (2008) Food-coping strategy index applied to a community of farm-worker households in South Africa. *Food and Nutrition Bulletin*. 29(1): 3–14.

Lemke, S. (2005) Nutrition security, livelihoods and HIV/AIDS: implications for research among farm worker households in South Africa. *Public Health Nutrition,* 8(7): 844–852.

Martins, J.H. (2006) Total household cash expenditures in South Africa by Living Standard Measure (LSM) group and product, 2005. Bureau of Market Research. Research report no. 347. Pretoria, South Africa.

Masemola, M. and de Jongh, P. (2009) Household Income Expenditure Patterns and Trends, 2008-2009. Bureau of Market Research, University of South Africa. Pretoria, South Africa. Available at: http://www.unisa.ac.za/contents/faculties/ems/docs/Press 395.pdf.

Masemola, M.E., Van Aardt, C.J. and Coetzee, M. (2010) Income and Expenditure of Households in South Africa, 2008–2009. Bureau of Market Research. Research Report no 395. Pretoria, South Africa.

Masemola, M.E. and Van Wyk, H.J. (2009) Income and Expenditure of Households in South Africa, 2007–2008. Bureau of Market Research. Research Report no 383. Pretoria, South Africa.

Masset, E. (2010) A review of hunger indices and methods to monitor country commitment to fighting hunger. *Food Policy* 36(S1), S102–S10.

Maxwell, D., Watkins, B., Wheeler, R. and Collins, G. (2003) The Coping Strategies Index: A tool for rapid measurement of household food security and impact of food aid programs in humanitarian emergencies. Field Methods Manual. CARE and World Food Programme, Nairobi, Kenya.

Medical Research Council (MRC) of South Africa. (1991) Food Composition Tables, Third Edition. Cape Town, South Africa.

National Agricultural Marketing Council (NAMC). (2007, 2008, 2009, 2010, 2011) Food price trends. *Press releases.* Accessed Febraury 2011. Available online at www.namc.co.za

National Food Consumption Survey (NFCS). (1999) Children aged 1–9 years in South Africa, NFCS group. Accessed 22 August 2008. Available on line at: http://www.sahealthinfo.org/nutrition/foodconsumption.htm

National Food Consumption Survey Fortification Baseline 1 (NFCS-FB-1). (2008) Executive summary. *South African Journal of Clinical Nutrition Supplement.* 21(3): 254, 261–262.

Nel, J.H. and Steyn, N.P. (2002) Report on South African food consumption studies undertaken amongst different population groups (1983–2000): average intakes of foods most commonly consumed. Directorate of Food Control, Department of Health, Pretoria, South Africa.

Oldewage-Theron, W.H., Dicks, E.G. and Napier, C.E. (2006) Poverty, household food insecurity and nutrition: coping strategies in an informal settlement in the Vaal Triangle, South Africa. *Public Health* 120: 795–804.

Organization for Economic Cooperation and Development (OECD). (2008) *Food Outlook 2008*. Paris, France.

Ortiz, I., Chai, J. and Cummins, M. (2011) Escalating Food Prices: The threat to poor households and policies to safeguard recovery for all. UNICEF Policy and Practice. Social and Economic Policy Working Paper. United Nations Children's Fund, New York.

Prahalad, C.K. and Hart, S. (2006) Making a market among the poor. *Food and Beverage Reporter,* August,1–2. South Africa.

Rose, D. and Charlton, K.E. (2002) Prevalence of household food poverty in South Africa: results from a large nationally representative survey. *Public Health Nutrition* 5(3): 383–389.

Ruel, M.T., Garrett, J.L., Hawkes, C. and Cohen, M.J. (2009) The food, fuel and financial crises affect the urban and rural poor disproportionately: a review of the evidence. *The Journal of Nutrition*, published ahead of print as doi:10.3945/jn.109.110791.

Sibrian, R. (2009) Indicators on undernourishment and critical food poverty at national and sub-national levels. Statistics Division, Food and Agricultural Organization of the United Nations, Rome.

South African Advertising Research Foundation (SAARF). (2006) *Segmentation handbook: based on AMPS 2005 and AMPS 2006*. South African Advertising Research Foundation, Johannesburg, South Africa.

SAARF. (2006) Living Standards Measure: Introduction. Available online at: http://www.saarf.co.za. Accessed on 7 February, 2011.

South African Demographic and Health Survey (SADHS). (1998) Department of Health online. Available at http://www.doh.gov.za/facts/1998/sadhs98/. Accessed 21 August, 2008.

South African Demographic and Health Survey (SADHS). (2003) Department of Health, online. Available at http://www.doh.gov.za/facts/index.html/. Accessed 22 August 2008.

South African Government. (1993) Regulations governing the labeling and advertising of foodstuffs. Published under Government Notice No. R.2034 of 29 October 1993. As amended by Government Notice No. R. 129 of 2 February 1996.

South African Government. (1997) Government Notice No. R. 396 of 14 March 1997. Department of Health, Pretoria, South Africa. Accessed 22 August 2008. Available online at: www.doh.gov.za.

South African Reserve Bank. (2011) Online Statistical Queries—Consumer prices of goods: Food and non-alcoholic beverages (All urban areas). Available online at www.resbank.co.za/qbquery/timeseriesquery.aspx. Accessed on 7 February 2011.

Statistics South Africa. (2008) Statistical release P0302: Mid-year population estimates. Accessed 22 August, 2008. Available Online at www.statssa.co.za.

Statistics South Africa. (2011) Consumer Price Index (P0141): Index numbers and year-on-year rates, metropolitan areas—all items base year: 2008 = 100. Available online at www.statssa.gov.za/keyindicators/cpi.asp. Accessed on 7 February, 2011.

Svedberg, P. (2002) Undernutrition overestimated, *Economic Development and Cultural Change*, 51(1): 5–36.

Thorn-Lyman, A.L., Valpiani, N., Sun, K., Semba, R.D., Klotz, C.L., Kreamer, K., Akhter, N., De Pee, S., Moench-Pfanner, R., Sari, M. and Bloem, M.W. (2009) Household dietary diversity and food expenditure are closely linked in rural Bangladesh, increasing the risk of malnutrition due to the financial crises. *The Journal of Nutrition*, published ahead of print as doi: 10.3945/jn.109.110809

Tiwari, S. and Zaman, H. (2010) The impact of economic shocks on global undernourishment. Policy Research Working Paper 5215. The World Bank, Washington, DC.

Training Manual: Food fortification for environmental health practitioners. (2004) Tswane University of Technology, Faculty of Health Sciences, Pretoria, South Africa.

USDA Food Security Assessment. (2005) USDA Agricultural and Trade report. Available online at http://www.ers.usda.gov. Accessed 22 August, 2008.

Van Aardt, C.J. and Coetzee, M. (2010) Personal income estimates for South Africa, 2010. Bureau of Market Research. Research Report 396. Pretoria, South Africa.

Van Heerden, I.V. and Schönfeldt, H.C. (2011) The lack of food intake data and the consequences thereof. *South African Journal of Clinical Nutrition*, 24(1): 10–18.

Vermeulen, H., Traub, L.N., Meyer, F. and Schönfeldt, H.C. (2008) Implications of projected food price inflation on household food security. Paper presented at the 2008 Conference of the Agricultural Economics Society of South Africa, September 2008, Windhoek, Namibia.

Vorster, H.H., Love, P. and Browne, C. (2001) Development of food-based dietary guidelines for South Africa: the process. *South African Journal of Clinical Nutrition*. 14(3): S3–S6.

WHO Technical report on Diet, Nutrition and the Prevention of Chronic Diseases. (2003) Report of a Joint WHO/FAO Expert Consultation. WHO Technical Report Series 916. Geneva, Switzerland.

Witten, C., Jooste, P., Sanders, D. and Chopra, M. (2003) Micronutrient programs in South Africa. Medical Research Council, Tygerberg, University of the Western Cape, School of Public Health, Western Cape, South Africa.

Wolmarans, P., Danster, N. and Chetty, J. (2005) Energy and nutrient composition of South African maize meal. Technical Report. Medical Research Council, Cape Town, South Africa.

World Bank. (2008) High Food Prices: A Harsh New Reality. Available online at: http://econ.worldbank.org/WEBSITE/EXTERNAL/EXTDEC/0,,contentMDK:21665883~pagePK:64165401~piPK:64165026~theSitePK:469372,00.html. Accessed October 2008.

Yach, D. (2008) Invited Editorial: a personal view of food companies and nutrition for better health. *Public Health Nutrition,* 11(2): 109–111.

Yach, D., Feldman, Z.A., Bradley, D.G. and Khan, M. (2010) Can the food industry help tackle the growing global burden of undernutrition? *American Journal of Public Health*. 100(6): 974–980.

Chapter 11

Africa's Turnaround: From Crisis to Opportunity in African Agriculture

William A. Masters
Friedman School of Nutrition, Tufts University, Medford, Massachusetts

Abstract

The world food and financial crises of 2007–2008 caused significant declines in real income for many people globally. The impacts of higher food prices and lower rates of economic growth were particularly severe for the world's poorest. This crisis, however, created an opportunity for public investments to raise agricultural productivity. This chapter describes three major trends whose confluence raises the payoff from such investments, laying a foundation for rapid crisis recovery and sustained future growth. The first turning point discussed here is political. We analyze data from a recent World Bank study that shows how far African governments have gone to reduce policy-induced price distortions, greatly facilitating productivity growth and poverty alleviation. The second transition is demographic. Over the 1970s and 1980s, Africa's rural population grew rapidly, leading to prolonged declines in per-capita endowments of land and other natural resources. These trends began to reverse in the 1990s, creating a window of opportunity for new investment to bring larger increases in output per capita. The third turning point is technological: after decades of stagnation during the Asian green revolution, African yields have grown steadily over the past decade, in part stimulated by foreign aid to boost agricultural production. Taken together, these trends imply a gradual lifting of earlier severe constraints on African agricultural productivity and economic growth. They suggest that African countries may be poised to take advantage of the increased public investment needed to overcome the global food and financial crises.

Introduction

The world food and financial crises of 2007–2008 brought sharp cuts in real income for many people, threatening to reverse recent achievements in health and nutrition, political empowerment and economic security around the world. The impact of higher food prices and lower economic growth rates could be particularly severe for the world's poorest, who spend a larger portion of their incomes on food and have less in savings with which to smooth their consumption over time. But for those who gained the least from historical growth in the world economy—including most of sub-Saharan Africa—the present crisis could mark a turning point towards new opportunities.

Sudden shocks, however harmful, can also be useful. It is widely said that the Chinese character for 'crisis' is actually formed of two components, one for 'danger' and one for 'opportunity.' A more recent aphorism, attributed to the economist Paul Romer in 2004 and then-President Obama's Chief of Staff Rahm Emanuel in 2008, posits that 'a crisis is a terrible thing to waste.' In Africa today, a central opportunity not to be wasted is public investment in raising agricultural productivity. This chapter describes three major trends whose confluence raises the payoff from such investments, laying a foundation for rapid crisis recovery and sustained future growth. These three trends could be motive forces for the debated upturn in African economies that has been described by keen observers of the continent such as Ted Miguel (2009) and monitored on an ongoing basis in sources such as the Organization for Economic Cooperation and Development's (OECD) African Economic Outlook (2010).

Each trend described in this chapter involves a turning point in economic development whereby African societies experienced phenomena similar to those seen elsewhere but with different timing and magnitude. Given that many other factors intervene to determine local outcomes, the trends are not deterministic. Measurement errors also contribute to observed variation. The variance may be large for any given country and time period, but adding up these observations to compare continents over decades reveals unmistakable trends and new opportunities for African agriculture in the twenty-first century.

The first turning point discussed here is political. Africa's economic turnaround has many political dimensions; here we focus on just one aspect of policy, documented by new data from a World Bank study comparing farm policies around the world. The results of this study show how far today's African governments have gone to reduce the cost to farmers of export taxes, marketing boards and other interventions imposed by previous regimes. Africa's policy-induced price distortions peaked in the late 1970s and reforms since then have removed about two-thirds of that burden, greatly facilitating productivity growth and poverty alleviation. Further reforms could yield additional benefits, but most of the handicaps imposed on African farmers by post-colonial governments have now been removed.

The second transition described here is demographic. Demography is a rich and complex field; in this chapter we focus on broad trends, as census data compiled in recent revisions of UN population projections reveal the slowly-unfolding implications of African history. Generally speaking, it appears that most African households obtained access to modern medicine much later and more suddenly than people in other regions. The resulting improvement in child survival and increase in population growth rates during the 1970s and 1980s were faster than those seen earlier in Asia or Latin America, and although Africa's towns and cities were also growing at historically unprecedented rates, their absolute size was so small that they could absorb only a fraction of all the new workers. Consequently, Africa's rural population grew faster and for longer than any other in human history, with a correspondingly rapid and prolonged decline in per-capita endowments of land and other natural resources. The post-independence improvements in child survival also triggered a rise in child dependency rates, which also reached historically unprecedented levels in the 1970s and 1980s. Both trends began to reverse in the 1990s thanks to gradual fertility reduction and continued urbanization. As seen earlier in Asia, the slow-down in rural population growth and the reduced burden of child-care creates a window of opportunity for new investment to bring larger increases in output per capita.

The third turning point is technological. Again, many new technologies influence African economies, and this chapter focuses on just one narrow aspect of the turnaround: national estimates of cereal crop productivity show how, after decades of stagnation during the Asian 'Green Revolution,' African yields have grown steadily over the past decade, so that estimated cereal grain output per capita now equals that of South Asia. The start of this turnaround could be associated with the other two trends, as the cumulative result of increased labor per hectare and more favorable policies, but could also reflect the gradual spread of improved crop varieties that resulted from earlier investment in agricultural technology. The inflow of foreign aid to boost agricultural production did not rise until the late 1970s and peaked in the late 1980s, yielding payoffs some years later.

Taken together, these three trends imply a gradual lifting of previously-severe constraints on African agricultural productivity and economic growth, and hence new opportunities for public investment to yield increasing payoffs over time. The last two decades of global agricultural abundance, however, saw foreign donors' support for African agriculture decline steadily from its peak in the late 1980s to a historical low in 2006 of around one US dollar per year, per person in Africa. Looking forward, the political, demographic and technological trends described in this chapter put African farmers in a better position now than ever before to take advantage of the increased investment needed to overcome the global food and financial crises. This opportunity would be a terrible thing to waste.

The Food and Financial Crises of 2007–2008

Figure 11.1 provides a visual snapshot in the context of data from January 2006 through December 2010 of the food and financial crises in terms of world-market prices in US dollars for:

- major food commodities (as measured by the Deutsche Bank Agriculture index);
- major foreign currencies (as measured by the DB US Dollar index); and
- major corporate equities (as measured by the S&P 500 index).

The crises began slowly during the period of May–October, 2007, when food prices rose by about 20 percent in dollar terms. The rise in food prices was associated with an increase in the value of major foreign currencies against the dollar, so food prices in other currencies rose by much less than that. Equity values were also rising, but then from October 2007 through February 2008 the S&P 500 dropped by about 20 percent while food prices and foreign currencies kept rising. These trends paused in mid-2008, but a few months later all three measures plunged as food prices and foreign currencies moved in tandem with equity valuation and the whole world lost real income. Economic recovery since 2008 has involved upward trends in all three indexes, to levels in December 2010 that were roughly similar to those of December 2007.

Looking forward, the crises of high food prices in 2007–2008 and of falling equity values in 2008–2009 may have been temporary, but they could have huge long-term impacts through their influence on investment patterns. If the period of food scarcity leads to more investment in agriculture, farm prices could fall again; on the other hand, the period of low equity values and low real incomes could lead to less investment in farm production, which if outstripped by food demand would lead to a sustained rise in real food prices. The trends described in each of the next three sections—in agricultural price policies, rural demography and farm productivity—set the stage for how African farmers might respond to increased agricultural investments.

Figure 11.1. The food and financial crises of 2007–2008

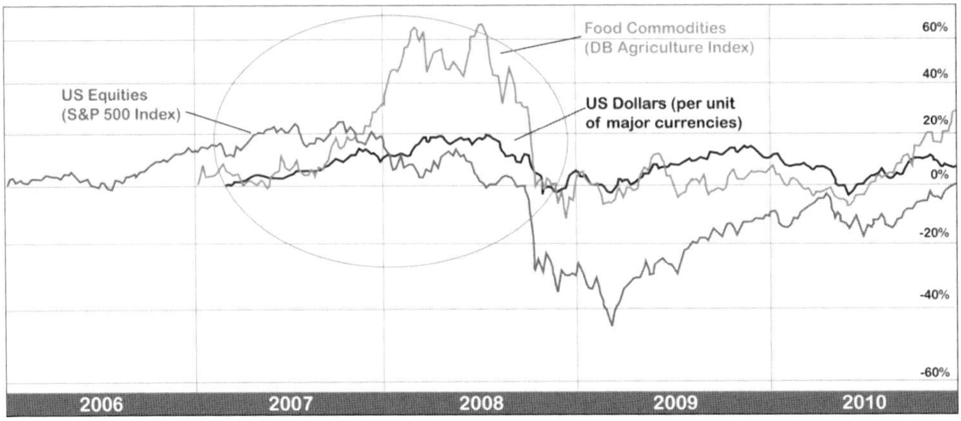

Data displayed using Google Finance, accessed December 29, 2010.
Note: In Figure 11.1, major food commodities are shown by the DB Agriculture Index Fund (NYSE:DBA), which tracks US dollar prices for trade in maize, wheat, soy and sugar, weighted at 25% each and rebased annually as the Deutsche Bank Liquid Commodities Index. Major non-US currencies are shown by the DB US Dollar Short Index Fund (NYSE:UDN), which tracks the price of selling US dollars to buy a basket of Euros, Canadian dollars, Japanese yen, UK pounds, Swiss francs, Australian dollars, and Swedish kroner, trade-weighted as the US Federal Reserve Bank's Major Currencies index. The S&P 500 index is a value-weighted sum of major publicly-traded corporations on US stock markets. The S&P 500 is shown from January 2006, while the DBA and UDN indexes started trading in early 2007; all data shown are through December 28, 2010.

Trends and Turning Points in Agricultural Policy

The magnitude of government interventions in agricultural prices around the world can now be described more precisely than ever before, thanks to a three-year World Bank project led by Kym Anderson. Results have been published in a global overview (Anderson, 2009) and four regional volumes including one on Africa (Anderson and Masters, 2009), with all data freely available online (World Bank, 2009).

The project's approach was to employ a common methodology in case studies of 68 countries covering more than 90 percent of the world's population and GDP, drawing on local expertise to measure taxes, subsidies, quantitative restrictions and regulations for that country's major farm products, in every possible year from 1955 through 2005. The studies covered a total of 77 commodities (an average of 12 per country), thereby tracking policy interventions affecting about 70 percent of global agricultural output. The simplest summary measure of these interventions is a Nominal Rate of Assistance (NRA), defined as the tariff-equivalent magnitude of policy-induced distortions, relative to what prices would be in competitive markets. An NRA above zero represents a subsidy to farmers, at the expense of others in that country, while a value below zero represents taxation of farmers to help others.

The two main tendencies we see in agricultural policy across countries and over time are a powerful development paradox, whereby governments in richer countries tend to subsidize farmers while governments in poorer countries tend to tax them, and a strong anti-trade bias, whereby governments tax international trade more than domestic transactions, thus raising local prices for importable products while lowering prices for exportables. Both patterns had been previously most fully documented by Krueger, Schiff and Valdés (1991), and are illustrated here in Figure 11.2 using a much larger number of observations.

Figure 11.2 shows smoothed regression lines through all of the new data set's 2,520 observations of a particular country and year, with total taxes or subsidies on all farm products in the left panel, and the subtotal for each country's exportable and importable products separately on the right. Governments in the poorest countries—including sub-Saharan Africa—have imposed heavy taxes on all kinds of farmers, mainly by taxing farm exports. Total tax rates move rapidly towards zero as incomes rise, thanks to reduced export taxes and increased protection of importables. This tendency is paradoxical insofar as it runs against policymakers' stated goals, transferring income within each country from the poorer majority to a wealthier minority.

Figure 11.2. National-average Nominal Rates of Assistance (NRAs) and Real Income per Capita, by Trade Status

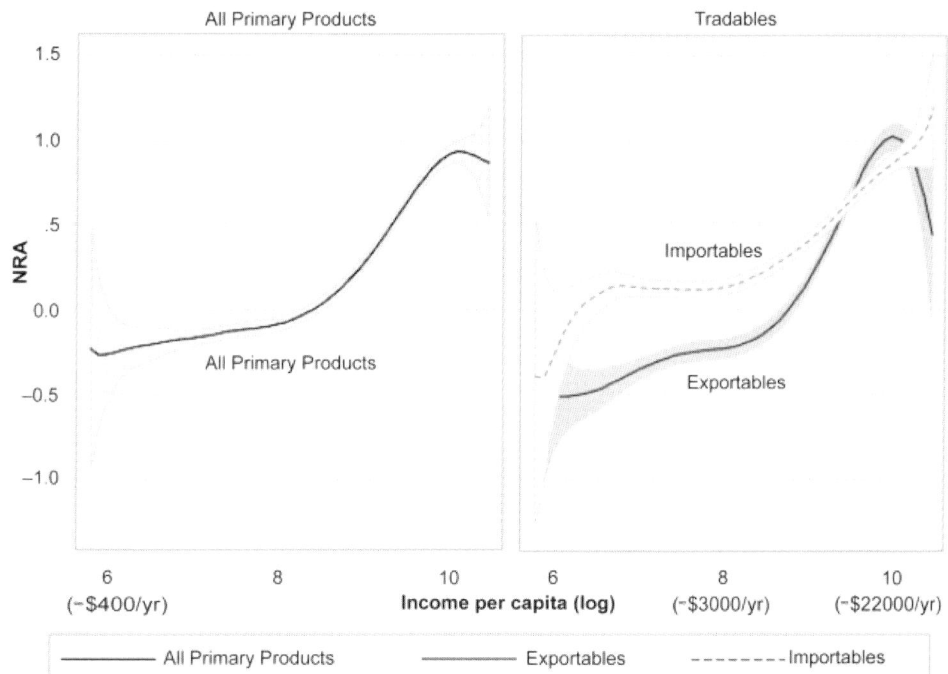

Note: Author's calculations, from data available at www.worldbank.org/agdistortions. Each line summarizes annual data for 66 countries from 1961 to 2005 (n=2520), smoothed with 95% confidence intervals using Stata's lpolyci at bandwidth 1 and degree 4. Income per capita is expressed in US$ at 2000 PPP prices.

Figure 11.2 combines cross-sectional and time-series variance for the world as a whole. To focus on Africa's opportunities over time, Figure 11.3 shows trends in assistance to agriculture for each continent separately. In Africa, we see a decade-long slide from the early 1960s to the early 1970s towards greater taxation of farmers, but this was gradually reversed in the 1980s and 1990s. The data for other regions show that in the past, as their incomes rose these regions generally provided increased subsidies to agriculture, but those market price supports have now been cut in favor of other channels for farm support. Africa thus remains the only region whose agricultural policies became more favorable to farmers during the 2000–2004 period.

Figure 11.3. National-average NRAs by region and year, 1960–2004

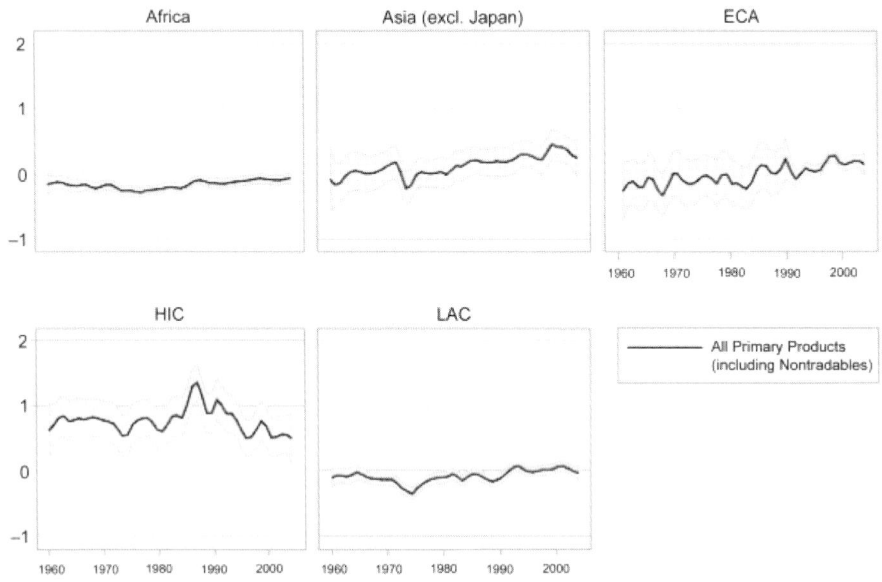

Source: Reproduced from W.A. Masters and A. Garcia (2009), which also provides estimation details. Regional designations are LAC – Latin America, ECA – Europe and Central Asia, HIC – High income countries.

Figure 11.4 combines the ideas in the previous figures, focusing only on the Africa data. Here there are fewer observations, so we show simple averages across countries over a five-year period. For each country and year, the data are a value-weighted sum of all farm products (the dashed line), some subset of which are imported (the top line) or exported (bottom line). These show clearly how African governments imposed steadily increasing taxes on exports and offered reduced protection from imports through the late 1970s. Since then, about half of the tax burden on exportables has been removed. Multiplying these tax rates times the value of output, it turns out that the total tax burden amounted to about US$134 per agricultural worker in the late 1970s but had been reduced to US$41 in the 2000–2005 period.

Figure 11.4. Average NRA across 16 African countries by 5-year period, 1955–2004

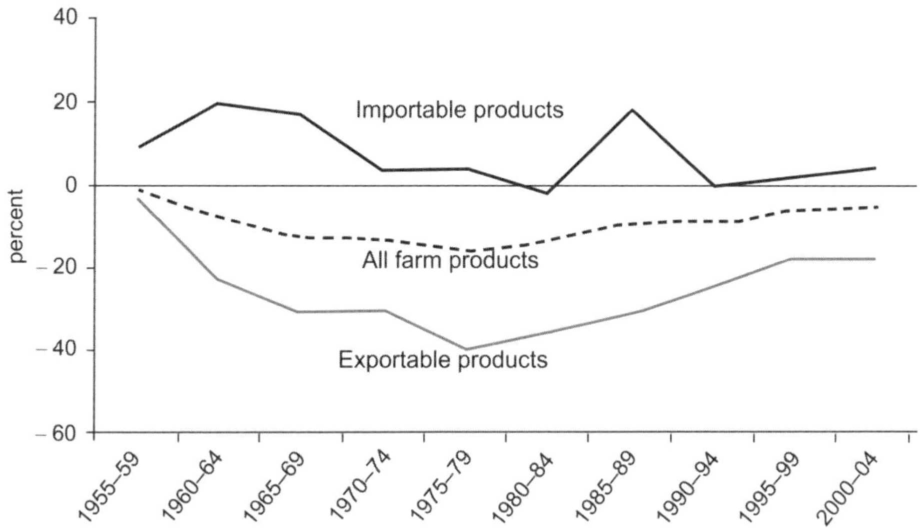

Source: Reprinted from Figure 1.3, in K. Anderson and W.A. Masters (eds), *Distortions to Agricultural Incentives in Africa*. Washington, DC: The World Bank, 2009.

Trends and Turning Points in Rural Demography

Government policies influence incentives, but farmers' ability to respond depends on the natural resources available to them and the technologies with which those resources can be used. A later section will focus on trends in farm technology and productivity. To address resource availability, this section focuses on two key aspects of population dynamics: the number of rural people, and the share of all people who are of working age.

The number of rural people determines the volume of natural resources available per rural worker. Not all rural people are farmers, and not all of farmers' incomes come from agriculture. Rural residence itself is not fixed, as individuals migrate to and from urban areas. Nonetheless, the direction and magnitude of change over time in the rural population indicates whether rural resources are becoming more or less abundant relative to the rural workforce.

Figure 11.5 presents the estimated total rural population of major global regions, found by subtracting each country's estimated urban population from its national totals. Census methods and data quality vary by country and year, but as with the policy measures in the previous section, aggregation to the continent and decade scale reveals enormous differences between Africa and other regions. To facilitate comparison, the data are shown as index numbers based in 1950. (Each region's current estimated rural population is shown as well.) Clearly, while the rural populations of Africa and Asia expanded at roughly similar rates in the 1950s and 1960s, the rate of increase slowed quickly in Southeast Asia, where the number of rural people peaked around 1995. Growth in South Asia became somewhat slower than Africa's beginning in the 1980s and is not projected to peak until 2025, while Africa's rural population is projected to continue rising beyond 2030.

Figure 11.5. Rural population estimates and projections, 1950-2030

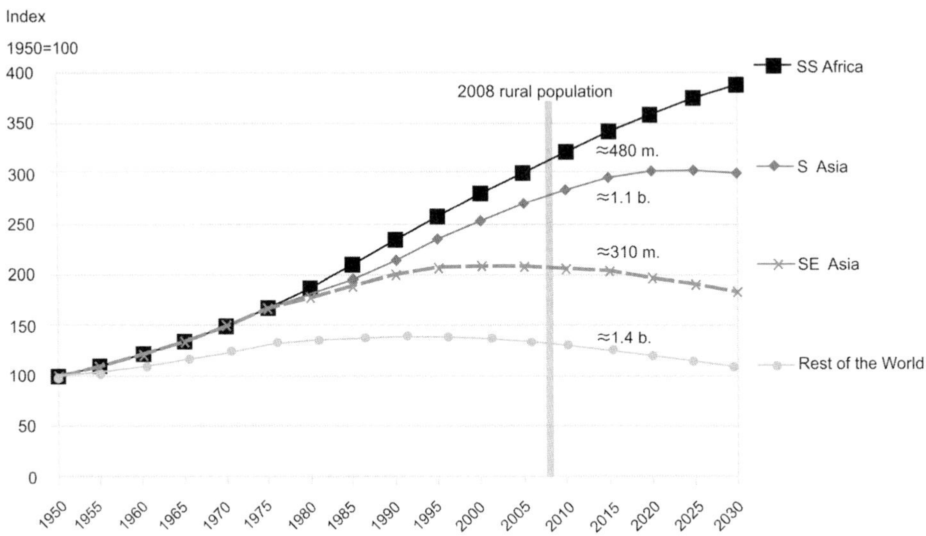

Source: Calculated from FAOStat (2009). Rural population estimates and projections are based on UN Population Projections (2006 revision) and UN Urbanization Prospects (2001 revision).

These data are shown in percentage-change terms in Figure 11.6. Each region's rural population growth rate reaches zero and crosses the dotted line in its peak year, when the absolute size of the rural population as shown in Figure 11.5 stops growing and begins to decline. The growth rates reveal how Asia's rural population expansion began to slow in the 1960s, even as Africa's kept increasing and remained above 2 percent per year for over three decades—a much higher level than was seen earlier in other regions.

One might think that Africa's rural population grew so quickly because its urban areas grew slowly. To check this intuition, Figure 11.7 shows the corresponding data for urban populations. In fact, Africa's towns and cities have grown much faster than those in other regions, at average rates around 5 percent per year during the 1950s–1980s. The explanation for rapid rural population growth is not slow urban growth, but a faster rate of total population growth and a smaller initial share of the population in towns and cities, so that even the world's fastest rates of urban growth could not keep up with the demographic shock associated with rapid reduction in child mortality.

Figure 11.6. Rural population growth estimates and projections by decade, 1950s–2020s

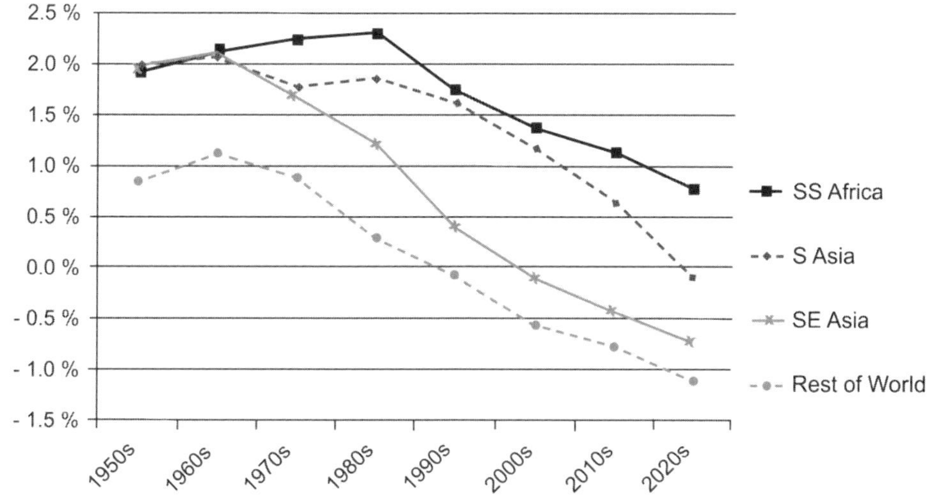

Source: Calculated from FAOStat (2009). Rural population estimates and projections are based on UN Population Projections (2006 revision) and UN Urbanization Prospects (2001 revision).

Figure 11.7. Urban population growth estimates and projections by decade, 1950s–2020s

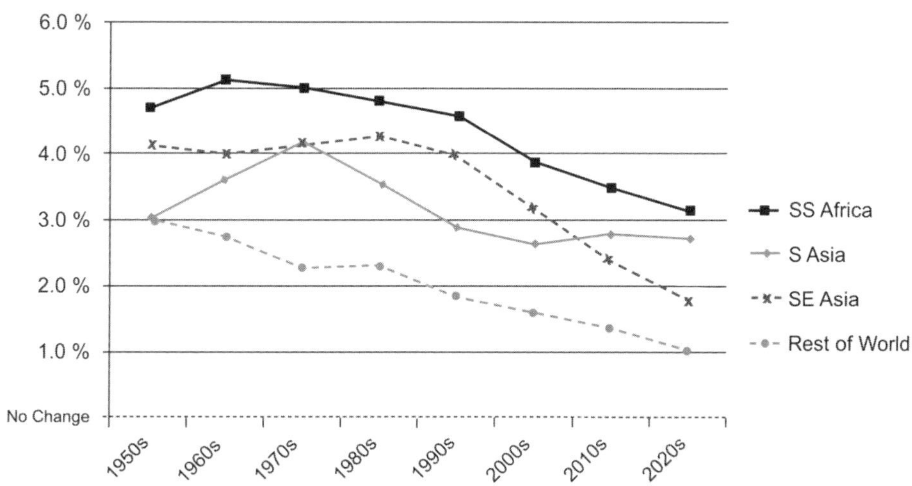

Source: Calculated from FAOStat (2009). Rural population estimates and projections are based on UN Population Projections (2006 revision) and UN Urbanization Prospects (2001 revision).

The magnitude and duration of rural population growth matters to the extent that the productivity of local cropland and livestock must rise even faster if the rural areas are to feed themselves and also produce a growing surplus. Africa's exceptionally high rural population growth rates during the 1970s and 1980s imposed a uniquely high hurdle that is now rapidly easing, in much the same way that a similar but lower challenge gradually faded earlier in Asia.

A population's changing dependency ratio imposes a somewhat similar kind of demographic burden, whereby those of working age must care for children or the elderly before per-capita gains can be achieved. The relevant data, based on the 2008 revision of the UN population prospects, are illustrated in Figure 11.8. Here we see sharp changes in the fraction of all people who are either children (0-14) or elderly (65+).

Figure 11.8. Estimated and projected total dependency rates (ages 0-14 and 65+) per 100 adults of working age, 1950–2030

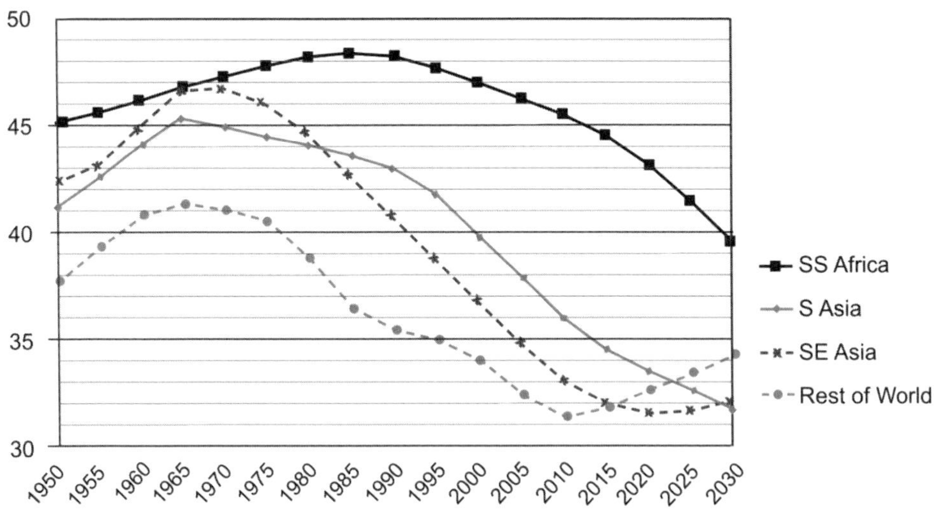

Source: Calculated from UN Population Projections, 2008 revision (March 2009), at: http://esa.un.org/unpp

In periods when the dependency rate is rising, education and health care costs grow even as the share of the population that is of working age declines. Conversely, when the dependency rate falls, the fraction of people who can work rises. If those new workers can be matched with high-productivity new investment, growth in output per capita can accelerate rapidly.

Trends and Turning Points in Agricultural Productivity

Farmers' responses to political and demographic influences, interacting with the technologies available to them, create the large differences in average cereal grain yields per hectare shown in Figure 11.9. This is a very partial measure of agricultural productivity, but more complete measures would require weights on the relative values of other crops and other inputs. The more transparent approach used here simply adds up the most comparable types of crops. Some cereals are more valuable than others, but all have roughly the same nutritional value. Cereals are also very widely grown, and every country formulates its own independent estimates of cereal grain areas and yields. As result, the inevitable errors are smoothed out over a large number of observations, and the huge differences shown in Figure 11.9 are clearly of great practical importance.

As shown in Figure 11.9, South Asia and Africa had similar cereal yields in the early 1960s, well below Southeast Asia and the rest of the world. In the late 1960s, yields began to grow in Asia and have continued to grow steadily since then at about the same rate as in the rest of the world. African yields fluctuated, with little growth until the late 1990s, but have risen steadily over the past decade at about the same rate as they did earlier in Asia.

Figure 11.9. USDA estimates of cereal grain average yield by region, 1961–2010 (mt/ha)

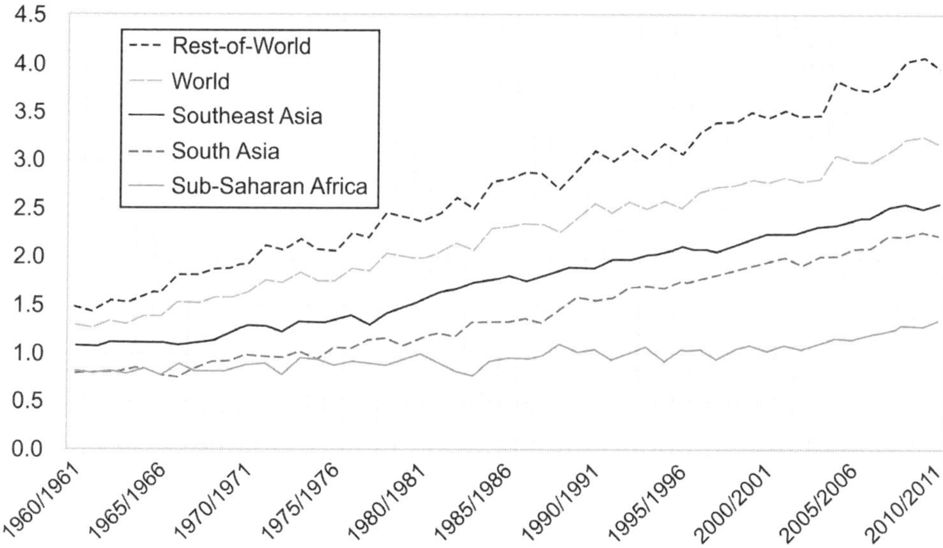

Source: Calculated from USDA, PS&D data (www.fas.usda.gov/psdonline). Results shown are each region's total production per harvested area in barley, maize, millet, mixed grains, oats, rice, rye, sorghum and wheat.

Africa's decade of normal yield growth is particularly important in the context of changes in area planted and the recent slowdown in population growth. These productivity gains can be attributed to a wide range of new technologies and production practices, many of which involve much higher labor use than was typical in the past, when rural population densities were lower. Increased labor has been applied to a variety of soil and water conservation techniques, more intensive management of livestock and manure, and more careful weeding and higher plant densities, as well as more use of inorganic fertilizer. Higher yields also involve new seed varieties that have been developed and released by the region's agricultural research services, much of the funding for which comes from foreign aid.

Figure 11.10 tracks the flows of all donors' Official Development Assistance (ODA) per person in Africa, in constant 2005 US dollars. The dark upper-most line, whose units are shown on the right vertical axis, indicates that total aid rose to about US$27 per person per year in the late 1980s, then fell to about $16 in the late 1990s before rising sharply after 2001 to over $36 in 2005 and 2006. The surge after 2001 was largely composed of debt relief (shown on the left vertical axis), which rose from about $3 to $14 per person during this period. There was also a substantial rise in aid for the health sector, from about $1 to about $4 per person. In contrast, aid for agricultural production, which had risen with total aid in the 1970s and 1980s, peaked in 1988 at about $5 per person and then fell steadily back to its 1973 level of $1 per person.

Figure 11.10. ODA commitments to Africa in selected sectors and total, 1973-2006 (real 2005 US dollars per capita)

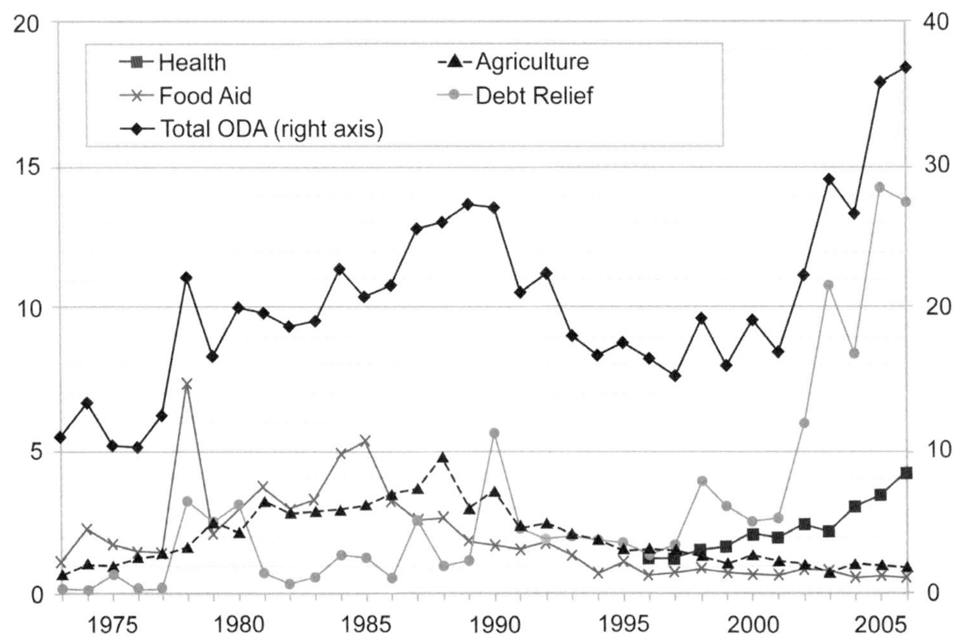

Source: Author's calculations, from OECD Development Assistance Committee (2008), Bilateral ODA Commitments by Purpose (www.oecd.org/dac), deflated by OECD deflator (2005=100) and divided by midyear population estimates for sub-Saharan Africa from the U.S. Census Bureau, International Database.

Conclusions

The food and financial crises of 2007–2008 caused great hardship for many people in Africa and throughout the developing world, raising the real cost of food and lowering real incomes. In an effort to limit its costs and avoid repeating the experience, governments and philanthropic donors around the world have committed themselves to increased investment in agricultural production in Africa. This chapter identifies three large-scale trends whose recent turning points suggest that Africa is poised to take advantage of such investment and produce rapid agricultural growth in the coming years.

First, African governments have now removed most of the policy distortions that kept farm-gate prices artificially low in the past. Doing so required wrenching reforms of deeply-rooted marketing boards, parastatal agencies, and trade regulations that were typically established by European colonial authorities and then actively used by post-colonial regimes to tax farmers and support city-dwellers. While there is ample scope for further reforms in favor of farmers, there is likely to be broad political support for those shifts as indicated by similar transitions in other developing countries. Furthermore, Africa's shift away from heavy taxation of its farmers occurs at the same time that other regions have reduced their price supports and found other means of supporting their agricultural sectors. The net result is a much more favorable policy environment for African farmers.

Second, African households have now absorbed much of the post-colonial demographic shock that gave Africa the world's fastest rates of population growth in the past. The continent's demographic transition was especially severe due to the sudden arrival of modern medicine, bringing sharp improvements in child survival at a time when the vast majority of Africans were still farmers. Africa's towns and cities grew quickly but from a small base, so both urban and rural population growth rates were faster than those previously recorded in other regions. As these growth rates slow down and a larger fraction of Africa's population enters the workforce, it becomes much easier for investment and technical change to raise per-capita output. Furthermore, this more favorable phase of population history occurs at a time when other regions have already passed through it, so that Africa will gradually become the only major region of the world to be experiencing this demographic dividend.

Third, African farms have now completed a full decade of rising cereal-grain yields, ending a long period in which output growth came primarily from expanding cropped area. Yield growth in the past decade has occurred at a similar rate as was experienced elsewhere in other Green Revolution periods, and far outpaces population growth. To the extent that new technologies continue to become available for adoption by African farmers, their relative land abundance could allow for rapid increases in total output, However, new technologies require public-sector agricultural investment, for which there was much more funding in the 1980s and early 1990s than there has been since. Given the inevitable time lag between those investments and the resulting productivity gains, Africans are only now reaping the benefits of past funding, and new programs will have to grow very quickly to limit the consequences of recent neglect.

Acknowledgements

A previous version of this paper was presented at the Institute for African Development, Cornell University in May, 2009 under the title 'The Political Economy of Agricultural Policy: Historical Trends, Recent Crises, and Prospects for Achieving the MDGs in Africa.' Many thanks are due to David Lee and several conference participants for their comments and suggestions.

References

Anderson, K. (ed.) (2009) *Distortions to Agricultural Incentives: A Global Perspective*. London: Palgrave Macmillan and Washington, DC: World Bank.

Anderson, K. and Masters, W.A. (eds.) (2009) *Distortions to Agricultural Incentives in Africa*. Washington, DC: World Bank.

FAOStat. (2009) Rural population estimates and projections, based on UN Population Projections (2006 revision) and UN Urbanization Prospects (2001 revision).

Krueger, A.O., Schiff, M. and Valdés, A. (eds.) (1991) *Political Economy of Agricultural Pricing Policy*. Baltimore: Johns Hopkins University Press.

Masters, W.A. (2009) 'Beyond the Food Crisis: Trade, Aid and Innovation in African Agriculture.' *African Technology Development Forum* 5(1): 3-15.

Masters, W.A. and Garcia, A.F. (2009) 'Agricultural Price Distortion and Stabilization: Stylized Facts and Hypothesis Tests.' In: Anderson, Kym (ed.) *Political Economy of Distortions to Agricultural Incentives*. Washington, DC: World Bank.

Miguel, E. (2009) *Africa's Turn?* Cambridge, MA: MIT Press.

OECD Development Assistance Committee. (2008) Bilateral ODA Commitments by Purpose. www.oecd.org/dac (accessed April 2011).

OECD African Economic Outlook. (2010) www.africaneconomicoutlook.org (accessed April 2011).

UN Population Projections. (2008 revision) http://esa.un.org/unpp (accessed April 2011).

US Census Bureau, International Database. (2010) www.census.gov/ipc/www/idb (accessed April 2011).

US Department of Agriculture. (2010) Production, Supply and Distribution Database. www.fas.usda.gov/psdonline (accessed April 2011).

World Bank (2009), The *Distortions to Agricultural Incentives* project. www.worldbank.org/agdistortions. Washington: World Bank.

Chapter 12

The Role of Public Policies and Policy Makers in Africa: Responding to Global Economic Crises

Vusi Gumede
University of Johannesburg, Johannesburg, South Africa

Abstract

After fluctuating greatly in the past few years, food and oil prices have recently returned to historically high levels. According to the World Bank (2011), food prices in late 2010 and early 2011 have risen to levels surpassing even the very high levels of 2007–2008. Oil prices in 2011 are hovering around $100 per barrel, implying that even if they decline, they will be much higher than where they were prior to the recent global economic recession. It is estimated that 925 million people are hungry or malnourished globally (Food and Agriculture Organization, 2011). The challenges emanating from the global food crisis of 2007–2008, and the financial and global economic crises that followed, remain unabated. Serious debates are taking place in many quarters regarding what public policies and policy makers could have done to avoid or mitigate the impacts of the recent crises. A number of factors need to be taken into account in determining an ideal mix of policies. Important lessons should be drawn from past food and financial crises. Sub-Saharan Africa, in particular, can learn from countries like Malawi, South Africa and Zambia that seem to have handled the challenges better in the recent past than in earlier times. This chapter discusses four areas of policy making where more informed policies would help mitigate a global economic crisis like the recent one. Broad economic policies and strategies should include a mix of policies that minimize job losses, in particular. Investment in economic infrastructure and regional economic integration are also part of the solution. Proper fiscal and monetary policies should be pursued if countries hope to mitigate the impacts of economic recession. Informed social policies are also key from the standpoint of protecting the poor and most vulnerable populations. Other types of urgent policy responses include those pertaining to food security and the environment, the financial sector, and the formation of 'social compacts.'

Introduction

What began as a downturn in the late 2000s in the US housing sector quickly became an entrenched global economic recession. According to the World Bank (2009), developing countries—with only a few exceptions—were at first sheltered from the worst elements of the turmoil but increasingly became much more vulnerable, with dwindling capital flows, huge withdrawals of capital, losses in equity markets, and a variety of other effects leading to declines in rates of economic growth. As a consequence of high food and fuel prices, many millions of people joined the ranks of the poverty-stricken. This was not only because of the global financial crisis *per se*, but also because the impacts of the concurrent global food crisis were not adequately addressed (Conceição and Mendoza, 2009). In addition, the 2007–2008 food crisis foreshadowed the more recent run-up in food prices in 2010–2011, which has been estimated to have added 44 million more people to the number of impoverished (World Bank, 2011).

The global economic recession reversed important, hard-earned gains that many sub-Saharan African countries had earlier achieved. The International Monetary Fund (2009) acknowledged that many countries in sub-Saharan Africa had enjoyed robust economic growth that had strengthened their balance sheets earlier in the 2000s. Sound economic policies were an important factor, as were the favourable external economic environment and increased external support in the form of debt relief and higher capital inflows. But the food and fuel price shocks that preceded the global financial crisis weakened the external position of food and fuel net importers, caused inflation to accelerate, and dampened their growth prospects. Although average growth rates on the African continent were expected to rebound to 4.5 percent in 2010 and 5.2 percent in 2011, the average growth rate for 2006–2008 was 6 percent, and fell to about 2 percent in 2009 (United Nations Economic Commission for Africa, 2009).

This chapter focuses on what public policy makers, working with the rest of society in their respective countries, can do to better manage a global economic recession and reduce its impacts on developing nations like those in sub-Saharan Africa. Significant analyses have been undertaken regarding the causes and consequences of the global food and financial crises (see several of the chapters in this volume, for example). This chapter will not dwell on those issues, though the next section summarizes some of the main findings of these studies. The following sections address public policy issues and elements that are critical in steering developing economies out of recessions and improving the economic prospects of the poor.

Factors Contributing to the Global Economic Recession

High Food Prices

Global energy and food prices shot up rapidly in 2007–2008. Although there have been both a later drop and subsequent major rise since then, food and energy prices have remained high compared to their historic averages. Even after the sharp price declines in 2009, for example, rice prices in March 2009 were 49 percent above their ten-year average; maize in April 2009 was 43 percent above its ten-year average; soybean prices in March 2009 were 36 percent above their ten-year average; and wheat in April 2009 was 31 percent above its ten-year average (Conceição and Mendoza, 2009).

In 2010–2011, the data indicate that food prices, in particular, continued to increase at an alarming rate. The FAO Cereal Price Index (2002–2004=100) averaged 156.0 in 2010 and increased to 209.1 in January 2011 (FAO, 2011).[72] Component indices experienced similar increases. As Blas (2009) argues, poor people were the most affected by the global economic recession of the late 2000s, but changes in consumption and production prices affect net consumers and net producers in different ways.

Lower global market demand for commodities pushes market prices down, reducing the profits of firms and the incomes of producers. As an example, the World Bank (2006) estimated that remittances to Kenya reduced the number of people living in absolute poverty by 8.5 percent, yet in 2008–2009, Kenya saw a fall in the international remittances of over 10 percent. In 2008, Kenya received a record US$611.2 million in remittances. However, the total remittances in the first seven months of 2009 stood at $342.3 million, down 8.4 percent from the same period of 2008 (but up 10.3 percent from the pre-recession period of January–July 2007 (Reuters, 2009)). In Ghana, remittances were reported to have fallen by about 10–13 percent in the same period (Green, 2009). As Green (2009) demonstrates in the case of Uganda, the declines in remittances may have induced families to remove children from school because many parents use remittances to pay for children's schooling in Uganda, as well as in most parts of Africa. The long-term human consequences of these impacts may be severe.

Loss of income to a poor household constitutes a serious external shock; many households have limited coping mechanisms and can easily plunge into severe chronic poverty, with far-reaching consequences. Increasing food prices have their greatest effect on poor and food-insecure populations, who may spend 50 to 60 percent or more of their income on food (USAID, 2009). According to the World Bank (2011), there was a 15 percent increase in food prices between October 2010 and January 2011, only three percent short of surpassing the 2007–2008 levels of food prices. This resulted in an estimated 925 million people recorded as hungry or malnourished, which makes up 13.6 percent of the estimated global population of 6.8 billion (FAO, 2011). Nearly all of the undernourished are in developing countries. During the recession of the late 2000s, countries in the Southern Africa region, for instance, reported that high levels of domestic food prices continued to negatively affect an estimated 8.7 million people in the region, including 5.1 million people in Zimbabwe, 353,000 in Lesotho, and 239,000 in Swaziland (USAID, 2009). Overall, the number of food insecure people in the region increased by nearly one-third between the 2007–2008 and 2008–2009 market years.

High Energy Prices

As pointed out by Capehart and Richardson (2008), energy costs affect all levels of the food production sector. Thus, crude oil prices in excess of $100 per barrel in 2008 substantially affected costs throughout the food supply chain. When energy prices are high, producers spend more for fertilizer (for which natural gas is a major input), crop drying and transportation, all of which raise production costs. At the processing, wholesale and retail

---

[72] The FAO Cereal Price Index is compiled by using the grains and rice price indices weighted by their average trade shares for the relevant years (in this case, 2002–2004). The Grains Price Index consists of the International Grains Council (IGC) wheat price index, itself an average of nine different wheat price quotations, and one maize export quotation. After expressing the maize price in its index form, the IGC index is converted to a base = 100 for 2002–2004. The Rice Price Index consists of three components containing average prices of 16 rice quotations: the components are Indica, Japonica and Aromatic rice varieties and the weights for combining the three components are assumed to be (fixed) trade shares of the three varieties.

levels, transportation costs and the costs of operating packing houses, manufacturing plants and retail stores all increase. Most, if not all, of these costs are passed on to consumers. In addition, high petroleum prices increase the competitiveness of ethanol, further boosting the demand for maize in ethanol-producing countries.

The energy-to-food price transmission mechanism disrupts development projects and economic growth prospects in those developing countries that are rebuilding their infrastructure and expanding their domestic markets, which are widely dependent on oil and agriculture. For example, Conceição and Mendoza (2009) state that oil prices in mid-2009 were still 20 percent above their 1998–2008 average. Significant increases in fuel and energy prices can create a crisis situation in countries that are unable to finance their development projects and needs. This challenge has not been sufficiently addressed.

As a result of the fall in global demand for raw materials and increased oil prices, sub-Saharan export revenues declined sharply in 2008 and into 2009, resulting in a deterioration of the current account, eroding foreign exchange reserves and generating major losses in trade tax revenues, the latter due largely to relatively elastic trade elasticities of the developing world.[73] Exports from sub-Saharan Africa began to recover in mid-2009, although they were still below pre-crisis levels (IMF, 2010).

Global Financial Crisis

The financial crisis in the US, which culminated in the global economic recession, is widely considered to be the greatest economic crisis since the Great Depression. Given the economic role of the US and global economic interdependence, the economic recession which began in the US was easily transmitted to other Organization for Economic Cooperation and Development (OECD) economies and subsequently spread widely around the world, with many countries finding themselves with related financial and economic problems. The financial crisis began with the real estate market in the US, specifically in the sub-prime mortgage market and with unscrupulous lenders (El-Baltagy, 2009). The resulting unsustainable real estate bubble began to collapse in 2006. The real estate bubble originated mainly as a response to the huge demand for financial assets. Since not many countries can actually provide such assets, in such situations, speculative bubbles can emerge in response to high demand and/or inelastic supply response to expressed demand. This was the case with the real estate bubble, and this ultimately was one of the main factors that led to the 2008–2009 global economic recession. In essence, the financial crisis was an outcome of sub-prime lending practices that escalated to an enormous problem of toxic assets.[74]

The global financial crisis affected advanced economies, emerging markets, and low-income countries in different ways. Advanced economies were hit mainly by the systemic banking crisis in the US and Europe in 2008–2009. Emerging markets with well-developed financial systems were initially mostly affected by cross-border financial linkages through capital flows, stock market investments, and exchange rates (International Monetary Fund, 2009). In financially less-developed countries, growth and trade effects dominated, with lagged impacts. Ultimately, the economic growth and trade effects became an issue for all countries.

---

[73] See previous studies (Gumede, 2000, 2004) in the case of South Africa, for example.

[74] Robert Hockett, in this volume, presents a detailed narrative of the dynamics that resulted in the recent global financial crisis.

Many countries in sub-Saharan Africa had enjoyed strong economic growth in the early 2000s. Factors contributing to this robust growth included a favourable external economic environment, strong demand for exports, and increased external support in the form of debt relief and higher capital investment inflows (ADB, 2009). However, this situation turned around with the onset of the global food and fuel price shocks and the subsequent global recession. Together these weakened export demand, adversely affected the trade balances of many net food importers, caused food price inflation to accelerate, and dampened the future prospects for growth. The financial crisis compounded the policy challenges confronting sub-Saharan Africa as countries sought to consolidate the region's economic gains and attempt to meet the Millennium Development Goals (ADB, 2009). While considerable advances toward the MDGs had been made in sub-Saharan Africa in recent years, particularly in reducing the number of people in poverty, it is estimated that the global economic crisis may have prevented 7 million people from rising above the poverty line of US$1.25 per day in 2009 (World Bank, 2010). In essence, African countries suffered these setbacks substantially as a result of the mistakes of the developed world.

In the wake of the global economic recession, economic growth rates in sub-Saharan Africa were reduced from levels that existed earlier in the decade. The International Monetary Fund (2010) estimated that growth in sub-Saharan Africa slowed sharply, from over 6 percent average annual growth in 2006–2008 to only 2.1 percent in 2009, although growth was projected to rebound thereafter.

The implications of reduced economic growth are especially glaring when related to the evidence on poverty. The World Bank (2009b), for instance, estimated that an additional 46 million people in developing countries were expected to fall into poverty in 2009 as a result of the financial and economic crisis; this on top of the estimated 100 million additional people still remaining in extreme poverty due to the food and energy crises of 2007–2008 (World Bank, 2009a). The number of people living on less than US$2 per day was expected to increase to over 1.5 billion globally, and the percentage of workers in Africa earning less than US$2 per day was estimated to increase from 82.2 percent in 2007 to 86.6 percent in 2009 (UNESCO, as cited in ADB, 2009). Poor people were disproportionately affected by the financial and economic crises for several reasons: first, because their sources of employment are frequently vulnerable (three out of five sub-Saharan African workers are considered among the 'extreme working poor'); second, because the poor rely heavily on primary sectors, which were deeply affected by the volatility of commodity prices; and third, because of the declines in foreign aid and inflows of remittances. With decreasing average incomes and soaring food prices, the poor were forced to allocate more income to purchasing food and, as a result, reduced expenditures on such household needs as health and education. Children from poor households were particularly affected (United Nations World Report, 2009).

Going forward, many African countries will face increasing pressures for debt repayment as international institutions and foreign banks not only tighten their lending policies but also seek to keep their reserves stable. Linked to this is the prospect that the after-effects of the global economic recession may result in a further slowdown in foreign aid and development funding to African countries due to the tightening of global credit.

More recent reports, on the other hand, suggest that Africa's prospects may not be so dire. The International Monetary Fund reported that remittances and official aid flows remained broadly unchanged from their 2008 levels, notwithstanding the recessions in advanced countries (IMF, 2010). Another positive development is that the World Bank (2011) reported that economic growth in sub-Saharan Africa rebounded strongly in 2010, with an increase in gross domestic product (GDP) of 4.7 percent, a trend that was expected to continue (projections for 2011 and 2012 were for growth rates of 5.3 percent and 5.7 percent, respectively). Sub-Saharan Africa is benefiting from the global recovery and from a boost in the demand for raw materials as well as from a rise in foreign direct investment and improved agricultural productivity. This is likely to have positive effects in mitigating against the poverty impacts of the global recession. However, high food prices and climate-related hazards threaten to undo the gains trickling down from renewed economic growth.

The Role of Public Policy: Some Perspectives

The global economic crisis has demanded that policy makers and other stakeholders be vigilant and do the right things at the right times. Any crisis at the scale of a global economic recession requires a particular kind of leadership—a leadership that is decisive and bold. To begin with, it would appear that the primary concern of policy makers should be to protect the most vulnerable, whilst simultaneously addressing macro-economic, fiscal and trade policy issues. The people who were already most vulnerable prior to the food and financial crises were the most affected. In South Africa, employment declined by 171,000 between the fourth quarter of 2009 and the first quarter of 2010 (Statistics South Africa, 2011). Elsewhere as well, African economies suffered and unemployment escalated. The most significant public policy initiative in response to the global recession in South Africa (SA), for instance, was the social pact between the government—through the Presidential Joint Economic Working Group—and its social partners, through the National Economic Development and Labor Council (NEDLAC). These parties committed to a collective response to the global economic crisis in December 2008. Important outcomes included the commitments by the private business sector to increase domestic investment. The government, for its part, recast its priorities to ensure that the most vulnerable were cushioned in various ways. The response that the country as a whole developed was debated in various platforms within and outside of the government. This was not unusual as policy (and strategy) making, law making and policy implementation are normally handled through a standard governmental process, the so-called 'cluster system,' before being debated by relevant stakeholders (Gumede, 2011).

Public policies can play an important role in cushioning the most dire impacts of economic crisis on the most vulnerable. Even though countries, whether in Africa or the developing world in general, are not homogeneous, some of these policies are generalizable. Indeed, multilateral assessments of the impact of the global recession on sub-Saharan Africa have shown that many SSA countries have experienced similar impacts.

Public policy responses in the developing world to the global economic recession were propelled by the reversal of three important developments experienced during the recent past: good financing, high commodity prices, and significant flows of cross-border and international remittances. As Griffith-Jones and Ocampo (2009) argue, these reversals called for a 'mix of policies to deploy including the macro-economic, fiscal and policy stance of countries and their dynamics' (p. 4). These economic policy actions were complemented by a set of social policy responses in the area of social protection, especially for the most vulnerable. These responses assumed different forms: public works programmes, cash transfer programmes, decreasing interest rates, and increasing expenditures on social services. In the context of the magnitude of a global economic recession, interventions such as these should not only be vigorously implemented but scaled up.

As an illustration, a variety of interventions were taken in South Africa. First, the South African government responded by easing monetary policy and introducing a fiscal stimulus package to support demand. The Monetary Policy Committee (MPC) of the South African Reserve Bank started reducing interest rates in December 2008, then progressively lowered the repurchase rate (NEDLAC, 2009).

Second, the South African government introduced the 'training layoff scheme,' which involved considerable investment (2.9 billion *Rand*) and expanded training programmes for those who faced retrenchment in order to cushion massive job losses, while temporarily reducing payroll costs for employers. Jobs in public works and community works programmes were expanded, and new training programmes were designed. This scheme, however, was not very successful, as it saved only about 70,000 jobs.

Third, public investments in infrastructure were critical in mitigating the impacts of the recession, through scaled-up public works with employment-intensive procedures. In the 2009 NEDLAC Agreement, the social partners approved a scaled-up second phase of the public works programme to improve its reach and impact. Although the first generation public works programme was successful in exceeding its job creation target, many of these jobs were short term and therefore were unable to prevent people from falling back into poverty. The second phase of the public works programme was subsequently designed to ensure that the total number of job-days offered increased tenfold, to two million one-year full-time equivalents. Some 4.5 million unemployed people are projected to benefit over the five-year period between 2009 and 2014, which would reduce unemployment by half (Nedlac, 2009). Incentives and investments in energy-efficient technologies and 'green jobs' (including those generated in response to future climatic changes) could play an even more important role in job creation and economic recovery in the future.

Another set of public policy responses is about creating and/or sustaining 'social compacts' in the affected countries, mechanisms in which nations work in unison and respond as a single unit to the effects of economic recession. It is unlikely that governments alone will be able to address all the societal challenges exacerbated by the global economic recession. This point is discussed further below, drawing from South Africa's recent experience.

A last set of public policy responses is more specific to food security. Important policy lessons should be drawn from the past food shortages and food price crises. For instance, countries such as Malawi, South Africa and Zambia seem to have handled the challenge of escalating food prices relatively well. In the food crisis in Malawi and Zambia in 2001-2003,[75] for example, early warning systems designed to protect the most vulnerable from lack of food, especially staple foods, became a critical component of crisis management responses. Inter-agency coordination among donors, government and non-governmental organizations (NGOs) also played a key role.

Lastly, there is a set of political issues that, at a global level, requires greater attention than it has received thus far. It has become glaringly obvious that the current global economic and power balance requires restructuring if the world is to be spared occasional, but devastating, economic recessions like that of the late 2000s. There are various individuals who have proposed ways to improve society—Emmanuel Kant, John Rawls,

[75] This crisis was caused by a multiplicity of factors, including drought and adverse weather conditions resulting in crop failure, lapses in the government's early warning system, mismanagement of food reserves and distortions in domestic markets (IMF, 2002).

Amartya Sen, and, most recently, Joseph Stiglitz are among the influential thinkers who have proposed some form of moral compass to guide policy making and implementation. Rawls (1999), for instance, proposed a particular definition of justice—'justice as fairness.' Under this conception of justice, the organizing principles for a society are based on all individuals existing at an initial position of equality, upon which further agreements and principles of social cooperation and governance are based. In their initial position, people are behind a 'veil of ignorance' and do not know their position in society or their fortune in the distribution of assets and abilities. The point of this hypothetical situation is to ensure that organizing principles agreed upon behind this 'veil of ignorance' should not be designed to favour any particular condition, but that they are the result of a process of fair deliberation and agreement.[76]

Broader Economic Strategies to Cope with Crisis

A main preoccupation of broader economic policies and strategies should be retaining existing jobs and expanding employment. This implies that even if economies go into a prolonged downturn, efforts must to be made to stabilize employment rates. This is where the issue of the proper policy mix becomes crucial. There are policy actions that countries have to pursue in order to save jobs whilst keeping the engine of the economy turning. One of these is trade policy. Africa is no exception—trade and industrial policies can be tailored in a manner that permits growing trade within the continent and its sub-regions wherever feasible. Since the early 1990s, many African countries have made significant progress in achieving higher economic growth in part through regional trading arrangements and regional economic cooperation. There is growing evidence that regional cooperation and long-term regional integration are likely to boost sub-Saharan Africa's path of economic growth. However, this is no substitute for increased and deepened linkages to the rest of the global economy.

Linked to regional and global integration is the matter of economic infrastructure. In South Africa, for example, a cabinet-level commitment to a major public investment programme amounting to approximately 800 billion *Rand* was made over the three fiscal years to cover the period to mid-2012. Investing in economic infrastructure provides a much needed strategic anchor to growing the economy whilst creating jobs. Both tailored trade and industrial policies and investments in infrastructure would help maintain the growth of African economies, in turn protecting jobs, while at the same time preparing economies for future growth as the world economy recovers. The challenge with this proposition—expanding investment in infrastructure and maintaining employment—is that, due to tight government budgets, the fiscal space for many countries on the African continent is very limited.

Many African governments have tried to minimize the impact of the global economic crisis on their economies through targeted interventions, including sector-specific rescue packages, training schemes and anti-poverty programs. However, as indicated above, the scope for implementing significant interventions is very limited in most countries. The key constraints facing these nations include declining government revenues and shrinking capital inflows, amongst which are declining remittances. In addition, African countries are

---

[76] This line of thinking characterizes a recent book on *Global Civics*, in which the editor, Hakan Altinay, describes global civics as a 'system of conscious responsibilities that we [humanity] are ready to assume after due deliberation and corresponding rights that we are ready to claim' (2011, p. 5).

increasingly unable to finance widening current-account deficits as foreign exchange reserves have continued to decline. In addition, the chronic gaps between savings and investment have been worsened by the global economic recession. According to the United Nations Economic Commission for Africa (2009), African countries would need on the order of US$50 billion to finance the savings-investment gap across Africa.

Most African governments need support from their development partners and international financial institutions to fill the financing gap and to help support short-term economic growth strategies while also pursuing their national long-term development plans (Khatiwada, 2009). Existing aid pledges are not enough to meet the rising demands from African countries, despite the continued growth in development aid even in the face of the financial crisis. In 2009, for instance, the rise in Overseas Development Assistance (ODA) in real terms, excluding debt relief, was 6.8 percent (OECD, 2010). Additionally, reforms in ODA are important because of the need to improve the capacities of African governments and non-governmental institutions to implement aid-driven projects and programmes. Such reforms would also address the concern that much of foreign assistance is returned to donor countries through practices covering everything from purchasing agreements to donor country consultants.

Fiscal Policy

In designing a fiscal stimulus, policy makers should be mindful of how different types of expenditures will affect the country's external position and economic activity. For instance, any counter-cyclical fiscal policy should not exacerbate the loss of foreign exchange reserves. Likewise, the unintended consequences of pro-cyclical policies need to be monitored.

Unlike in advanced economies, African government purchases of the machinery, equipment and materials associated with infrastructure spending have a significant import component that can cause leakages in foreign reserves. This leakage is parallel to the slowdown in domestic demand, which does not originate domestically as in some advanced countries, but externally. Such external dependence presents a challenge in that African countries faced with a global economic downturn must nonetheless muster meagre resources and funds to provide for the most vulnerable, who are the most afflicted by such slowdowns (Khatiwada, 2009). The challenge is particularly severe in heavily indebted poor countries.

In addressing the challenges faced during the global economic downturn and financial crisis, African countries will do well to create their own policy space to enable them to use appropriate fiscal policies to help fight the recession. Furthermore, existing African finance and development institutions, such as the African Development Bank, should be better empowered to analyze, plan, coordinate and respond to Africa's economic and social needs.

Monetary Policy

As inflation falls, monetary policy should be eased. The decline in fuel prices, along with the decline in food prices following the 2007–2008 crisis, permitted many countries to ease tight monetary policies to varying degrees (Africa Focus, 2009). On the other hand, countries still experiencing demand pressures and inflationary build-up may need to tighten monetary policy. An important related issue is the coordination of interest and exchange rate policies in the context of stimulating aggregate demand and job creation.

Using reserves to support a fundamentally overvalued exchange rate is likely futile. In situations where the capital outflow seems generalized or where a persistent current-account deficit can no longer be financed by the available inflows, a currency depreciation is generally necessary to help smooth adjustment of the exchange rate. However, this decision should be informed by an assessment of the possible negative balance sheet effects should the exchange rate weaken suddenly. This might warrant implementation of measures to address balance sheet weaknesses first so that the depreciation can support the adjustment (Africa Focus, 2009). Also, as the IMF (2009) recommends, introducing new controls on capital outflows should generally be avoided. Experience suggests that these are unlikely to be effective. In low-income sub-Saharan African countries in particular, capital controls have generally been ineffective even under normal conditions. Each country's own circumstances should nonetheless be independently evaluated; it is conceivable that capital controls could make sense under some specific circumstances (e.g., to reduce capital flight).

African countries also need to pursue measures to strengthen the banking sector through better risk assessment and monitoring, and through establishing adequate capital requirements (Balchin, 2009). This will facilitate savings mobilization and encourage private sector lending while minimizing credit risk. Banking sector regulation needs to be further strengthened by keeping pace with modern developments while at the same time giving priority to country-specific development strategies and remaining cognizant of national capacity and institutional constraints. Although these are potentially useful proposals, the real challenge emanating from the global economic system that lies behind the global economic recession remains addressing the underlying structural factors.

Trade Policy

Economic growth in Africa in 2008, at the onset of the recession, was 5.6 percent, down from 7 percent in 2007 (IMF, 2010); continent-wide growth declined further to 2.1 percent in 2009 and was expected to remain low until the end of the global economic recession. It has been argued that the main driver of recent economic growth in Africa was the rise in commodity prices, especially for oil. In recent years oil-exporting African countries have consistently grown more rapidly than non-oil exporting countries. As shown in Figure 12.1, annual real GDP growth among oil exporters averaged 7.9 percent in 2006–2008, compared to 3.8 percent for non-oil resource-intensive countries and 5.8 percent for non-resource-intensive countries (IMF, 2010). In addition to the stimulative effects of high commodity prices, it is important to underscore the fact that other key factors, especially good macro-economic policy and institutional reform, also helped underpin high growth performance in some African countries in the years immediately prior to the financial crisis. As many have argued, the adoption of sound and sustained macro-economic policy in these countries has helped boost the confidence of both domestic and foreign investors and thereby stimulated growth.

Expanding trade with other developing countries represents another potential means to soften the severity of the negative impact of global economic recessions on African economies. Global trade statistics suggest that trade among developing countries as a share of both total world trade and global commerce has been on the increase for quite some time. Merchandise trade among developing countries grew at an average annual rate of 13 percent between 1995 and 2007 and, in 2007, accounted for one-fifth of total world trade flows (ADB, 2009). It is critically important for the African continent to increase its share of this 'South-South' trade in order to offset the effects of possible declines in the demands for its commodity exports, such as those experienced during the global recession (Africa Development Bank, 2009). Gumede (2008) presents some proposals on what the South-South agenda could focus on. One of the critical matters that South-South cooperation can address is exchanging policy experiences—sharing experiences regarding how individual countries have dealt with previous financial and economic crises.

Figure 12.1. Economic growth in Africa—oil and non-oil economies, 2006–2008

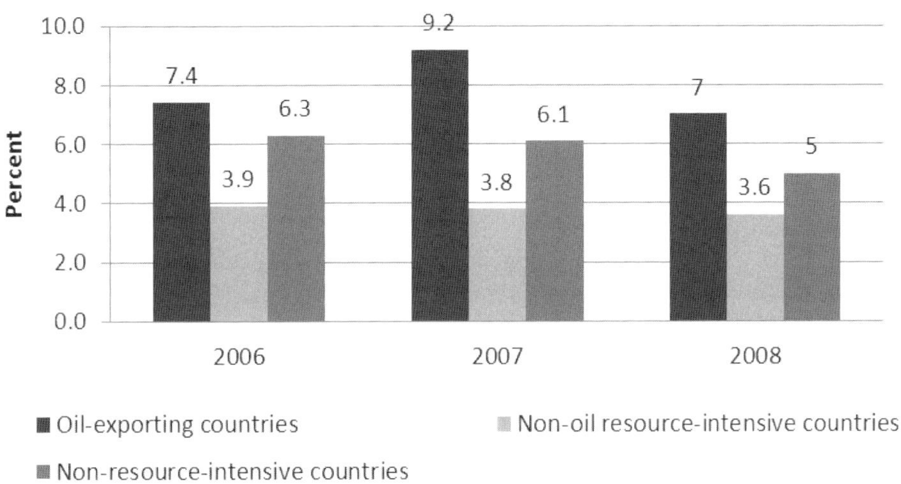

Source: IMF, 2010.

Agricultural Policy

The impacts of the financial and food crises would, of course, be expected to be more pronounced in agriculture-based economies. Price volatility has become especially pronounced in recent years, with offsetting effects on African net food producers and consumers. While the food price increases of 2007–2008 threatened the food security of net food consumers, the subsequent declines in prices, while beneficial to consumers, hit net food producers and exporters hard. In late 2008, export revenues shrank for a range of agricultural commodities. The hardest hit were the agriculture-dependent economies. For example, it is estimated that cotton and livestock make up 75 to 80 percent of Mali's annual exports, while in Burundi, coffee and tea represent 70 percent of exports. International prices of agricultural commodities declined substantially, by 25 percent for cotton and 19 percent for coffee, between the first quarter of 2008 and January 2009. The decline in prices was nevertheless compensated for by an increase in production due to good climatic conditions in countries such as Burundi. In some countries, while export receipts from agricultural products were rising, they fell short of pre-crisis targets. In Ethiopia, coffee exports in March 2009 were one-half of target levels mainly due to the decline in world prices (United Nations World Report, 2009). Then again, in late 2010 and early 2011, commodity prices surged again, rising to levels last seen in 2007–2008.

As a result of the global food crisis, the global agricultural and food systems once again became a priority—at least temporarily—on the international agenda at the behest of African governments. International agencies followed suit with financial support (although actual support has fallen far short of stated commitments). One concern voiced by FAO is that the global economic crisis might have shifted the focus to resolving the financial crisis at the expense of food security (FAO, 2009). This is not unexpected as the financial and economic crises worsened even as food prices were dropping in international markets. The long-term concern is that continuing global economic challenges may distract governments and international organizations from addressing the underlying structural factors that in part caused the earlier food price crisis (Conceição and Mendoza, 2009).

Reinvestment in agriculture is critical and overdue, while at the same time African governments must take into account the needs of small-scale farmers and other vulnerable groups dependent on primary agricultural production. Hunger, malnutrition and poverty reduction need to be placed at the center of agricultural policy and rural development. Smallholder farmers, for instance, are the most food insecure; therefore reinvestment in agriculture should prioritize their needs by measures such as ensuring that they have secure access to land, increasing farm productivity, improving their access to markets, and in other ways strengthening their livelihoods.

Governments should seize the opportunity to place poor, vulnerable, and food-insecure populations at the center of policy responses. This should be implemented through the adoption of social protection measures that address vulnerability and inequality, and that enable vulnerable populations to overcome the effects of shocks. These measures play a crucial stabilizing role in times of crisis, including the essential role of supporting spending on social services to protect income-insecure households (World Food Organization and World Bank, 2009). In addition, social protection measures play a critical role in consumption, smoothing and cushioning the impacts of micro-level household shocks.

One specific household-level response that can play a major role in supporting food security during food price crises is relying on household food gardens. There are many country experiences in which household gardens have been successful. Lesotho, for instance, has been lauded for its successful food garden programmes, and the success with which these have relieved households from the consequences of the food crisis. South Africa, Namibia and Swaziland also boast of relative success in promoting food garden programmes, which have done much to counter economic hardship (Levenston, 2010). The food-insecure are more than just farmers, however; they include a broad base of the poor population. Nonetheless, these efforts and initiatives are not in themselves enough to solve the food security challenges of Southern Africa without broader structural solutions.

Social Policy

The recent global economic recession reversed the gains earned from the enormous efforts of African countries and their development partners in the early 2000s to meet the Millennium Development Goals. According to the World Bank (2009b), infant mortality was projected to increase by 200,000 to 400,000 deaths annually to 2015 as a result of the global recession. The ADB (2010) reports that Africa, excluding North Africa, still accounts for half of all deaths worldwide of children under the age of five and that malnutrition and infant mortality have been exacerbated by the recent global economic recession. Low-income African countries that have made efforts to improve universal primary education and access to healthcare have also suffered setbacks as governments have been unable to finance subsidized educational and healthcare programs where poor households are not in a position to pay for school fees and attendant healthcare costs.

Sound social policies remain a core element in countries making progress in development in general, and in the case of sub-Saharan African countries specifically, they remain key mechanisms towards the achievement of the MDGs. The African Development Bank (2010) suggests that prior to the onset of the food and fuel crises and the global recession, African countries were making steady progress toward attainment of the MDGs. The recent global economic downturn, however, has dealt a severe blow to these nations' efforts.

The poor have inevitably been those most severely affected by the food and financial crises. In protecting the poor against global economic downturns, sub-Saharan African countries might learn from the experiences of social protection programs in Latin America. As highlighted in Gumede (2008), these include the following:

- The experiences of Brazil and Mexico suggest that large-scale social transfer programs are feasible and can be cost-effective;
- Comprehensive social protection programs (as in the case of Brazil and Chile) work better than piecemeal programs;
- Given that poverty reduction and social protection are responsibilities of the state, the capacity of the state to respond is key;
- Both centralized and decentralized approaches can work;
- Planning, coordination, and monitoring and evaluation are important; evaluation, in particular, is critical as it legitimizes the sustainability of these programs;
- Finally, targeting the extreme poor remains a particular challenge, compared to targeting the poor in general. Chile's *Solidario* programme provides evidence on this, as do the flexible approach followed in Brazil and programmes implemented in Mexico.

In essence, the lessons depicted above call for robust social protection interventions aimed largely at some form of income support. The main challenge of these interventions concerns budgetary constraints, especially as the public finances of many countries are precarious during periods of economic recession. Over and above cash-transfer types of programmes, public and community employment programmes should be scaled up to meet existing needs for employment creation. In addition, special targeted interventions should be pursued to address the needs of the most vulnerable groups through enabling them to gain access to credit, agricultural inputs, healthcare services, and social protection. These should be prioritized in national budgets, development programs, and plans to reflect a central focus on 'people-centerd' policy. Ongoing economic and social reforms in sub-Saharan Africa need to be made more pro-poor with initiatives such as public works programmes implemented to ensure greater employment opportunities, as in the case with South Africa (*African Monitor*, 2009).

Concluding Comments

This chapter has presented some thoughts on what public policies and policy makers in sub-Saharan African can accomplish in the context of global economic recessions. Two sets of policy responses, mentioned earlier, that fit into this conclusion are food security interventions and 'social compacts.' Regarding the first, I argue that policy makers should learn from experiences of relevant countries. Three countries in the sub-Saharan region that seem to have tackled the challenge of food security well are Zambia, Malawi and South Africa. Noticeable in all three was the crucial role of early warning systems in detecting supply shortages, substantive investments in trade support, regional solidarity and substantial inter-agency coordination among key actors. Other sub-Saharan African nations would do well to learn from these experiences.

As regards 'social compacts,' there is a need to construct and sustain social contracts; in other words, there is a need to build effective and concrete partnerships in which each stakeholder takes on some responsibility. South Africa provides a useful example. Led by the office of the Head of State, all social partners negotiated and agreed upon a set of specific actions and interventions aimed at dealing with the impacts of the global economic recession in South Africa. This idea of a social contract in times of economic crisis might be replicated elsewhere, for example, in the case of regional economic institutions to strengthen regional integration efforts.

The other two policy areas in which action is overdue are environmental policies and regulations pertaining to the financial sector. In relation to the financial sector, one main lesson is that toxic assets should be avoided in the future—in essence, the conduct of financial sectors needs to change. In the short term, many have argued for a review of capital requirements of development finance institutions. In relation to the environment, difficult policy decisions need to be made and tough actions implemented, particularly with regard to such concerns as climate change.

There are other interventions not of a policy nature that sub-Saharan African governments should consider in dealing with economic recession. The organization and capacity of the state needs reconfiguration in many instances in order to improve long-range planning and quick responses to economic shocks. This suggests a central role that only the government can play. The capacities of development finance institutions, locally and internationally, also need to be improved so that responses to economic crises can be speeded up and made more effective. Most important in this regard is the need to strengthen the international financial regulatory system by applying and enforcing stringent management standards in the banking and financial sectors. Second is the need to reform international financial institutions by increasing the representation of developing countries, strengthening the IMF's surveillance responsibilities, and reviewing the role and conditions of the IMF as the international 'lender of last resort.' Linked to this is the broader issue of reconfiguring global economic and power relations. The predominant global economic system has not worked well; it has benefited a few, often at the expense of the many.

Lastly, public policies and policy makers have to be agile in attending to the four sets of possible policy areas, discussed in this chapter, that require action. National economic policies and strategies warrant a mix of policies to focus on minimizing job losses. Investments in economic infrastructure and improving regional economic integration also must play a role. Fiscal and monetary policies, as suggested in many studies, must be effectively implemented to help mitigate the impact of recessions. Finally, social policies, particularly social protection measures, are key to addressing the needs of the poor and most vulnerable. Perhaps most importantly, countries should seize the opportunity presented by economic recessions to advance their respective structural reform agendas in order to boost prospects for long-term growth.

Acknowledgments

The author would like to thank Zukiswa Mqolomba and Thabileng Mothabi for valuable research assistance.

References

Africa Commission. (2009) Global Financial Crisis Calls for Action. *Africa Commission Newsletter,* Issue number 5, February, 2009.

African Development Bank. (2009) Africa and the Global Economic Crisis: Strategies for Preserving the Foundations of Long-term Growth. Paper Prepared for the 2009 Annual Meeting of the African Development Bank, 13–14 May, 2009, Dakar, Senegal.

African Development Bank. (2010) *Assessing Progress in Africa toward the Millennium Development Goals: MDG Report 2010*. Available at: http://www.afdb.org/fileadmin/uploads/afdb/Documents/Publications/MGDS 202010 20Eng.pdf

African Monitor. (2009) *Dialogue on Africa's Response to the Global Financial Crisis*. Available at: http://www.africanmonitor.org/Site/index2.php?option=com_content&do_pdf=1&id=109.

Africa Focus. (2009) *Africa: Global Economic Crisis*. March, 2009. Available at: http://www.africafocus.org/docs09/gec0904b.php.

Altinay, H. (2011) *Global Civics: Responsibilities and Rights in an Interdependent World*, Brookings Institution Press, Washington, DC.

Balchin, N. (2009) *The Impact of the Global Financial Crisis in Africa*. Available at: http://www.mthente.co.za/resources/reports-and-articles/mthente-in-the-news/The%20Impact%20of%20the%20Global%20Financial%20Crisis%20in%20Africa%20-%20Neil%20Balchin.pdf.

Blas, J. (2009) Poor still hit by high food prices. *Financial Times* 19 March, 2009.

Baxter, R. (2008) The Global Economic Crisis and its Impact on South Africa. Available at: http://www.reservebank.co.za/internet/Publication.nsf/LADV/21EFDE8DEE82935342257601003680B6/$File/Roger+Baxter.pdf

Capehart, T. and Richardson, J. (2008) *Food Price Inflation: Causes and Impacts*. Congressional Research Service: Report for Congress, Library of Congress. Available at: http://opencrs.com/document/RS22859.

Conceição, P. and Mendoza, R.U. (2009) Is the global food crisis over? Available at: http://www.voxeu.org/index.php?q=node/3459.

El-Beltagy, K. (2009) Global Economic Crisis. Available at: http://pathways.cu.edu.eg/news/news/uf/30/30293_4MPED-03-04.pdf

Food and Agriculture Organization. (2011) *2011 World Hunger and Poverty Facts and Statistics*, State of World Food Insecurity Hunger Notes. Available at: http://www.worldhunger.org/articles/Learn/Number_of_hungry_people_in_the_world.

Food and Agriculture Organization. (2009) The Right to Food and the Financial and Economic Crisis. Submission to the United Nations Conference on World Financial and Economic Crisis, United Nations General Assembly, 24–26 June, 2009, New York.

Green, D. (2009) *A Copper-Bottomed Crisis? The Impact of the Global Economic Meltdown on Zambia*. Oxfam, Oxford.

Griffith-Jones, S. and Ocampo, J. (2009) The Global Financial Crisis and its Impact on Developing Countries. United Nations Development Working Paper. UNDP, New York.

Gumede, V. (2011) Policy Making in South Africa. In: Landsberg, C. and Venter, A. (Fourth Edition), *South African Government and Politics*. Van Schaik Publishers, Pretoria, pp. 165–182.

Gumede, V. (2008) Social Protection in Latin America and Africa. *Africa Notes,* Summer 2008. Cornell Institute for African Development, Ithaca, NY.

Gumede, V. (2004) Export propensities and intensities of Small Manufacturing Enterprises in South Africa. *Small Business Economics: An International Journal*, 2004, Volume 22, Issue 5, pp. 379–389.

Gumede, V. (2000) Import Demand Elasticities for South Africa: A Co-integration Approach. *Journal for Studies in Economics and Econometrics,* 2000, Volume 2, Number 1, pp. 21–38.

Hussain, M.N., Mlambo, K. and Oshikoya, T. (2009) Global Financial Crisis: An African Perspective. African Development Bank, Tunisia, Tunis. Available at: http://www.afdb.org/fileadmin/uploads/afdb/Documents/Publications/00157618-EN-ERP-42.PDF.

International Monetary Fund. (2002) Malawi: The Food Crises, the Strategic Grain Reserve and the IMF. July, 2002. Accessed from: http://www.imf.org/external/np/exr/facts/malawi.htm.

International Monetary Fund. (2009) Impact of the Global Financial Crisis on sub-Saharan Africa. Available at: http://www.imf.org/external/pubs/ft/books/2009/afrglobfin/ssaglobalfin.pdf.

International Monetary Fund. (2010) *Regional Economic Outlook: Sub-Saharan Africa back to High Growth?* World Economic and Financial Surveys. IMF, Washington, DC.

Khatiwada, S. (2009) *Stimulus Packages to Counter Global Economic Crisis: A Review.* Discussion Paper, International Institute of Labor Studies, International Labor Organisation, Geneva.

Levenston, M. (2010) GardenAfrica works in South Africa, Swaziland, Namibia and Zimbabwe. Available at: http://www.cityfarmer.info/2010/05/16/gardenafricas-works-in-south-africa-swaziland-namibia-and-zimbabwe/.

Macias, J. and Massa, I. (2009) The Global Financial Crisis and Sub-Saharan Africa: The effects of slowing private capital inflows on growth. ODI *Working Paper Series*, Overseas Development Institute, UK.

Meegan, M. (2008) Africa and the Global Financial Crisis: Disaster or Opportunity? Available at: http://windyharbor.wordpress.com/2008/10/12/africa-and-the-global-financial-crisis-disaster-or-opportunity/.

National Economic Development and Labour Council (Nedlac). 2009. Framework for South Africa's Response to the International Economic Crisis. Saxonwold, South Africa. February 19. Available at: http://www.info.gov.za/view/DownloadFile Action?id=96381NEDLAC. (2009) Framework for South Africa's Response to the Economic Crisis. National Economic Development and Labor Advisory Committee. NEDLAC, Johannesburg.

Ngongi, N. (2008) Policy Implications of High Food Prices for Africa. Alliance for a Green Revolution in Africa. Available at: http://www.ifpri.org/pubs/books/ar2007/ar07essay03.pdf

OECD. (2010) Development Aid Rose in 2009 and Most Donors will Meet 2010 Aid Targets. Available at: http://www.oecd.org/document/11/0,3343,en_2649_34487_44981579_1_1_1_1,00.html

Rawls, J. (1999) *A Theory of Justice*. Harvard College, Cambridge, MA.

Reuters. (2009) *Remittances to Kenya Rise in July from 2008*. Available at: http://www.africagoodnews.com/pan-africa/diaspora/882-remittances-to-kenya-rise-in-july-from-2008.html.

Statistics South Africa. (2011) Stats On-line.

United Nations. (2010) Africa Economic Outlook. Available at: http://www.un.org/esa/dsd/resources/res_pdfs/publications/sdt_afri/AEO2010_part1_p76.pdf.

United Nations Economic Commission for Africa. (2008) Overview of Economic and Social Conditions in Africa. Meeting of the Committee of Experts of the Second Joint Annual Meetings of the African Union Conference of Ministers of Economy and Finance. Addis Ababa, Ethiopia.

United Nations Economic Commission for Africa. (2009) Economic Report on Africa. Available at: http://www.uneca.org/eca_resources/Publications/books/era2009/.

United Nations World Report. (2009) World Report, Available at: http//www.un.org/esa/policy/wess/wesp.html.

USAID. (2009) USAID Responds to the Global Food Crisis. Available at: http://www.usaid.gov/our_work/humanitarian_assistance/foodcrisis/.

Velde, D.W. (2008) The Global Financial Crisis and Developing Countries. Overseas Development Institute. Available at: http://www.odi.org.uk/resources/download/2462.pdf.

World Food Programme and the World Bank Group. (2009) Rethinking School Feeding: Social Safety Nets, Child Development and the Education Sector. Available at: http://www.un.org/en/ga/second/64/socialprotection.pdf.

World Food Programme and the World Bank Group. (2006) Global Economic Prospects. Available at: http://www-wds.worldbank.org/external/default/WDSContentServer/IW3P/IB/2005/11/14/000112742_20051114174928/Rendered/PDF/343200GEP02006.pdf

World Food Programme and the World Bank Group. (2009a) *Global Monitoring Report 2009: A Development Emergency*. World Bank, Washington, DC. Available at: siteresources.worldbank.org/INTGLOMONREP2009/Resources/5924349-1239742507025/GMR09_book.pdf.

World Food Programme and the World Bank Group. (2009b) Swimming against the Tide: How Developing Countries Are Coping with the Crisis. Background Paper prepared for the G-20 Finance Ministers and Central Bank Governors Meeting, Horsham, UK, 13–14 March.

World Food Programme and the World Bank Group. (2010) Global Monitoring Report: Achieving the MDGs in the Aftermath of the Global Economic Crisis. World Bank, Washington, DC.

World Food Programme and the World Bank Group. (2011) Global Economics Prospects Report 2011: Navigating String Currents. Washington: World Bank. Available at: http://siteresources.worldbank.org/INTGEP/Resources/335315-1294842452675/GEPJanuary2011FullReport.pdf.

Chapter 13

Lessons of the Food and Financial Crises: Renewing Sub-Saharan Africa's Commitment to Food Security and Economic Growth

David R. Lee, Derek Headey, Keith Wiebe and Muna Ndulo
Cornell University, Ithaca, New York
International Food Policy Research Institute, Addis Ababa, Ethiopia
Food and Agricultural Organization of the United Nations, Rome
Cornell University, Ithaca, New York

Abstract

This chapter synthesizes the main findings of the chapters in this volume and discusses a variety of policy alternatives for mitigating the effects of future food and economic crises in sub-Saharan Africa. The causes of the food crises were many and its impacts complex. Policies to address those causes are accordingly numerous and complex, as they must address both the various underlying structural causes of food price spikes and increased volatility as well as the consequences of shorter-term transitory shocks that reinforced the structural factors. Prominent among these interventions should be increasing public and private investment in agricultural productivity and in physical and social infrastructure, expanding trade, decreasing biofuels subsidies in industrialized countries, and dealing with long-term climate change. Africa played no role in the origins of the financial and economic crises but nonetheless suffered their consequences in the form of lower economic growth, macro imbalances, increased poverty and undernutrition. As a price-taker in most commodity and financial markets, mitigating the repercussions of future such crises means enhancing the resilience of African economies. This can be accomplished through measures ranging from improved short-term macroeconomic policies to longer-term growth strategies that emphasize economic diversification, reinvestment of export earnings, and increasing investment in infrastructure and human capital. Given the magnitude of poverty across the continent, more effective social protection programmes will also be important in cushioning the impacts of future crises on the poor.

Introduction

The global food crisis of 2007–2008 and the global financial crisis that followed were calamitous events. While not unprecedented, each in itself had severe consequences around the world, and the combination of the two reinforced their negative impacts on purchasing power, food security and other outcomes. For the poor—many of whom spend the majority of their incomes on food and whose employment often rests on precarious grounds—the food and financial crises had harsh consequences, in sub-Saharan Africa and elsewhere. Millions were estimated to have been thrown into the ranks of the poor and undernourished. Their welfare was, and continues to be, the concern of policy makers, international organizations, NGOs, and poverty and food security researchers who seek, first, to understand the effects of these crises and second, to redress their impacts in ways that are sometimes effective, sometimes not, and that sometimes, as in the case of trade protectionism, makes matters worse.

The chapters in this volume have reviewed at length the causes of the food and financial crises, both structural and transitory, and their impacts across sub-Saharan Africa, both at the aggregate level and for individual countries, regions and sub-national areas. Each of the book's chapters has also identified policy alternatives that might lead to more effectively dealing with the effects of such crises in the future, or to preventing them in the first place. The objective of this summary chapter is twofold: first, to synthesize the 'lessons learned' regarding the food and financial crises, both as related in this volume and from other evidence, and second, to present a consensus policy agenda that may help in mitigating the effects of future crises or enhance the likelihood of avoiding them to begin with. We discuss each in turn.

Lessons of the Food and Financial Crises

The causes of the food price crisis received much attention at the time and have since then. The passage of time permits a more nuanced perspective on the events of 2007–2008 than was possible at the time. First, it is clear that the food price crisis was the result of *multiple and reinforcing causes,* including both initial structural factors—which created the underlying economic environment and set the stage for food price rises—and subsequent transitory factors that reinforced the price increases. The former, structural causes included a set of interlinked factors. The first was *strong economic growth* earlier in the decade in a wide range of developing countries, principally in Asia and the Middle East, which increased underlying global demands for food and feed grains. Second, macroeconomic imbalances in the United States and surplus foreign exchange in other countries manifested themselves in a *declining US dollar* in the late 2000s. This induced nominal rises in food prices when denominated in US dollars—meaning that price rises in Euros and other countries were much less severe—but the weak US dollar also sustained higher foreign demand for US food exports. Third, *global grain stocks declined* from the late 1990s to the mid-2000s, due to various factors, including the demand for biofuels, surging food exports and stockholding behaviour on the part of key countries such as the US and China. Finally, *oil prices surged* beginning in 2005, and the rising price of oil itself had multiple effects: increasing food production and distribution costs; stimulating the demand for biofuels as oil substitutes, which, along with concurrent biofuel policies in the US and the EU fostered closer linkages between agricultural and energy commodity markets; and finally, contributing to increased speculative behaviour in financial and commodities markets as investors increasingly sought commodity-based alternatives to financial and mortgage-based investments. Real maize and soybean prices were the first to experience prices rises, in 2005 and 2006.

The upward pressures on commodity and food prices created by these initial structural factors were reinforced by a series of transitory factors that exacerbated price increases in 2007 and 2008. These consisted first of *weather shocks*, notably the Australian drought that led to sharp rises in wheat prices in 2007. This was reinforced by *government trade policies*, beginning with the Ukraine banning wheat exports in 2007, which led to several other countries also restricting or taxing wheat imports. As wheat prices rose, the demand for rice exports increased sharply in mid-2007, leading to increases in rice prices and in turn prompting a number of governments to restrict exports (India, Vietnam) or increase imports (the Philippines), further exacerbating the problem. Finally, as the financial crisis worsened in the US and other industrial countries, investors increasingly sought to diversify away from mortgage-based investments and invested in commodities. This *speculative demand* is likely to have contributed to the upward pressure on oil and agricultural commodity markets as food prices continued to rise in 2007–2008—as suggested by Songwe in Chapter 6 in this volume—although there is still much debate on this point.

Understanding the reasons for the food price increases of the late 2000s is important for many reasons, including the fact that consideration of preventive or ameliorative policy changes is best informed by a correct understanding of underlying causative forces. Policy is most likely to be effective if it addresses long-term structural causes of events, rather than transitory events. However, in the case of the food price crisis, distinguishing between structural and transitory factors is complicated by the fact that the latter were often manifestations of the former, and so cannot be dismissed as short-term aberrations. For example, long-term climatic changes manifest themselves at least in part in the form of increasing frequency and severity of extreme weather events such as droughts and floods. This suggests, as emphasized by Msangi and Rosegrant in Chapter 4, that policies would do well to address the underlying driver: greenhouse gas emissions and climate change. Energy price shocks—which, as indicated above, contributed to food price increases in multiple ways—were in part induced by the growing global energy demands expressed by China, India, and other rapidly growing developing countries. Thus policies addressing biofuel subsidies clearly have major implications for these linked markets and commodity and food prices. More closely linked energy and food markets are only one illustration of the longer-term integration of global financial and commodity markets, which accounted in part for the growing speculative demand for commodities as a result of the global financial crisis and its spillover effects in commodity markets. Thus, tightening regulation in financial markets may well have the secondary outcome of reducing the likelihood and extent of speculative behaviour in commodity markets and induced price effects.

Notwithstanding the transitory shocks that contribute to commodity price spikes, the longer-term structural trends together imply higher average food prices in the future, following many years of declining real prices through the early 2000s. These results are confirmed by the annual forecasts of OECD-FAO and USDA models (*OECD-FAO Agricultural Outlook*, 2010), which continue to forecast higher real prices in the next decade. This is important for various reasons. First, it suggests the difficulty of achieving human welfare, food security and poverty outcomes, such as the Millennium Development Goals (MDGs), in a price environment that looks very different from that which existed between the 1980s through the early 2000s, when real food prices were roughly stable and many countries were making progress toward the MDGs. At the same time, if higher prices remain in place, this, along with appropriate policies and infrastructure, will provide incentives for higher production and inducing the types of long-term investments that are necessary for agricultural production to respond long-term to higher demands: development of irrigation systems, agricultural research and technology development, and other long-term productivity-enhancing measures.

Shocks and price volatility—and their transmission to the food sector—were also important dimensions of the food price crisis. Many of the sources of volatility in 2007–2008 food prices reflected long-term structural trends and thus suggest the potential for continued future volatility: 1) growing links to energy markets; 2) long-term climatic changes and the increasing frequency of extreme weather events; and 3) the integration of commodity markets and associated speculative demands as part of portfolio balancing and risk management strategies of investors. All these will continue to transmit variability to agricultural commodity and food prices in the future and will increase the stakes in dealing with volatility, not just levels of prices. Medium and longer term economic models don't predict volatility for good reasons (Headey, Fan and Malaiyandi, 2010), and opinions regarding the extent to which past volatility will be reflected in future developments are unclear (Wright and Bobenrieth, 2009). But at a minimum, if average prices are in fact higher, stocks will most likely be lower, and thus greater volatility can be expected and may well be exacerbated by the above-mentioned factors. Additionally, the policy responses observed in the 2007–2008 crisis may also reemerge in future eras of high prices. Governments understandably seek to insulate their consumers from food price rises, which leads them to impose export restrictions and bans. In certain cases, trade insulation can reduce domestic price volatility, as in the cases of China, India and Indonesia in 2007–2008. Ultimately, however, a freer trade regime is perhaps the most effective long-run means of minimizing both international and domestic price variability.

The evidence suggests *highly heterogeneous country-level and local-level impacts* from global food price increases. This is confirmed by the evidence reported in several chapters in this volume—that on East and Southern African countries (Kenya, Malawi, Mozambique, and Zambia) in Chapter 8 (by Mason, *et al.*), Uganda in Chapter 9 (Simler), and South Africa in Chapter 10 (Schönfeldt, *et al.*)—as well as other research.[77] These diverse responses in part reflect the fact that farmers and consumers are differentiated by such factors as their status as net food buyers versus net food sellers, different distributions of land ownership, and different household coping strategies. Beyond the household level, other factors affecting the pass-through of global prices to local food prices include the lack of integration of many local and regional food markets with global markets due to poor physical connectivity and limited transportation and communications infrastructure (Benson *et al.*, 2008), differential exchange rate effects, and government protectionist policies which insulate domestic markets. Consequently, it is hard to generalize regarding the severity of country-level impacts.

In addition, aside from the developments in commodity markets (oil and food prices, changes in export prices and volumes, etc.), there were other relevant global economic developments. For example, we now know that some countries, although experiencing a slowdown as a result of the financial crisis and global recession, did experience sharply reduced growth, but recovered quite quickly. Even in Africa, the recovery was much more rapid than early indications suggested (see discussion below). Even within countries,

[77] See, for example, Minot (2010) on past price transmission effects, and the World Bank (2011b) regarding widely varying transmission effects in the 2010–2011 era of food price increases.

effects vary. Higher prices will offer opportunities to those farmers who are net sellers of commodities and who can take advantage of price incentives to produce and sell more (e.g. because they have access to information, credit, inputs, markets, etc.), but these opportunities are not equally distributed across large and small farmers or across rich and poor countries. Household-level responses on the consumption side are also very heterogeneous, as illustrated in Schönfeldt *et al.*'s review of the diverse coping strategies of vulnerable households in response to high food prices in South Africa (Chapter 10).

Estimates show that higher food prices and food price variability lead to *higher incidence of hunger and malnutrition* and can be expected to continue to set back achievement of the MDGs. FAO estimates the extent of global undernourishment rose from 848 million in 2005–2007 to 1.02 billion in 2009[78] before declining in 2010. These estimates, however, may overestimate the impact of food prices on hunger for several reasons: the lack of comprehensive data directly assessing hunger (versus proxy variables), household coping strategies that seek to maintain minimum food consumption levels when prices rise and incomes fall—but which may induce long-term negative impacts on schooling and other outcomes; and the exclusion of effects in key middle income countries—China, Brazil, Mexico, and others—which are rapidly growing (Headey, 2011). In Africa, price increases are likely to continue to threaten, or even reverse, progress made throughout much of Africa in the early to mid-2000s.

The linkages between economic growth rates and food prices are important. In high growth countries, strong economic performance will help offset the impacts of price increases on hunger, particularly if *price-induced wage increases* are maintained in inflationary environments. For instance, the evidence reported in selected East and Southern African countries by Mason and colleagues in Chapter 8 suggests this is more likely to have occurred in the formal wage sector—in urban Kenya, Zambia, and Mozambique—than in the informal sector, which employs more of the poor, who are more vulnerable to food price spikes. Similarly, Polaski *et al.* (2008) simulate the effects of wage changes in India and find that wage changes offset effects of prices on poverty.

Although not a primary focus of this volume, the *political dimensions of food price increases*—e.g. food riots—are critically important to understanding the broader environment within which food prices are experienced, especially in terms of how price rises interact with domestic concerns regarding national politics, poverty and governance. Food price increases contributed to food riots in countries as diverse as Haiti, Bangladesh, and Uzbekistan in 2008, and in Mozambique, riots were motivated in part by a proposed large-scale land deal involving a foreign firm. Most recently, in late 2010 and early 2011, political crises in North Africa and the Middle East have coincided with another era of high food prices—although underlying political and governance factors, along with youth unemployment, have played a dominant role. While high food prices are often identified as the proximate cause of civil unrest—they are highly visible, directly impact peoples' welfare, and are of paramount importance to the poor, who are often already food insecure and malnourished—it is the underlying structural factors that often create a fertile socio-political environment within which food price increases provide the 'spark' that ignites civil protest. These underlying factors include poverty (particularly urban poverty), unemployment, corruption, and non-democratic governance structures. It is the interaction

---

[78] FAO's estimates of current levels of global undernourishment combine USDA's region-specific estimated rates of change in the number of undernourished for 2009 and 2010 with FAO's baseline estimates of the number of undernourished by region in previous years. FAO's methodology is currently being revised.

of these forces that appears to have generated civil unrest in many African nations in the late 2000s (Berazneva and Lee, 2011). For example, there has long been very high urban unemployment in the Middle East, and these countries are large food importers. Egypt is the biggest wheat importer in the world.

Imports offer an alternative to domestic production, but *import dependence combined with low agricultural productivity and incomes* exacerbate Africa's food insecurity and the vulnerability of poor households, both urban and rural. Although the food price increases in Africa in 2007–2008 were sharp, they were more limited (63 percent in 2007–2008) than were increases in global prices, and the price transmission effects were highly heterogeneous, as described above. Import dependence is not a bad thing *per se*—imports permit households to consume beyond the level of domestic production capacity, and growing imports often reflect increases in real purchasing power. However, this assumes that households have adequate incomes to access food to begin with. In much of sub-Saharan Africa, this is not the case, increasing the importance of domestic food production capacity. Moreover, the opportunity cost for countries with limited foreign exchange may be reducing their capacity to invest in infrastructure, industry and other sectors. Agricultural productivity growth, although estimated to be rising in recent years in SSA (Fuglie, Chapter 7, in this volume), in part due to a better policy environment (Aryeetey and Moyo, Chapter 2, and Masters, Chapter 11), is still constrained by many factors that could enhance food production and food security across the continent.

Africa had nothing to do with the origins and initial impacts of the global financial crisis, but was nonetheless significantly affected by its results. Economic growth in 2009 declined sharply from 6.4 average annual growth in 2006–2008 to 2.1 percent in 2009 (IMF, 2010). As reviewed in several chapters in this volume (Chapters 1, 2, 5 and 6), the impacts of the financial crisis and global recession included: increased borrowing costs; a decline in the volume of cross-border lending, especially in countries with a significant presence of foreign-owned banks, and declining borrowing from industrial countries; stock market contagion effects (e.g., South Africa, Kenya, and Nigeria); reductions in employment, particularly in the garment and mining sectors (te Velde *et al.*, 2010); declines in foreign exchange reserves; and widespread currency depreciation. As the financial crisis transitioned into economic recession in late 2009, other impacts were experienced as a result of SSA's increased integration with, and dependence on, the international economy. These effects included declines in: remittances, as expatriate workers lost jobs and incomes (-5.5 percent in 2009 [World Bank, cited by GMG, 2010]); foreign direct investment and private capital investment, both of which dropped sharply in 2009 (Aryeetey and Moyo, Chapter 2); and overseas development assistance, which fell below target by $18 billion in 2010 as both private and public sources of capital dried up (OECD, 2011). In a region with a tremendous preexisting scarcity of capital, all of these declines adversely affected both consumption and investment.

As emphasized earlier in this volume, the recessionary impacts on the real sector were much more severe than financial sector impacts. These were led by the impacts in agriculture and natural resource-based industries due to falling demand for African exports, declining commodity prices in 2009–2010, and declining trade in general. Effects were broadly felt by African oil exporters, led by Nigeria, the minerals sector (Zambian copper), lumber (Ghana), and other exporters. In part, these declines appeared severe due to the prior trends of strong export demand and rising raw commodity prices throughout much of the 2000s up to 2009. The negative impacts on the tradable sector were exacerbated by a sharp drop in trade finance liquidity (Aryeetey and Moyo, Chapter 2).

For all these reasons, the pace of economic growth dropped sharply in 2009. The 2.1 percent annual growth in real GDP growth, combined with continued high rates of population growth, translated into -0.1 growth in per capita GDP (IMF, 2010). Combined with the food price crisis, progress stalled in addressing a range of development indicators—poverty, undernourishment, health, and political stability—jeopardizing earlier progress made toward achieving the MDGs. The good news is that economic growth resumed in 2010, with the IMF expecting 4.7 percent real growth in SSA in 2010 and 5.8 percent growth in 2011.

Notwithstanding the impacts described above and in this volume, why wasn't the economic crisis more severe, leading to larger impacts? A number of reasons have been proposed (IMF, 2010):

- Africa's financial system is much less integrated with the West than systems in Asia, Latin America and Eastern Europe;
- the absence of high household and sovereign debt (opposite of the industrial countries);
- African macroeconomic policy has improved over past years, and countries are more adept in pursuing counter-cyclical fiscal and monetary policies;
- shifts in regional trading patterns are occurring toward more rapidly growing parts of the global economy—notably, China and other rapidly developing Asian markets—which helps insulate SSA from economic trends in the US and Europe; and
- domestic demand remained stronger than in previous recessions, led by private consumption, government expenditures and exports.

While these developments are encouraging, newly rising energy prices and the threat of a new 'food price crisis' in 2010–2011 suggest the likelihood of recurring food price shocks and the continued vulnerability of SSA households to economic trends abroad. They also suggest the critical need to redouble efforts toward long-term solutions to addressing these problems.

Moving Forward—Improving the Policy Environment for Food Security and Economic Growth

The multiple causes, complex interactions, and mutually reinforcing—and sometimes, offsetting—economic relationships that led to the food price crisis and the financial and economic crisis as they played out in sub-Saharan Africa suggest that policy prescriptions should be similarly complex. Yet as much as the dual crises fueled widespread debate at the time (and since) regarding their causes and consequences, researchers and analysts largely agree on many of the policy alternatives that would promote a more effective response to similar crises in the future, or preferably, avoid them at the outset. Some key policy alternatives are outlined briefly below, first, in terms of dealing with future food price crises, and second, in reducing the severity of the impacts of future economic slowdowns.

In discussing policy options, a necessary caveat needs to be issued at the outset. While sub-Saharan Africa has a great deal at stake in terms of the behaviour of global food and commodity on the one hand and in terms of global economic growth impacts on the other, the continent, for the most part, is a 'price-taker' both in commodity markets and in global financial markets. Thus many of the most important policies that affect both the food and agricultural sector and the overall economy are forged in markets, countries and institutions in which African countries play a minor economic role. This should not be construed to imply that policy changes and institutional reforms in sub-Saharan African are not important—far from it. It is indeed precisely because of these types of reforms beginning in the 1980s—for instance, in improving the implementation of macroeconomic policy and in pursuing less protectionist trade regimes—that many African nations have begun to place themselves on higher paths to economic growth. However, in many cases, sub-Saharan Africa is going to be in a position of having to respond to international events outside its borders that, as in the late 2000s, can create serious domestic impacts. Thus, one dimension of the policy challenge for African countries is how to best position themselves to *respond to* international economic shocks and events in a way that mitigates the negative impacts on households, farms, firms and economic growth, in general, while supporting changes that lead to sustainable long-run growth.

Moderating Food Prices and Food Price Volatility, Increasing Agricultural Incomes and Food Security

As pointed out in many of the chapters in this volume, agriculture is at the heart of the African economy and in the livelihoods of its people. Thus, *increasing the productivity of African agriculture* is essential to improving the economic status of millions of rural smallholders who depend on agriculture for their livelihoods, as well as improving the economic growth prospects of many SSA economies and the purchasing power of urban consumers who depend on domestic production to meet their food needs. Fuglie, in Chapter 7, assesses changes in agricultural productivity region-wide in recent decades; his analysis, and that of Masters (Chapter 11), provide some room for optimism in that real agricultural GDP in sub-Saharan African has grown at healthy rates over the past decade or more. This has been due to various factors: improved macroeconomic policies, more market-oriented trade policies, and improving grain yields, for example. However, key to this growth have been positive terms-of-trade effects and the expanded use of land in agriculture, rather than strong growth in total factor productivity, which would reflect technological change and increased gains in efficiency and management.

Raising growth in total factor productivity will be harder to achieve as it will require sustained investments over the long-term—difficult to accomplish in countries that have experienced political instability (or worse) and where the formal institutions that support these sustained investments are often weak. What types of investments are needed? The legacy of low-level and declining expenditures on agricultural research and technology development must be reversed, not only in the public sector, historically the source of major investments in high-yielding crop varieties and irrigation systems, but in the private sector, which can play a key role in such areas as investing in productivity-enhancing agri-biotechnology and more widely and efficiently providing farm inputs—fertilizers, seeds, pesticides, machinery and equipment—to producers. Sub-Saharan Africa's widely degraded soils must be improved through the increased application of inorganic and organic fertilizers and soil amendments to make them more productive. Investments in physical infrastructure and in market development are also critical, both in providing inputs to farmers and in purchasing their outputs at competitive prices and delivering them to consumers.

Investing in human capital is critical in raising the underlying productive potential of Africa's people, its labor force and management capacity, not only in agriculture but economy-wide. Human capital investments are particularly necessary in education, health (disease control and prevention, nutrition, etc.) and skills development (World Bank,

2011a), all of which are essential not only to economic development but, more broadly, to creating fulfilling lives. Particularly given the key role of women in African agriculture, improving women's access to productive resources and inputs and providing increased schooling opportunities for girls and young women is of major importance. This is emphasized by Msangi and Rosegrant in Chapter 4, and is also a central conclusion of FAO's recent *State of Food and Agriculture Report* (2011), which emphasized the role of women and agriculture in development. Investments in farm productivity and in human capital are traditional consensus-type solutions, but the food price crisis has cast renewed attention on their importance. An era of higher commodity and food prices will help provide price-based incentives that may further encourage these investments.

Sub-Saharan Africa has some of the most underdeveloped infrastructure anywhere in the world. Forty percent of the population lacks access to safe water, and 60 percent to basic sanitation; only 30 percent of Africa's population has access to electricity, and only 30 percent of the rural population enjoys access to all-season roads; telephone and internet penetration are the lowest in the world (Kandiero, 2009). *Increasing investments in domestic infrastructure*—roads, bridges, ports, electricity, trade facilities, and communications—will thus play a central role in facilitating future growth in Africa. These investments contribute powerfully to raising agricultural productivity and the efficiency of domestic food systems and thus help keep prices low for consumers. Much of Africa is still severely restricted by poor physical infrastructure and communications, which limit the availability of inputs like fertilizers to farmers and the efficient functioning of product markets—and thus the ability of producers to receive fair market prices. Improved infrastructure also enables farmers to diversify their production to meet market demands beyond that expressed simply by local markets and helps provide the means for countries to pursue growth opportunities wholly outside agriculture, from mining to tourism. The financial and economic crisis threatened infrastructure investment in Africa, which was already low (2–3 percent of GDP); the African Development Bank estimates that closing the 'infrastructure gap' will require US$80 billion annually over a 10-year period by both public and private sectors (Kandiero, 2009).

While some of the causes of the global food crisis were transitory factors, over which policies are largely powerless, in other cases, trade policies exacerbated the crisis by restricting or controlling exports. These outcomes could have been avoided, or at least lessened, through *reducing tariffs and other import barriers* to increase access to imports, and *avoiding export bans and restrictions and other trade interventions* that limit supplies to international commodity markets. The effects observed in 2007–2008 were not only based on supply and demand fundamentals but on market psychology. One of the lessons learned is that the political and economic pressures on domestic governments to intervene in trade can be acute, but that these interventions can easily contribute to a market psychology of self-reinforcing price increases. The short-run motivations for these interventions are understandable, but they come at the expense of creating many tradeoffs: between the interests of consumers versus producers, between impacts felt in the short-term versus the long-term (wherein higher prices can trigger increased investment and induce higher production), and between restricting exports, which induces greater volatility in international markets, versus more targeted means of mitigating the domestic impacts of high and volatile prices on vulnerable populations. Such unilateral policies also undermine trust in trade and foster an environment of protectionism, making it more difficult to coordinate international efforts to maintain or increase trade openness (Abbott and Borot di Battisti, 2011). Domestic policy makers must remember that the international market itself is a way of mitigating domestic production shortfalls and volatility.

Another policy alternative that deals directly with problems of food supply shortfalls and price volatility has been proposed by the International Food Policy Research Institute, namely, a global system of regional food stocks, with some reserves managed by the World Food Programme to ensure regional food security (e.g. in Eastern Africa). While there are valid objections to reserve systems (wastage, cost, rules for management and release of stocks), regional stocks could be piloted at relatively small levels and then scaled up if feasible.

Of the long-term structural changes in the global food economy that contributed to the food price crisis in 2007–2008, none was more important than the growing link between food and energy markets. Yet an array of criticisms has accompanied this development. Biofuels such as maize-based ethanol not only compete with commodities used as food, but also compete for resources used in food production. Grains are highly substitutable in production: a rise in maize prices will lead to a rise in soybean prices—the two closely correspond and US farmers, for example, substitute maize for soybeans in allocating planted areas. Wheat prices, and pressure in wheat markets, will also contribute to rising market prices (Headey, 2011). As noted by Wiebe *et al.* in Chapter 3, a consensus estimate is that the demand for biofuels accounted for about one-third of the increase in the prices of maize and other staple foods. The claimed environmental benefits of biofuels like maize-based ethanol in reducing greenhouse gas (GHG) emissions have also come under increasing scrutiny as more refined life-cycle assessments have demonstrated earlier claims to be optimistic and estimates of GHG reductions to be highly sensitive to alternative feedstocks, refining technologies and discount rates (EPA, 2009).

At present, except for notable exceptions like Brazil's cane-based biofuels industry, much of the global demand for biofuels, especially in the US and Europe, is grounded on a range of policy interventions such as blending targets and mandates, trade restrictions, tax credits and other sources of direct support to producers and blenders, as detailed by Msangi and Rosegrant in Chapter 4. One additional effect of these subsidies and mandates is that their dependence on oil price movements makes food prices more sensitive to the business cycle volatility of financial markets (Lustig, 2009; Headey, Fan and Malaiyandi, 2010). Reducing the potential for the structural changes in energy and food systems to contribute to future food price rises, and avoiding other unforeseen economic and environmental outcomes of biofuels policies, could be accomplished by *eliminating mandates, subsidies and taxes that support the biofuels industry*. A competitive market-based biofuels industry may offer a partial alternative to reliance on fossil fuels, but not through subsidies and related trade barriers. If oil prices stay high, then subsidies are less relevant, as ethanol production will be profitable (unless feedstock prices are bid up as happened in 2006–2008).

Over the long term, *increasing climate change* and the variability of weather and climatic factors—temperatures, precipitation, and extreme weather events such as drought and flooding—are likely to have severe impacts on sub-Saharan Africa, its agriculture and its people. Indeed, many analyses have concluded that the continent is one of the regions of the world likely to suffer the greatest impacts of climate change. This is due to a confluence of many factors: projections of future temperature increases and shortfalls in precipitation; the tropical location of many of its people; its lack of irrigated land and reliance on rainfed agriculture; and high existing rates of poverty and human vulnerability. To counter these effects, it is important that African nations—and the many international organizations that assist African development—increasingly invest in measures to enhance climate adaptation and resilience, as well as mitigation. Wiebe *et al.* (Chapter 3) and Msangi and Rosegrant (Chapter 4) identify some of the needed measures, including: increased investments in irrigation and drainage; agricultural research including crop varietal development, especially drought-tolerant varieties; improved water harvesting technologies and practices; improved nutrient management for crops and soils; and improvements and adjustments in crop and grazing management, such as the use of conservation tillage and adjusting crop choice and planting/harvesting calendars. Many of these measures are 'win-win'—while improving agricultural productivity and incomes, they simultaneously enhance climate resilience and adaptation. They can also be self-reinforcing: as agricultural productivity and peoples' incomes rise, their capacity for adaptation and becoming more resilient is improved and they are better enabled to deal with subsequent climate-related crisis.

Policies to Deal with Financial and Economic Crisis and Human Vulnerability

As discussed above, most sub-Saharan African countries are small trading countries with little ability to influence international commodity prices and even less ability to influence international financial and capital markets. As a result, the policy challenge during the financial and economic crisis of the late 2000s was typically how to best deal with developments in the international economy and how, given both political and economic constraints, to insulate domestic economies and their peoples from the ensuing negative impacts. In the face of the major economic events of this period, the 'policy space' available to most SSA countries to deal with the consequences was limited (Mayer, 2008), particularly as African economies have increasingly been brought into the global economy and have bought into WTO-type multilateral trade disciplines. Yet, as te Velde *et al.* (2010) have emphasized, the vulnerability of developing countries to economic crises is not only a function of their exposure to its impacts, but also the way in which those impacts are moderated by the resilience of their financial and economic institutions. Achieving that resilience is a function of both informed short-term measures to deal with immediate financial exigencies and long-term strategies oriented toward achieving economic growth objectives.

The sustained economic growth that much of sub-Saharan Africa achieved in the late 1990s and through much of the 2000s was in part due to strong export prices and revenues, but also due to improved country policy environments: better macroeconomic policies, savings and domestic reinvestment of oil revenues, the expansion of domestic debt markets, and the diversification of export markets away from Europe and the US toward rapidly growing Asian markets. Central to renewing the strong economic growth of the recent past will be a return to many of those same policies, following the use of counter-cyclical fiscal and monetary policies to get countries through the recession.[79] This will likely mean less accommodative fiscal policy, given the widespread fiscal imbalances induced by the recession, and maintaining a flexible monetary policy while at the same time restraining inflationary pressures as economies rebound (IMF, 2010). The growth in export revenues resumed in late 2009 and 2010 with the resurgence of oil and commodity prices, although imports increased as well, leaving trade balances relatively less affected. From the macroeconomic side, it is easy to understand why the IMF concluded in its annual regional assessment in 2010 that overall "the prospects for the region are promising" (2010, p. 7).

While in the short run the fact that most African economies are not highly integrated into international capital markets shielded them from some of the worst effects of the

[79] Macroeconomic policy in sub-Saharan African has historically been strongly pro-cyclical, particularly among oil exporters and other resource-intensive exporters, so recent developments represent an important departure from the past (UNCTAD, 2010a).

financial crisis, in the long run those same markets are a source of international capital that is a source of future growth. Murinde (2009) notes that while Africa's four largest economies have undertaken financial sector reforms, much of the rest of the continent remains vulnerable to financial contagion effects. Real credit to the private sector has grown only slowly, even as other macroeconomic indicators have rebounded after the recession (IMF, 2010).

If strong economic growth is to be sustainable, it will be necessary for the region to continue to attract private investment, including foreign direct investment (FDI), and to promote further development of the domestic banking sector and capital markets, improve deepening of the financial market and increase competition. But avoiding the problems of the recent past will also require financial sector reforms such as those discussed by Hockett (Chapter 5) and Songwe (Chapter 6), including strengthening coordination, monitoring and risk management capacity in the global financial system and implementing stronger international financial regulatory standards under the new Financial Stability Board. In developing-country agriculture, domestic private investment (including that by farmers themselves) remains by far the largest source of investment. Agriculture is the mainstay of the African economy; thus attracting private investment, including that of farmers themselves, will be key to future growth of that key sector. FDI also plays an essential role in Africa, as it accounts for about one-fifth of gross fixed capital formation and is particularly important in the mining and manufacturing sectors (UNCTAD, 2010b). Addressing other aspects of the overall policy and regulatory environment—including property rights, marketing institutions, and the physical and communications infrastructure—is also important not only in creating an attractive investment environment but in providing the necessary conditions for achieving sustainable economic growth itself.

Much foreign investment in sub-Saharan Africa is drawn by the continent's rich natural resources—oil, natural gas, minerals, and agricultural land. While foreign investment in SSA continues to be overwhelmingly from industrialized countries, there is growing investment from developing countries. Much of this is from resource-seeking countries and state-owned enterprises in developing Asian economies—principally, China, India and Malaysia—which now account for a major part of interregional FDI flows among developing countries (UNCTAD, 2010b). Foreign investment in farm land in SSA has been accelerating rapidly (from a very small base) and continues to be controversial; at a minimum, it should be accompanied by suitable safeguards for local stakeholders.

Although private investment in SSA can be expected to grow in the future, development lending, including concessional loans, and official development assistance (ODA) will continue to be an important source of investment in key sectors like agriculture, infrastructure development, education and health. It has been estimated that to reach the necessary 7 percent growth rate to achieve the MDGs, Africa would require an additional \$117 billion in financial resources (Kaberuka, 2009). Traditional sources of development lending like the World Bank, International Finance Corporation, and the African Development Bank have in recent years been strengthened by special initiatives such as the NEPAD-OECD Africa Investment Initiative and the Emerging Africa Infrastructure Fund, a private-public partnership to finance the construction and development of private infrastructure across much of the continent. Increasing ODA commitments are another means to sustain investments in infrastructure and key productive and social sectors. ODA reached its highest level ever in 2009, US\$47.6 billion (OECD, 2011). Even before the financial crisis, however, ODA commitments were falling short of their targets established at the G-8 Gleneagles Summit in 2005, and those shortfalls are likely to widen in light of the effects of the economic recession in major donor countries, mainly the US and Europe (NEPAD-OECD, 2010). Increasing all of these sources of investment will be needed to meet Africa's development challenges.

Expanding trade is often at the front of the agenda for promoting African development and growth. The size of the continent, its restricted physical connectivity, limited consumer purchasing power, and trade protectionism have all constrained the growth of regional trade in the past. However, as noted by Masters in Chapter 11, in Africa's largest economic sector, agriculture, most African countries have long since undertaken massive policy reforms, reducing substantially the toll that policy-induced price distortions had formerly played in constraining agricultural trade and growth. Beyond agriculture, African nations have a mixed record in terms of their trade regimes and openness to trade (te Velde *et al.*, 2010). Many observers believe that significant payoffs lie in promoting greater interregional trade, subject to surmounting the above-mentioned, and other, constraints. Key to this are infrastructure investments that better connect consumers and producers and promote the efficient functioning of markets, and continuing the movement toward decreasing protectionism, whether within the context of the WTO's multilateral framework or regional trade agreements, of which Africa has many. Other mechanisms to promote trade include support for trade financing, which was hit hard by the economic recession, and increasing market access to developed countries through such preferential trade programs as the US African Growth and Opportunity Act (AGOA) and the European Union's EBA (Everything but Arms) initiative.

In the long run, it is important that African economies begin to diversify beyond sectors based solely on the exploitation of natural resources. While these sectors—agriculture, oil, natural gas, mining, etc.—build on Africa's inherent comparative advantages, they invariably lead to 'boom and bust' economic cycles and often to Dutch Disease problems. Most of the African economies hardest hit by the financial and economic crisis were in fact those most highly dependent on export earnings from one or a few sectors—oil, copper, coffee, cocoa, and cotton. Declining export earnings adversely affect everything from consumer demand and government revenues to maintaining employment and levels of public investments. Thus diversifying natural resource-dependent economies away from a strict focus on agriculture and resource extraction is a key strategy for long-term growth. Logical sectors in which to promote diversification include agro-processing, some manufacturing and value-added industries, and tourism. The informed use of 'windfall' export proceeds can be used to support economic diversification strategies, for example, through investment in the public sector to help fund human capital development investments (see discussion in the previous section), the growth of non-traditional export sectors, and even the creation of a Chilean-type trust fund to help buffer export price volatility (te Velde *et al.*, 2010). Botswana's Pula Fund, for example, is a sovereign wealth fund, financed by foreign exchange reserves earned from diamond and mineral exports, that invests primarily in industrialized country assets. Whatever strategies are followed, the solutions must be country-specific, as countries seek to diagnose their own situations and sources of comparative advantage.

Finally, no matter how effective the short- and long-term strategies identified above may be, economic downturns are bound to occur, inevitably leaving poor and vulnerable populations at the mercy of market forces beyond their control. Many of the countries that most effectively coped with the recent global recession had in place social protection programs to help moderate the impacts of financial and economic shocks. African nations must continue efforts to strengthen these programs through the targeting of especially vulnerable groups with cash and food transfers, vouchers, school feeding programmes, social insurance, labor market programmes, and other mechanisms. While these programmes are more prevalent in Asia and Latin America, a handful of African countries have shown that poor people can in fact be protected via these programmes, especially with donor support. In South Africa, the 'training layoff scheme' described by Gumede in Chapter 12 was implemented on the heels of the recession to cushion the threat of layoffs, enabling workers to re-train for new jobs while still receiving a salary and receiving social benefits. In a much poorer country, Ethiopia, the Productive Safety Nets Program (PSNP) has been quite successful in providing social protection and contributing to asset accumulation for around 9 million people, mostly in food-insecure and famine-prone regions in the north of the country. The PSNP offers food and/or cash in exchange for work on public goods such as roads or irrigation schemes. The PSNP also demonstrates some of the challenges of implementing such programs, especially in an environment of rising food prices (Sabates-Wheeler and Devereaux, 2010). Even so, social protection programmes can play a central role in helping cushion the impacts among vulnerable populations to future food and economic crises that will inevitably arise.

References

Abbott, P. and Borot de Battisti, A. (2011) Recent global food price shocks: Causes, consequences and lessons for African governments and donors. *Journal of African Economies* 20 (Supplement 1): i12–i62.

Benson, T., Mugarura, S. and Wanda, L. (2008) Impacts in Uganda of rising global food prices: the role of diversified staples and limited price transmission. *Agricultural Economics* 39 (November 1): 513–524.

Berazneva, J. and Lee, D.R. (2011) Understanding the African food riots of 2007–2008: An empirical analysis. Working Paper, March 2011. Cornell University, Ithaca, NY.

Environmental Protection Agency. (2009) *EPA Lifecycle Analysis of Greenhouse Gas Emissions from Renewable Fuels.* EPA-420-F-09-024. US EPA Office of Transportation and Air Quality. May.

Food and Agricultural Organization of the UN. (2011) The State of Food and Agriculture 2010–2011: Women in Agriculture: Closing the Gender Gap for Development. FAO, Rome, Italy.

Gilbert, C. (2010) How to Understand High Food Prices. *Journal of Agricultural Economics* Online version (April 2010). 1–28.

Global Migration Group. (2010) Fact-Sheet on the Economic Crisis and Migration, Remittances and Children Left Behind. Prepared by UNICEF. Available at: www.globalmigrationgroup.org/pdf/UNICEF_Fact%20Sheet_MigrationRemittances_and_Children%20Left_Behind_May_2010.pdf

Headey, D. (2011) Rethinking the global food crisis: The role of trade shocks. *Food Policy* 36 (2): 136–146.

Headey, D., Fan, S. and Malaiyandi, S. (2010) Navigating the Perfect Storm: Reflections on the Food, Energy, and Financial Crises. *Agricultural Economics* 41 (S1): 217–228.

International Monetary Fund. (2010) *Regional economic outlook: Sub-Saharan Africa 2010: Back to high growth?* April 2010. World Economic and Financial Surveys. Washington, DC.

Kaberuka, D. (2009) Start This Engine: Africa's Policymakers Should Prepare for Global Recovery by Priming Their Private Sectors. *Finance and Development*. June. 54–55.

Kandiero, T. (2009) *Infrastructure Investment in Africa*. Development Research Brief Number 10. Development Research Department, African Development Bank. August.

Lustig, N. (2009) *Coping with rising food prices: Policy dilemmas in the developing world*. February 2009. The George Washington University, Institute for International Economic Policy, Washington, DC.

Mayer, J. (2008) Policy Space: What, for What, and Where? UNCTAD Discussion Paper 191. United Nations Conference on Trade and Development. October.

Minot, N. (2010) *Transmission of World Food Price Changes to Markets in Sub-Saharan Africa*. Unpublished research report, International Food Policy Research Institute (IFPRI), Washington, DC.

Murinde, V. (2009) Global Financial System: Implications for Africa's Financial System. Birmingham Business School, University of Birmingham, Birmingham, AL.

NEPAD-OECD. (2010) Aid to Africa. *Policy Brief* No. 1, October. Africa Investment Initiative, United Nations Office of the Special Advisor on Africa.

OECD-FAO Agricultural Outlook 2010–2019. (2010) Organization of Economic Cooperation and Development and Food and Agricultural Organization of the U.N. Available at: www.oecd.org/pages/0,3417,en_36774715_36775671_1_1_1_1_1,00.html

OECD. (2011) Development Assistance Committee. Development Aid at a Glance: Statistics by Region—Africa. Available at: www.oecd.org/dataoecd/40/27/42139250.pdf

Polaski, S., Ganesh-Kumar, A., McDonald, S., Panda, M. and Robinson, S. (2008) *India's Trade Policy Choices: Managing Diverse Challenges*. Carnegie Endowment for International Peace, Washington, DC.

Sabates-Wheeler, R. and Devereaux, S. (2010) Cash Transfers and High Food Prices: Explaining Outcomes on Ethiopia's Productive Safety Net Programme. *Food Policy*. 35(4): 274–285.

te Velde, D.W., Ahmed, M.M., Alemu, G., Bategeka, L., Calí, M., Castel-Branco, C., Chansa, F., Dasgupta, S., Foresti, M., Hangi, M., Ingombe, L., Iqbal, A., Jalilian, H., Jemio, L.C., Kabuya-Kalala, F., Keane, J., Kennan, J., Islam Khan, T., Lunogelo, H.B., Massa, I., Mbilinyi, A., Mudenda, D., Mwega, F.M., Ndulo, M., Nina, O., Ossemane, R., Rahman, M., Reyes, G., Ssewanyana, S., Wild, L. and others. (2010) *The global financial crisis and developing countries: Phase 2 synthesis*. ODI Working Paper 316. March. Overseas Development Institute (ODI), London, UK.

United Nations Conference on Trade and Development. (2010a) The Financial Crisis, Macroeconomic Policy and the Development Challenge in Africa. UNCTAD Secretariat. April.

United Nations Conference on Trade and Development. (2010b) *World Investment Report 2010*. UNCTAD, New York and Geneva.

World Bank. (2011a) Building Human Capital in Africa. Africa Region, Human Development. Available at: siteresources.worldbank.org/INTHUMDEV/Resources/WBHDbrochureweb.pdf

World Bank. (2011b) Food Price Watch. Poverty Reduction and Equity Group. Washington, DC. April. Available at: www.worldbank.org/foodcrisis/foodprice watch/april_2011.html

Wright, B. and Bobenrieth, E. (2009) The Food Crisis of 2007/2008: Evidence and Implications. FAO Food Outlook, Global Market Analysis, December 2009.

Index